Salem

Salem

Place, Myth, and Memory

EDITED BY

Dane Anthony Morrison
Nancy Lusignan Schultz

Northeastern University Press ✦ *Boston*

Published by University Press of New England

HANOVER AND LONDON

NORTHEASTERN UNIVERSITY PRESS

Published by University Press of New England,
One Court Street, Lebanon, NH 03766
www.upne.com

First Northeastern University Press / UPNE paperback edition 2005
Printed in the United States of America   5   4   3   2   1

ISBNs for the paperback edition:
ISBN-13: 9781555536503
ISBN-10: 1-55553-650-6

Frontispiece: Seal of the City of Salem, 1836. Courtesy of the City of Salem.
Photo by Kim Mimnaugh.

Library of Congress Cataloging-in-Publication Data

Salem : place, myth & memory / edited by Dane Anthony Morrison,
Nancy Lusignan Schultz.
p. cm.
Includes bibliographical references and index.
ISBN 1-55553-609-3 (cloth : alk. paper)
1. Salem (Mass.)—History. 2. Salem (Mass.)—Social conditions.
3. Group identity—Massachusetts—Salem. 4. Human
geography—Massachusetts—Salem. 5. Salem (Mass.)—Intellectual life.
6. Salem (Mass.)—Biography. I. Morrison, Dane Anthony.
II. Schultz, Nancy Lusignan, 1956–
F74.S1 S33 2004
974.4′02—dc22
2003023134

Dedicated to the students of Salem State College,
past, present, and future

Contents

Illustrations

Acknowledgments

This book on Salem draws on the contributions of many people. The fourteen contributors, including photographer Kim Mimnaugh, who accepted the challenge of interpreting one place across time took especial pains to study Salem afresh and to think deeply about what this place has meant to each generation. In addition, many other people and organizations supported this project, and we wish to express our thanks to the following: John Acres, John Adams, Lisa Adams, the American Philosophical Society, Brad Austin, LaGina Austin, Emerson Baker, Barbara Baldassarre, Alice Bianchi, Asenath Blake, Patricia Buchanan, Deborah Burkinshaw, the City of Salem, Kristena Cowles, Elaine Cruddas, Donald Cutler, Alison D'Amato, Destination Salem, Phyllis Deutsch, Thomas Doherty, Susan Edwards, Marc Glasser, Amie Marks Goodwin, Bob Gormley, John Hampsey, Nancy Harrington, Harvard University's Center for the Study of World Religions, Johannah Henson, Historic Salem, Inc., the staff of the House of the Seven Gables, Chris Idzek, Elizabeth Kenney, Rod Kessler, Alexandros Kyrou, Diane Lapkin, Will LeMoy, Gregory Liakos, Carolyn Lusignan, Henry Lusignan, Cynthia McGurren, Martha Jane Moreland, Anne Marie Nicholas, Robert Orsi, the Peabody Essex Museum, Phillips Library, Michelle Pierce, Arthur Riss, the Salem Athenaeum, the Salem Maritime National Historic Site, Jackson Schultz, Jackson Schultz III, Jonas Schultz, Anita Shea, the Society of the Cincinnati, Jim Stoll, Adam Sweeting, Carol Thistle, Margaret Vaughn, Donna Vinson, the Yellow Dog Café, Peter Walker, Michael Weber, John Weingartner, and Patricia Zaido.

Preface for the General Reader

This is a book about place, particularly one place, Salem, Massachusetts. But, more than that, it is about the people of Salem and what this place has meant to those who lived and died here. The essays in this collection ask what Salem has meant to the families that came and never left, to the individuals who passed through on their way elsewhere, to those who called it home, or way station, or Mecca, or port of call, or destination, or history. It tells stories of how people influence a place and how a place influences people.

The essays in this collection examine fourteen generations of Salemites. For each, the experience of Salem, the fabric or texture of the place, has meant something different. But, for all, the impressions left were lasting and formative. By examining this place and its people, we learn much about the human condition—in its patterns and variations. And we learn much about our relationships with specific places—those we inhabit, those we leave, those to which we return—and how a sense of place is built.

Two maps, now lost, or that may have never existed, illustrate the ways in which people can imagine a place like Salem. One appeared in venerable maritime histories of Salem and is described as "an engaging map, likely drawn by a Chinese artist about 1800, which depicts the United States from the Atlantic to the Mississippi as 'SALEM.'" The other, described by voyagers who saw it in the hands of a native merchant of Calcutta, noted just two place names: *Boston,* marked by a dot, and the name *Salem* stretched across the entire continent of North America. Though historians have diligently searched for these maps, they have yet to be found. Yet, mythic or real, they tell us something about the ways in which Salem was conceived in the East as a city of global significance. A sense of place is constructed as much by what is left out as by what is included in the map. Each generation has its own idea about the meaning of a place, and that idea can change over time.

The essays will introduce you to Elias Hasket Derby, Benjamin Goodhue, and Nathaniel Bowditch, who spent most of their lives in Salem and whose individual successes made the city famous across the globe. Derby's commercial genius guided America's earliest voyages to the Baltic, Manila, and Calcutta; Goodhue devoted his life to public service; and Bowditch placed Salem at the forefront of scientific inquiry. You will read about Harriet Low and Nathaniel Hawthorne, both expatriates, but for whom leaving Salem meant something different. Miss Low was a lively ingénue who pined for parties and sewing circles from far-off Macao; Hawthorne was a struggling writer haunted by the legacy of his Puritan ancestor who sent twenty townspeople to their deaths for the crime of witchcraft. And you will meet Charlotte Forten and Thomas Maimoni, who came to Salem from elsewhere and moved on, but who left indelible impressions on the town. Forten was an African American schoolteacher who broke the color line a century before the civil rights movement; Maimoni was a sociopath whose murder of Martha Brailsford shocked the country.

General readers will find that this book mirrors the vibrant, engaged, democratic texture of life in Salem. A mix of styles and range of approaches mark the essays, poetry, and photography. The collection presents fresh ways of thinking and new information that will attract scholars, but in words and images that will appeal to the general reader.

In a sense, *Salem: Place, Myth, and Memory* may be considered an alternative guidebook to Salem. When you explore the living history museum, Salem in 1630, bring along chapter 1, "Salem as Frontier Outpost," and learn how Native Americans and Puritans adapted to each other's presence. As you tour the Salem Witch Museum, visit the city's historic churches, and browse in the occult shops, read chapters 2 and 11, "Salem as Religious Proving Ground" and "Salem as Witch City." As you stroll through Salem's Maritime National Historic Site and along Pickering Wharf, refer to chapter 3, "Salem as Enterprise Zone." Visitors with an interest in Salem's distinguished literary history will want to peruse chapters 7 and 12, "Salem as Hawthorne's Creation" and "Salem's House of the Seven Gables as Historic Site." If Salem State College is on your campus visit list, be sure to take a look at chapter 6, "Salem as the Nation's Schoolhouse." When you make the eminent Peabody Essex Museum and the Salem Athenaeum your destinations, you will undoubtedly want to consult chapters 4 and 5, "Salem as Athenaeum" and "Salem as Citizen of the World." Chapters 8 and 10 offer excellent walking guides to Salem's byways. "Salem as Architectural Mecca" describes Asia's influences on the mansions that line Chestnut Street and Washington Square. "Salem as Crime Scene" offers a glimpse of a dark underside of the Salem experience. For a gritty view of modern Salem, visitors will also want to read chapter 9, "Salem as a Global City," and the coda poem, "Montage of Brick and Water." Kim Mimnaugh's photographs capture many of the sights you will see as you meander through historic Salem.

A passage through Salem connects you to the four centuries of its recorded history—as well as its thousands of years of prehistory—and to the experiences of those who lived here. *Salem: Place, Myth, and Memory* will guide you to a deeper appreciation of the multiple meanings of this place. Understanding what Salem has meant to others can enrich your own sense of place wherever you go.

Preface for Instructors and Students

Why would we want to study a place, any place, over time—even a place as filled with history as Salem, Massachusetts? The novelist Eudora Welty suggests that the answer lies in a paradox: there is much to be learned from the small view. She tells us, "One place comprehended can help us understand other places better." Creative artists such as Welty evoke a powerful sense of a particular place, yet give it universal meaning. We experience this sense of place in the writing on New England by Nathaniel Hawthorne and Harriet Beecher Stowe, on the American South by Eudora Welty and William Faulkner, and on the American frontier by Willa Cather and James Fenimore Cooper. In the same way, Georgia O'Keeffe's images of the Southwest and Ansel Adams's landscape photography vividly capture the essence of place. Nathaniel Hawthorne anticipated Welty's point that understanding one place can help us understand other places better. In his 1838 story, "The Sister Years," he notes that Salem was, in effect, America writ small: "[H]uman weakness and strength, passion and policy, Man's tendencies, his aims and modes of pursuing them, his individual character and his character in the mass, may be studied almost as well here as on the theatre of the nations."

Salem: Place, Myth, and Memory has been designed with American Studies students in mind, following a route marked by Hawthorne and Welty. The interdisciplinary methodology of American Studies, combining the perspectives of history, literary studies, and the arts, offers a promising means through which we can understand how knowledge of a particular place can lead to a broad comprehension of the local and the national. From this perspective, the American experience can be seen in microcosm as Salem's experience.

Salem: Place, Myth, and Memory challenges readers to resurrect the neglected pasts of a historic site and to reflect on the many ways that a place can be imagined and reinterpreted. It offers Salem as a case study in which a variety of scholars examine the question of place through a number of disciplinary perspectives: archaeology, religious history, maritime history, local history, literary studies, architecture, economic history, and popular culture.

To facilitate your exploration of one place across time, we suggest some representative categories of inquiry. We are aware, however, that analysis has its dangers; in particular, it can create constructs that seem fragmented and arbitrary. We do not wish to dis-member the experience of Salem as a place, but to re-member it. The purpose of the book is to recall, for each of fourteen generations, the texture and tapestry of life in one location. We hope to recreate the experience of what it felt like to live in this place, what the place meant to each generation, and how those meanings changed over time. To this end, you might consider examining Salem through the following groupings of essays:

Religion in American Culture

In what ways does a place influence the ways in which spirituality is manifested among its inhabitants? How does the history of a place force religious expression into conventional channels? How do competing religions negotiate for space in the public sphere? How is the historical record of a place interpreted, and according to the needs and sensibilities of which historical age? Pairing the essays "Salem as Religious Proving Ground" and "Salem as Witch City" offers a fresh perspective on questions of religious experience in American culture.

Literature in American Culture

What is the relationship between a writer and the place in which he or she writes? In what ways does a writer draw upon the materials of her environs to create a distinct sensibility and to even perpetuate a mythology of place? How does an author represent his setting so powerfully that it becomes an icon that can dominate the American literary landscape, indeed, so that its very name plants foreboding in a reader even before opening the book? We find answers to these questions by linking "Salem as Hawthorne's Creation," "Salem as Crime Scene," and "Coda: Montage of Brick and Water."

Race and Ethnicity in American Culture

In what ways does a place become an arena of contestation and negotiation for racial and ethnic groups? How can we see a place through the beliefs of competing cultures, and how do these groups understand the fundamental conceptions of the "other"? The essays "Salem as Frontier Outpost," "Salem as the Nation's Schoolhouse," "Salem as a Global City," and "Salem's House of the Seven Gables as Historic Site" address these questions.

Education in American Culture

The study of education opens a window into the core values of a community. Through an examination of a community's openness to education, whether in formal institutions or vocational learning, we can examine the fundamental issues that characterize a place, such as time, change, and social hierarchy. The spirit of educational innovation is explored in the essays "Salem as Enterprise Zone," "Salem as Athenaeum," and "Salem as the Nation's Schoolhouse."

Communities as Economic Entities

Why are some communities sites of energy and enterprise while others stagnate? Why do these "enterprise zones" rise and fall? The essays "Salem as Enterprise Zone," "Salem as Athenaeum," "Salem as Citizen of the World," and "Salem as a Global City" suggest ways in which we can address issues of economic vitality and cultural adaptation.

Popular Culture

In popular memory, American places evoke association with the great and the mundane. How does this process of mythmaking occur? Our introductory essay, "Salem Enshrined," and the essays "Salem as Architectural Mecca," "Salem as Hawthorne's Creation," "Salem as Witch City," and "Salem's House of the Seven Gables as Historic Site," as well as the accompanying photographs and illustrations, explore the construction of one of the most famous myths in our popular culture.

Other areas to which this book contributes are urban studies, gender studies, and consumerism.

Salem: Place, Myth, and Memory also helps readers to better understand the intersection of the local, the national, and the global. Today, American Studies scholars are revisiting the conception of the "American experience" in broader, more global contexts. This expanded conception is replacing a traditional, narrow emphasis on "American exceptionalism"—a view that privileged the United States as both unique and separate from the rhythms of international developments. An artifact from Salem's history explodes this convention and illustrates how an "isolationist" view of America is a false construct.

After Salem was incorporated in 1836, 210 years after its founding, the community imagined by city leaders was a much more globally connected entity than conventional histories have depicted. They called for a city motto, *Divitis Indiae usque ad ultimum sinum*—"To the farthest ports of the rich East"—that served as a reminder of Salem's intimate connections with the trade of China, India, and Sumatra, the pepper-rich island in the South Pacific. The city council commissioned a design by pepper ship owner George Peabody to represent Salem's global connections. It portrays an Atjehnese man, surrounded by palm trees and a pepper plant, holding a parasol to shade himself from the hot Sumatran sun, and wearing traditional attire—a flat red turban, red trousers and belt, a yellow knee-length robe, and a blue jacket—common to the Atjeh province of the island. In the background, a Salem vessel, with sails unfurled, navigates the harbor. Filling out the emblem are compass rose motifs and the image of a dove bearing an olive branch. The Salem city seal may be read as text that illustrates this new direction in American Studies, offering a fresh way to envision connections, not just between the local and the national, but also among the local, national, and global. This expanded perspective on America's place in a global community may be seen in the essays "Salem as Citizen of the World," "Salem as Architectural Mecca," and "Salem as a Global City."

A globally connected approach to American Studies builds on Eudora Welty's observation, "One place comprehended can help us understand other places better." Understanding Salem, then, helps us to better understand the world.

Salem

Window display in downtown Salem shop. Photo by Kim Mimnaugh.

Introduction

Salem Enshrined:
Myth, Memory, and the Power of Place

NANCY LUSIGNAN SCHULTZ AND
DANE ANTHONY MORRISON

*Still, there will be a connection with the long past—a reference to
forgotten events and personages, and to manners, feelings, and opinions, almost or
wholly obsolete—which, if adequately translated to the reader, would serve to illustrate
how much of old material goes to make up the freshest novelty of human life. Hence, too,
might be drawn a weighty lesson from the little-regarded truth that the act of the
passing generation is the germ which may and must produce good or
evil fruit in a far-distant time.*

—Nathaniel Hawthorne, *The House of the Seven Gables*

 N a Sunday morning in October 1918, under arching elm, oak, and maple branches resplendent in vermilion and gold, an eerie emptiness possessed the stately streets of Salem, Massachusetts. Only the occasional crackle of electric trolleys and the clop of horses' hooves broke the stillness in intersections that on other Sundays had resounded with the rumble of Model T engines and the trumpeting of their horns. Like other patriotic Americans in the wartime nation, Salemites were obeying Fuel Administrator Harry A. Garfield's rationing edict that banned automobile driving on Sundays. But even if they could have driven, there were few places in Salem they could go. The local Committee on Public Safety had ordered the closing of the city's churches because of another foreign threat: "Spanish" in-fluenza. The killer "grippe" had already shut down Salem's workday destinations, including its schools, theaters, poolrooms, and bowling alleys. Nuns staffed emer-gency medical wards, and the Board of Health warned against "riding in jitneys and cars."[1] Headlines pushed aside news from the front to announce the latest medical statistics and proclaimed "Gasolineless and Churchless Sunday."[2] By the time World War I had ended, thousands of Salem's citizens, many in the prime of life, had fallen victim to "the flu," a mysterious epidemic that had cut across the

globe with staggering speed. In 1918 alone, nearly a thousand Salem residents died. From a historical perspective, the body count in Salem is not especially significant or unusual, and the Great Influenza Epidemic is no more or less remembered in Salem than elsewhere. What is remarkable is that the immense loss of life—five hundred thousand Americans and an estimated 25 million people around the globe—is nearly absent in historical memory. We maintain that this amnesia originates in a disconnection between the event and an identifiable location.

Much more conspicuous than these thousand deaths in Salem's four-hundred-year history are the twenty executions during the years 1692–1693 in the brief but horrific affair known as the Salem Witch Trials. Nineteen people, mostly women, were hanged for the crime of witchcraft, and one man, Giles Cory, was pressed to death by stones piled one at a time upon a plank on his chest. Not remembered in these figures are those who died during their imprisonment, the emotional trauma of Dorcas Good—a four-year-old locked in a dank cell for nine months and deranged ever after—and the emotional wounds that scarred everyone involved. Yet the witch trial legacy has lingered long after, haunting the writing of Nathaniel Hawthorne and finding a measure of resolution only 310 years later, when Massachusetts governor Jane Swift reprieved the final five accused.[3] The witch trials have so seized the American imagination that the event has come to stand for the place itself, consecrating Salem as a civic shrine. In most cases, when commentators refer to "Salem," they mean the witch trials.

Why are these twenty remembered when thousands of Salem's influenza victims have been nearly forgotten? Why do we commemorate the nineteen who were hanged, but not the 4,743 Americans lynched between Reconstruction and the civil rights movement?[4] Why has Salem, the place, become almost synonymous with the witch trials?

We believe that place takes on a particular mnemonic resonance when associated with extraordinary human events, most often involving tragic, sometimes wasteful sacrifice. A place is remembered far more vividly for those who suffered or died in it than for those who lived in it, and the most memorable places are often those where, it seems, lives were squandered. Tragedy can transform a place into a shrine; a historicizing phenomenon we call an "enshrining event" is an occurrence of such magnitude and cultural resonance that the place of origin is forever remembered and, indeed, mythologized. Memory transforms the site into a memorial and calls for commemoration—a conscious and selective process performed repeatedly in memorializing ritual, in countless separate acts for years, decades, or even centuries afterward. These "commemorating moments," as we term them, invoke heightened meaning for their observers, who read into original events significance that resonates in the conflicts, cares, and concerns of their own times.

Enshrining events are recognized as such once the process of memorializing a place begins. Commemoration—the investment of significance or meaning in a site—can evolve over time or can begin almost immediately, as in the days after March 6, 1836, when U.S. newspapers called upon Americans to "Remember the Alamo" and exact revenge for the massacre of 187 Texans by Santa Ana's army of 4,000.[5] In the hands of self-interested parties, commemoration can also become an act of political expediency. When an explosion ripped through an American battleship in the port of Havana on February 15, 1898, headlines in the *New York Sun* and *New York Herald* recast the Texas slogan as "Remember the *Maine,*" thereby enshrining the ship as a tomb at the bottom of the harbor. Secretary of the Navy Theodore Roosevelt blamed the explosion on Spain's "dirty treachery," and the *Maine* immediately became a patriotic symbol for the ensuing Spanish-American War, which netted the United States both Cuba and the Philippines. The story that "the blame for the *Maine* lies mainly with Spain" was fiction—in fact, the explosion on the ship has been traced to a faulty boiler—but the remains of the ship resting at the bottom of Havana harbor still resonate as a sacred space.

Pearl Harbor illustrates how commemoration both builds on and invents tradition. It shows as well how commemorating moments can be immediate, politically expedient, and cumulative. The surprise Japanese attack on American forces on December 7, 1941—historicized in President Franklin Delano Roosevelt's words as "a date which will live in infamy"—was the enshrining event of World War II. Echoing the battle cry that originated a century before in Texas, "Remember Pearl Harbor" commemorated a Pacific outpost. The effect of the slogan was cumulative, recalling at once the Alamo, the *Maine,* and countless other patriotic sacrifices and crystallizing public sentiment.

In their exhortation to "remember," commemorators choose the word whose etymological roots denote both "mind" and "body." The Latin *memor* means "mindful," and the Latin *membrum,* akin to the Goth *mimz,* means "flesh." Commemoration, therefore, is an imaginative reconstruction—a re-membering of the body politic—that enshrines the site of sacrifice, and, thereby, restores to the collective memory the lives that were lost there.

As Roosevelt astutely observed, a few dates may live in public memory—infamously or otherwise. References to 1776, the Sixties, and the terrorist attacks of September 11, 2001—what we know simply as 9/11—show how dates can come to stand for enshrining events. In this historicizing phenomenon, *dates* are substituted for *place* as a mnemonic device when the enshrining event occurs across a wide swath of geography and time. Lacking the particularity of place, a date becomes the default signifier. In popular memory, the shorthand for the American Revolution is 1776, telescoping events that took place between 1763 and 1783. "The Sixties" coalesces a decade of social unrest that included assassinations, race riots, antiwar demonstrations, and a host of countercultural movements. The abbreviation 9/11 describes the terrorist attacks that culminated in the destruction at the World Trade Center and the Pentagon and of United Airlines Flight 93 in western

Pennsylvania. Because these tragedies took place simultaneously in three different locations, the default mnemonic device becomes the date, 9/11—too recent to even include the year. As living witnesses to the enshrining events of September 11, 2001, this generation is able to watch the unfolding of commemorating moments that will construct a cohesive narrative of 9/11 and fix the tragedy in the public memory.

A tragedy may not immediately be recognized as an enshrining event—but, over time, its trajectory to enshrinement becomes clear. In the weeks following the 1834 mob attack on an Ursuline convent in Charlestown, Massachusetts, press reports, investigating committees, and even Catholic leaders characterized it as an aberration.[6] But, from this base, the nativist movement gained ascendancy in the public arena, peaking in the 1850s with the Know-Nothing Party. In the twenty years that followed, it became clear that the burning of the convent was not at all an aberration, but a catalyst and harbinger of things to come: it was the enshrining event of nineteenth-century anti-Catholicism.[7]

Commemoration privileges some events over others, even when those other episodes have touched a greater number of lives more profoundly. Salem is, in fact, a place of many significant events and many histories. The Great Fire of 1914 leveled whole neighborhoods in Salem, but it is barely remembered by the grandchildren of its victims. Thus even dramatic local occurrences can lack the cachet of an enshrining event: in local catastrophes, lives may be lost, but the story of their deaths yields no moral. Other local events—the birth of a famous author or the founding of a college—may be historically significant but not on the magnitude and not with the cultural reverberation of an enshrining event.

The occurrence of an extraordinary event in a particular place enriches the progression from enshrining event to national myth and calls for remembrance, tradition, and commemoration. Events such as the witch trials become mythologized when their tragedies are perceived to be beyond the realm of ordinary human experience. Lacking the particularity of place, even devastating global epidemics lose their resonance and the bounded character that defines them. Epidemics, like tornadoes, floods, and fires, are natural occurrences that invoke victims without villains, loss without a redeeming moral. Because the events of 1692–1693 signify some perceived injustice within a bounded geography, *Salem* has become associated with a whole constellation of beliefs about intolerance, persecution, and the abuse of authority. The power of place is illustrated in the fact that the name *Salem* is now even more powerful than the history of the place itself. The deaths of twenty people in the Salem witch trials are magnified and mythologized. The fate of other victims is obscured. Examples abound of the ways that our history story is distorted or forgotten. No witches were burned in Salem. The Pilgrims did not land on Plymouth Rock.[8] The Battle of Bunker Hill actually took place on Breed's Hill.

We have already suggested that place becomes inextricably linked to tragedy when the loss of life is perceived as especially wasteful or unjust. The particularity of a place allows the mythologizing to begin. In the mythmaking that follows, deaths occurring in such a way are elevated to the level of sacrifice, interpreted as exemplifying a principle, and they complete the christening of the place into sacred ground. Primitive and formative events are imaginatively reenacted on the soil. Regardless of how it begins, the event comes to stand for deeply held values and beliefs and for ideological conflicts decided there. But how are these myths created? Or, as Native American poet Ron Welburn asks, "In whose hands is the telling of the tale?"[9]

In Hawthorne's hands, the accused witches hanged on Gallows Hill became martyrs for tolerance, and *The House of the Seven Gables* is their memorial. For Ralph Waldo Emerson, the "embattled farmers" at Concord's North Bridge became "those heroes [who dared] to die, and leave their children free." In his "Concord Hymn Sung at the Completion of the Battle Monument, July 4, 1837," Emerson pledged:

> On this green bank, by this soft stream,
> We set to-day a votive stone;
> That memory may their deed redeem,
> When, like our sires, our sons are gone.

Emerson's "votive stone"—a more lasting and permanent marker than a flickering flame—is erected by the sons of the minutemen. His verses paid tribute to both the enshrining event of 1775 and to the commemorating moment of 1837. Emerson's language of civic religion, "On this green bank, by this soft stream," captured the mythologizing spirit of his times. The poet understood the danger that succeeding generations might forget this place and its enshrining event of April 19, 1775. So that "memory may their deed redeem," the memorializers chose, not the anniversary of the event, but Independence Day for the commemorating moment, enshrining at Concord the sacrifice of "our sires"—men who died without knowing that their deaths would give birth to a new nation. By dedicating the site on July 4, and through Emerson's use of religious language to commemorate this dedication, the enshrining process is complete. In Emerson's hands, a musket ball fired in a provincial skirmish became "the shot heard round the world."

The Civil War brought forth fresh episodes that called for commemoration—events in which observers felt compelled to pay tribute to "those who . . . gave their lives that that nation might live." Wrenching the consciousness of all Americans, blue or gray, was the decisive battle of the war, the vicious three-day struggle at Gettysburg that left 23,049 Union and 28,063 Confederate casualties. The horrific human tragedy and monumental historic consequences enshrined this rural township as a national symbol. In Abraham Lincoln's hands, the fallen soldiers at Gettysburg died for the cause of unification. In creating the sense of place that is Gettysburg, Lincoln's speech elevated it above other terrible Civil War battlefields. The address was far too modest. It privileged the enshrining event above the commemorating moment. Lincoln claimed that "we cannot dedicate—we cannot consecrate—we cannot hallow this ground. The brave men, living and dead, who struggled here, have consecrated it, far above our poor power to add or detract. The world will little note, nor long remember, what we say here, but it can never forget what they did here." Some sevenscore and four years later, who but scholars and Civil War buffs would note and remember the lists of dead and wounded? What schoolchildren commit to memory are, in fact, Lincoln's words, not Gettysburg's numbers. Even more than the soldiers who "gave the last full measure of devotion," Lincoln's address hallowed and consecrated the "great battlefield of that war." Like Hawthorne's Salem and Emerson's Concord, Lincoln's Gettysburg resonates powerfully in the American mind; but how many of us recall that Gettysburg is in Pennsylvania, and not in, say, Virginia?

Salem, Concord, and Gettysburg have all been canonized by "enshrining events." The civic consecration of a place can be so powerful that it obscures much more than the facts of what happened there. The public's fascination with the extraordinary erases the everyday history that makes a place meaningful to others who lived there before or after the enshrining event, especially in Salem. We know about the fate of the twenty accused. But what do most of us know about the lives of the thousands who occupied this dot on the map called Salem both before and after the enshrining event? Of Anne Burlak or Harriet Low? Of Charlotte Forten or William Bentley? Of Laurie Cabot or Martha Brailsford? Of Benjamin Goodhue or Black Will? Of John Turner or David Moulton? This book opens a window into their lives and the lives of representative others as it considers many facets of Salem's history—to, as the poet Welburn says, tell their tales as well.

Salem: Place, Myth, and Memory

Salem: Place, Myth, and Memory examines an essential American Studies question: What creates a sense of place? In this collection, fourteen scholars take the history of Salem, Massachusetts, as their template to examine the ways in which fourteen generations have experienced this place. Against a backdrop of commemorating moments that celebrate significant Salem anniversaries—the 1944 establishment of Historic Salem, Inc., the 1854 founding of Salem State College, the 1804 birth of Nathaniel Hawthorne—this collection challenges readers to reconsider the notion of place, including the ways in which the local intersects with the national and the global. Like Salem, every American community has ample occasion for commemorating moments, and these present opportunities for reexamining their myths and legacies. Few communities, however, have the power of place conferred on Salem by the enshrining events of 1692, and Salem offers scholars a rare opportunity to explore issues of both enshrinement and commemoration. Yet, this volume aims at more. *Salem* challenges readers to move beyond the conventional, to resurrect the neglected pasts of a historic site and reflect on the many ways that a place can be imagined and reinterpreted.

This collection builds upon an important body of scholarship that challenges Americans to look around them and to recognize the importance of place in the shaping and reshaping of our culture. *Salem: Place, Myth, and Memory* fits into this literature because it examines the power of place, but it is deeply centered in the local, examining a single place over time. Many studies paint with a much broader brush. In *Common Landscape of America, 1580 to 1845* (1982), John R. Stilgoe provides a sweeping survey of the way wilderness was transformed from chaos to landscape, which was "created by men intent on ordering and shaping space for their own ends."[10] Simon Schama extends this interpretation in *Landscape and Memory* (1995).[11] "[L]andscape is the work of the mind," Schama tells us. "Its scenery is built up as much from the strata of memory as from layers of rock." In this treatment, the relationship between culture and space is paradoxical; indeed, despite mankind's disruption, even devastation, of the environment, our occupation of the landscape "is a cause not for guilt and sorrow but for celebration." For Schama, a paradox lies in the fact that even in the appreciation of wilderness, "the very act of identifying [a] place presupposes our presence." Landscape and culture, then, are complementary aspects of the human experience.[12]

A second trend in studies of place is represented by treatments that emphasize historical methodology or the uses of memory in representing historic sites, such as John Lewis Gaddis's historiographical excursion, *The Landscape of History: How Historians Map the Past* (2002).[13] Gaddis's work offers worthwhile reflections on the relationships between place and the past, invoking the uses of metaphor and representation in the experience of locality, biography, and history. In an earlier groundbreaking study, *Mystic Chords of Memory: The Transformation of Tradition in American Culture* (1991), Michael Kammen examines collective memory, national identity, and historic place.[14] Kammen focuses on the dynamics of American tradition, particularly "when and how a tradition can have ideological consequences and help to define a culture or subculture." These dynamics are frequently negotiated between local and national constituencies, and they are selective in their orientation. Kammen observes that "memory is more likely to be activated by contestation, and amnesia is more likely to be induced by the desire for reconciliation."[15] Seen through the lens of place, however, memory can be grounded in the "enshrinement" of momentous events in particular places. And, as our example of the Great Influenza Epidemic illustrates, historical amnesia can originate also in the disconnection between an event and any identifiable location.

In *Race and Reunion: The Civil War in American Memory* (2001), David W. Blight builds on Kammen's assertions about the origins of public memory, taking as his domain the contested meanings of the Civil War: "Exactly what those lessons should be, and who should determine them, has been the most contested question in American historical memory since 1863."[16] He observes that the Civil War provided a lens through which "contending memories clashed or intermingled" around "the tangled relationship between two profound ideas—*healing* and *justice*." Sites such as Gettysburg provided the scenes on which these contests of memory and meaning were waged, and, indeed, provide the foundations on which memory is anchored. Blight's examination of memory in American culture is profound and stimulating. We disagree, however, with his generalization that "nations rarely commemorate their disasters and tragedies, unless compelled by forces that will not let the politics of memory rest."[17] We maintain that tragedy, in fact, provides a more poignant and powerful dynamic than victory or achievement in coalescing and preserving memory. Furthermore, the essays in *Salem: Place, Myth, and Memory* demonstrate that commemoration is not necessarily or always compelled, and that other forces—culture, economics, religion—anchor their traditions in a sense of place. This collection finds its niche in the perspective of locality. The essays uncover fresh insights into the study of place that can be gleaned only by focusing on one place over time, and thus showing how closely memory is tied to place.

A third approach to the examination of place and memory is to define a regional identity. In *The Eastern Frontier: The Settlement of Northern New England, 1610–1763* (1970), Charles E. Clark has examined the complexities of a New England identity.[18] He observes, "To most students of the American past . . . the phrase 'colonial New England' calls forth a cluster of associated images. . . . The trouble with such images is not that they are false . . . but that they are incomplete." Clark concludes, "Regions are both historically grounded and culturally invented, [and] components of their identity . . . change over time."[19]

Another study on New England is James M. Lindgren's 1995 history of the Society for the Preservation of New England Antiquities (SPNEA) during the progressive era, *Preserving Historic New England: Preservation, Progressivism, and the Remaking of Memory*, which examines the "cultural politics of remaking the New England memory."[20] For Lindgren, "[h]istoric preservation in New England . . . embodied a contest, sometimes of crisis proportions, over the definition of the past, present, and future." He shows us how the saving of historic landmarks was not so much an effort to preserve sites in their original forms as it was a process of redefinition in which these sites were "born anew to foster patriotism, Anglo-Saxonism, and acceptable Yankee values." Whereas Lindgren's important study shows how a "select band" used the preservation of place to further an agenda of conservative reform and, in so doing, engage in "the making of memory" and "the remaking of history,"[21] we seek to show how generations of ordinary Americans transcended the historic significance outsiders attributed to Salem and instead sought to give meaning to the lived experience of the place they knew. In a study published the same year as Lindgren's, Dona Brown examines the ways in which an emergent tourist industry went about fashioning regional identity to appeal to middle-class consumerism.[22] *Inventing New England: Regional Tourism in the Nineteenth Century* argues that, by the late nineteenth century, "tourism helped to forge a new landscape . . . driven by a profound 'sentimentalization' of New England, a new vision of the region . . . a mythic region called Old New England— rural, preindustrial, and ethnically 'pure.'" In American popular culture, "New England came to mean . . . an imagined world of pastoral beauty, rural independence, virtuous simplicity, and religious and ethnic homogeneity."[23]

The formation and characteristics of a New England identity are also the focus of Joseph A. Conforti's excellent work, *Imagining New England: Explorations of Regional Identity from the Pilgrims to the Mid-Twentieth Century* (2001).[24] Consonant with recent trends in the scholarship of region, Conforti discusses "real places but also historical artifacts whose cultural boundaries shift over time." He is concerned with continuities and changes, traditions and trends that maintain a sense of geographic coherence yet allow adaptation to the forces of history. In surveying "America's first strongly imagined region," Conforti recognizes that New England has been continually imagined and redefined in narrative—"stories that have been continually revised in response to new interpretive needs generated by the transformations of regional life."[25]

A fourth approach, encompassing the intersection of locality and experience, is the niche in which *Salem: Place, Myth, and Memory* lies. It is represented by texts such as *Mapping American Culture* (1992), a collection of essays edited by Wayne Franklin and Michael Steiner that grew out of the 1990 conference of the California American Studies Association.[26] Although a great many monographs have been written on the subject of place, we believe, with Franklin and Steiner, that a collection is the best vehicle through which scholars can study place, offering a "polyvocal community of scholars, with questions that transcend and therefore elude the concerns of a single discipline." The organizing theme of *Mapping* is the idea that "[s]pace is the driving force in American culture, but the closer attachments of place . . . may be more influential" for our sense of history, both national and local, as well as for personal identity.[27] Much like the *Salem* essays, *Mapping American Culture* aims "to grasp how space and place permeate the grand acts as well as the ordinary events of American life." However, complementing the westward orientation of the conference theme, *Mapping* discusses the relationship between open spaces and a sense of place; unlike *Salem*, it focuses on the varied experiences of different places rather than on one locality across time.

Because Salem, Massachusetts, has been a touchstone for seminal beginnings and decisive turning points in American culture, it is an excellent choice for a reconsideration of place.[28] This collection traces the development of one place as a local, national, and global entity from its seventeenth-century origins, depicted in the essays "Salem as Frontier Outpost" and "Salem as Religious Proving Ground," through the nineteenth century ("Salem as Enterprise Zone, 1783–1786," "Salem as Athenaeum," and "Salem as Citizen of the World"), and into the modern era ("Salem as a Global City," "Salem as Crime Scene," "Salem as Witch City," and "Coda: Montage of Brick and Water"). Of particular interest during 2004, the text's own "enshrining event" of publication, are the essays that directly relate to the sixtieth anniversary of Historic Salem, Inc. ("Salem as Architectural Mecca"), the sesquicentennial of Salem State College ("Salem as the Nation's Schoolhouse"), and, of course, the bicentennial of Nathaniel Hawthorne's birth ("Salem as Hawthorne's Creation" and "Salem's House of the Seven Gables as Historic Site"). Yet all the essays in the collection pose questions about place in ways that reverberate beyond 2004.

In the opening essay, "Salem as Frontier Outpost," archaeologist and historian Emerson Baker II challenges us to see Salem through two sets of eyes—those of Native Americans and those of English Puritan settlers. He also challenges one of our most fundamental conceptions—the very notion of place as a fixed construct. In Western cultures, a sense of place usually has to do with history, with events associated with a particular site. In Salem, an American sense of place began to diverge almost immediately from traditional assumptions through the accommodation of Native American and Puritan perspectives. It was this dynamic interaction of cultures that transformed both peoples' sense of place. Baker examines the site's Native American origins as Naumkeag, "the fishing place," which was occupied for thousands of years before the arrival of the first English settlers in 1626. Salem started as a "borderland—a place of negotiation" between Native American and British cultures. Even as the Native American people dwindled in number and Salem evolved into a commercial entrepôt, the frontier was never far away. In 1675, during Metacomet's War (called King Philip's War by the colonists), English residents felt the closeness of the frontier so much that they walled in the town to protect it from Indian attack. This initial theme of Salem as frontier would echo throughout the subsequent history of the community.

In chapter 2, "Salem as Religious Proving Ground," Christopher White, a historian of religion, examines several manifestations of spiritual experience throughout Salem's history. White makes the point that the historical record of a place is interpreted selectively, according to the needs and sensibilities of the historical age in which the explanations are written, no matter how infelicitous the connection to its history. Chronicles of religion in New England usually locate Puritan theology and ecclesiology at the center of life in the region. Without a doubt, Puritan traditions powerfully shaped the mind and mindset of New Englanders and, later,

Americans more generally. But White's evidence from Salem suggests that early Americans took their Christianity with more than a measure of ambivalence. Many New Englanders, from both early and later periods, knew surprisingly little about basic Christian beliefs; others were unsatisfied with conventional Christianity and supplemented it with pagan practices and notions; still others deliberately opposed Puritanism. By examining Salem as a place of religious contestation—by investigating how believers lived and competed with each other in this small community—White departs from traditional interpretations to assert that religious New England might best be understood as an ongoing negotiation between Protestant groups and others. Both marginal and mainstream groups were shaped by contact with the "other" in their midst. That fact comes quite clearly into focus when we analyze the diversity of religious experience in Salem, where contact, compromise, and, sometimes, conflict have shaped religious identities into the twenty-first century.

Local historian Robert Booth, whose essay, "Salem as Enterprise Zone, 1783–1786," takes a modern economic concept as its reference point, contributes the third chapter. In the wake of independence, Salem was part of an infant nation that stagnated in economic crisis. As a remedy, many Americans, including leaders such as Jefferson and Madison, looked to the frontier, forging paths through the post-Revolutionary wilderness that would become the new America. Their view was landlocked; they dreamt of conquering lands to the west and south and of spreading their political and economic systems to the Pacific. Booth's essay addresses how Salem's entrepreneurs emerged from the Revolution determined to carry forward the success of their wartime privateering and trading into the postwar commercial arena. As Salem's merchants reestablished trade with traditional markets, they also experimented with markets and trade routes that had been forbidden to them as British colonials. This spirit of innovation, unleashed by new republican freedoms, also animated the town's politics and civic culture. Merchants and politicians went beyond self-interest to identify themselves with the success of their community and with the republican ideals by which all might share in that success, Salem's residents embraced innovation and enterprise, and talented and ambitious outsiders chose to move in and join them. At a time when most of America was suffering from a prolonged economic depression, Salemites were prospering by venturing further into the untried areas—commercial, social, political—that transformed their town into a new kind of place that could not have existed under British rule, and that proved to be extraordinarily fruitful for decades to come.

Before Boston emerged in the mid-nineteenth century as New England's hub of scientific enterprise, Salem was the center of northern New England intellectual life. In chapter 4, maritime historian Matthew G. McKenzie examines how Salem's learned societies emerged from the Revolution with a commitment to intellectual pursuits that fueled the town's commercial prosperity. Salem savants organized local societies that drew on the community's practical foundations in trade and fishing, and they applied the scientific method to test and refine their knowledge of the seas. Historians have traditionally understood colonial American scientists as passively accepting the authority of Europe's learned societies. However, McKenzie's groundbreaking study of vocational science in Salem presents a different picture, revealing a moment when newly independent Americans established learned societies outside the academy that were based on community service and citizenship. These societies played a brief, but crucial, role in transitioning from community-based colonial science to the academically based science that emerged in the 1830s.

Whereas Emerson Baker's essay considers Salem as a western frontier or borderland outpost of European civilization, historian Dane Anthony Morrison's study, "Salem as Citizen of the World," emphasizes Salem's identity as a cosmopolitan seaport community engaged in global commerce. This fifth chapter illustrates the ways in which Salemites who sojourned abroad linked the town to the exotic cultures of the East and stoked its distinctive multicultural character. Hundreds of journals, logs, and diaries formed the mythology of a once-glorious Salem. Shared with friends and family, incorporated into newspaper reports and public lectures, the stuff of conversation long after, these recollections of faraway lands and peoples made Salem a unique place among American cities. More sophisticated, more cosmopolitan, more worldly and experienced, Salem of the China Trade stood out as a "citty upon a Hill" quite different from Puritan expectations, one that contributed to the nation's economic might, material culture, and literary imagination.

The national movement to create a public school system had important roots in Salem during the period 1830–1860, as education historian Rebecca Noel illustrates. In chapter 6, "Salem as the Nation's Schoolhouse," Noel shows that Salem's educational pioneering drew its inspiration from three sources: industrialization, European-inspired idealism, and the antebellum spirit of reform. Salem was the site of their convergence, the epicenter of this vast and lasting social reform. Leading reformer Horace Mann had strong ties to Salem through his marriage to Salem teacher Mary Peabody, whose sister Elizabeth founded the nation's first kindergarten and whose sister Sophia was married to Nathaniel Hawthorne. These connections enabled Mann to make Salem a laboratory of educational innovation and led to the development of the normal school and to the institution that became Salem State College. This model quickly spread from eastern Massachusetts to the rest of the nation.

The seventh chapter, "Salem as Hawthorne's Creation," by literary historian Nancy Lusignan Schultz, examines how Hawthorne's works helped to create our perceptions of Salem as a place. "Nathaniel Hawthorne invented Salem," Schultz tells us, and her cultural history of Salem as an imaginative setting reveals the ways in which Hawthorne's Salem became the powerful icon that dominates the American literary landscape. Hawthorne's sense of American identity—in particular its penchant for intolerance, narrowness, and persecution—offers an ironic counterpoint to the national myth of religious freedom. Hawthorne's Salem has been tapped as an alternative myth by writers of every subsequent generation, most notably by Arthur Miller in his famous probing of 1950s political persecution in *The Crucible*.

In the next chapter, "Salem as Architectural Mecca," John V. Goff observes that architecture reveals important lessons about place as a subliminal force in popular culture. Before Salem became infamous as America's "witch city," Goff asserts, the urban center was appreciated and promoted as one of the country's best-preserved "colonial" cities, valued for its exceptional and well-preserved New England architecture. The great antiquity of the settlement, combined with the superb preservation of many significant early landmarks from the seventeenth, eighteenth, and early nineteenth centuries, lured American architectural students and historians to Salem, especially after the nation's 1876 centennial celebrations. During the Victorian era, Salem was showcased nationally as a site in which both the earlier Colonial and the more recent Colonial Revival styles of architecture could complement one another. Proponents of the Colonial Revival style, drawn to Salem to study its colonial buildings, published measured drawings and photographs of its historic landmarks in both popular and professional journals. The publicity further promoted Salem's renown as an architectural Mecca, while also drawing new architectural talent to Salem. Goff's work contributes to our understanding of the built environment. He concludes that the decisive factor underlying Salem's first urban renaissance was the town's significance as a global seaport and birthplace of New England's China Trade. From an examination of common local patterns and design motifs in Salem balustrades, fence designs, and windows, Goff shows that early trade connections with the East gave a unique international flavor to many of its buildings, particularly in the form of adapted Chinese motifs.

In chapter 9, "Salem as a Global City, 1850–2004," Latin American historian Aviva Chomsky offers an exciting, multidimensional perspective on place. Salem's history, she asserts, is generally written as if it ends in the eighteenth century. In fact, Salem in the nineteenth and twentieth centuries reveals a very different city— one of rapid industrialization, immigration, and intense labor struggles. By the late twentieth century, Salem had become a place of deindustrialization as factories moved to the U.S. South and then abroad. A new generation of immigrants arrived in the city, this time from Latin America, and another cycle of increasing global ties developed.

In "Salem as Crime Scene," the tenth chapter, mystery writer Margaret Press asks, "Why would a crime writer choose Salem as a locale?" She considers the question "Is murder more sinister when committed here?" The author of *Counterpoint* takes on these questions as she examines how and why mystery writers have mined Salem as a setting for their stories and why real crimes committed within its borders seem to resonate with its notorious past. She also probes case histories and criminal investigations from the past and present, and she explores how members of the current Salem Police Department view crime in their city. The very name *Salem* plants foreboding in every reader before he or she opens the book. It hardly matters whether a writer builds on preconceptions, corrects misconceptions, uses them as a foil, or ignores them entirely. The reader will have begun the journey with a twinge of fear, a hint of mystery, and an expectation of the extraordinary. A writer can ask for little more than to live in a place like Salem.

In the eleventh essay, Frances Hill, author of *A Delusion of Satan: The Full Story of the Salem Witch Trials* and *Hunting for Witches: A Visitor's Guide to the Salem Witch Trials,* looks at "Salem as Witch City," that strange fantasy land of witch hats, devil masks, pentagrams, and wands that reaches its apotheosis each year on October 31. Why should a series of trials for witchcraft held in the Salem town house in 1692 bequeath this place its primary economic and cultural identity? And why should those trials of innocents on false charges lead not to exhibits and displays about the trials themselves but to bizarre entertainments based on playing at being frightened of witches and spirits? The journey from witch trials to Halloween tourism was never inevitable. Treating readers to a transatlantic perspective, this British author describes how Salem arrived at this place, and in so doing illustrates some of the ironies of mythmaking.

Archaeologist Lorinda B. R. Goodwin structures the final essay, "Salem's House of the Seven Gables as Historic Site," to reflect the layers uncovered at a dig. Goodwin looks back in time to present the notion that history is informed by levels of myth similar to layers of strata uncovered in fieldwork. The Turner House, as a twenty-first-century historic site, trades on its associations with Nathaniel Hawthorne, its identity as a home to sea captains, its status as an example of seventeenth-century architecture, and its tenuous connections with the witch trials of 1692. The "respect of place" that the house enjoyed during the seventeenth century ensured that every generation that came after would reinterpret and reinforce the site's almost mythological cachet; the preservation ethic that prevailed in Salem during the first half of the twentieth century reified these ideas. Research and ongoing interpretation have added other, self-conscious reinventions of the place in a long, evolving succession of traditions.

Poet J. D. Scrimgeour's coda, "Montage of Brick and Water," shatters Salem's cherished mythologies to offer a gritty image of a place uncomfortable in the present, yet unable to breach its "connection with the long past," its ties to "manners, feelings, and opinions, almost or wholly obsolete." Scrimgeour's Salem is a city of broken promises, of groaning consequences, of forlorn meanderings, of dirty air and stagnant water, of remembrance and remorse, recalling Hawthorne's ambivalence about his birthplace. In Scrimgeour's hands, the city's enshrining event, the unshakable witch trials, darkens every day in Salem. It is a place that hungers for glory days gone by yet wallows in the blackest moment of its history. Like Nathaniel Hawthorne, Salem is caught in Judge Hathorne's shadow, obsessed with the deeds of its patriarchs. Pinned under "weighty lessons," Salem is hobbled by the belief "that the act of the passing generation is the germ which may and must produce good or evil fruit in a far-distant time." Yet Scrimgeour's poem is also a paean to the city that has survived; it embraces Salem as a place where even the haunted Hawthorne could find "the freshest novelty of human life."

It is this ever-renewing aspect that the photography of Kim Mimnaugh, featured throughout the collection, also asks us to recall as part of the Salem experience. Like Scrimgeour's poem, Mimnaugh's impressions illustrate "how much of old material goes to make up" this "freshest novelty of human life." Alongside a history of fires and flu outbreaks, faded glories and fallen angels, her work is a montage of present glories and of Salemites who are decidedly not "slaves . . . to bygone times." In her images of Salem, with its Chinese balustrades and colonial breakwaters, its Dominicans and divines, Mimnaugh reminds us that the vitality of a place is a matter of how the present uses its past.

Every October, as leaves resplendent in vermilion and gold fall from arching elm, oak, and maple branches, the vitality of this place is apparent in every corner of the city, from Chestnut Street to Witchcraft Heights, in Salem's creative uses of its enshrining event. From the bawdiness of Haunted Happenings to the solemn respect of candlelight vigils for tiny Dorcas Good and the twenty executed, Salem's navigation through a sea of myths and memories, in this season of dying things, makes it a place forever new.

Notes

1. *Salem Evening News,* September 25, 1918.

2. See, for example, *Salem Evening News,* October 5, 1918.

3. Paula Keene, a graduate student in history at Salem State College, learned of the plight of the five remaining accused in a course on witchcraft in Old and New England. She was instrumental in bringing the issue before the state legislature.

4. Of these 4,743, it is estimated that 3,446 were African American. The greatest number of hangings in a single year occurred in 1892, when mobs lynched an average of 4 African Americans each week.

5. The selective nature of the commemorative process is apparent in the privileging of San Antonio, site of the Alamo, over Goliad, where, on March 20, over three hundred Texans were

slaughtered after they had surrendered. At that time, however, American battle cries recalled both the Alamo and Goliad. Michael Kammen takes a different approach to the remembrance of these and other sites in *Mystic Chords of Memory: The Transformation of Tradition in American Culture* (New York: Alfred A. Knopf, 1991). Kammen warns historians to "be very cautious . . . about taking for granted the cohesion, clarity, and retentiveness of either civic or popular memory" (9). However, we believe the evidence shows that the association of the "enshrining event" with a place reinforces the mnemonic power of the event. The public's knowledge of the witch trials, the Alamo massacre, the *Maine* explosion, or the attack on Pearl Harbor may not be particularly cohesive or clear, but in these cases the concrete imagery of place reinforces retention of the event in popular memory.

6. Nancy Lusignan Schultz, *Fire and Roses: The Burning of the Charlestown Convent, 1834* (Boston: Northeastern University Press, 1st paperback edition, 2002).

7. In recent history, we have seen similar developments in the enshrinement of Ruby Ridge, Idaho, and Waco, Texas, by antigovernment extremists. For Timothy McVeigh, the bombing of the Alfred P. Murrah Federal Building in Oklahoma City on April 19, 1995, was a diabolical "commemorating moment" appropriating the 220th anniversary of the battles at Lexington and Concord and the second anniversary of the burning of the Branch Davidian compound at Waco, Texas, on April 19, 1993, to raze a federal building, not to raise a memorial.

8. For a nice discussion of the memory and meaning of Plymouth Rock, see John D. Seelye, *Memory's Nation: The Place of Plymouth Rock* (Chapel Hill: University of North Carolina Press, 1998).

9. "Apess after Words," *Quarter after Eight* 2 (1995): 11–14, cited in Dane Morrison, ed., *American Indian Studies: An Interdisciplinary Approach to Contemporary Issues* (New York: Peter Lang, 1997), 7.

10. John R. Stilgoe, *Common Landscape of America, 1580 to 1845* (New Haven: Yale University Press, 1982), 3.

11. Simon Schama, *Landscape and Memory* (New York: Alfred A. Knopf, 1995).

12. Schama, 7, 9.

13. John Lewis Gaddis, *The Landscape of History: How Historians Map the Past* (New York: Oxford University Press, 2002).

14. Michael Kammen, *Mystic Chords of Memory: The Transformation of Tradition in American Culture* (New York: Alfred A. Knopf, 1991).

15. Kammen, 11, 13.

16. David W. Blight, *Race and Reunion: The Civil War in American Memory* (Cambridge, Mass.: Harvard University Press, 2001), 1.

17. Blight, 1–3, 9.

18. Charles E. Clark, *The Eastern Frontier: The Settlement of Northern New England, 1610–1763* (New York: Alfred A. Knopf, 1970).

19. Clark, viii.

20. James M. Lindgren, *Preserving Historic New England: Preservation, Progressivism, and the Remaking of Memory* (New York: Oxford University Press, 1995), 4–5.

21. Lindgren, 3–5.

22. Dona Brown, *Inventing New England: Regional Tourism in the Nineteenth Century* (Washington: Smithsonian Institution Press, 1995).

23. Brown, 8–9.

24. Joseph A. Conforti, *Imagining New England: Explorations of Regional Identity from the Pilgrims to the Mid-Twentieth Century* (Chapel Hill: University of North Carolina Press, 2001).

25. Conforti, 2–7. Readers may follow the development of a New England identity in the primary sources collected by Andrew Delbanco in *Writing New England: An Anthology from Puritans to the Present* (Cambridge, Mass.: Harvard University Press, 2001).

26. Wayne Franklin and Michael Steiner, eds., *Mapping American Culture* (Iowa City: University of Iowa Press, 1992). Joseph A. Amato's *Rethinking Home: A Case for Writing Local History* (Berkeley: University of California Press, 2002) also treats the theme of place as home, but in a midwestern setting.

27. Franklin and Steiner, 3–12.

28. There is a rich scholarship on Salem, Massachusetts. Readers will enjoy the illustrated *Salem: Cornerstones of a Historic City* (Beverly, Mass.: Commonwealth Editions, 1999) by K. David Goss, Richard B. Trask, Bryant F. Tolles Jr., Joseph Flibbert, and Jim McAllister. Most studies address the conventional themes, particularly the witch trials. Readers may refer to Paul Boyer and Stephen Nissenbaum, *Salem Possessed: The Social Origins of Witchcraft* (Cambridge, Mass.: Harvard University Press, 1974); George Malcolm Yool, *1692 Witch Hunt: The Layman's Guide to the Salem Witchcraft Trials* (Bowie, Md.: Heritage Books, 1992); Bernard Rosenthal, *Salem Story: Reading the Witch Trials of 1692* (New York: Cambridge University Press, 1993); Phyllis Raybin Emert, *The 25 Scariest Places in the World* (Chicago: Contemporary Books, 1995); and Frances Hill, *The Salem Witch Trials Reader* (New York: DaCapo, 2000).

Puritans and Naumkeag Indians. Campus mural, Salem State College. Photo by Kim Mimnaugh.

Chapter One

Salem as Frontier Outpost

EMERSON W. BAKER II

. . . the pavements of the
Main-street must be laid over the red man's grave.

—Nathaniel Hawthorne, "Main-street"

EFORE there was *Salem,* there was *Naumkeag.* The Native
American name, from the ancient Algonkian language, trans-
lates as "the fishing place" and explains why, for centuries before
the arrival of English settlers, Native American peoples set their
villages along the harbor. Overlooking Massachusetts Bay, reed-
thatched *weetos,* or wigwams, nestled within a ring of wooden palisade fencing.
Lazy smoke drifted upward through openings at the tops of these traditional native homes, and wafted over the sparkling waters. It was to the fishing place at
Naumkeag that the first wave of English settlers came to plant their Puritan village
in 1626. They christened it Salem, after the Old Testament city of peace, a condition they hoped to find in a New World that would be safe from the harassing policies of their king and church.

Puritan Salem began as an outpost on the margins of the English world. It was
the original settlement of the Massachusetts Bay Colony. It was, as well, a borderland—a place of negotiation and accommodation between English and Native
American cultures. In time, Salem would come to be known as a bustling cosmopolitan port with a substantial hinterland and numerous overseas trading spheres.
It is difficult for us to imagine this community as contested ground, yet in the first
half of the seventeenth century, Salem was such a place—a frontier in which natives and pioneers struggled for control. The geographic reality of Naumkeag's
rich resources influenced seventeenth-century Salem profoundly and echoes
throughout the subsequent history of the town.[1]

Naumkeag, Native American Homeland

For modern readers, *Naumkeag* and *Salem* are just two names for the same place. For seventeenth-century Algonkians, however, the names invoked much more. To them, *Salem* was a name imposed on the place by newcomers. They were told the name meant "peace" in Hebrew and expressed the newcomers' intention to build a community that would be devout in spirit and in harmony with their neighbors—although the Puritans' armor and blunderbusses may have raised some skepticism. The name *Naumkeag* carried no such ideological connotations. Instead, "the fishing place" was a practical description of a harbor and river that provided the bounty important for the Algonkians' survival. It was the name given by their ancestors, who had occupied the land for generations and who even called themselves "the Naumkeag" to express their integration into this place. Furthermore, the Naumkeag extended the meaning of the name to encompass a tribal territory that occupied much of the coastal north shore of Massachusetts Bay. So, while Naumkeag was a distinct location, the word also referred to a people and to their larger homeland. Existing side by side during the 1620s, these names— *Naumkeag* and *Salem*—implied to Native American and English inhabitants the collision of cultures that would necessarily come about in a contested space. As the history of this place unfolded, the Native American inhabitants may have begun to recognize the irony that the founding of a city named for peace would result in so much death and misery.

The renaming of Naumkeag is an example of what can be called an "imperialism of the map." English settlers and explorers very quickly renamed the landscape of New England, to give it a more familiar feel, to promote the region to potential settlers and financial backers, and to make a clear statement of their possession of the land. John Smith had begun this process in 1616 when he created his map of New England. Smith knew the Native American place names, but he renamed these locations after English towns and citizens. Naumkeag became Smith's "Bristol." Although this name, like most of Smith's labels, did not stick, the English continued to rename and thus affirm their ownership of the region.[2]

The names *Salem* and *Naumkeag* carry additional layers of meaning for the modern historian who researches through dusty documents to gain an understanding of different peoples' sense of place and of the significance of *toponomy*— the meanings of place names. An examination of surviving seventeenth-century court records and other legal documents reveals the complete English takeover of Salem's toponomy. We discover that English colonists very quickly imposed familiar English names on landscape features such as rivers and ponds, replacing existing Native American terms. Naumkeag River became Bass River, and Mashabequa River became Forest River. Only a handful of Native American names survived long enough even to be written down by the colonists. Furthermore, the Essex County court records contain few references at all to the Naumkeag's occupation of the land. One of the few documents that survives is a 1666 mortgage for seven hundred acres of land "at the head of Salem to the northwest from said town . . . there being at that place a hill where an Indian plantation sometimes had been."[3]

Because of this "imperialism of the map," it is difficult to imagine that just a few years before explorer John Smith described Naumkeag, the "fishing place," as a substantial and prosperous Native American community, occupied by a "multitude of people."[4] The people of Naumkeag were a band of the Pawtucket Tribe, an Algonkian-speaking group who occupied coastal New England from the Mystic River northward to Saco or Casco Bay. Their neighbors to the west were the Nipmuck. To the south were the Massachusett, who occupied the Neponset estuary and the south side of Massachusetts Bay. Further south, inhabiting Cape Cod and surrounding lands, were the Pokanoket, led by Massasoit. The Pawtucket, the Massachusett, and the Pokanoket all spoke the same language and were closely related by alliance and trade.[5]

The Pawtucket recognized no supreme sachem (chief) but divided themselves into regional groups under individual ruling families. From the accounts of early explorers such as Samuel de Champlain and John Smith, it is clear that the Pawtucket occupied a series of densely populated farming communities along the harbors and rivers of the region. There were three major groups of Pawtucket within Massachusetts—the Naumkeag, who occupied the lands from Salem to the Mystic River, the Agawam of Ipswich and northern Essex County, and the Pennacook, who occupied the Merrimac River. These various groups were affiliated through kinship, trade, and military alliance.[6]

Because Naumkeag was unusually abundant in natural resources, the people were able to survive comfortably by moving from place to place. One strategy for growing their traditional crops of corn, beans, and squash—quite different from English farming practice—involved cycles of slash-and-burn farming in which fields were quickly cleared, planted, and abandoned. Because they did not fertilize the fields, when crop yields began to drop a village would move a few miles to another location where the soil was more fertile. Another strategy was to move with the seasons, taking advantage of a bounty of natural resources. They fished from the ocean and rivers, hunted for game and wildfowl, and gathered roots, nuts, and berries. But despite the Naumkeag's mobility, they were tied closely to their homeland. They believed they had occupied it since the beginning of time and it was the sacred resting place of their ancestors. They were intimately acquainted with each stream, marsh, and hill, and all the animals were imbued with Manitou, or spirit power. Thus the land did not just provide food and shelter to the Naumkeag; it was linked to their heritage and even their cosmology.[7]

For English colonists, too, Naumkeag was a place apart—one very different from the homeland they had left behind. The Reverend Francis Higginson, one of the early English settlers to Naumkeag, represented the place as he wanted others to see it in his 1630 book, *New England's Plantation, or a Short and True Description of the Commodities and Discommodities of That Country.* This was a promotional piece designed to lure other Puritans to the New World, and in it Higginson developed the first mythology of Salem, based on the native experience of Naumkeag. Higginson represented Naumkeag as the mythical land of abundance Puritans came to label *Salem.* For Higginson, Salem connoted not a place of peace, but rather a place of abundance. More than anything else, he was struck by this world of plenty, which contrasted sharply to an England of dwindling natural resources. He used the word *abundance* repeatedly in referring to items as diverse as herbs, wood products, fish, farmland, and fat turkeys: "For wood there is no better in the world I think, here being four sorts of oak differing both in the leaf, timber, and color, all excellent good. There is also good ash, elm, willow, birch, beech, sassafras, juniper cypress, cedar, spruce, pines and fir that will yield abundance of turpentine, pitch, tar, masts and other materials for building both of ships and houses."[8] The bounty of the waters, where the "abundance of sea-fish is almost beyond believing," matched the bounty of the forest. The fishermen's "nets ordinarily take more than they are able to haul to land, and for want of boats and men they are constrained to let many go after they have taken them, and yet sometimes they fill two boats at a time with them." Higginson also greatly admired the fertility of the soil. He wrote, "It is scarce to be believed how our kine and goats, horses and hogs do thrive and prosper here and like well of this country. In our plantation we have already a quart of milk for a penny, but the abundant increase of corn proves this country to be a wonderment. Thirty, forty, fifty, sixty[fold] are ordinary here. Yea, Joseph's increase in Egypt is here outstripped with us. . . . It is almost incredible what great gain some of our English planters have had by our Indian corn."[9]

Despite English mythologizing of Pawtucket lands such as Naumkeag, the place was far from idyllic. For the native population, living off the land could be difficult, particularly in the late winter when food was scarce, a time they referred to as the "starving time." Compounding the challenges to survival, the Pawtucket had enemies who coveted what food and resources they did have. In 1607, war broke out between the Pawtucket and their allies and the Micmac of Nova Scotia. From the beginning, the war went badly for the southerners, and they suffered from a series of devastating Micmac raids that inflicted substantial casualties. One of the victims of the war was Nanapeshamet, the sagamore (chief) of the Naumkeag, who was killed by Micmac raiders about 1619. After his death, his widow and two eldest sons ruled his domain. Her name has been lost, for surviving documents refer to her only as the "Squaw Sachem"—a reference to this woman's unusual position of authority. The eldest son, Wonohaquaham (known to the English simply as John), was the sagamore at Mystic (now Medford, Massachusetts). The second son, Montowompate (dubbed James by the English), was sagamore of Saugus. The last raid of the war took place at Agawam in 1631, while the Agawam were entertaining their neighbors, the Naumkeag. The Micmac killed seven and wounded many more, including John, James, and the Agawam sagamore, Masconomet.[10]

Scarce resources and war were not the only trials the natives of Naumkeag had to face. A tragic result of European contact was that more native peoples succumbed to disease than to warfare, and this experience, also, shaped the meaning of *Naumkeag*. From 1616 to 1619, a great pandemic raged among the Pawtucket and their neighbors in coastal New England. Historians have not discovered the specific disease; however, this clearly was a "virgin soil" epidemic—a European disease that spread rapidly through a Native American population that had no prior exposure, and therefore no resistance. In such circumstances, "harmless" childhood diseases such as chickenpox and measles, which arrived with European explorers, soon became killers. The great pandemic killed an estimated 70 percent of the native population of coastal Massachusetts. In some communities, the devastation may have gone as high as 90 percent, as contagion spread through densely populated villages. Although the lack of solid data makes it extremely difficult to determine pre-epidemic populations, one estimate has placed the pre-1616 Pawtucket population at twenty-one to twenty-four thousand; after the plague, they numbered in the hundreds. In 1631, Thomas Dudley wrote that Sagamores John and James "command not above 30 or 40 men for aught I can learn. Near to Salem dwells two or three families."[11] Historians estimate that for each warrior in a tribe, approximately eight persons might be added to calculate the total in the community. This provides us with a rough estimate of three hundred American Indians between the Mystic River and Naumkeag in 1631, with only a couple of families left in Naumkeag. The Naumkeag bore the brunt of the epidemic, for Dudley estimated that Passaconaway, the Pawtucket sagamore on the Merrimac River, commanded four hundred to five hundred men. These numbers would see an even greater reduction in 1633, when a smallpox epidemic hit eastern New England. The impact of this attack was particularly devastating, for the victims included Sagamore John, Sagamore James, "and most of his folks." There were so few Naumkeag left that, before he died, John asked Boston's Rev. John Wilson to raise his orphaned son. At this point, the leadership of the few remaining Naumkeag fell to the Squaw Sachem and her youngest son, Winnapurkit, alias Sagamore George or George No-Nose.[12]

The result of this warfare and recurring disease was a near disintegration of Pawtucket society. Naumkeag was a very different place when English settlers first arrived in 1626 than it had been even ten years before. A relict population, living in what has been described as a "widowed land," greeted them. Francis Higginson observed that the Indians "do generally confess to like well of our coming and planting here; partly because there is abundance of ground that they cannot possess nor make use of, and partly because our being here will be a means both of relief to them when they want, and also a defense from their enemies, wherewith (I say) before this plantation began, they were often endangered."[13] The English were a source of coveted European trade goods, including knives, axes, kettles, fishhooks, and woven textiles. They also were welcome allies who could provide protection against the onslaught of the Micmac. In their greatly weakened state, it is not surprising that the Naumkeag welcomed the English settlers. Still, one suspects that Higginson, the promoter, exaggerated the Native American zeal for English settlers and their willingness to share the land and bounty of Naumkeag. Indeed, Higginson stated that he neither feared nor trusted the natives, "for forty of our musketeers will drive five hundred of them out of the field." Clearly the English were prepared to take what they wanted, should the Naumkeag not prove agreeable.[14]

The Pawtucket sachems soon realized that their security depended on their becoming allies of the Puritans. Yet, as their numbers dwindled, they rapidly slipped from a position of alliance to one of dependency. On March 7, 1644, the Squaw Sachem, Masconomet of Agawam, and two other Massachusett sachems signed a pact of submission in which they formally agreed to, "of our owne free motion, put ourselves, our subjects, lands, and estates under the government and jurisdiction" of the Massachusetts Bay Colony. With this act, they relinquished not only their lands but their culture as well, going so far as to open the door to Puritan indoctrination and allow their people "from time to time to bee instructed in the knowledge and worship of God."[15]

This was the last known reference to the Squaw Sachem, who died in 1650, leaving the leadership of her dwindling band entirely to Sagamore George.[16] The act of 1644 reveals the changing meanings of place in frontier Massachusetts Bay. By midcentury, around the gentle blue harbor of Naumkeag, a traveler would no longer find a palisaded village of thatched *weetos* or fields of maize, beans, and squash. Instead, he would see scattered clapboard farmsteads, cordoned fields filled with wheat, rye, and barley, and stark meetinghouses. For the Puritans who settled their kin and kine over native graves, the image spoke of promise, prosperity, and a new beginning. For the former native inhabitants, however, Naumkeag was a place of the past, of war, pestilence, and cultural invasion.

Although the treaty of 1644 placed Naumkeag firmly under English authority, for a time the English and a few remnant Naumkeag shared Salem. Surviving documents suggest that one or two Native American families lived within the town's bounds, maintaining a small settlement on the north side of the North River (near the corner of present-day North and Osborne Streets). It appears that George and his band usually lived close by, near the substantial wetland the English called Rumney Marsh—named after Romney Marsh on the coast of Kent. The marsh was principally within that part of Lynn that is present-day Saugus and Revere. One branch of George's family even appropriated "Rumney Marsh" as their surname. This was one of the few accommodations to English culture the Naumkeag would make, and the Reverend John Eliot complained that only one Saugus Indian ever showed any interest in converting to Puritanism. As he complained in a 1649 letter, "Linn Indians are all naught, save one, who sometimes cometh to hear the word, and telleth me that he prayeth to God; and the reason why they are bad is partly and principally because their sachem is naught, and careth not to pray to God."[17] The unnamed sachem was almost certainly Sagamore George.

Although George remained true to his native beliefs, some members of his family adopted Puritan practices, becoming what the English referred to as "Praying Indians." Most of New England's Puritans believed that a proper conversion to Christianity required a complete rejection of "heathen" ways. They encouraged Praying Indians to adopt English dress and occupations, and they urged converts to construct fixed English-style homes within sedentary Praying Towns. These permanent hamlets were strikingly different from Native American villages that were relocated from season to season, and even from one year to the next. Under the guidance of Roxbury's Rev. John Eliot, the Puritan ministry grafted fourteen Praying Towns onto the vestiges of established native villages. Remnant Native Americans established the principal Praying Town at Natick in 1651, and others soon followed in more interior locations, away from Puritan settlements. Battered by warfare and disease, many Praying Indians had come to believe that their native gods had abandoned their ancient homeland. They converted to Christianity and moved to Praying Towns. Sagamore George's sister Yawata and her family lived at Natick. Yawata's sons, James Rumney Marsh and Thomas Rumney Marsh, were leaders of the Natick community who remained loyal to the English during King Philip's War of 1675–1678. Sagamore George also had kinsmen at the Praying Town of Wamesit (on the Merrimac River in present-day Lowell). Yet some Naumkeag remained in their native lands. In his later years, Sagamore George lived "sometime of Rumney Marsh, and sometimes at or about Chelmsford," presumably at or near the Praying Indian town of Wamesit.[18]

An Ambiguous and Contested Frontier

The English settlers of Salem certainly benefited from this widowing of the land and the resulting native diaspora. But it was also in the colonizers' interest to downplay the remaining native presence. They no doubt perceived a vast expanse of empty land, which they assumed was unclaimed and unused. They also assumed that this commodious agricultural land, cleared by long-deceased Indians, was available for—and virtually awaiting—English farmers. To cement their claims to legal ownership, colonial logicians depicted Naumkeag as a *vacuum domicilium,* an "empty land," a legal status meaning vacant or unoccupied land. One of the most effective promoters of this view was Francis Higginson, who observed, "For all the country be as it were a thick wood in general, yet in divers places there is much ground cleared by the Indians, as especially about the plantation. I am told that about three miles from us a man may stand on a little hilly place and see divers thousands of acres of ground as good as need to be, and not a tree in the same."[19] Some of the settlers of Massachusetts Bay saw the warfare and epidemics as an act of Divine Providence, a sign of God's favor for the Puritan colonization of New England. Many Puritans made legal and moral arguments to justify the English claim of ownership. Some stressed that the Indians did not make proper use of the land, or could not use all their land. For example, Higginson observed that "[t]he Indians are not able to make use of the one fourth part of the land, neither have they any settled places, as towns to dwell in, nor any ground as they challenge for their own possession, but change their habitation from place to place." By stressing the fact that the Indians had no fixed abode, Higginson was attempting to negate Native American claims to the land. In this manner, the English inaugurated the myth of the New World as virgin land; in the process, they effectively erased Naumkeag.[20]

This *vacuum domicilium* was a frontier in the classic Western sense—an ambiguous space in which different groups competed to define its meaning. The ways in which Native Americans and Puritans met in this "empty place" established the frontier tradition that so profoundly shaped the American national identity. To the native inhabitants, it was Naumkeag, a fishing place in which microenvironments were occupied or not, according to the seasonal cycle of farming, hunting, fishing, and gathering, as their ancestors had done for hundreds of years. To English settlers, it was Salem, a farming and trading place of homesteads that were used continuously, as their ancestors had done for hundreds of years in England. Because of their inherently ambiguous nature, frontiers have always been places of contestation and violence. Naumkeag/Salem followed this pattern.

The Massachusetts Bay Charter of 1629 set the precedent for Salem's development as a Puritan community, ignoring the Native American presence on these lands. Instead, this royal charter, issued by an English king to English subjects, presumed that the ultimate authority to grant lands in North America belonged to European royalty, through the doctrine known as the "right of discovery." However, the Reverend Higginson and other settlers had to adjust to a very different reality when they arrived. The charter essentially granted the Massachusetts Bay Company the support of their king for title to and jurisdiction over all lands they claimed to find unoccupied. In those areas that natives did inhabit, it was incumbent upon the colony to negotiate occupation and jurisdiction. Indeed, when

John Endicott was sent over to Naumkeag to help organize the nascent Massachusetts Bay Colony in 1629, he was instructed to purchase title from the Indians if "any of the Savages pretend Right of Inheritance."[21]

Under the leadership of John Winthrop (governor for a total of eleven years between 1629 and his death in 1649), the Massachusetts Bay Colony pursued a policy that initially avoided purchase from the Indians. Winthrop maintained that Indian land that was possessed and improved should be purchased; however, he decreed that hunting and fishing grounds—the bulk of Indian lands—were unimproved, and therefore, according to English legal theory, *vacuum domicilium*, free for the taking by anyone who would "improve" it. In this way, the Puritan settlers of the Massachusetts Bay Colony used English law to justify taking native land. This stance may have been merely a ploy by the Puritans, rather than signifying a real cultural difference with the Native Americans over ownership and use of land. After all, the royal forests and hunting grounds of England were not improved, yet Winthrop would never have dared to question the king's ownership of these tracts. Winthrop further justified the taking of "unimproved" lands by asserting that there was more than enough to support the dwindling Native American population.[22]

In 1634, Roger Williams, the articulate, renegade young minister of Salem, initiated a direct challenge to Winthrop's construction of place. Williams claimed that the natives, not the Massachusetts Bay Company, held title to the land. Indeed, he went so far as to call the king a liar for claiming he had the right to grant sovereignty and land to the Massachusetts Bay Company. The next year, the General Court banished Williams from the colony. Many historians view the banishment as resulting from Williams's extremist and uncompromising religious beliefs. However, a focus on the significant role of place adds much to our perspective. Williams's stance on Indian land ownership rendered him a dangerous man in the eyes of colonial leaders, and certainly contributed to his forced departure. Williams fled to the Narragansett Bay region, where he purchased land from the Indians and founded the colony that ultimately became Rhode Island.[23]

The 1634 dispute with Williams, however, prodded the colony to formulate a land policy; later that year, the General Court passed an act defining and regulating Indian lands. This policy confirmed the Indians' title to their improved lands and guaranteed them their hunting and fishing grounds. The act also regulated English purchase of land from the natives, stating that such lands could be purchased only with the permission of the General Court. In the ensuing years, numerous Englishmen made such purchases from various Bay Colony Indians. The Squaw Sachem and her followers received payment for land from the towns of Concord, Charlestown, and Cambridge. The tribe received twenty-one coats, three bushels of corn, and a considerable quantity of wampum from Charlestown, and it retained the right to farm, hunt, and fish and occupy its small parcel of land during the life of the Squaw Sachem. Some land sales even predated the actions of the General Court.[24]

In such an ambiguous frontier, however, land sales and Native-English relations were complicated and could end in violence, as in the case of Poquanum. In 1632 or 1633, Nathaniel Baker testified that in Nahant he had "met with an Indian called Poquanum or Black Will who had on a stuff suit of clothes that were pinked." Poquanum asserted he had bought his elegant English clothes from Thomas Dexter, "giving him Nahaunt for them."[25] Thus Nahant passed peacefully into English hands. Unfortunately, Poquanum's fate would not be so pleasant. Not long after the sale, Poquanum traveled north to the coast of Maine. On Richmond's Island he was seized by a group of Englishmen who were searching for the Native Americans who had murdered Walter Bagnall, a fur trader on the island. There was no evidence that Poquanum had anything to do with Bagnall's death, a crime that had taken place over a year before he or his executioners actually arrived at the island. Indeed, Poquanum's sale of Nahant suggests that he enjoyed friendly relations with the English. Unfortunately, he appears to have been in the wrong place at the wrong time, an early victim of "frontier" justice, for the vigilantes hanged him.[26]

As English settlement transformed Naumkeag into Salem, English courts were established to impose English order upon frontier ambiguities. After the Squaw Sachem had placed Naumkeag under English authority in the treaty of 1644, native people who had differences over land with Englishmen were required to seek justice in English courts. Appeal to the court system was the strategy pursued by Sagamore George, who tried to maintain ownership of the Naumkeag's remaining tribal lands, despite English incursions and even the execution of his father-in-law, Poquanum. George's first recorded appearance in court was in 1642, when he and "Edward, alias Ned of Wight" sued Francis Lightfoot of Lynn over a piece of land. The result of the case is not recorded. In 1651, Sagamore George attempted to assert his title to lands at Rumney Marsh. The English inhabitants protested the claim, saying it interfered with their own claim of title to the land. The General Court, as the colony's legislature was known, stepped into the dispute and ordered the English landholders to give Sagamore George twenty acres of good farmland in lieu of his claim. Apparently, however, George believed he had not received ample compensation for any of his claims, for in 1669 he again unsuccessfully petitioned the court regarding the same lands.[27]

Along with property disputes and violence, trade in firearms and alcohol has been a historic feature of the American frontier. Indeed, the Naumkeag and their kin were much more likely to show up in the records regarding these actions than they were in property disputes. As early as 1630, the Massachusetts Bay Colony took steps to prevent firearms from being traded to the natives. Puritan authorities permitted prominent sagamores only, including the Squaw Sachem and Masconomet, to own Puritan firearms; even then, they needed permission from the General Court just to receive powder and shot or to have their guns repaired. Despite strong prohibitions, many natives greatly desired European weapons, and colonial officials were hard pressed to prevent a growing illicit trade. Essex County men were repeatedly prosecuted for selling powder and shot to the Indians. As this demand increased and fears of a native uprising waned, the General Court finally yielded. In 1668, the legislature passed a law allowing a limited trade in firearms, but only through licensed merchants whose records were closely scrutinized by the government.[28]

Court records indicate that the trade in alcohol to Native Americans proved equally difficult to enforce. Puritan officials wanted to regulate this trade closely, for fear that natives, unaccustomed to alcohol, could not control their drinking. Essex County court files contain references to quite a few cases of public drunkenness of Indians, as well as to fines against those Englishmen who sold natives liquor. Despite the laws against such sales, there were always English suppliers for the Native Americans who were willing to buy virtually any form of alcohol. In 1658, Jeremiah Belcher was charged with selling "strongwater" to his servant Nedacockett, alias "Indian Ned." Belcher offered a rather lame defense, claiming he had sold liquor to Ned on only two occasions, and only three gallons each time. Furthermore, he asserted, it was real rotgut, "which was so fusty that the English would not buy it." Belcher tried to further rationalize his behavior by accusing Hugh Gullison of selling fifty gallons of liquor to the natives. Even respected citizens faced such charges. In 1672, John Hathorne was hauled before the court because "many Indians had been much disguised with drink" in his Lynn tavern.[29] Hathorne's nephew and namesake, Col. John Hathorne, would subsequently serve as a judge during the witchcraft trials and was ancestor to Salem's Nathaniel Hawthorne.

In seventeenth-century frontier outposts such as Salem, alcohol was a social problem of moral and practical dimensions. Puritan ministers considered public drunkenness a moral infraction in itself, for drunkenness was a sin, but it also led to sins of the flesh. For example, in 1664 when Samuel Archer of Salem was accused of being reeling drunk in the streets, a deponent suggestively added he was "leading an Indian woman by the hand," presumably toward a sexual assignation.[30] For their part, Puritan magistrates feared that drunken Indians would be a danger to themselves. Peter the Indian, for one, became so intoxicated that he passed out in the snow and froze to death in Marblehead in late November 1665. Several English passersby "strove to raise him but he would not let them, and said there were Indians at Mr. Boud's getting liquor for spoons, who would help him. He smelled so of liquor that they could not stand by him."[31] In Lynn in 1672, several English women voiced concern for the personal safety of their families, insisting that Indians who became drunk at the Hathorne tavern were more liable to commit acts of violence. Their concern was not entirely unfounded. For example, in 1652 the constable of Newbury claimed to have been assaulted by drunken Indians. And in 1668 an intoxicated Penacook man had killed Thomas Dickenson, one of the agents of a Merrimac River trading post, after Dickenson sold a huge quantity of liquor to the tribe.[32]

Traditionally, as already mentioned, the native peoples of Naumkeag had traveled to take advantage of the bounty of the land. By the mid-seventeenth century, they had been forced to trade this movement for the new and uncertain mobility that the poor and dispossessed must face in their struggle to survive. Their seasonal rounds of foraging were replaced by trips to the taverns, where they traded hand-carved wooden spoons and burl bowls for liquor. These desperate circumstances reduced some of the Naumkeag to servitude and even slavery. Sometimes the Essex County courts ordered Native Americans into servitude to pay off debts; however, they could also sell themselves or family members into indentured servitude. The earliest recorded case in Salem was Hope, the servant for the Reverend Hugh Peter. In 1639 Hope was whipped for running away and being drunk. Another example was Nedacockett, a debtor who served Jeremiah Belcher for a time. Belcher was brought before the court after he gave Ned some powder and shot so that Ned could shoot some fowl for his master. Ned is known to have sold land to Belcher, so perhaps this is how he freed himself from debt. In 1660 Ned was found guilty of owing a debt of £8. On the way to jail he escaped from the marshal—perhaps fearing another term of indentured service.[33]

There seems to have been considerable movement of bound native people both into and out of Essex County. Judging by her name, Mary Agawam was a Native American inhabitant of the Ipswich area; however, by 1659 she was a servant of George Walton, working in his tavern in Portsmouth, New Hampshire. When Mary gave birth to a bastard son, the child was indentured to Walton until his twenty-fourth birthday. Even as Mary left Ipswich, other Indians came into Essex County as servants. For example, there was a 1666 complaint against Richard Oliver for "taking an Indian from Nantuckett without the consent of his father, who was there living, and said Oliver having an indenture signed by the boy, with the consent of an Indian who pretended to be the uncle of the boy as a witness."[34] Most scholars assert that Tituba and Indian John, the famous servants of the Reverend Parris who were caught up in the witchcraft outbreak of 1692, were Native Americans. However, they almost certainly came from outside the region. As such, they were part of the diaspora of the seventeenth century, in which Native Americans both entered and left Essex County.[35]

Dispossessed and enslaved, even in death native people could not always find peace in their homeland. In 1667 Robert Cross Jr. of Ipswich was found guilty of exhuming and defiling the grave of Masconomet, the sagamore of Agawam. Cross went so far as to carry the skull upon a pole, bragging to friends that he would "make a grease pot of the skull for his wife." Initially, Cross was assisted by John Andrews. Andrews dug down about half a foot when, he told the court, "my hart misgave me." Andrews freely confessed and said he was "heartily sorry for what he had done." The court was clearly shocked by this "barbarous and inhuman act." Cross was fined £6, placed in the stocks, imprisoned, and ordered to rebury the remains. Although the court's action shows that such behavior was unacceptable by Puritan authorities, the very fact that two men would initiate such an action shows that at least some planters had a callous disregard for Native Americans.[36]

Yet there were others in the area around Salem, men like Daniel Epps, who did care deeply for the welfare of the Pawtucket. For a number of years, Epps and his family worked hard to help and safeguard one Native American family. In 1670, a family of Indians had appeared at Epps's Ipswich farm. They consisted of an old squaw, her son Robin, her daughter, and the daughter's two very young children. The old squaw was infirm, her daughter was terminally ill, and Robin was apparently unable or unwilling to work. They were refugees fleeing from the upper Merrimac, where Mohawk raiders had killed several members of the family. They came to Epps's farm because in past years they had dwelt upon the land, knew Epps, and apparently had no other place to turn for help. Epps observed that they "had nothing" and were "poore and desplicable [*sic*], and not in any ways capable of keeping themselves, at least towards a living, all the other Indians Quickly leaveing them rather laughing at their pitty full case." Epps took pity on them, providing them with food and supplies. After a few months, the young squaw passed away, but on her deathbed she asked Epps to look after her young son—still less than one year old. The boy was named Lionel—after Epps's son. The Indians continued to live on Epps's land, with his support, for about nine years. Then the old squaw moved away, and Robin sold his young nephew Lionel into servitude to pay for gambling debts. Epps tried for several years to get Lionel freed from his alleged owner, Henry Bennett. He initially lost the case, but he won on appeal to the Court of Assistants.[37] Daniel Epps and Robert Cross demonstrate the extremes of response to the Native American presence in Essex County. Such views kept Naumkeag an ambiguous and disputed frontier for much of the seventeenth century.

Daniel Epps's protection of this family is all the more remarkable because it continued through King Philip's War (1675–1678), a tumultuous era in Anglo-Indian relations. During the conflict, Salem's English residents saw their place in a new, more troubling light—so vulnerable to native attack that they constructed a lengthy palisade around the entire core of the settlement. The cost of this and other wartime fortifications for Salem totaled £254—a daunting sum, especially when the community already had to bear the burden of taxes imposed by the governor and legislature, who desperately needed money to fight the war. Salem and surrounding towns contributed to numerous militia companies and suffered seri-

ous losses in the war. Two of the most famous English defeats took place when Essex County companies were virtually wiped out. Lathrop's Company, often referred to as the "Flower of Essex," was wiped out at Bloody Brook in September
1675. Swett's Company was similarly ambushed and suffered extremely heavy casualties in Maine in June 1677. The war produced numerous widows and orphans,
often in need of the community's support, and some crippled veterans also returned to Salem. Collectively, these people served as a constant and painful reminder of the war.[38]

The summer of 1677 was particularly hard for Essex County; the fishing fleet,
at work off the coast of Maine, came under native attack. In July of 1677, Wa-
banaki warriors seized nearly twenty fishing boats, mostly from Salem and Marblehead. They killed or took captive the ships' crews and seized any foodstuffs or
supplies they could find. Finally, the crew of one of these shallops were able to turn
the tables on their would-be captors and sailed back to Marblehead with two native prisoners. Word quickly spread along the waterfront, and an angry mob of
women seized the captives and decapitated them, even pulling the flesh off their
bones. At one level, this grisly attack reveals how threatening Native Americans
were to the inhabitants of Salem and Marblehead. More profoundly, it tells us
something about the mutability of roles, values, and behaviors on the frontier. In
Marblehead of 1677, we see Puritan women transform themselves into the very
"savages" they feared and detested. It shows how war in a frontier setting transformed not only social and gender roles, but also the basic sense of order in which
"civilized" societies take pride.[39]

Salem

During the war, even Praying Indians who remained loyal to the English had
been viewed with suspicion, and these fears lingered long afterward. In 1679 the
town of Salem ordered that no native person would be allowed to spend the night
in the town, further extending native dispossession and loss of Naumkeag. Now
Native Americans could only be visitors in their homeland.[40]

The meaning of this place shifted again during the next decade. During the
mid-1680s, King James revoked the charter that had legitimized the existence of
the Massachusetts Bay Colony and ordered Governor Edmund Andros to sub-
sume the Puritan Commonwealth under a new, artificial amalgam of New England, New York, and New Jersey, to be known as the Dominion of New England.
Ironically, despite their profound distrust of their native neighbors, Salem Puritan
settlers found it necessary to actively seek out the remaining Naumkeag Indians to
safeguard title to their town. In 1686 Andros challenged the validity of the claim
of Essex County towns to common lands within their borders. He threatened to
revoke title to these lands, claiming ownership had not been approved by the king.

As a result, many Essex County towns bolstered their ownership by purchasing title from the surviving Indians. In 1686, Salem's selectmen sought out the heirs of Sagamore George to purchase title to the town from them.[41] George had apparently joined the native cause in King Philip's War, perhaps not a surprising fact considering the fatal injustice his father-in-law had suffered at English hands. Although there are no references to the aged sagamore in the war, one deposition refers to the fact that he had come home from Barbados. This island had been the destination of many defeated Indians, who had been sold into slavery. A 1675 reference in the *Boston Book of Possessions* does mention that seven Indians, including one named George, were sentenced to be sold into slavery. Possibly this was a reference to Sagamore George. Regardless, it seems that somehow George had been able to pay for his freedom and to return home. Perhaps his kinsman, James Rumney Marsh, arranged his homecoming. James was a Praying Indian who had remained loyal to the English during the war. Indeed, in about 1680 Sagamore George died at James's house.[42]

Because Sagamore George had died, in 1686 the town fathers of both Salem and Lynn had to seek out his heirs when they wanted to purchase native title to their townships. Eleven of his heirs and relatives signed the deed to Salem; six of them lived at Wamesit, and five at Natick. The family received £20 for officially signing off on the land they no longer occupied. It may have been seen as a windfall to people who had long ago moved away and who had given up any practical claim of ownership on property occupied by so many Englishmen. Had Roger Williams not died just three years before, he might have gained a measure of satisfaction for even this symbolic transfer of ownership. As the Native Americans had moved away, Naumkeag had gradually ceased to exist as a place; now, it legally passed out of existence for the nominal price of £20.[43]

Governor Andros and the Dominion of New England were overthrown in the wake of England's Glorious Revolution of 1688. However, by this time New England was already engaged in King William's War, another frontier conflict that proved almost as devastating as King Philip's War. The conflict went badly for New England, as frontier settlements were attacked and many settlers killed or taken captive. By 1692, Essex County was in the grip of an extreme war panic, which historians believe was a major contributing factor in the famous outbreak of witchcraft throughout the county that year. Revealingly, some of those who claimed that Satan tormented them indicated that he was a "tawny man, like an Indian."[44] Many who participated in the witchcraft trials, including the afflicted, were either refugees from native attack or had other ties to the war on the frontier. Some had ties to the Naumkeag themselves. For example, in 1679 John Proctor was convicted of selling cider and liquor to the Indians, who were frequent guests in his home just south of the Salem Village line in present-day Peabody. One of the deponents against Proctor was his neighbor, Giles Cory. Proctor was executed for witchcraft, and Cory was pressed to death when he refused to confess. There were even several "Indians" resident in Salem Village in 1692. Rev. Parris's servant, Tituba, was one of the first to be accused of witchcraft, and her confession led to the widening of the prosecutions into a major outbreak.[45]

After 1692 the native populace of Essex County faded further into obscurity. A nineteenth-century Salem historian, Joseph Felt, observed that "credible tradition relates, that down to 1725, and subsequently" a company of native people made an annual visit to Salem and encamped on a side of Gallows Hill—presumably because it was just about the only common land left in Salem. At this time, there were still three Indian families residing in Ipswich on a year-round basis, occupying "Wigwam Hill." Recently, scholars have determined that the Native American people of eastern and central Massachusetts did not become extinct. Rather, they tended to "go underground," living in marshes and other marginal lands or blending into the population by taking English surnames and livelihoods. So, while observers like Nathaniel Hawthorne, Joseph Felt, and William Bentley believed that the Naumkeag and Agawam had completely disappeared from their homelands, a relict population presumably remained—living in shadows at the margins of society.

Despite this "disappearance," the Native American presence would continue to be felt in a variety of forms. Throughout the nineteenth century, native relics often came to light during construction, a reminder of the original inhabitants of Naumkeag. Throughout Salem and surrounding towns, cemeteries and occupation sites revealed themselves. "Pothunters" recovered literally thousands of prehistoric stone artifacts, ranging from spear points and knives to axes, gouges, and fishing weights. Shell middens, essentially prehistoric trash dumps, could be found along the shoreline. One in Marblehead, on Throgmorton Cove, was "a great heap of shells" that was "removed about the year 1850, for utilization of its material as a fertilizer. It contained about thirty cords of shells and ashes, among which were found bones of a large deer, together with pieces of crudely ornamented pottery, bits of copper, and stone implements." During the course of development, several Native American cemeteries were found, resulting in the disturbance of dozens of burials. Such discoveries are the ultimate reminder that Naumkeag existed before Salem.[46]

Salem's most famous nineteenth-century resident, Nathaniel Hawthorne, alluded to such discoveries when he sadly observed in "Main-street" that "the pavements of the Main-street must be laid over the red man's grave."[47] The story recounts the early history of Salem, showing the demise of the Squaw Sachem and her people, the destruction of their wilderness, and the rise of an increasingly urbanized and industrialized landscape. Hawthorne was fascinated also by frontier warfare—a common theme in his works. Sometimes he spoke to the "savagery" of Indians and their warfare, though he is more often the defender of Native Americans and denounces what Europeans and Americans had done to them. For example, in the "Gray Champion," Hawthorne complains of "the veterans of King Philip's war, who had burnt villages and slaughtered young and old, with pious fierceness, while the godly souls throughout the land were helping them with prayer."[48] Often, the influence of Native Americans hides in the shadows of Hawthorne's works, but it is there nonetheless. It even lurks in *The House of the Seven Gables,* in which a major plot element is the disappearance of the deed to thousands of acres of lands in Maine sold to Judge Pyncheon by native sagamores. In these and other ways, Hawthorne demonstrates the haunting links between ancient Indians and the Salem of his day.[49]

Naumkeag Redux

With his fascination for the past, Hawthorne must have been quite interested to see the reemergence of the name *Naumkeag* in 1845, when a new textile company, the Naumkeag Steam Cotton Company, was born in Salem. The Naumkeag mills quickly became a significant force in Salem's industry, selling principally under the *Pequot* brand name. The choice of both names follows a tradition of the New England textile industry that borrowed names from Native American individuals, tribes, and places. However, both are interesting choices. By 1845 the Naumkeag people were such a distant memory that they posed no threat to the establishment, and the Pequot of Connecticut, the first tribe to be removed by the English, had been destroyed in 1637. By the 1840s, the name *Naumkeag* harkened back to a pastoral ideal that was increasingly distant to the urban dwellers of Salem. Indians were now only occasional visitors to the city, as were the two Penobscot chiefs who aroused only curiosity and no fear when they passed through town in 1818. In the twentieth century, the Naumkeag mills faced economic decline. They became a victim of the changing economic landscape of Salem and Essex County that witnessed the relocation of the textile industry to the South, and then overseas. In 1947 the mill finally closed its doors, leaving another generation to ponder the demise of the Naumkeag.[50]

Notes

1. Sidney Perley, *The Indian Land Titles of Essex County, Massachusetts* (Salem, Mass.: Essex Book and Print Club, 1912), 8.

2. J. B. Harley, "New England Cartography and the Native Americans," in *American Beginnings: Exploration, Culture and Cartography in the Land of Norumbega,* ed. Emerson W. Baker et al. (Lincoln: University of Nebraska Press, 1994), 296–304.

3. The quote is from *Records and Files of the Quarterly Courts of Essex County* (Salem, Mass.: Essex Institute, 1911–1975), III, 322. See also Perley, 13; and Sidney Perley, *The History of Salem, Massachusetts* (Salem, Mass.: Sidney Perley, 1924), I, 42.

4. John Smith, "A Description of New England," in *Sailors' Narratives of Voyages along the New England Coast, 1524–1624*, ed. George P. Winship (Boston: Houghton, Mifflin and Co., 1905), 240.

5. The close relationship between the Pawtucket and the Massachusett has led to difficulties among modern historians in determining the exact bounds and memberships of these groups. This essay uses the terminology and tribal divisions delineated by the *Handbook of North American Indians,* which is a widely accepted authority. In particular, see Bert Salwen, "Indians of Southern New England and Long Island: Early Period," in *Handbook of North American Indians,* ed. Bruce Trigger (Washington, D.C.: Smithsonian Institution, 1978), XV, 160–76. For the northern limit of the Pawtucket, see Emerson Baker, "Finding the Almouchiquois: Native American Families, Territories and Land Sales in Southern Maine," *Ethnohistory,* in press. Some scholars believe that the Naumkeag were part of the Massachusett, rather than the Pawtucket. For example, see Dane A. Morrison, *A Praying People: Massachusett Acculturation and the Failure of the Puritan Mission, 1600–1690* (New York: Peter Lang, 1995).

6. Salwen, 160–76; W. L. Grant, ed., *Voyages of Samuel de Champlain, 1604–1618* (New York: Charles Scribner's Sons, 1907), 90–92.

7. Salwen, 160–66; Neal Salisbury, *Manitou and Providence: Indians, Europeans, and the Making of New England, 1500–1643* (New York: Oxford University Press, 1982), 13–49.

8. Francis Higginson, *New England's Plantation, or a Short and True Description of the Commodities and Discommodities of that Country* (London, 1630); reprint, Everett Emerson, ed., *Letters from New England: The Massachusetts Bay Colony, 1629–1638* (Amherst: University of Massachusetts Press, 1976), 32.

9. Higginson, 31.

10. Salisbury, 121, 183–84; Baker, in press; William Wood, *New England's Prospect,* ed. Alden T. Vaughan (Amherst: University of Massachusetts Press, 1977), 79–80; Richard Dunn, James Savage, and Laetitia Yeandle, eds., *The Journal of John Winthrop, 1630–1649* (Cambridge, Mass.: Harvard University Press, 1996), 55.

11. "Letter of Thomas Dudley to Lady Bridget, Countess of Lincoln, March 28, 1631," in Emerson, 68–69; Salisbury, 25–28; Salwen, 171–72.

12. The quote is from Dunn et al., 105; see also Salisbury, 190–91; and Joseph B. Felt, *Annals of Salem* (Salem, Mass.: W. and S. B. Ives, 1845), I, 14–16.

13. Higginson, 37. For the term *widowed land,* see Francis Jennings, *The Invasion of America: Indians, Colonists, and the Cant of Conquest* (New York: W. W. Norton, 1976), 15–31.

14. Higginson, 37.

15. Nathaniel B. Shurtleff, ed., *Records of the Governor and Company of the Massachusetts Bay in New England* (Boston: Press of William White, 1854), II, 84; III, 55–56.

16. Testimony by Richard Church (Middlesex County Court Files). See Thomas Weddle, "John Tontohqunne, Cicely's Son," manuscript published in serial form in *The Saugonian,* 2002–2003.

17. Perley, *History of Salem,* 45; see also Felt, 16; and Massachusetts Historical Society Collections, ser. 3, IV, 88.

18. For the quote, see David Kunkshamooshaw et al. to the Selectmen of Lynn, September 4, 1686, Essex Deeds XVIII, 150; the deed is transcribed in Perley, *Indian Land Titles,* 68–75. See also Alden Vaughan, *New England Frontier: Puritans and Indians, 1620–1675* (New York: W. W. Norton, 1965), 235–59; and Weddle. For an overview of the Praying Indians, see Morrison.

19. Higginson, 30.

20. Quotation is from Higginson, 37. See also Salisbury, 175–77, 197–200; and William Cronon, *Changes in the Land: Indians, Colonists, and the Ecology of New England* (New York: Hill and Wang, 1984), 55–82.

21. Shurtleff, I, 394; see also Yashuhide Kawashima, *Puritan Justice and the Indian: White Man's Law in Massachusetts, 1630–1763* (Middletown, Conn.: Wesleyan University Press, 1986), 42–48.

22. Kawashima, 47–48; Salisbury, 175–77.

23. Richard P. Gildrie, *Salem, Massachusetts, 1626–1683: A Covenanted Community* (Charlottesville: University Press of Virginia, 1975), 30–38; Dunn et al., 107–9.

24. Kawashima, 48–49; Salisbury, 199–200.

25. *Quarterly Courts of Essex County,* VII, 126. A pinked suit would have a scalloped, fringed, or otherwise decorated edge, making it a fancy piece of clothing.

26. Perley, *Indian Land Titles,* 49–50.

27. *Quarterly Courts of Essex County,* I, 43; Shurtleff, IV, pt. 1, 68–69; IV, pt. 2, 428.

28. Vaughan, *New England Frontier,* 226–30; Shurtleff, III, 44; *Quarterly Courts of Essex County,* I, 44, 233; II, 117.

29. *Quarterly Courts of Essex County,* I, 72–73, 88; II, 117; IV, 160, 214, 370–71, 400, 424; V, 61; VII, 80, 113. *Fusty* means stale smelling, or musty.

30. *Quarterly Courts of Essex County,* III, 180.

31. *Quarterly Courts of Essex County,* I, 268–69, 282; II, 297.

32. *Quarterly Courts of Essex County,* I, 268; V, 59–63; Massachusetts Archives XXX, 154–61.

33. *Quarterly Courts of Essex County,* I, 11; II, 61, 70, 117, 212; III, 180, 299; Massachusetts Archives XLV, 213–14. For other references to Indians selling their woodware, see *Quarterly Courts of Essex County,* III, 333; VII, 66. Perhaps marshall Samuel Archer let Ned escape, for several years later Archer was observed drunk and in the company of an Indian woman.

34. Isaac W. Hammond, ed., *Documents Relating to Towns in New Hampshire,* New Hampshire State Papers Series, vol. 12 (Concord: State of New Hampshire, 1883), 672–73; *Quarterly Courts of Essex County,* III, 366.

35. The clouded origins of Indian John and Tituba have undergone considerable debate; however, there is very little chance that either was a Naumkeag or even a Pawtucket. More likely they were from the southern colonies of the Caribbean. See Elaine Breslaw, *Tituba, Reluctant Witch of Salem: Devilish Indians and Puritan Fantasies* (New York: New York University Press, 1996), 1–20; Peter Hoffer, *The Devil's Disciples: Makers of the Salem Witchcraft Trials* (Baltimore: Johns Hopkins University Press, 1996), 1–16, 205–10; and John McWilliam, "Indian John and the Northern Tawnies," *New England Quarterly* 69 (1996): 580–604.

36. *Quarterly Courts of Essex County,* III, 400.

37. *Quarterly Courts of Essex County,* IX, 251–53; John Noble, ed., *Records of the Court of Assistants of the Massachusetts Bay Colony, 1630–1692* (Boston: Suffolk County, 1901), I, 259.

38. Emerson Baker and John Reid, *The New England Knight: Sir William Phips, 1651–1695*

(Toronto: University of Toronto Press, 1998), 135–37; *Town Records of Salem, Massachusetts,* II, 211, 229, 231–32, 240, 318, 323–26; III, 9. Although some historians see the death of Philip in 1676 as the end of King Philip's War, fighting continued on the northern frontier until 1678.

39. James Axtell, "The Vengeful Women of Marblehead: Robert Roules's Deposition of 1677," *William and Mary Quarterly* 31, no. 4 (1974): 647–52.

40. *Town Records of Salem,* II, 304. For more on the fear of Praying Indians, see Kristina Bross, "'That Epithet of Praying': The Vilification of Praying Indians during King Philip's War," in *Fear Itself: Enemies Real and Imagined in American Culture,* ed. Nancy Lusignan Schultz (West Lafayette, Ind.: Purdue University Press, 1999), 53–67.

41. David S. Lovejoy, *The Glorious Revolution in America* (New York: Harper and Rowe, 1974), 186–87, 197; Perley, *Indian Land Titles,* 64.

42. Perley, *History of Salem,* 43. There is no specific reference to George's death, but he is mentioned as deceased in December 1681. See Weddle.

43. Perley, *Indian Land Titles,* 77–84.

44. For a selection of the growing literature on the "frontier" interpretation of the witchcraft outbreak, see James Kences, "Some Unexplored Relationships of Essex County Witchcraft to the Indian Wars of 1675 and 1689," *Essex Institute Historical Collections* 120 (1984): 181–211; Carol F. Karlsen, *The Devil in the Shape of a Woman: Witchcraft in Colonial New England* (New York: Norton, 1987), 226–30, 245–46; Baker and Reid, 134–55; Emerson Baker and James Kences, "Maine, Indian Land Speculation, and the Essex County Witchcraft Outbreak of 1692," *Maine History* 40, no. 3 (2001): 159–89; and Mary Beth Norton, *In the Devil's Snare: The Salem Witchcraft Crisis of 1692* (New York: Alfred A. Knopf, 2002).

45. *Quarterly Courts of Essex County,* VII, 135; Breslaw, 97–132; Norton, 20–22, 27–30.

46. Perley, *History of Salem,* I, 27–37.

47. William Charvat et al., eds., *The Centenary Edition of the Works of Nathaniel Hawthorne* (Columbus: Ohio State University Press, 1962–1980), XI, 55.

48. Charvat, IX, 11. This paragraph draws heavily upon Margaret B. Moore, *The Salem World of Nathaniel Hawthorne* (Columbia: University of Missouri Press, 1998), 128–31.

49. Baker and Kences, 181–82.

50. William Bentley, *The Diary of William Bentley, D.D., Pastor of the East Church, Salem, Massachusetts* (Gloucester, Mass.: Peter Smith, 1962), IV, 502.

The First Church of Salem. Photo by Kim Mimnaugh.

Chapter Two

Salem as Religious Proving Ground

CHRISTOPHER WHITE

Just think a moment,
and it will startle you to see what slaves we are to bygone times.
—Nathaniel Hawthorne, *The House of the Seven Gables*

N a clear December day in Salem, everything except the dry snow, which blew in circles on the city streets, seemed quiet and still. There were no tourists or pilgrims, no one selling Salem's history or its haunted places. Stores and restaurants looked open but were empty. It was my first visit to the "witch city," and, though it was inadvertent, I did meet a witch. She was sitting at the back of a store full of incense, spells, and other sacred things, taking inventory, when I ducked inside to escape the cold of the street. In the usual way of store clerks, she asked how I was and if she could help me, and I suspected nothing out of the ordinary. But when I started talking to her I realized that she was, in fact, quite extraordinary, and that the place she inhabited might be as well.

Among other things, Karyn Rego told me that everything—history, life, human nature—was a circle. As she explained it, the concept seemed simple enough, a bit like karma: everything you did came back to you. She called it the "threefold law," which I took to mean that by some cosmic calculus everything we did was multiplied by three and returned to us. She assured me that there was in fact more to it than this. She said that the circles she referred to obtained on larger scales as well, in the weighty matters of reincarnation, history, and time's cycles. We took her life as an example. As a psychic and someone sympathetic to "Wiccan" (that is, modern witchcraft) beliefs, she believed that human beings lived many lives and that long ago she, in fact, had dwelled here in Salem. She could feel it when she walked through the streets. She came back to Salem in the twentieth century on business and once settled had discovered that her connection to the place was deep indeed. Another Salem psychic told her that she might have an ancestor, someone in her family, from the area—perhaps an accused witch. When she did some research she discovered that this was true—that she was directly related to Elizabeth Howe, a witch trial victim hanged in Salem in 1692. This same psychic told her that her connection to Salem's past was even closer, that in a past life she had been Elizabeth Howe's younger cousin and that during the witch trials she had been forced to hide in a barn. She had been alive during the executions. Her life, she was certain, was moving in circles. She thought mine probably was, too.[1]

Karyn was not sure why she had circled back to Salem, but she was sure she had done so for a reason. Most witches and psychics in Salem have a similar sense of the miraculous or "magical" in their lives—a sense that the world is enchanted, full of purpose and meaning. The fact that she could make a living here and meet like-minded people surely was part of Salem's attraction (and in this her story is fairly typical of the two thousand or so modern witches living here). But like many Salem witches she came also because she had particular feelings and memories that drew her. Not everyone's memories were as clear or as detailed as hers, even among Salem's more perspicacious believers, but there is no doubt that religious people here feel connected to this place and its past. This essay is about how these people have remembered that past, especially the 1692 witch trials—and about how their memories of these events continue to shape the history of religion in the region.

I.

If Karyn Rego, like others in Salem today, find themselves drawn to the place by the cords of memory, Salem residents in earlier times were repelled by the town's association with violence and guilt. Even as far back as the mid-1690s, just a short while after the executions in 1692, a consensus developed that something had gone wrong in Salem. One local minister who supported the trials until his wife was accused, John Hale of Beverly, Massachusetts, provided some of the most anxious reflections. In a sad, honest book called *A Modest Inquiry into the Nature of Witchcraft* (1697), Hale admitted that "a great deal of innocent blood" had been shed "by proceeding upon unsafe principles in condemning persons for malefic witchcraft." Though he stopped short of saying that all of the condemned were innocent, he could see that many good people had been convicted on evidence that was, at best, "slender." Hale was willing both to take the blame himself and to assign it to other ministers, who, while they certainly did not "willingly depart from the rules of righteousness," also did not properly discern the signs of God or Satan in the world. "We walked in the clouds," Hale wrote remorsefully, "and could not see our way." Why exactly they had not seen their way was a vexing question, one that Hale responded to in standard Puritan fashion: New Englanders had committed "sins of lukewarmness" and were being punished.[2] That was it—that was the answer. They had not pursued with dedication or alacrity their special calling to be a new people in a new Jerusalem.

Hale was not the only one worried about the trials and their spiritual reverberations. Many of those who had witnessed or participated in the trials came to regret their involvement. In the same year that Hale wrote his *Modest Inquiry*— 1697—twelve of the jurors involved in the trials signed a document in which they fretted that they had "been instrumental with others, tho Ignorantly and unwittingly, to bring upon our selves, and this People of the Lord, the Guilt of Innocent Blood." What were the consequences of accumulating such guilt? Around the same time, January of 1697, one of the prosecuting judges, Samuel Sewall, also became increasingly "sensible of the reiterated strokes of God upon himself and [his] family" and, fearful and repentant, publicly confessed his guilt. A similar combination of anxiety and regret informed other confessions. In a private diary entry the day after Sewall's public declaration, a tearful Cotton Mather worried that God would punish his family "for my not appearing with *Vigor* enough to stop the proceedings of the Judges, when the Inextricable Storm from the Invisible World assaulted the Countrey." His only consolation was that "having the *Righteousness* of the Lord Jesus Christ pleading for us, *Goodness and Mercy* should follow us"; and he hoped with what he thought was some "assurance of the Lord" "that Marks of [God's] Indignation should not follow my Family."[3] Puritans believed that sins caused affliction, sickness, and death and that the consequences of sin were transmitted to family members and descendants. This made their remorse acute. They worried about their children and their children's children.

So it was that in the years after the trials there were many retractions, qualifications, and apologies. Those involved in the trials expressed doubts about how to read correctly the signs of God and Satan in nature; they wondered whether victims or judges had been duped by the devil; and they argued about legal procedures that in hindsight seemed unfair and untrustworthy. None of them, however, questioned the existence of Satan or his minions or the very real problems they caused in the world. And none of them doubted God's existence or his ubiquitous good works. Puritans lived in a world inhabited by supernatural forces that were both good and evil, an enchanted world of wonders, portents, and apparitions. Dreams revealed the future; sudden deaths or monstrous births were signs of God's displeasure; comets and shooting stars signaled imminent danger. Nothing was due to chance. In the witch trials, the problem was that innocence and guilt, life and death, turned on these supernatural events and how human beings interpreted them. When it became evident that wrongheaded interpretations had led to deadly errors, the danger of trying to read ambiguous supernatural signs became clearer than ever. In the short term, the result was the end of witch trials as a practice. In the long run, the mentality of the supernatural, the interest in signs and

portents and visions, itself became vulnerable. In Salem in particular, believers became wary of religious enthusiasms of all kinds, preferring cool, rational religions
to hot, evangelical ones. But that is a story for the eighteenth century.

II.

In early-eighteenth-century New England, declining church membership was
both a perception and a reality. In Salem, for example, church membership by 1700
had declined to no more than 10 to 15 percent. Sixty years earlier it had been closer
to 50 percent.[4] There were many reasons for this decline. One was that Salem, like
other coastal towns, had its share of sailors who (like sailors in other times and
places) were willing to dispense with Puritan restraints. Eighteenth-century Salem
was increasingly prosperous, increasingly cosmopolitan, and increasingly filled
with unholy diversions (such as pubs). Another reason, one more particular to
Salem, had to do with guilt about the witch trials and the decline of the supernatural mentality that seemed to follow in its wake. The reluctance to hunt or prose-
cute witches that overtook the area was directly related to a reluctance to persecute
deviant believers in general, and in Salem the result was an expanding religious diversity. This new openness was greeted with the usual range of attitudes—indif-
ference, dismay, resignation—but in the end Salem accepted diversity more readily than neighboring towns.[5] By the first third of the eighteenth century, the
religious situation in Salem had diversified considerably: there were three Congregational churches (First Church, East Church, and Third Church), one Quaker
meetinghouse on Essex Street, and one Episcopal church on Prison Lane (now St.
Peter's Street).[6] Captain Francis Goelet, a British trader who visited Salem in 1750,
said the "Small Sea Port Towne" consisted of one main street, "abt 450 Houses,
Several of which are neat Buildings, but all of wood," and "One Curch [*sic*], 3 Pres-
biterian and One Quakers Meeting." "The Situation is Very Prety," he concluded.
(Neighboring Marblehead was by contrast a "Dirty Erregular Stinking Place.")[7]

The splintering and decline of older congregations—and the emergence of
newer ones—worried more conservative Salem residents. The cure for this dangerous condition was the same one tried with great effect in other towns: revival.
There were indigenous and imported varieties. The great British revivalist George
Whitefield toured the area in 1740 and wrote about it in his journal. He, too, preferred Salem over Marblehead: "Got to Marble Head, a large town twenty miles
from Boston. About eleven preached to some thousands in a broad place in the
middle of the town, but not with much visible effect. Rode to Salem and preached
there also to about 2000. Here the Lord manifested forth His glory. In every part
of the congregation persons might be seen under great concern and one, Mr.
Clark, a good minister as is granted by all I conversed with, seemed to be almost
in heaven."[8]

It is possible that Whitefield was right and that thousands of lay believers responded with alacrity to his message; and yet, aside from the good reverend Peter Clarke, local clergy seem to have wanted little to do with Whitefield. One historian of religion in Salem, Thomas Henry Billings (who lived in Nathaniel Hawthorne's time), searched for lasting evidence of Whitefield's Salem revival and could not find any. His conclusion that "many ministers did not like Mr. Whitefield or his methods and were suspicious of the whole movement" is supported by one fact above all—that no one from Salem came to a regional meeting convened to promote revival methods. Though cautious not to lose sight of the fact that "there were many genuine reformations of life" in the revival, Billings nevertheless concluded that it did not have "official approval" and did not produce "any permanent effects" locally. Billings explained Salem's "aloofness" in this way: "No matter how [participants] may have explained it, [indifference to the revival] was probably due in part to the vivid memory of the witchcraft delusion and its horrible results. Men still in active life during the decade from 1740 to 1750 would remember Judge Sewall's recantation and apology and the shame that attended the recovery from the madness of those terrible days. The community had experienced a purgation of those emotions on which the fear of the supernatural rests."[9] In eighteenth-century Salem, memories of the witch trials worked against revivals and other manifestations of the supernatural mentality.

There is other evidence that this was the case. In the late eighteenth and early nineteenth centuries, liberals such as the Unitarian cleric and public figure William Bentley (1759–1819) pointed to the trials as an example of what happened when supernaturalism and irrationality spun out of control. Bentley was a paradoxical figure. In public, he lobbied for religious freedom and tolerance; in private, he harshly criticized Baptists, evangelicals, Universalists, and others. In Catholic histories of Salem, Bentley emerged as something of a local hero, his congregation an island of good will in turbulent seas of Puritan anti-Catholicism. Louis Walsh, the Salem historian who wrote *Origin of the Catholic Church in Salem* (1890), praised Bentley for hosting the first Catholic priest in Salem (a convert from Congregationalism) and for helping him find and organize Catholics—mostly French refugees from England—in the 1790s.[10] In his diary, Bentley proudly recorded the same events, remembering that he took time to care for and visit Catholic immigrants, even conversing with them in their native tongue.[11] He took pride in these enlightened acts. Bentley also was among the first to exchange pulpits with Anglicans (resolutely and intensely disliked in the Revolutionary period), and he invited others—Methodists, Presbyterians, Congregationalists—to preach to his congregation. A believer in both Christianity and the Enlightenment, faith and reason, Bentley hoped for progress and peace among the religions.

But there were limits to his ecumenism. He was, for example, staunchly opposed to revivalists and revivals. He had nothing but condemnation for "the stupid ass at the Tabernacle"—Joshua Spaulding, minister of the Tabernacle Church—for embroiling local churches in controversy and schism and for bringing other illiterate and ill-informed preachers to town. Though certain that Spaulding could not distinguish the severest satire from "the most happy compliments," Bentley nevertheless composed a satire in Spaulding's honor (which he kept to himself):

> On tubs to preach you are design'd,
> But to your fate quite well resign'd.
> To teach, or think, you know not how,
> but have no blush upon your brow,
> For thinking is a devilish plan
> To favor reason, & the God in man.[12]

Bentley was sure that such preachers, "without a public or regular education [into the ministry]," had everywhere caused "convulsions, separations," and "zeal." The continued activity of these groups, especially Baptists—a group, Bentley quipped, that immersed "disciples in water and ignorance"—left long legacies of confusion and nonsense. When a Baptist congregation was assembled in Salem in 1805, a year after Hawthorne's birth, Bentley called it "a dark day."[13] Deeper reflection on these matters brought Bentley's mind to the history of fanaticism in the area, which in turn reminded him of the witch trials. The problem was not religion itself, of course, but an unenlightened, credulous attitude, a belief that armies of demons and angels inhabited the world. Bentley always was surprised when encountering that mindset. "Found that the notions of *Witchcraft* & the belief of the facts of 1692 were not eradicated," he confided to his diary in 1798. "An aged lady sat with the greatest composure and delivered her firm assent to wonders of wonders more wonderful."[14]

Bentley's concern about fanaticism and irrationality was fairly common in an age worried about factions, parties, and republican stability. These were, after all, the years after the American Revolution. The "tornado of passions" recently concluding the French Revolution made Americans uncertain that their masses might learn to rule themselves and hold the new nation together. New England ministers in particular warned of "the propensities and passions peculiar to human nature" and the many "destructive courses of error and delusion," and everyone worried about the "mad rancor of party and faction." Inside and outside Salem, politicians and theologians used Salem as a metaphor for factions, fanaticisms, and foolishness of all kinds. In any case, Bentley, always ready to stand up for his town, took heart that Salem in the eighteenth century was on the right track. "The greater progress of society in Boston & Salem has changed the scene," he commented hopefully. "The latitude of religious freedom has made religious sects mingle freely in these Towns, while NewburyPort is possessed by the most bitter devotees on the Continent. . . . One of the Clergymen in NewburyPort, from a personal aversion, would not attend the funeral of the father of another nor of his child, nor in his company at the funeral of a clergyman dying upon a visit to the place, or the wife of another."[15] Witch trials notwithstanding, Bentley hoped Salem was becoming a beacon of reason and progress.

III.

But Bentley and his enlightened coterie were not successful in banishing Salem's ghosts forever. In fact, no century wrestled with Salem's dark past more than the nineteenth, and no single Salem resident imagined and evoked this past more powerfully than Nathaniel Hawthorne.

Hawthorne had reasons to wrestle with the past. One of his direct ancestors—his father's great-great-grandfather—was a seventeenth-century magistrate who condemned some 1692 witches to death. At least according to Hawthorne tradition, Judge John Hathorne was cursed by one of the accused as she proceeded to the gallows. Though that curse—and the 1692 trials in general—appear not to have bothered John Hathorne, they preoccupied his descendants considerably, especially the melancholy Nathaniel Hawthorne, who dealt with his family's guilt by writing stories about sin and shame, fathers and sons, transgression and repentance. In an autobiographical preface to *The Scarlet Letter* (1850), a novel in which hiding one's guilt is the deadliest sin and admitting it the loftiest redemption, Hawthorne spoke briefly about these issues and how they had played out in his own life. "The figure of that first ancestor [in Salem], invested by family tradition with a dim and dusky grandeur, was present to my boyish imagination, as far back as I can remember," he recalled. The witch trial judge John Hathorne "made himself so conspicuous in the martyrdom of the witches, that their blood may fairly be said to have left a stain upon him. So deep a stain, indeed that his old dry bones, in the Charter Street burial-ground, must still retain it, if they have not crumbled utterly to dust!" The macabre images were standard fare for Hawthorne, capturing both his anxiety about the past and his mood in the present. "I know not whether these ancestors of mine ever bethought themselves to repent, and ask pardon of Heaven for their cruelties," Hawthorne worried, "or whether they are now groaning under the heavy consequences of them, in another state of being. At all events, I, the present writer, as their representative, hereby take shame upon myself for their sakes, and pray that any curse incurred by them" "may be now and henceforth removed."[16]

Hawthorne had enough of the Puritan in him to know, as the Scripture says, that a father's sins might well be visited upon his sons. He took the family curse quite seriously. Unfortunately, his efforts to throw off this curse, to confess and repent in *The Scarlet Letter,* were not enough to drive away all of his anxiety and guilt. In other ways, by other devices, he continued to try to escape the past and its claim on him.

How he negotiated his religious identity was part of it. Both William and John Hathorne and their families had gone to the only meetinghouse in Salem, a Congregational church near the southeast corner of what is now Washington and Essex Streets. By Nathaniel's time this single congregation, through the usual disputes and schisms, had broken into six—three orthodox Congregational meetings (Tabernacle, South, and Howard Street) and three more liberal congregations (First, East, and North). There also were several newcomers on the scene: an Episcopal Church, a Baptist Society and a Free-Will Baptist offshoot, a Quaker meeting, Roman Catholic and Methodist congregations, and some Universalists. The Hawthornes went to First Church, which claimed descent from the original church but which had, by the early nineteenth century, softened its Calvinism considerably. The transformation of Calvinist orthodoxy into Unitarian (and transcendentalist) liberalism at Hawthorne's church was the same transformation witnessed at Bentley's East Church (and the same transformation that took place all over coastal New England). In any case, however softened the Calvinism in Nathaniel's time, apparently it was not soft enough. Above all Nathaniel recalled the rigor of his old church, remembering the "good old silver-headed clergyman" and "the old wooden meeting-house in Salem which used, on wintry Sabbaths, to be the frozen purgatory of my childhood."[17] Hawthorne continued to be propelled toward liberal positions, moving even to transcendentalism, a romantic religion of nature often critical of traditional Christian symbols and practices.

Hawthorne used his fiction to work himself out of old positions and into new ones, but his liberation never was complete. In *The House of the Seven Gables* (1851), written just a year after his *Scarlet Letter,* Hawthorne fictionalized the curse put on his family by telling a story about Matthew Maule's curse on the arrogant Colonel Pyncheon and his descendants. With the hangman's noose around his neck, Maule blurts out: "God will give him blood to drink!"[18] This curse and the ways it influenced the present were a persistent theme, but several characters in the book were created to throw off the burdens of the past, especially Holgrave, Phoebe, Hepzibah, and Clifford Pyncheon. In a crucial chapter, Hepzibah and Clifford flee from the House of the Seven Gables—a symbol of Maule's curse, old traditions, and the past—to the train, a vehicle of freedom and a new, spiritualized faith. As the train carries them away from the town, Clifford has a conversation with a conservative gentleman dubious about the train and other new experiences. Clifford agrees with the man that the past can never be wholly transcended, but he arrives at a compromise position: some things change, some things stay the same. "You are aware, my dear sir," Clifford concludes, "—you have observed it in your own experience,—that all human progress is in a circle; or, to use a more accurate and beautiful figure, in an ascending spiral curve. While we fancy ourselves going straight forward, and attaining, at every step, an entirely new position of affairs, we do actually return to something long ago tried and abandoned, but which we now find etherealized, refined, and perfected to its ideal." This was a transcendentalist metaphor—everything was a circle, an ascending spiral.[19] It was a vision of history that these travelers accepted only with ambivalence, a time line that both predicted change and recognized its impossibility. For this reason it elicited hope and resignation in about equal measure.

These contradictory emotions bumped and clashed in Hawthorne's mind as well. There was a time when Hawthorne, like Clifford, had been more certain that the train (and everything it represented) might help him "substitute something better" for "stale ideas of home and fireside." Years before writing both the *Scarlet Letter* and the *Seven Gables*, Hawthorne himself had used this strategy to escape. He left Salem and moved to a transcendentalist community near Boston called Brook Farm, an experience he later fictionalized in *The Blithedale Romance* (1852). Initially, he embraced the idea of a self-sufficient intellectual and spiritual community, and he went to Brook Farm hoping to find these things and more time to think and write. The reality of the place, however, was quite different. "You cannot make a silk purse out of a sow's ear," Hawthorne complained near the end of his stay, "nor must you expect pretty stories from a man who feeds pigs."[20] In short, the practical matters of farm living—loading manure, cutting hay, milking cows—overwhelmed and depressed him. And these were not his only problems. The advent of transcendentalism had helped him in certain ways, but Hawthorne never could quite embrace its resolute recantation of sin; he was irritated by the optimism of Brook Farmers and could not see how evil, death, and the dark past could so easily be wished away. Near the beginning of his *Scarlet Letter,* he wrote that "the founders of [New England], whatever Utopia of human virtue and happiness they might originally project, have invariably recognized it among their earliest practical necessities to allot a portion of the virgin soil as a cemetery, and another portion as the site of a prison."[21] The contrast with Brook Farm was revealing: when someone did die at Brook Farm—Zenobia in *Blithedale*—these transcendentalists discovered that they had not planned a cemetery. How had such an oversight been possible? It had been possible, Hawthorne suggested, because transcendentalists had not even considered the possibility of suffering or death. To a man who always sensed the nearness of sin and suffering, this attitude was inexplicable. Hawthorne left Brook Farm just six months after arriving.

IV.

By the late nineteenth century, others in and around Salem shared Hawthorne's ambivalence about the liberal trajectories of Puritanism. They, too, wondered whether Unitarians and transcendentalists had eroded New England's strong sense of sin and guilt, its legendary commitment to duty and responsibility. Had New Englanders lost the sense of purpose that had followed so naturally from a firm belief in Divine Providence? Hence it was that by the late nineteenth century new interpretations of Puritanism and the witch trials in particular came into focus—interpretations that aimed not to liberalize or alter old ways but to revive them. Many turned to Puritans to rediscover virtues they saw in short supply, especially things like discipline, obligation, and conviction.

The attempt to recover the lost power of the Puritans was part of a nationwide "colonial revival" that recalled with nostalgia an old New England undisturbed by immigration and industrialization. The sentiment that informed it varied from fear that foreigners had diluted native bloodlines to hope that old-style Calvinism might settle modern nerves or cure world-weariness. The strength of this colonial revival is suggested by the fact that on the eve of the bicentennial of the witch trials, an amateur historian named Alice Earle published a sympathetic and immensely popular study called *Sabbath in Puritan New England* (1891). During its first year, the book sold nearly twelve thousand copies; in a decade, it went through twelve editions. In the book, Earle evoked the moral and physical power of the Puritans, describing, among other things, the rough texture of their religious lives. "Strange and grotesque decorations did the outside of the earliest meeting-houses bear," she wrote; "grinning wolves' heads [were] nailed under windows and by the side of the door, while splashes of blood, which had dripped from the severed neck, reddened the logs beneath." This fanciful encomium to New England's ancestors was intended to improve and edify a tired, contemporary generation: "Patient, frugal, God-fearing, and industrious, cruel and intolerant sometimes, but never cowardly, sternly obeying the word of God in the spirit and the letter, but erring sometimes in the interpretation thereof,—surely they have no traits to shame us, to keep us from thrilling with pride at the drop of their blood which runs in our backsliding veins."[22]

In an age that praised Puritans in these ways, memories about the witch trials had to be reconstructed cautiously. Some of the most creative glosses on the 1692 events came from descendants of witch trial victims, many of whom by the nineteenth century had organized themselves into prosperous associations that convened religious services, memorial gatherings, and other commemorative events. The family of one of the first witch trial victims, Rebecca Nurse, held a bicentennial commemoration of Rebecca's death in Danvers (formerly Salem Village) in 1892, during which they and the family's minister reflected on the trials. Instead of blaming the Puritans, they praised them for ending witch hunts and other superstitious practices. Witchcraft "delusions" had "lived through thoughtless centuries," one Nurse descendant noted, until "the superior average strength and character of the early New England settlers and their immediate descendants" finally subjected those delusions to a "searching scrutiny." As Salem minister and historian A. P. Putnam put it in 1892, "Therefore, 1692 was a crisis in the history of witchcraft, because 1692 saw the culmination of thoughtful intelligence, and of spiritual discernment, in a degree far greater than had ever appeared in any ancient state. To these sources we trace the stream of beneficent New England influence along whose banks may peace and good will to men flourish in abundance ever-more."[23] In this clever late-nineteenth-century view, Puritans were not responsible for perpetuating credulity and intolerance; they were responsible for *ending* these things.

Of course, these kinds of selective memories were conjured to solve very specific problems in the present. Caroline Emmerton, a wealthy philanthropist from an old Salem family, had the ingenious idea that a restored House of the Seven Gables museum and heritage center might educate and Americanize immigrants then flooding into Salem. When she bought and began restoring the House of the Seven Gables in 1908, her settlement house association in the Turner Street area had been operating for several years, offering services to Polish, Russian, and Irish immigrants and classes on sewing, handicrafts, and dancing. Once the House of the Seven Gables was restored and open to the public, she had more money to buy additional buildings and expand her settlement work. Eventually, the House of the Seven Gables Settlement Association was able to offer a variety of uplifting pro-grams—citizenship classes and patriotic pageants, with immigrants playing star-ring roles; lessons in cooking and housekeeping; and lectures on our American heritage delivered in foreign languages. One of the biggest events was a "Pageant of Salem," a four-day event in 1913 that involved over a thousand actors. The pag-eant, like Emmerton's other work, reaffirmed a sense of community (and a com-mon history) for Salem residents new and old. Of course, the witch trials could not be entirely avoided. It was admitted (though not emphasized) that in the Pu-ritan character there was an infelicitous "strain of superstition and intolerance." The pageant used the witchcraft "delusion" as a way to call for a renewed tolerance, especially for Salem's new immigrants.[24] But monuments to this past never were chiseled in stone or installed permanently in the local landscape. For many years prominent Salem citizens, including Hawthorne, had called for a memorial on Gallows Hill, perhaps a column or "lookout" that might remind people of the in-firmities of human nature in a dark time. But the idea was met with inertia, dis-taste, and, occasionally, hostility.[25]

There was one last and quite crucial development in late-nineteenth- and early-twentieth-century glosses on Salem, and that was the explosion of medical and scientific interpretations. Though Puritans themselves had developed a cer-tain amount of skepticism toward the supernatural and enlightened Christians like Bentley disliked credulity, these earlier figures had held on to a belief in God, the Holy Ghost, and (depending on Bentley's mood) evil spirits. But many in late-nineteenth-century America were determined to snuff out the supernatural altogether, and they did it usually by redescribing the supernatural in natural terms. As far as Salem witchcraft was concerned, medical and psychological interpretations flourished, especially interpretations that reduced the strange behavior of the "possessed" girls to some kind of hypnotism, hallucination, or hysteria. In 1928 James Putnam, a professor of neurology at Harvard, articulated what had become conventional wisdom in his article "Some Medical Aspects of Witchcraft": "We are, therefore, altogether justified in assuming that the descriptions given of the performances of those bewitched, of the sights seen and the sounds heard and the damage done, will find explanation on the basis of demonstrated laws of mental life, discounting always the perverted imaginations of the chief actors in the play. The appearances of imps and familiars so often described were doubtless actual animals or persons, transformed at times into satanic forms to satisfy the fear or fancy of the observer, an entirely analogous experience to the effect of fear under ordinary conditions, but naturally exaggerated through the emotional abnormality of the time." Putnam's conclusion was that the outburst at Salem was "an example merely of what, under different conditions, has occurred in every part of the world, and will continue to occur, modified only by what we call the progress of civilization and of liberal thought. To us the scenes at Salem in 1692, especially the mental condition of the 'afflicted children,' bear the stamps of 'group hysteria,' in which suggestion, self-protection, a feeling of domination, in an atmosphere of profound belief in the actuality of witchcraft, played a dominant role."[26]

By the early decades of the twentieth century this kind of interpretation had gained wide acceptance, making it hard to escape the conclusion that real demons, angels, and other wonders no longer lurked in either Salem's living present or its remembered past. *The place and its history, we might say, had become disenchanted.* But the twentieth century saw one final development in Salem, one final irony that changed things again. A new group of witches, faintly resembling the old, arrived. They had their own memories of Salem's past and very particular ways of using them.

V.

Visitors' guides before the middle of the twentieth century did not play up Salem's connection to the 1692 trials. A 1908 guidebook promoted a range of historical sites—some "fine old residences," two museums, the Charter Street Burial Ground, the Custom House, Hawthorne's residence, and Derby Street. Nor did businesses at the time capitalize on Salem's witch history. A few local companies tried out witch themes for commercial purposes in the late nineteenth century— a "witch city" brand of fish sold by Pettingell's Fish Dealers on Derby Wharf, a "Salem Witch Spoon" marketed by Daniel Low, and "Ye Witchcraft Game" by

Parker Brothers (doomed because of negative local reaction)—but that was about it.[27] The shame and guilt of the trials—notwithstanding heroic revisions during the colonial revival—still outweighed the benefits of selling Salem's curious and inexplicable history.

By the 1950s the mood had changed a little. Though Arthur Miller thought Salem residents in 1952 still were a little touchy about the trials—"You couldn't get anyone to say anything about it," he complained—in fact the city was beginning to incorporate the trials into its historical identity and commercial pursuits.[28] In 1948, it restored the former residence of witch trial judge Jonathan Corwin, creating a "Witch House" that would serve as an "everlasting monument to courageous men who broke the shackles of theocratic authority and paved the way for that freedom of thought which has made this country great." (Why a judge's house was chosen as such a reminder is a mystery.) In 1972, the first for-profit witch attraction also opened, the Salem Witch Museum, taking over a Gothic Revival church that was the home of Salem's East Church (Bentley's congregation, though during his lifetime located in a different building on Essex Street). Then the cast and crew of the television comedy *Bewitched* came and filmed two Halloween episodes. This undoubtedly increased the place's visibility and probably also reinforced a growing sense that Salem's infirmities, safely ensconced in a distant past, might now be comfortably laughed about.

Thus Salem already was well established as the "witch city" by the time modern witches, or "Wiccans," started arriving in the late 1960s. When they did arrive the irony of the situation did not escape them. One of the first to come was Laurie Cabot, who needed to relocate in the area but felt it would be "crass" for a real witch to do so. When it happened that she found an "irresistible" home in Salem she decided to come, but she also resolved to keep her religion private. In a year or so she had assembled a congregation (or "coven") of witches around her to practice their faith, and her notoriety was spreading. Of course, she was partly to blame for the buzz; she is not a shy, retiring presence. She is an outgoing, clever soul with a sense of humor, a modern witch who walks the streets of Salem in flowing black robes. In her two magic shops she sells serious ritual objects—pentacles, crystals, incense, herbs—but also things like black conical hats. We've "reclaimed the conical hat as a spoof," she explained once. "We've got to have some fun."[29] So by the time the *Bewitched* cast was discovering Salem, the American public was discovering Laurie Cabot. All of the major media outfits came to interview her—*National Geographic, Time, Newsweek,* the networks—and her face, fast becoming the face of modern witchcraft in Salem, became an important part of the place as well. (In the mid-1970s Governor Dukakis proclaimed her the "official witch" of Salem, a move that elicited criticism from cynics and anxious reflection from other witches. Cynics complained that this was another way for Cabot to make a buck; witches were sure that a psychic, not a politician, should have made such an important decision.)

What do modern witches like Cabot believe? As with any religion, modern witchcraft encompasses a spectrum of beliefs and practices. This is especially true for this religion, which eschews hierarchies and values individualism above all. Witches believe that the world is full of magical powers, that individual lives are meaningful and eternal, and that history is, to use the old Puritan word, *providential.* They also believe that the spiritual forces (or "energies") that sustain all life and undergird all religions can be used in special rituals to heal and help people. (Witches have a complex calendar of seasonal rituals that is similar to ritual cycles in indigenous cultures.) They believe that the consequences of one's beliefs and actions come back threefold (this is the karma-like "threefold law"). They believe in god and goddess figures (usually one each, but sometimes more). And they believe in reincarnation. They do not believe in Satan—a "Christian concept," Cabot grumbles—and they do not practice what could be called "black magic" (that is, manipulating the energy in the world to accomplish evil ends). The image of an evil, green-faced witch casting spells is a stereotype, they point out, a scary fantasy used by Christians to justify centuries of persecution.[30]

That history of persecution is crucial to most witches' sense of identity and sacred history. Modern witches see themselves as inheritors of ancient pagan (especially Celtic and Druid) traditions that went underground during what they call (with capital letters) "The Burning Times," a reference to the church's persecution of pagans, Jews, and anyone else unorthodox or deviant. In a 1990 video in which Laurie Cabot introduces viewers to modern witchcraft, she uses fairly standard language. "During the [ancient] time that we had been alive and living well and practicing for hundreds of thousands of years, along came another religion, Christianity, and when they moved into Great Britain their only way of course of conquering was to demean or get rid of existing religions." This was a scourge that "people don't even whisper about" today, a "holocaust of nine million people" "burned and hanged as witches." "We survived that," Cabot adds, triumphantly, and "have reared our children and taught them the ways of healing and psychological balance and protection, meditation, and herbalism—and it [has] carried through [to] today."[31]

Those who practice witchcraft in Salem today remember the 1692 events in different ways. The best-known rituals of remembrance are the ritual circles performed near Gallows Hill in Salem every October 31, one of which is followed by an immensely popular candlelight vigil from Gallows Hill to the witch trials memorial. These are not Halloween celebrations. (Witches in Salem, I was surprised to discover, do not celebrate Halloween. On my first day in Salem I asked one witch what she did last Halloween, and she answered, good-naturedly, "I think I went out for Chinese food.") Though witches do not celebrate Halloween as such, there is a holy day on October 31 that is important to them, a day to celebrate the harvest and remember passed loved ones, a day they call Samhain (pronounced

"Sow-en"). On this day, they say, "the veil between the worlds is the thinnest."[32] Because of this, it is the perfect time to remember and even communicate with Salem residents dead and gone.

The Samhain rituals in Salem vary a little bit, but the basics are the same. Witches gather in circles, where they call on the spirits of the four directions. An officiant in the center of the circle draws these spirits into the group by turning to the four directions with outstretched hands or a long staff extended toward the horizon. At the center of the circle is an altar with different symbols of nature and the gods—the fruits of the harvest, frankincense and myrrh, incense, flowers, crystals. Then the officiant talks a bit about the meaning of the event. In one of Laurie Cabot's Samhain circles, everyone raises their palms to the sky and Cabot begins with these words: "We come to this sacred place to commemorate those who died for our freedom. We remember these, and we are the living commemoration of the nine million witches that were tortured, burned, and hanged in the Burning Times." In some Samhain circles the names of victims are then recited—the list can be quite long, moving through hundreds or even thousands of witch martyrs from the Burning Times; or it can be very short, limited only to those women and men killed in Salem.

In the Samhain ritual in particular, but also in daily life, Salem witches think of themselves as a part of the Burning Times, as emotionally and existentially connected to earlier witches and their underground, secret rituals. Hence, Cabot says that in antiquity "we" were alive "and practicing for hundreds of thousands of years." *She was there.* This is not a rhetorical flourish; she actually recalls a past life in which she participated in these historical events. Because the circles of reincarnation meaningfully connect all events and things, modern witches are ancient witches—Salem witches, perhaps—reincarnated. And if modern witches are ancient ones reincarnated, modern critics also might be ancient judges reincarnated (a warning to both skeptics and captious historians). These facts, too, give the Samhain ritual an emotional power. As Cabot herself says, "I'm still angry at the accusers of the witch trials in 1692. . . . there is some anger left because I think the same people are reincarnated and living in Salem now."[33] If ever there was a mentality of the supernatural, this is it.

The final irony to this story, then, is that as powerfully as Christians used the witch trials to limit, reduce, and expunge the mentality of the supernatural, in the end modern witches have brought it back. This is not to say that all witches approve of how Cabot practices the faith—or how she renders the Samhain rite in particular. Many witches are quick to criticize Cabot and others who do not distinguish between medieval witches, accused Puritan "witches" in 1692, and modern Wiccans. One skeptical witch, a bright, roguish woman who humorously called herself the "bad witch of Salem," wondered why modern witches commemorate the 1692 trials at all. "What do the accused 'witches' have to do with us?" she said, exasperated. "They weren't real witches—they were *Puritans*. If they were alive today they would want to *burn and hang us!*" Though scholars now wonder if some of the accused *were* real witches—almost certainly a few did dabble in divination and the occult—the criticism remains sound.[34] Certainly, the accused were not members of a harassed minority pagan faith clamoring for recognition and civil rights, as Cabot sometimes makes them out to be. Cabot is aware of these criticisms but remains unruffled. Some of the accused may have been witches, she says, some not. In any case, to Cabot the trials usefully symbolize other important things, such as the dangers of religious (specifically, Christian) intolerance and fanaticism. This seems to be a meaning embraced by everyone in Salem today—that through the hate and fanaticism of the trials we might learn not to hunt witches and scapegoats in the present. That seems like a reasonable legacy.

Still, to this researcher there was something vaguely unsettling about how these witches reclaimed the 1692 victims as their own. The victims of 1692 were not actual witches; they were Puritans wrongly charged and convicted—didn't everyone know this? But the more I thought about it, the more the meanings of these trials seemed obscure, and the more I wondered whether Laurie Cabot had a point after all. Perhaps the difference between my perspective and hers had less to do with the facts of the case and more to do with the prejudices we both brought to the past. This point became clearer to me as I did the research for this chapter. William Bentley worried about the chaos and disorder of the Revolution and saw the witch trials as a lesson in irrationality and its fearful consequences. Caroline Emmerton and John Nourse wanted to build a culture of belonging for new immigrants and they saw the trials as a moment of turning to tolerance and freedom of conscience. I don't need to belabor the point that we all foist upon the past our present hopes and fears.

So I wonder, putting my question in more specific terms, if the difference between Cabot and me is that, like most modern Americans, I no longer believe that magical or supernatural powers control events in my daily life. This fact, of course, influences how I interpret history and Puritan culture in particular. One commentator said it well: "Because we no longer believe in the supernatural power of witches we have assumed that individuals executed at Salem were innocent."[35] Because we no longer believe in witches or magical powers, we must find other ways of explaining what happened to the accusers and the accused in 1692. If this is the case, if this disenchanted mentality defines us today, the source of it has to be the scientific twentieth century, which reduced explanations of many religious things (including witchcraft) to quite specific medical and scientific diagnostic categories—"hallucination," "hysteria," mental imbalance. My point is not that we should do away with these modern explanations, but that for very particular reasons they seem less plausible to witches like Laurie Cabot. Like seventeenth-century Puritans, Cabot and other witches live with a mentality of the supernatural in which transcendent energies, refracted in different ways through human feelings and actions, produce real effects in the real world. In a surprising way, that mentality makes real witches and real witchcraft in 1692—and many other things—possible all over again.

Maybe Karyn Rego was right; maybe spirits from the past come alive in the present, making it sacred over and over again. Maybe in Salem at least, things do move in circles.

Notes

The author thanks the many witches, Puritans, and skeptics in Salem who helped make this article possible: Mulysa Gurrierro, Toni and Marie Gurrierro, Karyn Rego, Kathleen Rulo, Donna Story, Robert Craigie, Alison D'Amario, Patty MacCloud, Tina Jordan, and Tim Reagan. I also want to thank the librarians at the Phillips Library and Richard Trask at the Danvers Historical Society.

1. Karyn E. Rego, interview by author, Salem, Mass., December 10, 2002. Also Karyn E. Rego, phone interview by author, January 12, 2003.

2. Quotations are from Charles W. Upham, *Salem Witchcraft, With an Account of Salem Village and A History of Opinions on Witchcraft and Kindred Subjects* (Boston: Wiggin and Lunt, 1867; reprint, Mineola, N.Y.: Dover Publications, 2000), xiii.

3. Quoted in Bernard Rosenthal, *Salem Story: Reading the Witch Trials of 1692* (Cambridge, U.K.: Cambridge University Press, 1993), 201–2.

4. Jon Butler, *Awash in a Sea of Faith: Christianizing the American People* (Cambridge, Mass.: Harvard University Press, 1990), 170–71; Richard P. Gildrie, *Salem, Massachusetts, 1626–1683: A Covenant Community* (Charlottesville: University Press of Virginia, 1975), 85. Arriving at precise percentages is difficult; it depends on whom we count. Gildrie pointed out that before 1650 only "eighty families out of 238 that held land were not represented within the church." In other words, 66 percent of landowning families were represented in the church. Counting individual church members yields other results. Doing just that, James Duncan Phillips pointed out that 34 percent of males were church members in 1650; the percentages were significantly higher for women. James Duncan Phillips, *Salem in the Seventeenth Century* (Boston: Houghton Mifflin, 1933): 353–56.

5. A couple of people have pointed out that Salem accommodated itself quickly to religious diversity. See Butler, 170.

6. The religious landscape here has been reconstructed in two places: James Duncan Phillips, "The Life and Times of Richard Derby, Merchant of Salem, 1712 to 1783," in *Sketches about Salem People* (Salem, Mass.: The Club, 1930), 32–33; and Charles Osgood and H. M. Batchelder, *Historical Sketch of Salem* (Salem, Mass.: Essex Institute, 1879).

7. Quoted in Phillips, "Richard Derby," 33.

8. George Whitefield journals, quoted in Thomas Henry Billings, "The Great Awakening," in *Sketches about Salem People,* 1.

9. Billings, 14–16. Another historian noted a similar situation during the Second Great Awakening of the early nineteenth century, pointing out that "the evangelical zeal and the frantic revival meetings" of the period were "notably lacking in Salem." Anne Farnam, "A Society of Societies: Associations and Voluntarism in Early Nineteenth-Century Salem," in *Dr. Bentley's Salem: Diary of a Town* (Salem, Mass.: Essex Institute, 1977), 36. Christine Heyrman presents a more complex story of the First Great Awakening in maritime Massachusetts, though Heyrman too points out that local revival enthusiasms reminded Salem residents of the witch hysteria. Christine Heyrman, *Commerce and Culture: The Maritime Communities of Colonial Massachusetts, 1690–1750* (New York: Norton, 1984), 378.

10. Louis S. Walsh, *Origin of the Catholic Church in Salem, and Its Growth in St. Mary's Parish and the Parish of the Immaculate Conception* (Boston: Cashman, Keating and Co., 1890), 1–5.

11. William Bentley, *The Diary of William Bentley, D.D.* (Gloucester, Mass.: Peter Smith, 1962), I, xxxi.

12. Quoted in Robert C. Stewart, "Reading Dr. Bentley: A Literary Approach to a Historical Diary," in *Dr. Bentley's Salem: Diary of a Town* (Salem, Mass.: Essex Institute, 1977), 9.

13. Quoted in William McLoughlin, *New England Dissent, 1630–1883: The Baptists and the Separation of Church and State* (Cambridge, Mass.: Harvard University Press, 1971), II, 1071.

14. William Bentley, *The Diary of William Bentley, D.D.,* ed. Marguerite Dalrymple, 4 vols. (Gloucester, Mass.: Peter Smith, 1962), II, 284; III, 67–68.

15. Quotation from Bentley, I, 253. Other quotations and information are from Philip Gould, "New England Witch-Hunting and the Politics of Reason in the Early Republic," *New England Quarterly* 68, no. 1 (March 1995): 61–63.

16. Nathaniel Hawthorne, *The Scarlet Letter* (New York: W. W. Norton, 1988), 9.

17. Quoted in Margaret Moore, *The Salem World of Nathaniel Hawthorne* (Columbia: University of Missouri Press), 103, 109.

18. Hawthorne family tradition remembered Sarah Good spitting this curse at Judge Hathorne, though the historical record (apparently unknown to Nathaniel) indicates that the Reverend Nicholas Noyes actually was her target.

19. From George P. Lathrop, ed., *The Complete Works of Nathaniel Hawthorne, with Introductory Notes* (Boston: Riverside Press, 1883), 307–8. See also Alfred Rosa, *Salem, Transcendentalism and Hawthorne* (Cranbury, N.J.: Associated University Presses, 1980), 130–31.

20. Quoted in Robert L. Gale, *A Nathaniel Hawthorne Encyclopedia* (New York: Greenwood Press, 1991), 60.

21. Lathrop, 307–8; Rosa, 127–28.

22. Alice Earle, *The Sabbath in Puritan New England* (New York: C. Scribner's Sons, 1891), 11, 70–71, 96, 187, 259, 327. Quoted in Joseph Conforti, *Imagining New England: Explorations of Regional Identity from the Pilgrims to the Mid-Twentieth Century* (Chapel Hill: University of North Carolina Press, 2001), 216–21.

23. John W. Nourse, *An Address Delivered at Danvers, July 29, 1892, Before the Nurse Family Association* (Salem, Mass.: The Salem Press, 1894), 10–11. The minister presiding at this meeting agreed, pointing out that Puritan hardheadedness paved the way for a decline in theocratic no-

tions and clerical influence in the United States. A. P. Putnam, "Rebecca Nurse and Her Friends: Address at the Dedication of a Tablet in Honor of Forty Friends of Rebecca Nurse, of Salem Village" (sermon preached on July 29, 1892), Phillips Library, Salem, Massachusetts.

24. Conforti, 250–61.

25. Rosenthal, 207; "The Proposed Memorial 'Look Out' on Gallows Hill, Salem," *Putnam's Monthly Historical Magazine* 1 (May 1892–April 1893): 295–96; Zachariah Mudge, *Witch Hill: A History of Salem Witchcraft* (New York: Carlton and Lanahan, 1870).

26. Putnam's article is excerpted in Fred Gibson Robbins, "Witchcraft," in *Sketches about Salem People* (Salem, Mass.: The Club, 1930), 23. For more on the history of witchcraft interpretations, see Marc Mappen, ed., *Witches and Historians: Interpretations of Salem* (Malabar, Fla.: Krieger Publishing, 2002).

27. For background information in this and subsequent paragraphs I am indebted to Richard Trask, interview by author, Salem, Mass., December 18, 2002; and K. David Goss, Richard B. Trask, Bryant F. Tolles Jr., Joseph Flibbert, and Jim McAllister, "Salem Then and Now," in *Salem: Cornerstones of a Historic City* (Beverly, Mass.: Commonwealth Editions, 1999), 125–26.

28. From an interview with Arthur Miller in the *Boston Globe,* December 15, 1996. Quoted in McAllister, 123.

29. Quoted in Alexander Stevens, "Bewitching Business," *North Shore Sunday,* November 1, 1992. I have drawn information on Cabot from this article and from Robert Rosenthal, "Salem's New Witch Weaves a Spell," *Boston Globe,* October 31, 1974.

30. Mulysa Gurrierro, interview by author, Salem, Mass., December 10, 2002; and Elizabeth Reis, ed., *Spellbound: Women and Witchcraft in America* (Wilmington, Del.: Scholarly Resources, 1998), xi–xxiii. Also, Toni and Marie Gurrierro, interview by author, Salem, Mass., January 8, 2003; and Kathleen Rulo, interview by author, Salem, Mass., December 13, 2003.

31. *Laurie Cabot and the Witches of Salem, Massachusetts in . . . The Discovery of Witches* (New York: White Light Pentacles/Sacred Spirit Productions, 1990), videorecording.

32. Mulysa Gurrierro, interview by author, Salem, Mass., December 10, 2002.

33. *Laurie Cabot and the Witches of Salem.*

34. In a now-classic book, Chadwick Hansen argued that some of the 1692 witches intentionally worked black magic. Chadwick Hansen, *Witchcraft at Salem* (New York: G. Braziller, 1969). The debate is still lively. See Jon Butler, "Magic, Astrology, and the Early American Religious Heritage, 1600–1760," *American Historical Review* 84, no. 2 (April 1979): 332; John Demos, "Underlying Themes in the Witchcraft of Seventeenth-Century New England," *American Historical Review* 75 (1969–1970); and Kenneth Minkema, review of *The Devil's Disciples: Makers of the Salem Witchcraft Trials* by Peter Hoffer and *Tituba, Reluctant Witch of Salem: Devilish Indians and Puritan Fantasies* by Elaine Breslaw, *William and Mary Quarterly* 54, no. 3 (July 1997): 642–45. See also David Hall, *Worlds of Wonder, Days of Judgment: Popular Religious Belief in Early New England* (Cambridge, Mass.: Harvard University Press, 1990), 100, 146–47.

35. Mappen, 43.

View of Derby Wharf from the Salem Custom House. Photo by Kim Mimnaugh.

Chapter Three

Salem as Enterprise Zone, 1783–1786

ROBERT BOOTH

While we fancy ourselves going straight forward, and attaining,
at every step, an entirely new position of affairs, we do actually return to something
long ago tried and abandoned, but which we now find etherealized,
refined, and perfected to its ideal.

—Nathaniel Hawthorne, *The House of the Seven Gables*

TWENTY years after the close of the Revolutionary War, in 1803, Salem was no longer a Massachusetts town or even an American seaport, but the capital of a worldwide trading empire, with closer ties to the merchants and markets of Arabia, India, Sumatra, and China than to New York, Philadelphia, or Charleston. Salem was among the most glamorous and exciting seaports in the young nation, famous for its intrepid sailors and far-sailing ships and for the sights, sounds, and aromatic smells of its waterfront, for the beauty of its streets and parks and the excellence of the architecture of its mansions and public buildings, for the immensity of its wharves and the wealth and taste of its merchants.

The home of ten thousand people by 1800, Salem supported two newspapers, ten churches, many schools, and a thriving local culture that drew on the arts, crafts, foods, and fashions of Europe and Asia.[1] So profound was the importance of the Far East that, once a year, the many shipmasters of Salem's new East India Marine Society dressed up in the turbans and silks and linens of the pashas and potentates with whom they traded, and solemnly paraded through the town—a sight seen nowhere else in America. And nowhere else, outside of the largest cities, did one encounter the richness of Salem's business and cultural resources: banks, publishers, insurance companies, charitable organizations, libraries, bookstores, a municipal water system, a museum of Orientalia and natural history, concert halls and assembly rooms, marine societies, free schools, private schools for adults and children, and choral and instrumental groups. With its learned professionals, its wide experience in dealing with the nations of the world, and its superb knowledge of finance and commerce, Salem addressed itself directly to a national audience, and was heard respectfully.

How had Salem—a somewhat staid, hierarchical community before the Revolutionary War—effected such a remarkable cultural and economic transformation? What did Salemites hope to achieve in the new nation? What did it mean to live in an early enterprise zone that was emerging as a major player on the global stage? What did this mean for Massachusetts? For America?

Salem's prominent place in the nation was the result of actions taken and opportunities seized twenty years before, in the confusing days after the end of the Revolutionary War. This essay focuses on the spirit that animated Salem during the critical years 1783–1786, a period during which local leaders initiated foreign trade with the Orient, exerted statewide and national political influence, and fostered new cultural forms in architecture, education, science, and religion. In these first few years of peace, Salem continued the Revolution at the civic level, and its leaders set a course that would make their town the showplace of the new America and of the riches and richness that American freedoms made possible.

Salem entered peacetime life with four important assets that could be directed into arenas of maritime enterprise: a great deal of new money, hundreds of able-bodied and experienced mariners, a large fleet of armed trading vessels, and a Viking-like spirit of conquest and adventure. After years of successful privateering and wartime trade, Salem's merchants and sailors believed they could go anywhere and succeed as traders and as warriors.[2] Most American ports had lost heavily during the war, as trade had dwindled, merchants had failed, and vessels had been lost to the enemy or had rotted at the dockside. In Salem, the opposite was true. After the war, there were more rich men than before the war; and Salem's wealthiest citizens sought eagerly to invest their war winnings productively. They soon learned that it was not safe to revert to old patterns in the brave new commercial world of Massachusetts and America under the Articles of Confederation. Even though they had the political right to trade freely and faced few barriers to importation, American merchants were now restricted in their choice of trading partners and were hard-pressed to find cargoes and lines of credit, thanks to Britain's postwar commercial reprisals.

Salem's foreign trade, which had been interrupted by the first years of war but had resumed in 1779, continued and expanded in 1783. The merchants and mariners were not interested in small profits—they wanted big returns on their investments. The war had taught the merchants that they had a very high capacity for risk, and privateering mariners had learned that playing the quasi pirate and possibly hitting the jackpot was greatly to be preferred to taking wages for wearing a sea furrow to and from the Caribbean or Europe. If someone could point them in the right direction and promise them a shot at big money, they were ready to go to the ends of the earth to get it.

Most important for the town's future were the high-achievers willing to stay in Salem rather than move on to Boston or some other larger port. Merchants Stephen Higginson and his Cabot kinsmen, having left Salem during the war or just before, had, in their new homes of Boston and Beverly, prospered beyond all expectations. It was widely believed that they had become the richest men in Massachusetts. Salem, the place they had left, had been an excellent wartime privateering center, but it might not prove the ideal postwar trading port for ambitious merchants and mariners. Boston had resumed its traditional status as the mercantile and maritime center of Massachusetts, with the largest population and the best distribution system to western and southern markets. A merchant in 1783 had to wonder about the opportunities that Salem afforded, especially because the nearby town of Marblehead, formerly a rich and populous market for Salem, had sunk very low because of wartime losses. For those whose business was to seek overseas markets, to trade for valuable goods, and to sell them at home at the best prices in the strongest markets, Boston beckoned. And, as capital of the new state, Boston was the place where legislators could be buttonholed and made to understand what merchants needed in the new order of things.

Against the obvious attractions of Boston, Salem could offer an excellent harbor and abundant human and shipping resources, the network of valuable connections and relationships, and the skills and vision of a commercial community determined to create a new center of economic and political gravity, complete with a satisfying social and cultural life. Such a conception was not unrealistic. Salem in 1783 was a place of talented merchants, mariners, artisans, lawyers, doctors, ministers, and teachers, some quite young. Still in their prime were the merchants Elias Hasket Derby, forty-four; Capt. Benjamin Goodhue Jr., thirty-five; and the renowned scientist and physician, Dr. Edward Augustus Holyoke, fifty-five.

Goodhue, Harvard-educated and widely popular, was among the town's post-Revolutionary political leaders.[3] During the next few years, he struggled between competing private and public interests: the love of commerce and the riches it brought him and his family, and the need for effective government, to which his conscience and his ego called him. Holyoke, now as in the past twenty-five years, was a distinguished intellectual who attracted a circle of brilliant and devoted young men who took a keen interest in science ("natural philosophy"), education, mathematics, and mechanical invention. During the war, Holyoke had helped to found both the American Academy of Arts and Sciences and Salem's Philosophical Library; now, he wanted Salem to become a beacon of enlightenment and scientific progress. Derby, the rich owner of a fleet of armed vessels, was facing the end of the wartime privateering and trading that had made him truly wealthy, and the start of a peacetime commerce that would be conducted under the flag of a new nation with new trading policies that he hoped would not hinder his hunt for high profits.

Less notable but hardly less able were Jonathan Ropes, Jonathan Gardner, and John Pickering, astute politicians and competent leaders who represented the sizeable class of homegrown merchants and shipowners. Like the town's stalwart sailors and sea captains and its skilled artisans, many professional men had come from other towns and even other nations, drawn by Salem's wartime prosperity and postwar prospects. Altogether, they lit the fires of talent, ambition, and energy that made Salem, in spite of its smaller size and its location in the shadow of Boston, shine forth as one of the brightest stars in the new republic.

ੴ

Salem's postwar riches and success could not have been predicted. In the 1760s, dominated by a Tory ruling class, Salem had fallen astern of Marblehead in both population and wealth. In the mid-1760s, the Marbleheaders had jettisoned their few Tory leaders in favor of the rebels Jeremiah Lee, Azor Orne, John and Jonathan Glover, and their firebrand spokesman, Elbridge Gerry—the very men who had outstripped Salem in merchant trade. Salem had no comparable leadership group in the 1760s, but it did have a growing Whig faction led by some young Harvard graduates and bankrolled by a few rebel-party merchants, chief among them Richard Derby (1712–1783) and his sons Richard Jr., Hasket, and John.[4] In the decade before the war, the house of Derby had been a successful family trading firm in which all shared alike and which, like most such firms, dealt primarily with the Caribbean. They had a fair amount of capital and a small fleet of midsized trading vessels, including, as early as 1769, one named the *Free American*. Among the Salem rebel faction, no one had more influence or more assets than the Derbys, and no one was quicker to buy up gunpowder and cannon for use against the English.[5]

During the years and months just before the war, things took a remarkable turn. Col. Jeremiah Lee, Marblehead's merchant prince and militia leader and owner of a very large fleet, suddenly died in May 1775. The loss of his leadership was keenly felt in the seaport, where his money and vessels would be tied up in probate rather than deployed for war. The other great shipowners of Marblehead, Robert "King" Hooper and Maj. John Pedrick, were Loyalists and not inclined to send their vessels against the British. As a consequence, Marblehead was unable to do much privateering or trading during the war, and hundreds of Marblehead men, generally considered to be the finest mariners in New England, wound up sailing instead on Salem privateers and letters-of-marque.[6]

Like Marblehead, Salem had experienced sudden and unexpected change. In the months between October 1774 and March 1775, the town's leading Tories fled to Boston, Halifax, and London. Overnight, it seemed, more than a century of economic and political leadership vanished, and the kinship ties and political-economic connections of the royalist gentry were thrown to the winds. Into this vacuum stepped Salem's rebel leaders. Foremost was Richard Derby Jr., Salem's representative to the rebel provincial congress. He found support from politicos John Pickering and Benjamin Goodhue Jr. Hasket Derby, having served as a selectman, representative to the legislature, and member of the committee of correspondence, soon gave up politics and focused on running the family business and procuring arms. Other leaders, like Timothy Pickering Jr. and Richard Ward, went into the Continental army and served for years. Colonel Pickering, the head of the Salem regiment and a former legislative representative, would join Gen. George Washington's inner circle and serve as quartermaster general of the army.

During the eight years of the Revolution, Salemites had adapted to completely new conditions in which the hazards of war loomed large: loss of life and property, loss of trade and fisheries, loss of vessels and capital through privateering or wartime trade, loss of trading partners and routes, and loss of heads of households incarcerated, sometimes for years, as prisoners of war. Amid all of this turmoil, Hasket Derby had adeptly picked his way. He had tried, at first, to keep the Derby vessels trading in the West Indies; but after three of them had been taken by the English, he had commenced privateering, which amounted to licensed high-seas robbery of British transports and merchantmen. Derby had not skimped: he had armed his vessels heavily, and employed bold masters and crackerjack crews. To his great relief, privateering had proved to be a highly profitable way to employ his assets: some of his vessels captured as many as ten well-supplied vessels in one cruise. Whether conducted on his own or in partnership with others to spread the risk and expenses, Derby's privateering luck was phenomenal, and his wealth and reputation had grown rapidly in the direction of legend. All of the best captains and crewmen wanted to sail for Derby, and Derby chose astutely among them, with preference given to his own relatives. Most proved to be excellent sea wolves, and very few of them or their men were captured or killed. As the years went by, Hasket Derby became by far the richest man in Salem, with a private navy that was nearly indefatigable. Young sailors dreamed of sailing on his vessels and striking it rich. "King" Derby achieved an almost mythical status in Salem, as all of his voyages turned to gold. In Marblehead and Newburyport, the stories were often written in blood and disappointment. Derby and Salem had been singled out for great good fortune; and, in a religious age, there was little doubt as to the cause.

As a winner in the high-stakes game of privateering, Derby had pushed his luck farther in 1779 and sent out armed letters-of-marque vessels, laden with cargoes, on trading voyages. As with his privateering, Derby's wartime trading was hugely successful. His vessels generally arrived safe at their destinations with cargoes that won a high price, and they returned with cargoes worth much more. For three years, Derby traded without any setbacks or losses and with a huge increase in his personal wealth. Toward the end of the war, his masters and men were not so fortunate as before, yet they remained the most successful privateers and traders in America.

Peace came in the spring of 1783, and Hasket Derby was the great man of Salem. He had no rivals: his brother Richard was dead, and Timothy Pickering had become a Philadelphian. Other merchant shipowners had made or lost small fortunes, and many a common sailor had become a wealthy man, with shares in several privateering vessels and ownership of a shop full of prize goods. The fortunes of war had not discriminated among Salemites on the basis of character, education, or background. The group of truly rich citizens numbered seventy-three, and many others were affluent.[7] Among the wealthiest were men from old merchant families like Orne and Pickman; but to their names had been added those of Forrester, Peirce, Waitt, Leach, Turell, Carpenter, Rust, Dewing, Richardson, and Peabody, none of whom was Salem-born, and some of whom had come to town only after the war had started. Of them all, Samuel Orne, who had just died, and William ("Billy") Gray were twice as rich as the rest, except for Hasket Derby, who was twice as rich as either of them, based on the town assessors' property valuations.

ૐ

Drawing on their own new capital and on the ambitions of the privateersmen, Hasket Derby and the other merchants were ready to hazard their new fortunes, starting with the good old West Indies trade. Derby had kept up that trade, in a limited fashion, during the war; but peacetime brought new problems. The British West Indies markets were now closed off to American shipping, so the entire trade (other than smuggling) went to the French, Spanish, and Danish Caribbean colonial islands. Salem merchants were hard-pressed to supply even this diminished market, for they had little in the way of desirable exports. The great prewar staple, salt cod, was in short supply because of Marblehead's inability to restart its decimated fishery. Lumber from Maine, rum from seaport distilleries (Salem had several), produce and livestock from farms, and even items like hats and shoes were marshaled for export, as were some captured goods that had been warehoused during the war. Most Salem shippers settled for a trade mainly in their own hemisphere: 54 voyages were made to other states (including 23 short trips to Maryland and Pennsylvania), 15 more to the Canadian maritime provinces, and 84 to the Caribbean. Only 9 voyages were made directly to Europe and the wine islands, and none directly to France, although 7 vessels that voyaged out to other places returned via French ports. From these tentative beginnings, Salem's trade gained momentum. During much of the year, only 12 to 15 vessels sailed from Salem monthly, but by December conditions had changed, and in that last month of the first year of peace, Salem cleared a fleet of 32 vessels, almost all to the West Indies, and fully 20 of them in just one week. In sum, the record for eight months of recorded Salem voyages in 1783 was an impressive 162 clearances. Records for arrivals are less complete; only 104 are known at Salem for the same time span.[8]

In that year, some unusual commercial events affected all of America, Salem included. Before the war, "English goods" had been the high-end items in American homes, including the beautiful cloths and carpets of India and porcelains of China, which had come by way of England and the British East India Company. Even in wartime Salem, as in Boston, some English goods had always been available, in varying kinds and quantities, from the sold-off cargoes of captured British vessels; and Americans had not lost their taste for these luxury items. With the announcement of peace in April 1783, British and French merchants saw the opportunity and dispatched their vessels to the major seaports of the new nation, which had no manufacturing capacity of its own. Americans, giddy with victory and the coming of peace, celebrated with a buying frenzy that was enabled by generous terms of credit (British and domestic) and sustained by a great appetite for the new and the beautiful. Although few could really afford these items, everyone embraced the freedom to appear affluent and to outdo their neighbors in the acquisition of handsome textiles and leather goods and the latest fashions in hats, shoes, clothing, and accessories.

Salemites, like other Americans, were ready to indulge themselves, and these new shipments created a sensation. Passing over the Caribbean imports, people lined up to purchase the English and French "luxury" goods. Impressed, Hasket Derby was happy to feed their appetites, and he sent his *Astrea* to Virginia in June 1783 to get tobacco for London, which accepted American products for which there was no British source. By the time Captain West had begun the homeward voyage with English goods, two more Derby brigs were on their way to London with tobacco.[9] Derby saw no need to advertise his new luxury shipments, but in September 1783 the *Salem Gazette* ran its first ad for goods "just from London."[10] Significantly, these goods—broadcloths, calicos, ladies' caps, gold pins, boys' fustian frocks, Barcelona handkerchiefs, Irish linen, "books of different sorts, well bound, and wrote by good authors," writing paper, buttons, crockery, and more— were offered by William Pruden, probably an English sales agent. Pruden's advertisement was gone by December; but English and French agents certainly did overrun Boston and contribute to the buying frenzy in 1783.[11] Toward the end of the year, Salem's own retailers had finally acquired English goods from London vessels arriving in Boston; and Samuel Page, John Hathorne, John Appleton, William Vans Jr., George Abbot, and William Lang were taking out large ads in the *Gazette*.[12]

Clearly, America was in a mood to celebrate its independence, and all sorts and classes of people participated in this purchase-fest, which did not abate as more and more goods became available. Some observers became uneasy at this mass indulgence and contended that, for many, luxury items and peace itself had brought no relief from the sufferings of war. Taxes were very high and regressive, and many families could not pay them; other families, having lost their breadwinners, had to rely on charity or public relief and could not be ignored. But while some Salem families suffered, things were much worse elsewhere. In nearby Ipswich, seaborne commerce, an important prewar business, had ceased altogether. In gallant Marblehead, the conflict had left three hundred widows and gangs of fatherless children begging in the streets—a stark and disturbing contrast to the relative affluence of Salem. Some must have regarded the Marbleheaders' suffering with alarm, for the state government seemed incapable of relieving it.[13] Newspaper writers pointed out that the craze for English goods hurt the local West Indies business and, much worse, enabled Britain to bring about the economic defeat of America by absorbing much of its credit and commerce. Beyond these perils was rampant wealth-obsession and its corruption of public morals—a concern expressed by Boston's soldiers, who, at their Fourth of July celebration, drank an admonitory toast, "May luxury never prevail to the prejudice of morality and national dignity," followed by one full of hope: "May the arts and sciences flourish in America."[14]

In Salem, a favored and flourishing town with much new wealth spread among many people, Hasket Derby was by far the most favored of all, and he was widely recognized as the shining star who would lead them onward into the American promised land. He was a model of republican rectitude and remained modest in his personal appearance and faithful in his attendance at church. Beneath him were other stars and would-be stars who, in the new democratic firmament, were scrambling (with their wives and children) to assert themselves by virtue of wealth, military honors, hospitality, and personality. Amid the general frenzy of consumption and fashion, in which it was not easy to discern real wealth and taste from the illusory version, those who were intent on social ascendancy soon found a way to self-identify: music, singing, and dancing, those very un-Puritan pastimes, took Salem by storm. Once associated only with rich Tories and British colonial officials, concerts and formal dances had begun among Salem rebel society as early as the spring of 1782, along with the singing of nonsacred choral music. So popular were these activities that a group of the new gentry rushed to subscribe shares in a singing-school building. Built in the west end of town, the structure, with murals, was finished by the end of December 1782 and immediately came into use as a concert hall. The first concert at the new Assembly House, held on New Year's Day, 1783, was preceded by "a dance for the young gentry at Mrs. Pickman's." Next day, there was another such concert, with music from two violins, a French horn, and a drum.[15] The sensation was great, and everyone seems to have understood the import of this cultural innovation: Salem's new society was being formed, dance by dance, concert by concert, and the young and the youthful were taking over.

The lawyer William Pynchon, sixty, recorded in his diary that the private dances and the assembly concerts "engross the conversation & attention of the young & gay; the elders shake their heads with, 'What are we coming to?'" Pynchon, a Loyalist who had never left town, was, as a remnant of the discredited Tory upper class, inclined to dismiss Salem's dancing gentry as parvenus (he once called the Assembly House "Tradesman's Hall"); however, as the father of young adult children who were thoroughly American and wholly caught up in the social swirl, he could not afford to be too critical. On January 13, the day a crystal chandelier was installed in the Assembly House, the Hasket Derbys hosted a dance at their new home in the west end. This, no doubt, raised the level of excitement that much higher—even those who were lame came hobbling into the Derbys' dancing party. Within a few weeks, such private dances were augmented by formal dances at the Assembly House itself, which became a ballroom and even had a gambling table in an anteroom; and within a few months Mr. Pynchon and most of the old guard were themselves taking dancing lessons. What was fashionable—what one wore, whom one knew, what one enjoyed, where one resided—became very important, and all sorts of moves were made, figurative and real: many of those who did not reside in Salem's west end quickly made arrangements to do so.

Dressed in gorgeous new finery, dancing the latest steps, gathering to rehearse for concerts of vocal music, forming audiences for instrumental performances, the Salemites found the perfect medium in which to be recognized for the graces, elegances, and talents of the new age. It is as if Salem's strivers had found a sound track for their new social aspirations and sense of community. Pynchon noted that the jostling for position was fierce: "Jealousies, slanders, envying, among several of the assembly folk. Parties are forming, and a little more tattling and imprudence throw the whole into confusion."[16] Throughout 1783, Salem's parties, dances, and assemblies were constant celebrations of the freedom to move to the music, to sing out in harmony, to be part of something altogether new and exciting. Republican and accomplished, youthful and knowing, the participants rapidly created a social milieu that preserved most of the old uprightness but to it added measures of grace, glamour, and pleasure. This cult of music defined a smallish, powerful in-crowd in the new Salem—people with talent, taste, money, and ambition. As they intended, few others could keep up with them, and in fact they and their children would soon form the nucleus of a notable aristocracy. In the meantime, their musical pursuits suddenly elevated a few members of the artisan class: Samuel McIntire, a young carpenter and draftsman from the tough Knocker's Hole neighborhood, won acclaim as a violinist, as did Samuel Blyth, a housepainter who, like McIntire, made and repaired musical instruments, including organs (Blyth's brother Benjamin, also a housepainter, had already crossed over into art as a portraitist). McIntire, who probably designed the Assembly House, and Blyth, who painted its murals, were capable of reading and interpreting music for their patrons; McIntire, at least, seems also to have been a composer. A few years earlier, his talents would have been trivial curiosities, essentially wasted in a fellow without the education or standing to develop them; but in this Salem, newly artistic and newly appreciative, a man like McIntire could become a hero.

Though it would soon subside, the craze for music and parties and socializing was wonderfully expressive of a people who had discovered their own beauty and were embracing a new way of being. It was a declaration of independence from the old, silent, devout, strict, regimented ways of colonial society. Joining hands, they moved forward together into a more colorful, spirited, and dynamic culture. It was exhilarating, and a little frightening; but it was what they wanted, and in Salem they could have what they wanted, for their American God had smiled on them and rewarded them for carrying out some larger plan, whose end, perhaps, was not yet in sight. There is little doubt that the Salemites felt themselves to be children of destiny who could indulge in the new fashions and freedoms without losing their way or forgetting the seriousness of their purpose. It is notable that Salem's infatuation with music and dancing, which coincided with a craze for European luxury goods, seems not to have drawn criticism for its frivolity and "degeneracy" as would a similar social circle in Boston less than two years later.[17] The lack of criticism may be understood in political terms, in that the Boston episode tied into a bitter gubernatorial election; but it may also have been that Salem, hardheaded and profit oriented, was simply not in danger of sybaritic excess. The Derbys attended the assemblies, and so did the ministers, and, when the music was over and the next day came, everyone was working hard to achieve the rewards for their eight years of risk and loss and sacrifice. Most people knew that winning the war and throwing parties were not enough to sustain their new culture: now they would have to start winning the competitions of peacetime and see what they could make of their great chance to prosper as an independent people.

Commerce fell off sharply in 1784, as Salem shipowners evidently found it more difficult to assemble cargoes, or simply refrained from doing so. Perhaps they had saturated the domestic market for Caribbean sugar, molasses, and rum. Only 118 clearances occurred (versus 162 in eight months of 1783): 72 voyages to the West Indies, and 46 elsewhere, including just 29 to the other states, already choked with European goods.[18] Hasket Derby saw that these new conditions curtailed the profitability of the old West Indies trade, and he looked around for better opportunities. In May and June 1784, the Cabots, of Beverly and Boston, sent out vessels bound for Russia. In June, Derby countered by dispatching the large brig *Light Horse,* under Capt. Nehemiah Buffinton, to Kronstadt, the port of Saint Petersburg.[19] The Baltic was only the first move that Derby made as he redefined the terms of the game of trade. And who could stop him? He was a free American.

Derby had the drive to succeed against a strong current of bad news. In 1784, a formerly secret congressional report was released as a public warning to the states that, unless they gave Congress "powers competent to the protection of commerce, they can never command reciprocal advantages in trade; and, without these, our foreign commerce must decline, and eventually be annihilated."[20] But there was no political will to endow Congress with those powers, and the English and French continued to send over shiploads of consumer goods.

Those who had fought so hard to create a new nation now wondered if it could long survive, as it quickly drifted from the wartime ideals of "piety, justice, moderation, temperance, industry, and frugality," which John Adams had thought to be "absolutely necessary to preserve the advantages of liberty, and to maintain a free government."[21] America's willingness to wallow in a flood of luxury goods no doubt reminded some of a similar inundation, not long before, in Britain and by way of the East India Company. The corruption it had brought to government had been a major factor in England's inability to respond to American discontent in a way that might have averted war. William Pitt, so admired by the American revolutionaries, had written at that time, "For some years past there has been an influx of wealth into this country which has been attended with many fatal consequences, because it has not been the regular, natural produce of labor and industry. The riches of Asia have been poured in upon us, and have brought with them not only Asiatic luxury, but, I fear, Asiatic principles of government. Without connections, without any natural interest in the soil, the importers of foreign goods have forced their way into Parliament by such a torrent of private corruption as no private hereditary fortune could resist."[22]

Salem, of course, was in the business of importing foreign goods, and always had been; but no Salem merchant had sent his vessel toward the Orient. In 1784 the town took in sail and traded modestly in hopes of better weather, while in America at large the storm hit, and confusion and instability swept over the land. There were no safe harbors for people's money: no retail banks, factories, or stock companies existed. The Confederation Congress was unable to set policies that would overcome the rivalries and differences of the various states. American merchants were in hock to Europeans. The nation had massive overseas public debts and a weak government unable to raise the money or get the credit to pay those debts. Federal currency was valueless, and each state's currency was volatile and highly inflated. Former soldiers were still looking for their pay. The needs of the new nation overwhelmed the frail structure that had been created, during the war, to hold things together. Commentators issued apocalyptic predictions of a luxury-besotted America's impending doom and implored people to stop purchasing foreign goods and make do with less; but it was too late: they had already stopped, and now the goods were piling up unsold. English and European creditors called in their loans, which the importers could not pay. The economy, with nothing to prop it up, crashed.

At the moment that most places in America were sagging, Salem was betting on itself and attracting believers. As others were leaving for Ohio and the big cities, most people in Salem stayed put. Those who had come for the privateering had done well enough; and now, in the face of economic depression, many others—relatives and friends, and sometimes strangers—moved to Salem from Medford, Ipswich, Danvers, Lynn, Marblehead, and even Boston and Charlestown. Some came from Canada, and others from Britain and Europe.[23] They saw Salem as the center of something, a place of destiny, without knowing exactly why it was so. It may well have been that Salem's waterfront—with boats and ships constantly in motion, with customs officials surveying and inspecting, with goods being loaded and unloaded, and with sailors roaming the streets and visiting the stores and taverns and grogshops—formed a persuasive image of activity and prosperity. That picture also included the more substantial presence of brand-new mansions being erected, the paving of streets, the renovation of older homes, and the replacement of colonial public buildings with handsome new ones in a style befitting an independent republic.

On one Salem road, known as the New Street, just down from the Assembly House, the large three-story homes of Rev. John Prince, Col. John Page, Capt. John Leach, and the two Sanderson brothers all went up from 1782 to 1784, and they stood in a very impressive row. Four of these five men had come from other places and made their fortunes in Salem. Just down the street stood the best house of all, built in 1782 for another in-migrant, Jerathmeel Peirce, a native of Medford who had been a leather dresser with Aaron Wait, a Marblehead transplant; together, they had expanded into privateering and wartime trade. The architect of Peirce's famously beautiful mansion was none other than the musical carpenter, Samuel McIntire, twenty-five, whose artistic genius had won him the admiration of Salem's rising moneyed class and had led them to employ him as their architect.[24] Nearly as handsome were other likely McIntire compositions, Capt. Francis Boardman's house on the common (far from the west end) and Joshua Ward's, on a main street overlooking the inner harbor. Hasket Derby, having decided not to complete an ungainly McIntire-designed house in the East Parish, had purchased a three-story uptown brick manse in 1782 and hired McIntire to redesign its interior right away. This work was followed, in 1785–1786, by new wooden facades in the Peirce-house manner, topped by a Marblehead-style glassed-in "lookout" cupola on top.

Derby's renovated house stood near the town's brick schoolhouse, which, although not old in 1785, did not make the right statement for an important place like Salem. The townsmen, ready to build schools in the eastern and western parts of town and concerned that the courts might be moved to Ipswich, voted in March to tear down their old town house and their schoolhouse and to contribute toward the cost of a new, spacious Essex County courthouse that would also serve as

Salem's town house. Again, the architect was Samuel McIntire. He was being given the opportunity to transform Salem's appearance, building by building, much as Charles Bulfinch would later do in Boston. The practice of architecture was not then a recognized profession, nor was town planning; but Salem's merchants, long connoisseurs of naval architecture and beautiful lines, saw that good design could remake their old seaport into an epitome of modern elegance. They were happy to patronize McIntire, who, for a workman's paltry fees, gave them detailed plans of buildings they could not have dreamed of. He was the first man in America to play that role, and Salem was the first place in the new nation to make a conscious effort to build in the style of a republic. In 1785 the new County Court House went up at the highest point in the middle of the main street of the town: it made a noble appearance as a red-brick, pedimented, Roman meetinghouse, topped by a belfry and tower and decorated with beautiful trim and elegant paintings inside.[25] Though smaller than some of the new public buildings of Boston and Portsmouth, it was perfect for Salem and inspired more construction around it, and it was much admired by all who visited and saw what money and taste could do.

As Hasket Derby watched the Court House go up, he must have felt pride in what he was accomplishing both at home and at sea. For two years he had sent out vessels and men on many voyages, some to the West Indies, some to England and Russia, some even to France and Spain; but Derby, with his one brown eye and one blue, usually saw things differently; and already he had decided that those routes, even if profitable, were too crowded with competitors and needed to be discontinued in favor of something new and better.[26] Looking out over Salem from the aerie of his cupola, he could easily see down the busy inner harbor to the expanse of Salem Bay, eastward to Marblehead and its harbor, and farther eastward out to the North Atlantic and the horizon of the whole world. Derby saw that world as his trading empire and Salem as its capital; and he was determined to make his vision a reality.[27]

The East and the riches of the Indian Ocean were Hasket Derby's real objects. Salem's well-armed ships and brave men could outsail anyone's; and if Salem was too small as a consumer market, Derby could always sell his wares in New York, Philadelphia, or Europe, or in the ports of the Far East. The main thing was to open the trade and deal with the markets directly, just as the British East India Company and other European monopolies were doing. He could see no reason not to try, for he was not averse to the "influx of wealth" from "the riches of Asia" that Pitt had once excoriated. Derby knew that a New York City vessel, the *Empress of China,* backed by the merchant prince Robert Morris of Philadelphia, had already sailed for Canton; but Salem's own prince thought there was no need to go quite that far. In June 1785, the canny Derby must have smiled to read in the local newspaper that, for $300, he could buy a share in a New York ship being fitted "for the India trade" and that some New York merchants, having discussed "the embarrassed and critical situation to which the trade of America is reduced," had urged that Congress be given "full and ample powers to regulate" the nation's commerce.[28] Elias Hasket Derby, without help from New York or Congress, was opening that very trade himself, for, late in 1784, he had sent Jonathan Ingersoll, lately one of his privateer commanders, as master of the ship *Grand Turk* on a trip to Africa's Cape of Good Hope in search of a cargo of goods from the East.[29]

≈

In an America that had few cultural bright spots, Salem was becoming known as a place where the pulse of life was quick and the promise of the new republic was being met. Drawn by the town's prosperity and mercantile activity and by a local culture that extolled learning, art and music, and sociability, educated and inventive young men moved to Salem and there found inspiration in the person of the great Dr. Holyoke.

Edward A. Holyoke (1728–1829) was one of the few remaining members of the prewar Monday Night Club, a group of college-educated Salem men who had gathered weekly to discuss literature, philosophy, and scientific topics. Tory gentlemen all, the Club members had struggled to stay in Salem, but most had fled as war approached. Dr. Holyoke, unimpressed by the king but unconvinced of the need for a war of independence, had stayed on in his beloved Salem, healing people, conducting experiments, teaching young medical students, and accepting the new order installed by the rebels. Within a year or two, he was thriving in a republican society that seemed to welcome innovation and experimentation.

As an eminent scientist and physician, Dr. Holyoke had no equal in Massachusetts as an organizer of the voluntary organizations that were emerging as a characteristic feature of life in the early republic. In 1779, he helped to found the American Academy of Arts and Sciences, a coterie of learned men dedicated to scientific research and to publishing their findings. Holyoke, of course, contributed an article to the first issues of the academy's journal and later served as its third president. He helped to incorporate, as well, the Massachusetts Medical Society (1781), of which he was the first president. In 1783, largely through his efforts, Harvard Medical School was established as the first such school in America, and he was the recipient of its first Medical Doctor degree. He would continue to take into his house and train a steady stream of young physicians, most of whom moved on from Salem to other towns and cities throughout New England and the republic, carrying with them their mentor's values and methods. The doctor's studies led him to publish several contributions to the medical literature, including one in the American Academy's journal. He was a keen astronomer and meteorologist, and he published several papers (including one in 1783 and one in 1786) of his observations of climatic effects on the health of Salem's people.

Dr. Holyoke's fame added luster to Salem's cultural and intellectual life, which continued to grow impressively. At a time when books were relatively rare and few were written or published in America, Salem had its own bookseller, its own newspaper and book-printing press, and its own learned society, made up of the shareholders in the Philosophical Library, a small group that had rescued a scientific library at a Beverly privateer auction in 1781. Dr. Holyoke, Rev. John Prince, Rev. Joseph Willard (the president of Harvard since 1783), and a few other local men formed the core group, but the membership grew as additional shares were sold. They met weekly for dinner, discussions, and reviews of publications and even hired their own librarian. Through their enterprise, they made Salem a national center of scientific thought and accomplishment.[30]

Other groups arose in Salem as people realized that they were free to associate and that the old class distinctions and family connections meant much less in their new republic. The Marine Society at Salem, which had existed since the 1760s, became a more powerful force for scientific and navigational inquiry by its members, the town's shipmasters and merchants. In 1783, local leaders founded the Independent Cadets, a military social organization, and the Essex Lodge of Freemasons. These organizations welcomed men from varied backgrounds: Irish American sea captains, French artisans, Quaker shopkeepers, and former privateersmen who had been farmhands just a few years earlier.

Among the new arrivals in 1783 was Nathan Read, a recent Harvard graduate and former college librarian who had already briefly taught school in Salem. Read placed himself under Dr. Holyoke, in whose house he boarded, to study medicine. By day he worked as an apothecary, and by night he pursued his interests in science and mechanics. Read filled a workshop with his models of steam boilers, engines, and other machines. He did not, perhaps, know where this fascination was leading, but he would eventually carry out all of his tinkering on a grand scale. With his marriage to a local heiress a few years later, he gave up his chemicals and potions and, in the 1790s, turned to the construction of dams, bridges, and mills. He took out patents on his inventions and founded and ran the very profitable Salem Iron Factory. In this enterprise, Dr. Holyoke was a major investor.[31]

Read's fellow Harvard newcomer in 1783, the Reverend William Bentley (1759–1819), had taught school in Boston and preached in Beverly before being called to Salem's East Church as assistant pastor. At twenty-four, Bentley was already noted as one of the most gifted young men in Massachusetts, with special interest in science, languages, and education. His decision to settle in Salem rather than Boston may have been influenced partly by the presence of scholars such as Dr. Holyoke and the cultural ferment that grew up around them. Bentley's early love for Salem would be sorely tested in the next few years, since the old minister, whom he was hired to assist, did all he could to discredit and drive off the newcomer. It was all in vain, for the parishioners, mainly seafaring families, had recognized in Bentley the very spirit of young America—smart, brash, brave, and exciting. They wanted to know what Bentley could teach them, not only as church parishioners, but also as citizens of a new country, hungry for knowledge and open to new ideas.

Within three years, young Mr. Bentley had silenced the old minister, who never resumed the pulpit. The East Church became Bentley's own, and the ship-masters and sailors and their families encouraged him to take a large role in their lives, serving as a kind of unofficial mayor of their parish as well as their minister. Alone of the town's ministers, in March 1785 he joined the Essex Lodge of Freemasons, into which he would recruit many of his parishioners over the years. In March of the following year, after the headmaster of the new public school in the East Parish left abruptly, Bentley personally resolved the crisis by assuming leadership of the school. "I feel myself obliged to declare," wrote Bentley, "that I am zealous to establish the liberal institution of a FREE SCHOOL upon the best foundation in my Society, and do really consider this institution as the most noble which my sphere of action presents."[32] It was a critical moment in the history of his parish. When the Salem town meeting had agreed to build a new school there in 1785, it had, for the first time, created the same educational opportunities as in the more-affluent West End, and to lose that chance was unthinkable. Bentley went to work with a will, reorganizing the classes and courses of study, introducing firm discipline and healthy meals, bringing in a writing master, and running things so well that the continuation of the East Public School was assured. Bentley took on the private tutoring of the most promising of the poorer boys so that they could learn accounting and navigation and even go on to college—a thing almost unheard-of before the war. Among those whom he helped with their studies was a young store clerk named Nathaniel Bowditch (1773–1838), who would go on to become the foremost mathematician and astronomer of his day and to win lasting fame in 1802 as the author of *The New American Practical Navigator.*

Bentley seemed never to rest in his studies, his preaching, his teaching, and his resolution to change the lives of his east enders for the better. In 1786 he augmented his pastoral and tutorial work by drafting petitions on behalf of military companies and other groups, translating letters from foreign merchants, writing a famous and much-copied column for the *Salem Gazette,* publishing a book of hymns that he had written, and organizing both a choir and a choral society. The east enders' singing may have been less polished than that of the west end, but it served well to bring Bentley's people together to express themselves in harmony and, in the process, to show the west enders that they did not own all of the town's talent. In April 1786, Bentley's singers were burned out of their practice space when a fire destroyed the house and school of Michael Walsh, twenty-three, a graduate of Trinity College in Dublin who would later write the first American book on commercial accounting and international trade. Although Walsh soon moved on to Newburyport, his brief presence in Salem (where he, too, taught Nathaniel

Bowditch) was one more indication of its ability to attract the best and the bright-est. In September 1786, Bentley and two other Salem ministers, Thomas Barnard Jr. and John Prince, began a course of public evening lectures on geography, the English language, and other topics intended to help educate the working people of Salem. Early in 1787, Bentley started a men's discussion group that met weekly at his house, and during the summer he printed and distributed to his parishioners two hundred copies of his own primer on grammar.

Through topical sermons, discussion groups, booklets, and lectures, Bentley steadily educated his congregation in the progressive political and scientific thought of his day. He was an admirer of the French Enlightenment and a firm be-liever in the power of education and the obligation of a republican society to serve all classes of people. In all that he did, he was driven to infuse the community with the principles of virtue, justice, charity, and opportunity celebrated in the Massa-chusetts 1780 constitution. Salem was his laboratory in which many cultures were channeled through the medium of commerce. In the noisy, bustling, buoyant re-publican seaport, its people, including lowly sailors, coopers, rope makers, and boat builders, could participate as full members of society with the assurance that their children would be educated and their talents developed. Bentley saw Salem as the perfect place for American potential to be realized. He later wrote in his di-ary, "It is confessed, that to commerce we owe our enlightened age: by it, the ge-nius of modern nations is formed, and their laws and religion. The political virtue of our mariners is more secure, as they are maintained in the social virtues, and love of their country."[33] Never before considered valuable as civic participants, sailors, Bentley maintained, would form the majority of the town's electorate and, therefore, deserved every encouragement toward becoming thoughtful and virtu-ous citizens.

Bentley was only one of three young ministers who had a profound influence on their parishioners and who made Salem a place unique among the towns and cities of the young republic. Rev. Thomas Barnard Jr. (1748–1814), of the North Church, and Rev. John Prince (1751–1836), of the First Church, were also religious progressives and enlightened thinkers, and they alternated with Bentley in deliv-ering the town's evening educational lectures. Barnard was the son of a Salem preacher, but Prince, like Bentley, came from Boston and, like Bentley, found in-spiration in the life and work of Dr. Holyoke. Barnard had many scientific inter-ests, but was best known for his work as a young schoolmaster whose star pupil had been an apprentice, Benjamin Thompson, the future physicist, inventor, and European military commander later known as Count Rumford. Barnard did no scientific writing himself, but he generously loaned out books from his library of six hundred volumes.[34]

Originally trained as a pewterer, Rev. John Prince set up a workshop in his house and engaged in scientific experimentation, making his own equipment and instructing pupils in the use of lenses and other apparatuses.[35] In 1783 he invented an improved version of an air pump and published his findings in the American Academy of Arts and Sciences' journal. Prince was an early member of the Philosophical Library, and after 1783 its volumes were shelved in his house. Between the library and his laboratory-workshop, he became a magnet for the scientific and the studious in Salem, generously sharing all that he had and knew. He made improvements on several other scientific devices, including the microscopes of the time. Over the years, his proficiency as a maker of scientific instruments earned for him a place at the front ranks of inventors in Britain and America. Like Barnard and Bentley, Prince was an innovator in religion as well, and he disseminated new ways of thinking throughout the town. He espoused a form of liberal Christianity and guided his congregation into the relatively uncharted waters of Unitarianism. At a time when that denomination provoked outrage in many other communities, three of Salem's largest congregations were happily making the journey away from the Puritanism of the prewar days.

Within each minister's congregation, certain persons and families ventured to assert social leadership, although none was certain of what constituted such leadership in a republic. The transformation from hierarchical to egalitarian norms presented a significant opportunity for the ministers to reform society. Anyone with ambitions and social pretensions would need the support of the pastor and his guidance as to proper tastes, behaviors, and limits. It is interesting to note that Prince and Barnard, ministers to the more affluent, attended the Assembly House concerts and left only when the dancing began (Bentley stayed away altogether). In addition to guiding Salem's people in new social and religious norms, all three of Salem's foremost ministers had a great interest in education and in broadening the base of opportunity for the children of the working and seafaring families; and all three insisted on the need for a virtuous culture and a society built on benevolence, in which the richest would support all forms of good works and cheerfully compete with one another in helping the poor and unfortunate.

The liberalism and idealism of the three parsons, and the relative youth of the ministers in all of the town's churches, ratified Salemites' interests in new values, foreign influences (that of France, especially), and new cultural models. As Henry Adams later contended, ministers and magistrates, usually conservatives who were threatened by new ideas, generally blunted the natural liberalism of post-Revolutionary America.[36] In contrast, Salem's ministers were actually agents of democratic change and educational opportunity, having been influenced by the progressive thinking at prewar and wartime Harvard College, by the writings of the English radicals, and by the words and deeds of their own mentors, themselves rebel ministers who had assisted their congregations in throwing off their British and Tory masters. Salem's judges, too, like John Pickering and Richard Ward, were youthful men who had earned their places through success as Revolutionary politicians. The Tories found no foothold in the ruling ranks of postwar Salem; and a freethinking, open-minded populace, eager to partake of the excitement of new forms and fashions, found itself quite willing to be guided by the smart young ministers, ambitious shipowners, and enlightened magistrates.

ॐ

Rev. William Bentley, a sharp-eyed lookout for incoming vessels, may have been the first to see Hasket Derby's *Grand Turk* come surging into Salem Bay in August 1785, home from adventures in new seas and unfamiliar ports. Unlike Derby's postwar endeavors in the Atlantic, such as the dismal return of the *Light Horse* from Russia, this voyage brought in a healthy profit. Yet the *Grand Turk's* success had been due more to the improvisations of Capt. Jonathan Ingersoll than to any sound basis for trade with the East. In fact, Derby had been mistaken in his assumption that it was possible to trade at the Cape of Good Hope with English vessels returning from India and China. Happy with his profit, but concerned about his failure to find a predictable means of gaining access to Asian goods, Derby was considering whether to push into the unknown waters beyond the Cape, when suddenly came news that American vessels had been welcomed at the French-held islands of Île de France (Mauritius) and Île de Bourbon (Reunion) in the Indian Ocean, within striking distance of Calcutta. Henceforth, Derby would try his luck in those waters, and his luck, as usual, would prove to be spectacular.

In 1785, Salem's maritime commerce was reviving from wartime chaos and was more active than it had been in the year previous, with 131 clearances (118 in 1784) and 160 arrivals (117 in 1784). As before the war, most voyages were made to the West Indies and the other states (70 and 42 clearances, respectively); but now, 9 trips were made to Spain and the Wine Islands, indicating a revival of the fishery and barrel-stave trade.[37] Although Hasket Derby kept vessels engaged in these markets, he was, typically, quick to exploit the opening with France's overseas possessions. After securing letters of introduction to the governors of Île de France and Bourbon from the French consul in Boston, Derby sent out the *Grand Turk* under Capt. Ebenezer West in December 1785, bound for the French islands and Canton.[38] He did so even though he could not be sure of securing insurance for the voyage, and in spite of a thrown-together cargo of everything from butter and iron and beef to sugar, candles, rum, beer, salt fish, earthenware, and prunes.[39] The highly competitive Derby was furious that a former employee, Capt. Benjamin Carpenter, had already set out in the schooner *Benjamin* for Cape Town, and Derby was determined to beat him and everyone else in the race for Indian Ocean ascendancy.

By 1786, Salem's merchants were directing their commerce to the same places and in roughly the same proportions as in 1785. The exception, again, was the house of Derby. In the second half of the year, Hasket Derby committed four large vessels to the East Indies trade and sent them out in sensational fashion. His interest in the East was underscored by his dispatching his namesake eldest son, who had washed out of Harvard College, to England at the end of 1786 and then on to France to spend a year learning French, making connections, and gathering commercial and political intelligence about the Orient.[40] In September 1786, Derby's brig *Three Sisters,* under Capt. Daniel Saunders, set sail for Cape Town, followed by John Norris's Salem brig *Adventure,* under Capt. Henry Clark, bound for Île de France. In December 1786, two additional voyages commenced: Capt. Jonathan Lambert sailed in command of the brig *Hope,* co-owned by Derby and Jacob Ashton and bound for Cape Town; and Capt. Ichabod Nichols cleared in Derby's ship *Three Sisters* for the Cape of Good Hope and on to Île de France.[41]

Derby's decision to pursue the Indian Ocean trade in force was a fateful stroke toward elevating Salem's place in the new republic. His strategy of multiple voyages to multiple ports preempted other merchants and won for Salem the route from the west, while Boston shippers settled for the longer eastward route around South America and across the Pacific. Derby's shipmasters, courageous and youthful, had the drive to seek adventure and new markets, and to build for themselves the knowledge and wealth that would give rise to a new generation of merchants, bred as young privateersmen and as teenaged sea captains, confident that they could do anything and compete with anyone, and not afraid to fight their way forward.

During the critical years of 1785–1786, Capt. Benjamin Goodhue Jr., himself a former shipmaster, experienced his own sea change. Goodhue, a state senator, had held one public office or another since his days as moderator of the rebel town meetings. With a growing family and many opportunities to expand his shipping partnership, the lure of money was strong. Yet, he had little faith in the economic future, especially under the hapless national government created by the Articles of Confederation. As a member of the state's constitutional convention, he came to believe that he could help lead the state and nation in the right direction, based on principles rather than ego or opportunism. Now, the civic-minded merchant finally had to make a choice between his own interest and the people's, between business and politics.[42]

While serving his first term in the Massachusetts senate, Goodhue came to a decision: he would make public service his calling and would set his course for federal office. In this, he was unlike any other politician in Salem, but not unlike Hasket Derby and Edward Holyoke in their determination to extend their influence as far as it would go. Like them, he saw things in the big picture, well beyond the boundaries of Salem and Massachusetts but rooted in the values and friendships of his home place. A high-powered political life had no precedent in America and came with no guarantees of election or popular acceptance of his principles and decisions. It would require huge sacrifices, not least of personal gain; however, he realized that such sacrifices were required if America was to survive. Many others had made the ultimate sacrifice in the expectation that the best men would come forward to create that new thing, a national republic, and sustain it through the hard work of government.

ᘒ

Early in 1785, the vainglorious John Hancock announced that he would resign from the governorship, and Goodhue made his move. In March, he wrote to the Massachusetts senate president that he wanted to pursue a lifetime career in public service, not least because of his dismay at "the prospect of such illiberal, ignorant, and designing characters as you mention filling the most important stations in government."[43] It was clear to him that the people deserved able and honorable leaders, that America could not thrive under the Articles of Confederation, that a strong central government was essential, and that the states needed to cooperate in making policy to regulate commerce and to require American access to British markets in exchange for British access to America.

As a politician, Goodhue was, of course, aware of the deplorable state of the nation and the commonwealth, and the sense of societal desperation. Throughout Massachusetts, the citizens of rural districts had been holding conventions to protest the government's failure to reduce the crushing tax burden and its inability to lift the economic depression that was forcing them off their farms and into debtors' prisons. Tragically misreading the farmers' appeals, newspaper editors and statehouse orators urged people to be frugal and industrious, to work hard in their fields and at their trades, to make their own goods, to go without if need be, and to refrain from buying foreign goods. Goodhue could not agree. As a merchant, he knew the importance of commerce, and he also knew that the United States, without the means to produce what its people needed, would have to trade for it. He knew, too, that some statesmen still thought that trade was evil and had no place in a republic, where private gain was to be subordinated to the public good and where the biggest gainers, the merchants, could not be allowed to raise themselves to despotic heights.[44] As Congress tried futilely to develop an agreement on commercial regulation, some leaders grew so frustrated as to propose the abolition of trade altogether, whereupon John Adams tartly retorted that trade was not a matter of policy but a basic human drive. "The people of the seaports," Adams asserted, "are as aquatic as the tortoises and sea-fowl; and the love of commerce, with its convenience and pleasure, is a habit in them unalterable in their natures. It is in vain, then, to amuse ourselves with the thoughts of annihilating commerce."[45]

In fact, Goodhue saw commerce—the exchange of goods with foreign trading partners—as the solution, not the problem. His colleague, Hasket Derby, was showing the way. Government should encourage the opening of new markets for

American produce and products, as well as the acquisition of valuable and desirable goods, and use the duties on those imports for federal revenue. In April 1785, ten years after the beginning of the war, a committee of Boston merchants announced to other merchants that they were certainly losing the trade war and needed to band together to press Congress for a trade policy. For their part, the Boston merchants would no longer trade with resident British sales agents. In June, the Massachusetts legislature passed its own navigation act, prohibiting the export of goods in British vessels and setting additional duties on foreign imports. Yet, when a year had passed and few other states had joined in the Commonwealth's action, the act was repealed.[46]

If Americans would not stop importing and buying English goods, and if the states could not agree on policy, something had to give. In January 1786, James Madison and the Virginia legislature called a meeting of all the states "to consider how far a uniform system in their commercial regulations may be necessary to their common interest." To this call, Massachusetts was quick to respond. Benjamin Goodhue and three others were appointed by the legislature as representatives to the conference. The state's congressional delegation, however, replaced them with their own group, which opposed the meeting altogether on the grounds that Virginia and New York were trying to hold a political convention under the rubric of commerce. The conference, held on schedule in Annapolis, had delegates from five states, but not from Massachusetts. The conferees decided that it was important to have commercial regulation but more important to have a "constitution of the federal government adequate to the exigencies of the union," and so they called for a conference in Philadelphia in the spring.[47]

Goodhue was, doubtless, bitterly disappointed to have lost the opportunity to work at the national level. In 1786, when ill health brought John Pickering, Essex County's register of deeds, to the brink of death, Goodhue announced for the register's job, but Pickering recovered, and Goodhue withdrew. Like everyone else in Massachusetts, he felt impotent in the face of continuing economic and political problems. As William Pynchon wrote in his diary in March, "scarcity of cash is alarming" and "commerce ruined, cash is fled; debts to France, Holland, and Spain must be paid."[48] The despondent strain was heard, too, in a local newspaper, whose editor reminded everyone that "[t]his life, checkered with instability, misfortunes, and crosses, makes it necessary we should possess Job's patience, Moses' meekness, and Solomon's sapience. In war we anticipated happiness and peace; in peace we have our trouble, and sweet felicity keeps aloof from us."[49] Pynchon also reflected on his visit from the well-traveled prophetic old Tory, Robert "King" Hooper of Marblehead, who, in August 1786, gave "a dismal account of the credit of the neighboring states; all going together by the ears, poverty and distress are coming on, paper currency, party spirit, malice, mob's spite, and the Devil; another Revolution; some adhere to France, some to Britain; some curse the leaders,

some the Whigs, others Tories."[50] It was into this bleak political and social landscape that Benjamin Goodhue had resolved to venture forth, to grapple with monstrous problems. It was against this same gloom that Hasket Derby's remarkable
commercial achievements, and their tonic effect on Salem, may be seen in their
historic light, for in the rest of America and in the state as a whole, things were going from bad to worse. During the fall and winter of 1786, distraught farmers in
western Massachusetts, whose cries for help had never been answered, finally took
arms against the government. Shays's Rebellion was soon put down, but its gun-
fire echoed in every state. Clearly, federal taxes were needed to support a standing
army, if only to squelch uprisings by desperate former soldiers; but the larger point
was that America required a strong central government capable of making policy,
addressing national problems, and earning the respect and credit of other nations.
Fortunately, the springtime conference called by the Annapolis conferees was well
attended, and in May 1787 the delegates in Philadelphia began the work that soon
produced the Constitution of the United States.

Benjamin Goodhue, full-time public servant, had missed out on his first opportunity for service at the national level; but his principles would carry the day at
Philadelphia. As the United States Constitution was being framed, some of Hasket Derby's vessels returned from their long voyages to the East, and their cargoes
were soon filling Salem stores with spices, tea, coffee, porcelain, silks, and colorful
cotton fabrics. Derby's success in establishing trade with India and China—a
trade that once had been seen as a subversive act of the sort that had corrupted
Britain—now was celebrated everywhere as a sign of the young republic's heroic
ability to extend itself around the globe and make America's name known alongside those of the old powers of Europe. Similarly, American commerce in general,
formerly anathema to Revolutionary idealists, was now embraced as the best hope
for filling the coffers of the revised federal system of government, with its new military forces, federal judiciary, and executive branch.

In 1788, Benjamin Goodhue Jr. was narrowly elected a United States representative and took his place in the First Congress, and attended the inauguration
of President Washington. He was reelected thrice and developed a solid reputation
in commerce and finance. He was a notable proponent of the neomercantilist policies of Alexander Hamilton, who had recognized the national importance of Hasket Derby's foreign trade and its meaning for the years to come, and would bril-
liantly frame federal policy, in both the Washington and Adams administrations,
around the interests of merchants. Goodhue's stock rose very high, despite his
usual gloom about the future. In 1796 he was selected to serve an unexpired term
as a United States senator, after which he handily won election as senator on his
own. Among other notable pieces of legislation, he introduced the compromise
bill by which it was agreed that the nation's capital city would be built at a place to
be known as Washington, D.C. Goodhue, the first son of Salem to make high-

level electoral politics his career, retired from the Senate in 1800 and returned to his home port, where he engaged in trade for the rest of his life.

By clearly understanding the needs of the young nation, by believing that he could make a difference, and by giving up much of his life in service to his town, state, and country, Senator Goodhue proved to be an extraordinarily able and valuable public servant. His worth was so high, and his opinions so greatly valued, that for the next fifty years Salem was virtually invited to send its best men to the Congress, the Senate, the cabinets of presidents, and the United States Supreme Court. The town's voice in the highest counsels of public policy and law was therefore ensured, and for many years Salem would have more than its share of sway in the world, thanks to Benjamin Goodhue Jr. and his successors.

❧

Salem's postwar achievements, impressive in themselves, were even more remarkable for being nearly unique in the new nation. Within a decade, the significance of Salem's innovations of the mid-1780s would become abundantly evident in the qualities that set Salem apart in young America: the number and wealth of its merchants, the size of its fleet and cargoes, the general prosperity of its citizenry, the opportunities for its young people, the number of new immigrants, the excellence of its public and domestic architecture, the quality of its teachers and ministers, the new focus on education, the liveliness of its social scene, and the fact that, by 1796, two of its sons were serving at the highest levels of national government: President Washington's secretary of state, Timothy Pickering, and United States Senator Benjamin Goodhue.

In the late 1780s and into the 1790s, the United States got its money's worth out of Salem, as ship after ship went to the other side of the globe, to India and China and Sumatra, and came back laden with highly profitable cargoes that paid many of the expenses of the federal government. Derby's brave men, the former privateers and their older sons, entering an unknown world of trade, formed such strong ties with the merchants of the Indian Ocean that not even Boston could challenge Salem for dominion there. Derby's refusal to accept things as they had been, his drive to innovate and experiment, his willingness to take the risks that led to breakthroughs—these qualities made him Salem's great exemplar of the American entrepreneur. His competitiveness, his determination to stay in Salem and to make it great, his clear vision of what commerce could be, and his determination to carry it out were the key factors in Salem's rise to a height of commercial prosperity that made it famous the world over and that made Hasket Derby among the wealthiest men in America—its first millionaire, according to some. Alongside him, by the 1790s, were at least four other Salem merchants: William ("Billy") Gray, Joseph White, Simon Forrester, and Joseph Peabody, who invested just as heavily in the valor, intelligence, seamanship, and shrewdness of

Salem's mariners. Derby and the rest had made Salem very rich, and its wealth, though certainly used for private ends, also supported charity, comity, opportunity, and beauty and contributed to the security of the infant republic and the creation of a capital worthy of the great and valorous nation of Salem, conqueror of the East Indies.

No less than Goodhue and Derby, Holyoke and his admirers would find that Salem had given them the stage on which to develop a dynamic, progressive local culture and to lead rewarding lives. In the effort to create a more enlightened society, their influence was enormous, since their many students took with them their mentors' values, virtues, and ideals and spread them over the years and across America. Dr. Holyoke, by far the eldest of the three, survived Hasket Derby by thirty years and Benjamin Goodhue by fifteen years; he lived to be 101, dying in 1829. During the 1830s, when its commerce faltered and its national political voice was finally stilled, Salem's fame yet burned brightly in the dispersed inheritors of Holyoke and his circle: in Nathaniel Bowditch, the astronomer and mathematician; in the judge and industrialist Nathan Read; in Reuben Mussey and Daniel Oliver, physicians and chemists; in the educator Elizabeth Palmer Peabody and the pomologist and author Robert Manning; in Judge Joseph Story of the U.S. Supreme Court; in the lexicographer John Pickering VI, and, some years later, in the architects, sculptors, poets, inventors, philosophers, and novelists whose work went forth into every civilized port and hamlet of the world.

Notes

1. In 1800 the population concentration on Salem Bay was among the largest anywhere in North America, for Salem's close neighbor, Marblehead, was nearly as large in population, and its other neighboring port, Beverly, had perhaps four thousand residents. These ports had a farming hinterland that was reached by short but navigable rivers and a few good roads; they included Lynn, Danvers, Wenham, Ipswich, Middleton, and Andover.

2. A *privateer* was a private armed vessel under government commission that was permitted to attack enemy vessels and to confiscate both vessel and cargo as "prizes."

3. Richard Derby Jr., older brother of Elias Hasket Derby, had been Salem's leading political figure until his untimely death in 1781.

4. J. Duncan Phillips, *The Life and Times of Richard Derby* (Cambridge, Mass.: Riverside Press, 1929), 1–47.

5. Richard H. McKey Jr., "Elias Hasket Derby and the American Revolution," *Essex Institute Historical Collections* 97 (1961): 195.

6. A *letter of marque* was a government commission that allowed a merchant vessel to use force to defend itself and to capture an enemy vessel when attacked. A vessel that was so commissioned was called "a letter of marque vessel."

7. A review of the 1784 and 1785 postwar valuations of Salem shows that there were seventy-three heads of households who paid a tax on total estate value of £1,800 or more. Many more were not as wealthy but were still affluent and possessed of discretionary income for investment.

8. James Duncan Phillips, "Salem Ocean-Borne Commerce from the Close of the Revolution to the Establishment of the Constitution, 1783–1789," *Essex Institute Historical Collections* 75 (1939): 135–58. The figures for arrivals are much less reliable than those for departures ("clearances"). It would seem that the "arrivals," which he tallies at 104 for the eight months of records in 1783, pertained only to Salem vessels returning from a certain destination, and not to all vessels arriving from that port.

9. Robert E. Peabody, *Merchant Venturers of Old Salem: A History of the Commercial Voyages of a New England Family to the Indies and Elsewhere in the XVIII Century* (Boston: Houghton Mifflin, 1912), 52–53. See also Phillips, "Salem Ocean-Borne Commerce," 147: "Ship *Astrea,* N. West, cleared 5 June 1783 for Virginia." Her return is not recorded but perhaps occurred by September, perhaps in Boston.

10. *Salem Gazette,* September 25, 1783.

11. Thomas M. Doerflinger, *A Vigorous Spirit of Enterprise: Merchants and Economic Development in Revolutionary Philadelphia* (Chapel Hill: University of North Carolina Press, 1986).

12. *Salem Gazette,* December 12, 1783.

13. Marblehead's people and politics were very different from those of Salem, and the town had always been capable of defying its neighbor.

14. *Salem Gazette,* July 10, 1783.

15. William Pynchon, *The Diary of William Pynchon of Salem,* ed. F. E. Oliver (Cambridge, Mass.: Houghton, Mifflin, 1890), 140.

16. Pynchon, 140.

17. William M. Fowler Jr., "The Massachusetts Election of 1785: A Triumph of Virtue," *Essex Institute Historical Collections* III (1975): 298–300.

18. Phillips, "Salem Ocean-Borne Commerce," 135–58, 249–76.

19. James Duncan Phillips, *Salem and the Indies: The Story of the Great Commercial Era of the City* (Boston: Houghton Mifflin, 1947), 39.

20. Quoted in Norman A. Graebner, "New England and the World, 1783–1791," in *Massachusetts and the New Nation,* ed. Conrad E. Wright (Boston: Massachusetts Historical Society, 1992), 6.

21. John Adams, in Massachusetts Constitution, Declaration of Rights, art. 18.

22. Quoted in Bernard Bailyn, *The Ideological Origins of the American Revolution* (Cambridge, Mass.: Harvard University Press, Belknap Press, 1967), 134–35.

23. William Bentley, *The Diary of William Bentley, D.D.,* ed. Marguerite Dalrymple, 4 vols. (Gloucester, Mass.: Peter Smith, 1962). See also "Salem Warnings, 1791," *Essex Institute Historical Collections* 43 (1907): 345–52.

24. Fiske Kimball, *Mr. Samuel McIntire, Carver: The Architect of Salem* (Salem, Mass.: Essex Institute, 1940), 58–59.

25. Kimball, 61–62.

26. Freeman Hunt, ed., *Hunt's Merchants' Magazine,* February 1857, 166.

27. As early as 1790, Elias Hasket Derby, Salem merchant, addressed the U.S. Congress as "the guardians of the liberty and trade of the citizens of this rising empire," petition of June 10, 1790, quoted in *Hunt's Merchants' Magazine,* February 1857.

28. *Salem Gazette,* June 23, 1785.

29. Robert E. Peabody, *The Log of the Grand Turks* (Boston: Houghton Mifflin, 1926).

30. Harold L. Burstyn, "The Salem Philosophical Library: Its History and Importance for American Science," *Essex Institute Historical Collections* 96 (1960): 169–206.

31. Burstyn, 189–92.

32. Letter of March 14, 1786, quoted in Bentley, ix.

33. William Bentley, *Sermon . . . Occasioned by the Death of Jonathan Gardner, Esq. . . .* (Salem, Mass.: T. C. Cushing, 1791).

34. Burstyn, 180–81.

35. Burstyn, 179–80.

36. Henry Adams, *The United States in 1800* (Ithaca: Cornell University Press, 1971), 56–57.

37. Phillips, "Salem Ocean-Borne Commerce," 249–76.

38. M. Toscon to Elias Hasket Derby, November 23, 1785, Derby Papers, Peabody Essex Museum.

39. Richard McKey, "Elias Hasket Derby and the Founding of the Eastern Trade," *Essex Institute Historical Collections* 98 (1962): 65–70. Derby later learned that he had been refused insurance on the voyage because he had no experience in that trade route.

40. The French sojourn was prelude to another assignment for young Derby; a yearlong residence on Île de France, in the Indian Ocean, directing his father's shipping business. He was very successful.

41. James Duncan Phillips, "East India Voyages of Salem Vessels before 1800," *Essex Institute Historical Collections* 79 (1943): 117–32.

42. Clifford Shipton, *Harvard Graduates* (Benjamin Goodhue, Class of 1766), 359–61.

43. Benjamin Goodhue to Samuel Phillips, February 17, 1785, quoted in Shipton.

44. Shipton, 360–65.

45. John Adams to John Jay, December 6, 1785.

46. Peabody, 55.

47. Thomas Wentworth Higginson, *The Life and Times of Stephen Higginson* (Boston: Houghton Mifflin, 1907), 67–74.

48. Pynchon, 233–34.

49. *Salem Chronicle,* April 7, 1786.

50. Pynchon, 247.

Science text, Salem Athenaeum original collections. Photo by Kim Mimnaugh.

Chapter Four

Salem as Athenaeum

MATTHEW G. MCKENZIE

*Some have voyaged to the East Indies or the
Pacific, and most have sailed in Marblehead schooners to
Newfoundland; a few have been no farther than the Middle Banks, and
one or two have always fished along the shore; but . . . they have all been christened
in salt water, and know more than men ever learn in the bushes. . . . If the young men
boast their knowledge of the ledges and sunken rocks, I speak of pilots who knew the
wind by its scent and the wave by its taste, and could have steered blindfold
to any port between Boston and Mount Desert, guided only by
the rote of the shore,—the peculiar sound of the surf on each
island, beach, and line of rocks, along the coast.*

—Nathaniel Hawthorne, "The Village Uncle"

N a cold January day in 1804, Salem's docks stood quieter than usual. Crates teeming with Chinese goods, Indian spices, and European manufactures rested undisturbed in ships' holds as boxes, barrels, and crates of dried codfish stood by to take their place. There was little activity along the waterfront; instead, a crowd of Salem residents stood before their brick or clapboard homes just a couple of blocks from the wharves. Soon, music from a drum, a bassoon, a clarinet, and a flute echoed down the street. As the music grew louder, the assembled crowd watched members of the East India Marine Society round a corner, each carrying Pacific Island artifacts collected from the Far East. Four African American boys, masked, donned in the vibrant colors of Chinese "habits," and bearing an Indian palanquin, or enclosed litter, rounded out the procession of exotic curiosities. Once the parade arrived at the society's hall, the members celebrated the contribution these objects made to the advancement of higher learning in the new republic. They commemorated Salem's trade and the knowledge such trade opened up to them with toasts:

The riches which the arts give, may they find sacred to their support.
Natural history. May commerce never forget its obligations.[1]

While the society toasted the accomplishments of its members in the comfort of its well-appointed hall, far out in the Atlantic a handful of battered and weathered fishing vessels finished their season's last fishing fare. Cold and tired crews hauled on anchor hawsers as hands prepared their fish-filled holds for the passage back to Salem Harbor. As in most years since the seventeenth century, Salem's fleet had left in April, seeking prized North Atlantic cod from the Nova Scotia Banks to Newfoundland's Grand Bank. The fleet had returned home with full holds twice already that summer and had set sail for a last voyage in September. Now tired, dirty, smelly, and salt-encrusted crews trimmed their 40- to 60-ton schooners' sails to start pounding their way against wind and waves to the southwest and toward Salem Sound.

In considering Salem as a distinct place, we might well reflect on its role as an extended athenaeum, where formal academic learning and vocational knowledge blended in mutually beneficial ways. Between 1760 and 1812, Salem residents watched their town emerge as a New England center for two forms of higher learning. Beginning with the formation of the Salem Social Library in 1760, the town's cultivated residents organized to move Salem into a wider British world of science and learning. By the outbreak of war in 1812, their community boasted libraries, learned societies, and natural history museums that rivaled those of nearby Boston. Through the existence and creation of formal centers of learning, Salem's resident scholars participated in an Atlantic "republic of letters" that defined their position within a wider Western cultural world. At the same time, Salem was also home to a less commonly acknowledged center of learning. Outside the libraries and museum halls, the town's fishermen were also expanding their vocational knowledge of the Northwest Atlantic marine environment. As more fishermen sailed northeast to the Nova Scotia and Grand Bank cod fisheries, they, too, expanded their understandings of their wider world. Whereas formal learning allowed Salemites to better appreciate their place in the Western world, Salem's fishermen developed an understanding of the town's place in a larger maritime environment. Thus in both formal learning and vocational knowledge, Salem emerged in the early republic as a center of renewed energy, insight, and innovation that had profound influences upon the nature, growth, and character of American natural sciences in the nineteenth century.

To modern sensibilities, science and letters dwell in academic institutions, which are specifically set up for the formal, publicly acknowledged, and systematic expansion of learning pursued by credentialed scholars. Such a view, however, reflects the reorganization of academic research between 1800 and the 1830s. In this process, academics and technically trained researchers in Britain and the United States removed experimental science from public lectures and demonstrations and instead situated the pursuit of natural knowledge within academies and institutions, which have since been the uncontested centers of academic research.[2]

In the eighteenth-century Anglo-American world, however, such professionalism had yet to take place, and science lacked today's clear definition of what it was and who was qualified to pursue it. While we are familiar with formal centers of learning in early America, such as the college communities situated at Harvard College (1636), William and Mary (1693), Yale (1701), Princeton (1746), Brown (1754), or Dartmouth (1761), what has been largely forgotten in the historical record, obscuring our knowledge of science in early America, is the predominance and influence of lay individuals who sought to advance knowledge in their respective spheres of practical and vocational activity and who followed established, systematic methods of science to get answers.

In the early republic, a number of institutions emerged as links between structured and informal approaches to the advancement and dissemination of knowledge. Marine societies in Salem, Boston, New York, and Newburyport organized their resources to collect navigational information about their local coastlines. These data, in turn, were assembled and made available to other members, and in some cases they were published for the benefit of all who sailed into the port. John Churchman represented another, more individualistic approach. A surveyor in the mid-Atlantic states, Churchman used his limited familiarity with magnetic variation to postulate a new method for determining longitude. In doing so, he joined a growing army of other professionals who waltzed down the erroneous path linking variation to longitude.[3] Farmers' almanacs, a third strategy, based predictions of future weather on "nonscientific" and intuitive observations; even today, their accuracy sometimes rivals and surpasses that of predictions made by the national weather service. Not only did these approaches represent the presence of less formal, vocational uses of science, but they also remind us of the greater influence of lay investigators at this time.

Maritime commerce, both overseas and coastal, created many of the communication links that allowed Salem to construct its place in a wider world; Salem's fisheries brought to the town deeper and ever-advancing knowledge of the regional marine environment upon which the local economy depended. As Salem's fishing fleet grew, the town's fishermen developed better understandings of their local marine environment—knowledge that helped them make a more prosperous living. Thus the town's forays into the arts and sciences were inextricably linked to its fishermen's vocational understandings of the Northwest Atlantic marine environment.

Scientific Societies: Defining Salem's Place in Western Culture

Much has been written on the formation of Salem's academic learned societies. Walter Muir Whitehill, Harriet Tapley, Harold Burstyn, and a handful of nineteenth-century Salem memorialists have already described the Salem Social

Library, the Salem Philosophical Library, and the East India Marine Society's social makeup, activities, and significance.[4] These fascinating histories highlight the intellectual engagement that distinguished this community from other colonial seaports. Yet few scholars have examined how those scientific societies affected the ways in which Salem integrated itself first into an imperial commercial and cultural milieu, and later into the wider world that opened with American independence. More than just emblems of a town's erudition, Salem's centers of higher learning formed bridges to a larger world of ideas and behaviors that had significant implications for Salem and its place in that world.

Trade played a fundamental role in the town's intellectual pursuits. First and foremost, Salem's trade generated the wealth required to attract and support an educated professional class already trained, to varying degrees, in the pursuit of the arts and sciences. Trade also created the contacts that gave Salem access to the most recent correspondence and publications. If nothing else, trading ties gave its local savants access to agents in London, Paris, and other learned centers through whom they could communicate observations and purchase books. After American independence, Salem's trade also sent its mariners to distant parts of the globe. There, new plants, animals, and human societies attracted the attention of interested captains whose commercial voyages often doubled as scientific voyages of discovery and collection.

Not surprisingly, the merchants and traders who formed the Salem Social Library in 1760 gave higher learning an important role in the successful pursuit of trade. Many eighteenth-century traders saw higher learning across a wide array of fields as the best preparation for business success. Broad-based understanding of the arts, law, politics, classical literature, foreign languages, history, and sciences armed commercial men with the tools necessary to make profits. Law and politics gave businessmen the background from which to anticipate how international and domestic affairs would influence market conditions. Foreign languages, literature, and the arts and classics gave commercial representatives some common ground with other traders and officials from which productive working relationships could be established. Consequently, in their 1761 shopping list given to the Reverend Jeremy Condy, members of the Salem Social Library requested works on political philosophy, comedies, histories, the classics, astronomy, physics, religion, and anatomy.[5] Like other merchants in the British world, Salem's commercial men and women saw the sciences open new ideas that could help expand their commercial interests.

As historians of American science have argued, colonial American centers of learning served as a unique conduit through which colonists could gain access to imperial centers of patronage and research.[6] In French Saint Domingue, for example, natural researchers and Enlightenment ideals expanded plantation slavery until the end of the French monarchical government in 1789.[7] In the Carolina low country, a similar pattern developed. Wealthier, scientifically minded planters traded American plant specimens to members of the Royal Society of London for new agricultural methods, new commercial crops from elsewhere in the empire, and new innovations in swamp drainage and irrigation. Access to London research centers enabled this group to enhance their commercial success—success that, after the Revolution, solidified their political positions and allowed them to become the planter class of the antebellum South.[8] Science and social authority blended in the North, where the Boston Marine Society's role in navigational science allowed the organization to play indirect and direct roles in national policies, local development, and some of the commonwealth's more pressing postwar political crises.[9] In all these cases, science was not practiced as a pure, value-free pursuit of natural knowledge. Intellectual activities also generated real and distinct political, social, and economic influence.

Salem's intellectual interests served nonscientific functions as well. Like other learned communities in colonial America, the Salem Social Library and the Salem Philosophical Library attracted members of the town's professional and mercantile elite. Samuel Curwen, Benjamin Lyde, Nathaniel Ropes, Andrew Oliver, Edward Augustus Holyoke, and William Pynchon translated their Harvard educations into prominent legal, governmental, or commercial careers. Commercial men who lacked higher education also ranked among the libraries' members. Benjamin Pickman had made his fortunes in the fisheries, owning vessels and buying cargoes for resale in Europe. Timothy Orne also owned several vessels and ran a successful shipping business, and Stephen Higginson was a prominent merchant. In addition, these societies attracted younger men who were establishing their careers and their social roles within the town. Joseph Bowditch, William Vans, John Nutting Jr., Samuel Barton, William Jeffrey, and Richard Derby Jr. all joined the libraries to highlight their social distinction as educated men of the community and to gain closer access to their senior colleagues.

Salem's learned societies did more than assemble well-educated and distinguished local residents. They provided access to the latest European research, thus enabling their members to build national and international reputations as scientists and technologists. The Salem Philosophical Library, for example, helped Manasseh Cutler establish himself as one of America's prominent thinkers. Between 1781 and 1806, his most productive period, he borrowed most of the library's volumes of the Royal Society of London's *Philosophical Transactions,* the French Academy's *Histoire,* and Buffon's *Histoire Naturelle,* and he held on to Priestly's *Vision, Light, and Colors* for four years. Cutler made effective use of the opportunity, publishing four articles on astronomy in the *Memoirs of the American Academy of Arts and Sciences.* For his work, he was awarded an LL.D. from Yale University and named fellow of the American Academy, a member of the American Philosophical Society, and honorary fellow of the Massachusetts Historical Society.[10] John

Prince was another Salemite who used his Philosophical Library membership to construct an impressive international reputation. Through his mapmaking and instrument work, John Prince, pastor of Salem's First Church, acted as an intermediary between American colleges and academies and British instrument makers. Improving designs of air pumps, microscopes, and the kaleidoscope, Prince earned a well-deserved reputation among London colleagues. His favorable evaluation of one device so pleased a London instrument maker that it "was pronounced by him to be the highest encomium that could be bestowed."[11]

Salemites of the early republic appear to have understood the power of place. Robert Booth has described Salem as an early American enterprise zone, in which community leaders such as merchant Elias Hasket Derby, pastor William Bentley, and politician Benjamin Goodhue Jr. combined knowledge, experience, and resources to draw the talented and the daring to their town and to transform their community into an engine of economic growth.[12] Intent on reproducing this phenomenon, town leaders established a host of learned societies through the next decades, transforming their community into an extended athenaeum. In 1799, the town's shipmasters who had sailed the dangerous, unfamiliar waters beyond the Cape of Good Hope and Cape Horn joined to pursue greater knowledge of lands and peoples of the East Indies and the Pacific. In addition to recording their navigational observations, members in the East India Marine Society collected artifacts, plant specimens, and cultural objects during their voyages to bring back to Salem. These collections, assembled into a museum in the 1820s, challenged Salem's residents to situate themselves within something of a global framework, fundamentally altering the town's sense of place. Like the Social Library and the Philosophical Society, the East India Marine Society connected to the wider world, making Salem's residents see themselves, in Dane Morrison's phrasing, as "citizens of the world."[13]

Access to the world's varied cultures and international reputations enabled leading Salemites to demonstrate the "critical mass" that characterized Salem's interest in the sciences, arts, and letters. Consequently, science helped put Salem "on the map" within a larger British Empire and tied the town to imperial centers of cultural and scientific authority. In this way, Salem mimicked the experience of other British colonial communities in the late eighteenth and early nineteenth centuries. As Deepak Kumar has argued for the Indian experience, science was more than just an intellectual activity; it was also "an economic as well as a cultural intervention" that carried significant political, commercial, and imperial implications.[14] For the Australian case, Roy Macleod has argued that because of their role in force projection, transport, commerce, communication, and the spread of modern notions of "progress," "the bonds forged through science are indissolubly linked to political [and I would add cultural] development."[15]

Salem's interests in the arts and sciences were far more than a local affair. Intellectual interests and pursuits allowed its citizens to identify and define a place in a larger Western learned world that spanned the Atlantic and the Pacific. With a prominent role in an expanding American foreign trade, Salem was able to pursue science along the same lines that it pursued trade. As such links helped define a town's development, Salemites came to see themselves within a larger world whose goods, ideas, learning, and material artifacts came to their doorstep.

Vocational Science: Defining Salem's Place in the Northwest Atlantic

New England had long attracted fishermen who kept notes on fish behavior. As early as 1717, it was emerging as a center of the Northwest Atlantic fishery. In that year, the region pulled roughly 1,300 fishermen away from the Newfoundland fishery and into the New England fleet. One observer in 1728 commented that the Newfoundland fishery was not a nursery for British seamen, but "far from answering that end, [it] is become a dangerous drain from the Mother kingdom to increase the shipping of a [New England] negligent of the laws of navigation, frequently encroaching upon your Majesty's Royal prerogative and too much inclined to independence." The influx of so much higher-priced, skilled labor into the New England fishing fleet, however, did not drive up the cost of New England–produced fish, which in 1717 sold for a dollar per quintal less than Newfoundland fish in European markets.[16]

Antique map of North American fishing grounds, Salem Athenaeum collections. Photo by Kim Mimnaugh.

Salem and its surrounding towns soon took on a prominent role in New England's fishery. Salem had been settled in 1626 by the remnants of a Cape Ann fishing colony under Roger Conant. By 1747 it was exporting over fifty thousand quintals of dried codfish per year to both Europe and the West Indies. In 1756 it had thirty-four fishing schooners averaging about thirty tons each,[17] and in 1762 it owned 10 percent of the colony's 300-vessel fishing fleet.[18]

As Salem's fleet expanded, so too did the number of Salemites observing the environment in which they earned their living—the sea. As the fleet expanded and new apprentices received improved training before setting themselves up as independent fishermen or masters, this knowledge was reinvested in the town. Such slow, generational expansion of environmental understanding is difficult to trace.[19] But the speed with which Salem's fishery rebounded after 1763 shows how important environmental knowledge was to the recovery of Salem's fishing industry. The French and Indian War had all but shut down British fisheries in the Northwest Atlantic. With the expulsion of the French in 1759, however, Salem's fishery expanded greatly. In 1765 Salem's fleet almost doubled to fifty-three vessels ranging in size from thirty to sixty-two tons and employing roughly 350 to 400 men. This quick recovery suggests that Salem's merchants had extended credit lines to a large number of experienced and skilled masters. In investing in the fishery, they naturally favored masters with the skills, knowledge, and reputations to ensure profits and the safe return of vessels and gear. Consequently, Salem's rapidly expanding fishery in the 1760s suggests that Salem had a large number of fishermen with the skills, experience, and environmental knowledge to secure such confidence from investors.

After the American Revolution, however, Salem's fleet recovered only slowly. The war put an effective end to most of the state's sea fishery, draining commercial assets and resources. In the first twelve months of fighting alone, for example, Salem lost $70,000 in depreciated boats and equipment.[20] The war inflicted even greater human costs, however. As the conflict dragged on, most of Salem's skilled mariners signed onto privateers, entered into the army, or were captured by British cruisers operating offshore. Most never returned. While precise figures for Salem are difficult to determine, the history of other fishing towns suggests Salem's fate. Gloucester, for example, lost three hundred men from its fisheries, one-third of its able-bodied population. In Chatham (Cape Cod), the war diminished the fishing fleet from twenty-seven vessels to only four or five and filled the town with widows and orphaned children.[21] Marblehead suffered heavily as well. Before the war the town had 12,000 tons enrolled in the fishery and 1,203 taxpaying adult men. By 1780, however, only 544 men remained and the town only had 1,509 enrolled tons, or three-eighths of its former tonnage.[22] Even as late as 1789, the town was still home to 459 widows and 865 fatherless children.[23] As a center of shipping, fishing, and the fighting, Salem likely lost many of its skilled fishermen as well.

According to New England fisheries historian Raymond McFarland, the loss of so many men undermined the training that new fishermen needed. After the Revolution, "[m]en, too, had lost the habit of their old vocation in following varying fortunes of service in the army or navy. The younger generation of boys had received little training in the shore fisheries such as their fathers had, and none of them had acquired practical experience in deep-sea fishing by a trip to the Grand Banks as 'cut-tail' aboard a New England schooner."[24] Boys heading into the fishery traditionally spent three to four years in training as a "cut-tail." After that apprenticeship, they graduated to become "headers," learning more nautical skills on the vessels and taking their full share as part of the crew. Apprenticed for another six years or so, by age twenty young fishermen benefited from almost a decade of close supervision, training, and instruction that gave them a foundation to work on their own as crew or master.[25] The Revolution, however, interrupted that training by killing off or removing from the fleet skilled senior fishermen who could train new fishermen.

In spite of Salem's postwar wealth and the availability of investment capital, the loss of so much knowledge hampered the recovery of the town's fisheries, which took several years to regain their prewar health. Salem had emerged from the Revolutionary War with much more wealth than other Massachusetts port towns, and throughout the 1780s it had the capital to invest in its previously profitable fisheries. The town's merchant community also benefited early from the growth of American trade to the East Indies in the 1780s. From 1786 to 1790, however, Salem's average fleet dropped by a third from its prewar levels to twenty vessels, and it employed on average only 160 men.[26] Without the knowledge to ensure profits and the skills to preserve capital, investors were reluctant to extend credit lines.

As more young men gained fishing experience in the 1780s, that situation began to change. The first postwar generation of fishermen began to pass on their collective knowledge to their successors, and Salem's fleet expanded with fresh, more qualified masters operating their own vessels. By 1796 Salem's tonnage had almost doubled from its 1786 levels, and the three towns of Salem, Beverly, and Marblehead made up 22 percent of the entire U.S. fishing tonnage.[27]

Deep-water fishing has always been a risky endeavor, requiring skilled labor and significant start-up capital. As a result, fishermen have always needed significant sums of investment capital to buy lines, hooks, bait, nets, cordage, anchors (which were frequently lost), and expensive imported salt. Such funds were not open to just anyone, however. As Daniel Vickers has argued, fishermen have long relied upon credit lines and debt that would only be extended to the most capable and experienced captains and masters.[28] To achieve this competency, fishermen needed to develop a fundamental understanding of the marine environment in which they worked. These skills and this knowledge were as essential to the commercial success of the fishery as were labor and capital.

Historians have found it difficult to trace the development of the arcane body of knowledge that constituted the expertise of early American fishermen. Only a few terse logbooks, noting days of departure and arrival, weather and wind, and course changes, survive from the Atlantic fisheries before 1800. Despite these hurdles, however, even terse logs reveal fishermen's active interest in their environment and demonstrate the ways in which they used that knowledge to pursue their living. The log for the schooner *John,* for example, offers a good glimpse of what kind of information Salem's fishermen had accumulated by the 1760s. On April 24, 1764, the *John* braved early spring gales, sailed past the Gulf of Maine, anchored on the Western Bank, and took in several hundred fish in three weeks. Later, the vessel shifted to the Middle Bank, and in another month it took in several hundred more. These simple entries suggest that the master of the *John* knew that fish in the Nova Scotia stocks, which favored the water depths found on the Western and Middle Banks, were larger in the early spring and would fetch higher market prices.[29]

David Moulton's 1829 log of a voyage to the Bay St. Lawrence reveals similar understandings of the Northwest Atlantic marine environment. Although he sailed from Hampton, New Hampshire, Moulton's notes, like those of his numerous Salem colleagues, reveal similar acquaintance with this environment, including weather, marine food webs, and physical characteristics such as bottom conditions and water depths. For example, Moulton, like most mariners, had developed an understanding of weather cycles that allowed him to predict future conditions. Returning from the St. Lawrence on August 28, 1829, he noted that "at 10 PM wind died away calm and it remained so till 12 the clouds appeared like a N.E. wind." The next day he waited for the storm: "at 8 PM the weather look'd rather dul with sines of rain at 10 PM the wind rather gained." Finally, on the 30th, the storm came and blew for almost the next week, forcing Moulton to steer his vessel off its southwesterly course toward home.

Moulton's log also reveals a fundamental understanding of marine food webs. On June 29, his crew fished for bait mackerel for his cod hand lines. In his log, the captain remarked, "[T]he weather was clowdy and rainy at 4 AM went to fishing for bait found them considerable plenty, we went to fishing found them considerable plenty we caught 1170." Throughout the voyage, his log suggests a close attention to the relationship between the abundance of baitfish and the abundance of codfish. Moulton paid sufficient attention to the two to note surprise when they were not in direct proportion: "The weather was clear the fore part of the day the after part was clowdy with a few small showers we found [cod]fish scarce but bait a plenty." Moulton also noted occasions when other species were found feeding on the mackerel schools that attracted codfish. "August 22 . . . went to fishing found cod fish scarce but we found plenty of dog fish."[30] Current research suggests that Moulton was not too far off in his assessments. Dogfish have been long known by fishermen and scientists to temporarily ruin a fishery by voraciously feeding on cod.[31] Moulton's observations show that he had some awareness of this relationship.

The type of information that concerned fishermen comes into clearer focus through records generated later in the nineteenth century. After 1852, fishermen were required to submit more detailed logbooks to receive their federal bounty money. In them, masters wrote down observations that they had been trained to make in the course of their careers. The logs reveal the type of information fishermen noted—either mentally or on paper—between 1800 and the 1850s, shedding light on how they observed their environment. They indicate that early republic fishermen understood how water depth and bottom conditions defined areas more likely to host large groups of cod; consequently, masters noted the depth and bottom type before they anchored for fishing. In 1829 Moulton indicated he had some idea of this relationship when on June 12, his crew "sounded for fish." By the 1850s, fishermen had also noted the relationship between fish size and water depth. In 1839, the *Boston Sentinel* reported that "the principal of which is a different depth at which the fish are taken, the largest fish being taken in the deepest water."[32] The type of bottom also had a direct bearing on the presence or absence of fish. Nearly a decade and a half later, on April 29, 1852, Capt. Larkin West of the schooner *Torpedo* of Salem noted, "Have 59 fath. sandy bottom." On August 25, he noted, "this night and morning caught 450, hove up, tried to find some rough bottom, at 2 PM came to anchor." One week later he linked the bottom condition to catch rates: "this night caught 140, the bottom being rocky and fish scarce."[33]

Bottom conditions were so important to Salem's and Beverly's fishermen that masters often used soundings to navigate. In 1855, Capt. Andrew Woodberry used soundings in conjunction with his charts to fix his position on the Scotian Shelf banks: "by chart and by soundings, get soundings on Western Bank [and] anchor in 55 fath., Lat. 43°22'." On July 10, 1857, Woodberry wrote, "spk w/ [fishing vessel] Thomas Boden w/4,000 f[ish], Longitude by soundings, 62°20'." In May 1861, Capt. James Allen of the schooner *Ceylon* of Beverly knew bottom conditions well enough to note, "corrected my longitude by soundings, 40 fath., Long 61°10'."[34]

Salem fishermen also noted codfish daily feeding patterns. West indicated in his log that fish fed in the mornings and evenings. "[In the] morning had a spert [of fish feeding activity] as usual, PM clear, a number of vessels got underway, had a scattering pick of fish through the day, filled up the 1st bbl of oil." This master's knowledge of fish feeding behavior paid off two weeks later when he noticed an unusual lull in nighttime feeding. "[F]ish very scarce in the night and morning, but concluded to let her lay a spell to see if they would not take hold." His patience paid off—that day the crew hauled in 208 fish.[35] The *Sentinel* article of 1839 reported that "second fare fish," fish caught in early summer during a vessel's second trip to the banks, tended to feed at night; consequently, fishermen hand-lined through the night to take advantage of increased fishing activity.[36]

Salem fishermen also tried to make connections between weather and fish behavior. Moulton noted this on June 19: "at 4AM went to the fishing found them considerable the weather was thick and raining. we caught 1180." Four days later he noted, "at 4 o'clock AM went to fishing found them considerable plenty with the weather very moderate we caught 1285." In 1854, Capt. Abram Fiske of the schooner *Richmond* out of Beverly noted in a bit of frustration, "It seems as if everything comes together, no fish, no wind to get where there [*sic*] are any, and thick fog. Fish scarce and small." West had similar complaints in 1852. On June 22, he wrote, "Comes with moderate foggy weather and no fish."[37] Studies have shown that weather influences fish feeding habits. Southwesterly winds drive warm water from shore and create cold water upwellings that lead codfish inshore.[38]

These two approaches to the pursuit of knowledge—the academic and the vocational—were not as isolated as they appear in the histories or historiography of Salem in the early republic. Many of the prominent members of Salem's scientific societies established their wealth, social status, and influence through the extension of credit to fishermen. Families such as the Ornes and the Curwens, for example, made their money by owning fishing vessels that "made" the highly prized commodity that allowed them to extend their trade into southern Europe. Many of Salem's aspirant academics relied upon their fishing neighbors' knowledge and expertise to provide them with the leisure to pursue their intellectual interests.

The convergence of environmental knowledge and academic pursuits set the stage for Salem and the rest of Essex County to emerge as one of the nation's first centers of environmental research. In 1833 a group of interested gentlemen drew upon Salem's intellectual reputation and established the Essex County Natural History Society at Salem's Lyceum Hall. Marine life formed an important part of their early interests. They established a museum that included a collection of marine invertebrates and fishes commonly found in the Gulf of Maine.[39] The creation of this institution began a process by which Salem and Essex County would witness the blending of the two forms of learning. In 1866 George Peabody moved the process even further by establishing the Peabody Academy of Science, which served as a home to Louis Agassiz of Harvard University. By the second half of the nineteenth century, prominent marine researchers such as Spencer F. Baird and George Brown Goode had come to realize that fishermen, like the many skilled and experienced ones working out of the Salem area, carried a wealth of information about the marine environment, and they referred to fishermen's opinions to support their own scientific conclusions.[40]

"It is not for nothing," a colleague recently said to me, "that the federal government established one of the first fisheries research facilities in the country on Cape Ann."[41] Plenty of other areas had access to fishing fleets and institutions of higher learning where such a facility could be built. Salem, however, had a unique tradition of pursuing academic learning, fishing, and marine environmental observation that made Essex County the best possible place for such an establishment. In almost a direct line between Boston's universities and Cape Ann's fishing towns, Salem, as one of the nation's earliest centers of higher learning—an extended athenaeum—brought together two distinct learned cultures in an atmosphere that had long celebrated the practical pursuit of natural knowledge and higher learning. As formal learning situated Salem within a wider world of science and research, Salem's fisheries provided the expertise by which that learned culture could situate the town in its own marine environment.

Notes

I would like to thank Dr. Dane Morrison for his expertise and support for this article. I would also like to thank the UNH History of Marine Animal Populations (HMAP) Project members for access to their data and knowledge: Dr. William Leavenworth, Karen Alexander, Dr. Jeff Bolster, Glenn Grasso, and Dr. Andy Rosenberg.

1. See Walter Muir Whitehill, *The East India Marine Society and the Peabody Museum of Salem: A Sesquicentennial History* (Salem, Mass.: Peabody Museum, 1949), 16–20.

2. For a concise study of this process, see Jan V. Golinski, *Science as Public Culture: Chemistry and Enlightenment in Britain, 1760–1820* (Cambridge and New York: Cambridge University Press, 1992).

3. Patricia Fara, *Sympathetic Attractions: Magnetic Practices, Beliefs, and Symbolism in Eighteenth-Century England* (Princeton: Princeton University Press, 1996).

4. Cynthia B. Wiggin, *The Salem Athenaeum* (Salem, Mass.: Forest River Press, 1971); Harold L. Burstyn, "The Salem Philosophical Library: Its History and Importance for American Science," *Essex Institute Historical Collections* 96 (1960): 169–206; Harriet Sylvester Tapley, *Salem Imprints, 1768–1825* (Salem, Mass.: The Essex Institute, 1927); Lawrence Waters Jenkins, "The Marine Society at Salem in New England: A Brief Sketch of Its History," *Essex Institute Historical Collections* 76 (1940): 199–220.

5. See Tapley, 230–37, for a list of requests and actual purchases.

6. See, for example, George H. Daniels, *American Science in the Age of Jackson* (New York: Columbia University Press, 1968); George H. Daniels, *Science in American Society: A Social History* (New York: Knopf, 1971); Brooke Hindle, *The Pursuit of Science in Revolutionary America, 1735–1789* (Chapel Hill: University of North Carolina Press, 1956); Raymond Phineas Stearns, *Science in the British Colonies of America* (Urbana: University of Illinois Press, 1970); and Dirk Struik, *Yankee Science in the Making* (Boston: Little, Brown, 1948).

7. James McClellan III, *Colonialism and Science: Saint Domingue in the Old Regime* (Baltimore: Johns Hopkins University Press, 1992).

8. Joyce Chaplin, *An Anxious Pursuit: Agricultural Innovation and Modernity in the Lower South, 1730–1815* (Chapel Hill: University of North Carolina Press, 1993), 131–42.

9. Matthew McKenzie, "Vocational Science and the Politics of Independence: The Boston Marine Society, 1752–1812," (Ph.D. diss., University of New Hampshire, 2003).

10. Burstyn, 178.

11. Burstyn, 179–80; Benjamin Silliman, as quoted by Burstyn, 180.

12. See chapter 3 of this volume.

13. See chapter 5 of this volume.

14. Deepak Kumar, *Science and the Raj, 1857–1905* (Delhi and New York: Oxford University Press, 1995), 2.

15. Roy Macleod, "On the Moving Metropolis: Reflections on the Architecture of Imperial Science," in *Scientific Colonialism: A Cross-Cultural Comparison,* ed. Nathan Reingold and Marc Rothenberg (Washington, D.C.: Smithsonian Institution Press, 1987), 218.

16. Harold A. Innis, *The Cod Fisheries: The History of an International Economy* (Toronto, 1954), 147. A quintal was a measure commonly used in colonial America and equaled 133 1/3 pounds.

17. Innis, 161–62.

18. Salem figures from Raymond McFarland, *A History of the New England Fisheries* (New York: D. Appleton and Co., 1911), 99.

19. See Jeffrey Hutchings, Barbara Neis, and Paul Ripley, "The 'Nature of Cod' (*Gadus Morhua*): Perceptions of Stock Structure and Cod Behaviour by Fishermen, 'Experts' and Scientists from the Nineteenth Century to the Present," in *Marine Resources and Human Societies in the North Atlantic since 1500,* ed. Daniel F. Vickers, ISER Conference Paper Number 5 (St. John's, Newfoundland, 1995), 123–88.

20. McFarland, 123.

21. McFarland, 123.

22. Samuel Eliot Morison, *The Maritime History of Massachusetts, 1783–1860* (Boston: Northeastern University Press, 1979), 139.

23. McFarland, 124.

24. McFarland, 130.

25. McFarland, 151.

26. McFarland, 131.

27. *American State Papers, Documents, Legislative and Executive, Volume VII, Commerce and Navigation* (Washington, D.C.: Gales and Seaton, 1832), 386.

28. Daniel F. Vickers, *Farmers and Fishermen: Two Centuries of Work in Essex County, Massachusetts, 1630–1850* (Chapel Hill: University of North Carolina Press, 1994), 85–202.

29. Log of the Schooner *John,* LOG1762J, mfilm #91, reel 68 (Peabody Essex Museum, Salem, Massachusetts).

30. David Moulton, [Log], 1829. Private Collection.

31. See Bruce B. Collette and Grace Klein-MacPhee, eds., *Bigelow and Schroeder's Fishes of the Gulf of Maine,* 3rd ed. (Washington, D.C.: Smithsonian Institution Press, 2002), 54–57, 228–35. See also Richard H. Backus, ed., *Georges Bank* (Cambridge, Mass.: MIT Press, 1987), 480–82, 483–84.

32. *Boston Sentinel,* September 1839, as printed in George Browne Goode, *The Fisheries and Fishery Industries of the United States* (Washington, D.C.: U.S. Government Printing Office, 1887), I, sec. 1, 131.

33. Log of Schooner *Torpedo,* 1852, Box 88, Record Group 36, "Salem/Beverly Customs Records," National Archives and Records Administration (Waltham, Massachusetts); Collette and Klein-MacPhee, 229.

34. Log of Schooner *William Penn,* April 25, 1855, Box 91, Record Group 36, "Salem/Beverly Customs Records," National Archives and Records Administration (Waltham, Massachusetts); Log of Schooner *A. N. Clark,* Beverly, May 6, 1857, Box 53, Record Group 36, "Salem/Beverly Customs Records," National Archives and Records Administration (Waltham, Massachusetts); Log of Schooner *Ceylon,* Beverly, May 19, 1861, Box 58, Record Group 36, "Salem/Beverly Customs Records," National Archives and Records Administration (Waltham, Massachusetts).

35. *Torpedo,* 1852, June 11 and June 28.

36. Goode, 131.

37. Moulton; Log of Schooner *Richmond,* Beverly, June 6, 1854, Box 82, Record Group 36, "Salem/Beverly Customs Records," National Archives and Records Administration (Waltham, Massachusetts); *Torpedo,* June 22, 1852.

38. Collette and Klein-MacPhee, 234.

39. Ralph W. Dexter, "Essex County and the Development of American Marine Biology," *American Neptune* 49 (1989): 34–38.

40. Goode, sec. 1, 221.

41. Personal communication with Dr. William Leavenworth, March 15, 2003.

American vessel in Canton, reproduction painting by Philip von Saltza, Salem State College collections. Photo by Kim Mimnaugh.

Chapter Five

Salem as Citizen of the World

DANE ANTHONY MORRISON

*I thought of my own Town Pump in old Salem. . . . when I once
grasped the handle, a rill gushed forth that meandered as far as England, as
far as India, besides tasting pleasantly in every town and village in our country.
I like to think of this, so long after I did it, and so far from home, and am
not without hopes of some kindly local remembrance on this score.*

—Nathaniel Hawthorne, letter from Florence, June 1858

N April 1941, on the eve of a conflict that would pull Americans to Sumatra and Bombay and Canton, Dorothy Schurman Hawes was recalling the exploits of an earlier generation of Yankees in these distant locales for the readers of the *Essex Institute Historical Collections.*[1]
At a time when isolationism had captured the American imagination and Americans' knowledge of the Orient was bounded snugly between the yellow covers of *National Geographic* magazine, Mrs. Hawes hoped to draw her readers' gaze to locales that many Americans found strange and "inscrutable"—places that would soon become painfully familiar to all of them as the Pacific theater.[2] As a counterpoint to the coming global tempest, in the little city of Salem, Massachusetts, amidst the Federalist mansions and elm-shaded neighborhoods of Washington Square and Essex Street, sat an oasis of serenity—the elegant, wainscoted reading room of the Essex Institute's Plummer Hall. Here the dusty logs, letters, and journals that Mrs. Hawes pored over were lovingly housed, and here genteel amateur historians traced their ancestors' adventures. The records kept in the Essex Institute reminded Salem that it had once had an intimate acquaintance with the wider world, and had flourished in it.

Outside the whispered stillness of the Plummer Hall reading room, through the next four years, Salem's hopes and fears once again were linked with world events. Its schoolchildren stammered through the names of Pacific archipelagoes, their parents hovered anxiously in their parlors over paneled RCA cabinet radios as Edward R. Murrow brought news of the latest action on a new front, fathers pushed pins into maps to indicate the latest posting of a son or daughter, and moth-

Plummer Hall interior. Courtesy of Salem Athenaeum.

ers draped blue or yellow stars in bedroom windows. They collected scrap metal, troweled victory gardens and bought victory bonds, and rationed rubber from French Cambodia, petroleum from Dutch Indonesia, and sugar from Calcutta.

For most Americans of 1941, the places of the Pacific were strange, exotic, and erotic. For the deep-rooted families of Salem, however—descendants of the sea captains, business agents known as "supercargoes," and ordinary Jack Tars who had sailed these waters before—Mrs. Hawes's tales were as familiar as family yarns told around dining tables, as, indeed, they were. Like the mariners who were the subjects of her history, Hawes had been an expatriate American in Asian lands, the daughter of a U.S. minister to China and the wife of a naval attaché and representative to Chiang Kai-shek, living ten years in Shanghai and Beijing. The history of China Trade Salem likely stirred memories of her own past, melding history and biography, and forged, as well, a felt connection to the men and women in whose footsteps she had walked and to overseas travelers such as Harriet Low.

Miss Low was just twenty when she began a four-year sojourn (1828–1832) in Macao, the Portuguese stopover off of Canton, accompanying her merchant uncle and ailing aunt. Her journal recorded an ingénue's impressions of the East—images that became Miss Low's paper memories of time spent among mysterious and exotic cultures. It was one of hundreds of journals, logs, and diaries that formed the mythology of a once-glorious Salem. Shared with friends and family, incorporated into newspaper reports and public lectures, the stuff of conversation long after, these recollections of faraway lands and peoples made Salem a unique place among American cities. More sophisticated, more cosmopolitan, more worldly and experienced, Salem of the China Trade stood out as a "city upon a hill" quite different from Puritan expectations, one that contributed to the nation's economic might, material culture, and literary imagination.

For a brief period, Salem exerted a remarkable influence on American life. The town introduced exotics such as the elephant and giraffe to Americans, and it filled Yankee pantries with pepper, tea, and porcelain.[3] More so, its exploits shaped national character, and did so at a critical moment. By 1790, Salem's 7,921 residents had made it the sixth largest city in the new nation.[4] At a time when tariffs made up the bulk of all federal revenues, Salem's commerce—including such exotic cargoes as Patna opium, bêche-de-mer (edible sea worms), and birds' nests (for bird's nest soup)—contributed 5 percent to the national treasury. By the early 1800s, Salem vessels so dominated the spice trade of the South Seas that the region became known as the Salem East Indies.[5] Indeed, Salem dominated trade in a single foreign commodity—pepper—in a single part of the world in the first fifty years of the republic.[6]

China Trade Salem

Salem was not the first American seaport to send a vessel to the East. Once British mercantilist regulations had been overthrown in the War for Independence, Yankee vessels broke their enforced confinement to Atlantic waters and began to traffic in every part of the globe. In December 1783, the sloop *Harriet* sailed out of Boston to the edge of the Atlantic, reaching the Cape of Good Hope. The following year, the *Empress of China* departed New York to anchor off Canton.

Salem vessels soon followed, and when, during the 1786–1787 season, five American ships were reported anchored at Whampoa Reach (Huang-Po) in the Pearl River (Pei-ho), the *Grand Turk* of Salem was one of them.[7] From this start, Salem vessels ranged the globe in search of exotic cargoes for American cupboards—pepper and porcelain, Bohea tea and Indian bandanas, silks and sandalwood.

Within the infant nation, a republican experiment that "tottered with every step," as Washington fretted, Americans watched with care the precedents their country set, and newspapers boasted of first landings. The *Salem Gazette* and *Salem Mercury* placed their seaport among the most prominent that sent out vessels on "voyages of exploration and commerce." The citizens of China Trade Salem were among the first Americans to fly the stars and stripes in the emerald lagoons, bustling harbors, and restless bays of the Pacific. On April 30, 1785, under Capt. Jonathan Ingersoll, Elias Hasket Derby's *Grand Turk* was the first American vessel to weigh anchor off the mountains of St. Helena.[8] It was said that when the *Grand Turk* touched at the Arabian port of Mocha, "[t]he natives had never heard of America, and the strange vessel was a nine days' wonder." In 1789, the *Atlantic* of Salem first flew the stars and stripes at Calcutta and Bombay. The first American voyage to Batavia was made in a Salem vessel, the *Astrea,* about the time President Washington was taking office at Federal Hall in New York City. Between March 1806 and August 1807, Salem's *Eliza* opened the trade in Fijian sandalwood, and in 1800, Capt. Nathaniel West's ship, the *Minerva,* began the first circumnavigation of the globe by a Salem vessel.[9] For a brief period, Jonathan Lambert of Salem took possession of Tristan da Cunha in the South Atlantic, planting a trading post for passing vessels.[10]

Citizens of the World

The long voyages and extended stays required in maritime commerce meant that Salem would be not only a place transformed by contact with the East, but also a place transferred. One could find Salem men and women in the most far-flung regions during these years, freighting bits of Salem life on virtually every sea and to every port. Salemites, it seemed, were everywhere. The distances spanned during these voyages tell part of the story. So, Capt. Dudley Pickman noted in the log of the *Belisarius,* "September 11 [1800] arrived at Salem having run per log this passage, 13,950 miles," and in the *Derby,* "Distance this passage by log 14,583 miles."[11] Ship captains met one another in various parts of the world. Just two years after the end of the Revolution, as Maj. Samuel Shaw was returning from his second voyage to Canton, he encountered Salem's Jonathan Ingersoll, commanding the *Grand Turk* on its first voyage to the Cape of Good Hope.[12] Berthed in the Hooghly River at Calcutta in 1797, the log of the *Belisarius* recorded, "I find there have been here a great many American ships particular Salem vessels & that they have carried home a good deal of Sugar."[13] Anchoring in Calcutta on April 6, 1803, Capt. Dudley Pickman recalled that he "was happy to find Mr. P.T. Jackson of the ship *Pembroke* of Boston, and Messrs. Ellis and Cabot of the *Asia* of Beverly," but "[no] other Americans in port."[14] And in July 1803, Capt. Nathaniel Bowditch, scouring Sumatra for pepper, met, or in the terms of the times, "spoke" Captains Ward, Silsbee, and Carnes in the Bay of Sunda on the same errand.[15]

In fact, communities of expatriate Americans could be found from Canton to Calcutta, and from Macao to Manila to Mauritius, usually including someone from Salem. Most, it seems, moved about, following trading or missionary opportunities. Cosmopolitan Salemites, linked to a global expatriate community through a network of gossip, rumor, and occasional fact, were able to follow the journeys of friends and acquaintances from Macao to Bombay to New York. Harriet Low's sister was nevertheless just a degree of separation from a famous Canton-based physician, globe-trotting English tourists, and a host of missionaries and merchants. Harriet reported: "You have no doubt heard of Dr. Morrison. I believe he understands Chinese better than any English person. We then called on Mrs. Allport, a very interesting woman just from Calcutta. We then returned home, letters from Uncle soon after."[16] A surprising number made an exotic site their temporary home. The Lows sojourned in Macao for four years. Hasket Derby, son of the eminent Elias Hasket, held his post in India for three years "in the interests of his house, and firmly established an immensely profitable trade which for half a century was to make the name of Salem more widely known in Bombay and Canton than that of New York or Boston."[17] In July 1803, Capt. Nathaniel Bowditch noted the American presence on Île de France (Mauritius), having met up with Salem captains Ingersoll and Goodhue and with Mr. Cabot and Mr. Bonnefoy, a shipmate on the *Astrea* in 1795 who had decided to begin a new life on Île de France eight years earlier.[18] So common was it to encounter Salemites in these far-flung locations that Capt. Dudley Pickman of the *Belisarius,* berthed at Madras in 1799, confessed his disappointment that he had "met very few Americans, and, except in business, formed no acquaintaces with the English residents. Of the former, was Captain Cheever, born at Danvers where his relations now live, has been twelve or fifteen years in India, master of a country vessel, has acquired but little property and will probably never return to America. . . . Mr. Stephen Minot of Boston, lived for several years in Salem with Captain N. West, now trades between Isle of France, and Tranquebar and Madras, probably covering French property, principally prize vessels which he brings back from Mauritius for sale."[19] While it may seem astonishing to modern readers to learn that Pickman had encountered at least three North Shore expatriates in a single city in India in 1799, the Salem captain had clearly expected to meet many more.

What Pickman described was a social phenomenon of the early republic that has been understudied by historians—expatriate Americans, sometimes living singly, sometimes gathered in enclaves. Some rose to high position or participated in signal events. Among the more notable were John Ledyard of Connecticut, who served as a corporal of marines on Captain Cook's final voyage and then returned to the United States and mounted a one-man campaign to convince Thomas Jefferson, Robert Morris, and other prominent leaders to stake him to a voyage to America's Northwest Coast. Another Connecticut man, Elihu Yale, rose to high position in the British East India Company in Madras. His fortune became the initial endowment to the university named for him.

Home took on a particular salience for overseas travelers, whose voyages could keep them from the familiarity of hearth and neighborhood for years at a time. The loss and loneliness they experienced were a source of frequent commentary in their journals. Leaving sight of familiar places brought pangs of regret, as in the entry of William Augustus Rogers, supercargo aboard the *Tartar,* bound for Calcutta in 1817: [At Thatchers light off Cape Ann] "Here I cast one '*longing lingering look*' to the shores of my native land. And how fortunate was I in the consolatory thought that I left behind me many an anxious friend, who would rejoice at my prosperity or feel an anxiety for one who had left them in pursuit of an honorable independency."[20] Harriet Low's journal is as poignant, noting of her departure, "I left home at 5 o'clock with feelings not to be described, nor imagined. . . . I cannot say I enjoyed anything that took place that day. . . . however I behaved like a heroine, as I had resolved to be. . . . I stood at the stern thinking of home and all associated with that sweet place till I wished that I was there and not condemned in foreign climes." She had begun her journal to maintain a vicarious bond with the Salem she left behind, writing, "Embarked on board the ship *Sumatra* bound to Manilla from thence to Macao where I shall probably take up residence for the next 4 years and for you my Dear Sister shall this journal be kept." In a side note, she added, "This journal was commenced a week after we had sailed. It then appeared like a month."[21]

For these travelers, absence did make hearts fonder. Their days and their dreams were filled with the faces, voices, and landscapes of the places they had left behind, and which now figured more prominently in their minds. The most ordinary sounds and sights could recall familiar associations with home, neighborhoods, and community. The effervescent twenty-year-old Harriet Low described the sensation of meeting acquaintances from home: "Just before tea, Sail O was heard. We were all on deck in short time, a sound that makes us start like the cry of fire in Salem but which excites a great variety of feelings. A fear that it may be a pirate, though joy and hope predominate. A hope that she may be bound home. And a hope that she may have some of our friends in her." Once settled in Macao, Miss Low characteristically captured the excitement of finding friends in faraway corners of the world when she recalled for her sister, "We had the pleasure of seeing Mrs. Cleveland, her husband, and James. Can you judge of our delight these

Salem ladies meeting in Macao. Only think of it. So you see the thing that we were anticipating before we left America had come to pass. It seems almost impossible, as though it must be a dream that we are so far from home and together. . . . I can tell you it was delightful to see someone from home."²²

For post-Revolutionary Yankee voyagers, home took on deeper meanings than it had for earlier generations of colonial mariners, confined as they had been to the Atlantic by British mercantilist regulations. In the thoughts of earlier American "colonials," identity was integrally a part of place, but that place was local. They thought of themselves as from Massachusetts, New Hampshire, or Connecticut, but not as Americans. They were, after all, British. For the first generation of Americans, then, travels "eastward of Good Hope" inspired a stronger sense of national bonding than had existed before. As the *Tartar* made way for Calcutta in 1817, republican thoughts filled the head of supercargo William Augustus Rogers:

> The night was beautifully placid, the constellations vied with each other to compensate for the loss of the great luminary which had gone to illumine other lands and the western stars shone with heaven's purest light, to guide the oppressed emigrant to the cradle of freedom and the seaworn mariner to the land of his home. Fare well for a time my country, last child of nations, may ages roll on their unwearied courses and find thy sons as wise, as brave, and as virtuous as they now are. How proud were my feelings when I beheld the setting sun covering with his golden mantel the freest *"of all lands he shines upon"* the land of pure and rational liberty, uncontaminated with licentiousness, and unrestrained by tyranny, the asylum of oppressed humanity, the refuge of itinerant misery.²³

After five months and two oceans, in January 1818 he recorded, "At 6 a.m. R.S.R. discovered land from the fore yard. The high lands of Ceylon, . . . This is the first land I have seen for 135 days! . . . It seems like my native land. But that land, the loss of the dearest of all friends a son can boast, has deprived me of almost all pleasure when I think of it."²⁴ Eleven years later, Harriet Low voiced her sense of national belonging in an entry from Saturday, October 10, 1829, in which she sighed, "I saw a ship passing up to Canton from our door this morning. I watched it for a long time, hoping that I should see the stars and stripes, but could not make any thing of it but an English signal."²⁵ Home had become both Salem and America for this generation.

Why did they sail, separated from family and friends, for years, even decades? They went, their recollections tell us, to "see all that was curious."²⁶ The Salem that sent out its sails across the world was a place of enterprise, certainly. But, this community represented a liberal and progressive view of enterprise that was particular to the early republic. This salt air community esteemed "useful and entertaining knowledge," as Nathaniel Hawthorne styled it, as a proper course to set in their search for profits. Salem's voyagers kept their own detailed journals—paper memories—and, on their return, shared these recollections with their families and neighbors, embellishing the record and bringing home the experience of life abroad.[27] These journals connected Salem to the wider globe and made even those who never left land feel that they were citizens of the world.

Many entries read surprisingly like a *National Geographic* magazine or geography textbook, admirably emphasizing the accumulation of knowledge that was typical of Salem's penchant for scientific exploration and discovery. We find page after page of entries that represent the captain, the supercargo, the passenger as a sophisticated citizen of the world. Given the long voyages, the endless time, and the desire to break through the lace ceiling of social respectability, we are not surprised to encounter extended descriptions of the far reaches of the globe, as in Pickman's India entries:

> Calcutta is situated on the River Hooghly, a branch of the Ganges, and is about 100 miles from the sea, in twenty-three degrees north latitude and eighty-eight degrees east longitude. The English first obtained the Mongol's permission to settle here in 1690. It is now capital of Bengal and of all British India. In 1756 it was taken by the Nabob Surajah dowla, with 70,000 troops and 400 elephants, and 146 English prisoners were confined in the black hole prison during the night of June 20, where 123 died before morning. The next year it was retaken by the English, who have ever since held possession undisturbed.[28]

And the *Salem Mercury* of July 31, 1787, detailed a lengthy description of Indian customs, beginning with the "*Ceremony of a BRAMIN Marriage.* THE ceremony of their marriages is very remarkable [*sic*]. For as they account marriage one of the best actions of a man's life, it is ushered in, performed, and consumated [*sic*] in a very extraordinary manner."[29] As refined men and women of the world, Salem's global voyagers at times incorporated poetry, drawings, and even copied entries from the *Encyclopedia Britannica*.[30] On their return to Salem, they were swept up as premier lecturers in the storied halls of the East India Marine Society, at the porcelain-laden dining tables of prosperous merchant families, in the spice-laden coffeehouses of overseas traders, and among the scarred and weathered captains, mates, and mariners of bustling wharves.

Whether merchant, shopkeeper, or housewife, the citizens of China Trade Salem could not help but be interested in economic conditions around the globe. "Useful knowledge" of seasons, markets, and harvests was essential to the commonwealth of Salem. Dudley Pickman made his contribution to Salem's accumulation of commercial knowledge in his India entries:

Calcutta is the greatest place of trade in British India. A very extensive trade is carried on here with Europe, America, and the other parts of India. Here are fine docks for repairing vessels, and shipyards for building. It exports to Europe and the United States piece goods, cotton, sugar, indigo, ginger, etc. From Europe, it imports English goods of every description, liquors, etc. and specie from Europe. Raw cotton was formerly an article of import from Surat to Calcutta. It is now produced in Bengal and exported in very large quantities. Indigo is an important article of export. The cultivation of both is rapidly increasing. In July and August as the rivers rise, goods come in from the country, and from September to January, is considered the best times to purchase sugar, ginger and piece goods. Many more vessels are here at this, than any other period, and March and April sometimes are found better months for advantageous purchases, than earlier, from an anxiety in holders to push off their goods before new ones come in. The quantities at market are then, however, comparatively small, and a considerable demand would render them scarce and dear.[31]

To satisfy this need, in its February 19, 1788, issue, the *Salem Mercury* reprinted from the *Calcutta Gazette* the following:

By letters from China, we have received very melancholy accounts, . . . nothing short of what the late famine up the country afforded.

There has been so little rain during the last rice reason [*sic*], that a famine has been the consequence, and upwards of 30,000 of the poorer sort of people, up the country, have perished for want of this necessary article.[32]

Likewise, the important news for Christmas Day (but not reported until six months later) in the *Salem Gazette* came from the East Indies:

FOREIGN INTELLIGENCE. . . . The news brought from China by the late ships, has proved as we intimated in our last, not to be of the dismal complexion which report at first stated, the market was so declaredly good and rising, that opium has risen considerably in price here within these few days; and as so much was said some time since in the Calcutta prints, of the failure of Shikinqua; it is proper to mention, that advice is said on good authority, to have been received of his having made a payment of 40 per cent. on the amount of his debts.[33]

Salemites were just as curious about the peoples with whom they traded, and the town's newspapers frequently satisfied their wonder with articles that widened their understanding of other cultures. Still, they saw the world through the eyes of

China Trade Salem, and economic interest framed their curiosity. Thus when Dudley Pickman described Calcutta from the *Derby* in 1803, he noted, "The rainy season commences in May and continues till September, sometimes raining for several days almost without intermission, and scarcely a day passing without some showers."[34] Knowledge of the seasons was essential information for the merchant who sought the highest quality in cinnamon or opium, as well as for the captain who sought to navigate foreign waters. As Pickman's journal provided recollection for his conversations upon returning to Salem, the memories of William A. Rogers, aboard the *Tartar* along the Indian coast from 1817 to 1818, brought important navigational information to the captains of the Salem East India Society. Rogers's jottings warned, "In passing along the W. Coast of Ceylon, care should be taken to distinguish the Hooy Mount from Adam's Peak, which although very lofty still may be mistaken for one or other."[35] From discussions with Rogers and his colleagues, Salem mariners might learn as much about sailing the Malabar or Coromandel coasts as schooning outside Salem harbor.

However, it was the fluctuating conditions of trade, specifically, that occupied the minds of Salem's merchants—a need fulfilled by the town's expatriate citizens. From one of these, the *Salem Gazette* heralded the following news: "We further learn,—That our countrymen are not allowed to sell their Furs in China, is certain—and it is equally certain it is not, as has been said, thro' the British influence—as we find they equally suffer—in the London Price Current of the 20th April, the *General Coote,* Capt. Baldwin, from China, enter'd fifteen Cases of Sea-Otter Skins, bro't from Canton."[36] More than other early American communities, Salem had learned how to integrate a liberal appreciation for learning with "useful knowledge" that would alert its maritime network to opportunities and obstacles abroad, bringing economic advantage to the community as a whole.

In representing the peoples "eastward of Good Hope" to their own community at home, Salem's maritime writers sometimes portrayed the exotic "other" as a sharp counterpoint to the values they sought to celebrate and embellish. Trust, hard work and disciplined order, and progress ranked high among the traits they extolled. Therefore, they were sensitive to instances of untrustworthiness, lassitude, and inefficiency. When other peoples failed to conform to their expectations, these incidents were given due representation in their journals. For example, Pickman issued a warning in his instructions to Capt. Benjamin Shreve, piloting the *New Hazard* out of Salem in 1815: "The most important thing in your voyage is in securing your ship. You had better not employ a Man of doubtful character at any rate. Engage with a security merchant of the first Character even at rather higher prices for your goods and you will be sure to have a good cargo and without being delayed beyond the time stipulated for. There are generally about 12 security merchants, with one of whom you must engage of those who were in the Hong in 1805, when I was at Canton, 5 or 6 did much American Business."[37] An equally sophisticated sense of how the world worked can be seen in his advice for using Indian banyans, or middlemen:

> They are paid by the persons of whom the goods are purchased—at least nominally. Those generally employed are, Ramdulolday (who is also banyan to the very respectable English house of Fairlie, Gilmore, and Co.). He does most of the southern and some of the New England business, is very shrewd and capable, extremely avaricious, and possesses great talents for business. He is considered to be worth three to five million rupees. Ram Chunder Banorjea, a Brahmin, does some southern and a considerable proportion of the northern business. He is said to be worth five to ten lacs rupees and is a very smooth tongued man. Collisunker and Doorgapersaud Ghose do some southern and more northern business. The latter is a shrewd man and industrious when pressed by business. They are about as rich as Ram Chunder, and I was satisfied with the manner in which they managed the business I entrusted to them.[38]

The memories of William Augustus Rogers, Harriet Low, Dudley Pickman, and others became Salem's views of the wider world and acquainted Salem's residents with the peoples of the globe. The journal of Harriet Low provides a glimpse of how different the view from Canal Street was from that of Canton: "I suppose you will like to know what I thought of a Malay and how my modesty could withstand such a shock, as to see a man unclad, but I agree with Bishop Heber in thinking their colour serves as a covering. They seem like a different race of beings." In Macao, she noted, "One idea of the Chinese amuses me, that is that a vessel cannot go without eyes. They therefore have a large eye on each side of the bow which looks very singularly. If you ask them what these are for, they say, Hiyah, bow cannot see without eye." Low's observations reflected a characteristic common to voyagers' journals, the imposition of American values on other cultures. Salem was a place transferred through such means, as Low and others gauged Chinese or Indian practices against their own values and frequently found the latter lacking in morality or logic. In Macao, Miss Low was at an age when young women were often concerned with family and children, and she brought these matters to her sister's attention. Her entry described in the Pearl River "an immense quantity of Boats in which whole families live indeed 2 or 3 [?]. The women steer the boats and frequently have an infant slung to her back. The common mode of carrying children among the poor class and the poor little thing only has a shaking if it cries. They sometimes use their children very cruelly." And, in the same entry, she wrote, "I was astonished to see what immense loads these coolies carry on their shoulders. Everything is carried by them. Some little boys I see with two heavy loads slung on to a long pole and carrying it apparently with the greatest ease." Yet, alongside the wide-eyed awe, one hears also an emergent discrimination in Low's comparisons: "I am now in Manilla Bay. I cannot believe it. . . . The Cavita on one side, Manilla on the other. The Caseo's with the natives going from one place to another looks quite lively. . . These Caseo's are built out of solid wood or rather dug out of trees. There is a covering of bamboo, under which the family live. The wife was sowing. I should not have known it to be a woman at first, she had on nothing but trousers, the men are merely covered about their middle. I did not like the looks of them so well as I did the Malays. Their faces are not so intelligent."[39]

The world of Harriet Low, like that of Dorothy Hawes, was a dangerous place, and the remains of hundreds of Salem men molder unmarked in graves around the globe. Even in the familiar waters of the Atlantic and Caribbean, death was a part of the ebb and flow of maritime life, shaping the consciousness of communities such as Salem. When the Salem brigantine *Nabby* arrived in Surinam on January 28, 1808, she had already lost seven men, including her captain, Nathaniel Hathorne (father of the writer) to "yellow-jack."[40] The South China Sea, Endeavor Straits, and the Strait of Malacca posed greater threats still. The final voyage of William Augustus Rogers, to Batavia in the *Trexel*, ended not in Salem but in Bangkok when he was washed from a houseboat during a gale.[41] As Harriet Low neared Batavia in the *Sumatra*, she noted in her journal for Wednesday, August 26, 1829, "what a graveyard it has been, and still is, for foreigners."[42]

For tracing the dimensions of national character for American readers, maritime writers found that pirates were especially useful foils. "Algierine" or Malay, "faithless Mahomet" or French privateer, buccaneers played several roles in maritime literature. They functioned as a political threat to the free navigation of the seas and a cultural threat to national honor. The act of piracy violated the values that linked national character and commercial culture, traits such as honesty, trust, openness, and candor. Consequently, pirates were ever a menacing presence in the literature. Reflecting common concerns, William Haswell recorded his anxiety aboard the *Lydia* in 1801: "Now having to pass through dangerous straits, we went to work to make boarding nettings, and to get our arms in the best order, but had we been attacked, we should have been taken with ease. The pirates are numerous in their prows and we have but eleven in number." Captain Banard fretted about the safety of his vessel in Sambongue anchorage, recording, "put the ship into the highest state of defence possible, got all the boarding nettings up, and the arms loaded and kept a sea watch. This night a Spanish launch, as it proved to be afterwards, attempted to come on board, but we fired at it and ordered it to keep off."[43]

The threat of piracy was real. In the Philippine journal of Nathaniel Bowditch, for instance, an entry for October 5, 1796, reports, "Capt. John Gibaut in returning from China through the Straits of Malacca for Bengal was attacked by a number of Prows. . . . William Brown likewise was attacked there. . . . [The pirates] have been known to attack vessels even in Manilla Bay."[44] Such reports made their way into the newspapers of the Atlantic coast. A number of papers re-told the story of the ill-fated voyage of the *Essex* to Mocha:

> News is received here that Captain Joseph Orne in the ship *Essex* had ar-rived at Mocha, with $60,000 to purchase coffee, and that Mahomet Ikle, commander of an armed ship, persuaded him to trade at Hadidido, and to take on board 30 of his Arabs to help navigate her thither while his vessel kept her company; that on the approach of night, and at a con-certed signal, the Arabs attacked the crew of the *Essex,* and Ikle laid his ship alongside, and that the result was the slaughter of Captain Orne, and all his men, except a Dutch boy named John Hermann Poll. The *Essex* was plundered and burnt. The headless corpse of Capt. Orne and the mu-tilated remains of a merchant floated on shore and were decently buried. It was soon after ascertained that the faithless Mahomet was a notorious pirate of that country. He kept the lad whose life he had spared, as a slave until 1812, when Death kindly freed him from his cruel bondage.[45]

As trust was essential to overseas enterprise, treachery was inimical to com-merce. Corruption, deceit, or treachery compromised commercial voyages to the East and endangered the lives of their crews. In the early republic, when business was considered a personal endeavor and character mattered greatly, Americans were acutely sensitive to bad conduct. The lens of commerce shaped how they per-ceived and depicted the peoples they encountered in the East, and what they per-ceived as corrupt behavior in the "ordinary" practice of business figured promi-nently in their depictions. Native custom and governmental regulation could be as confounding as navigating the Endeavor Straits, as chiefs, headmen, rajahs, viceroys, commanders, and mandarins displayed a myriad of unnerving ways to add time and cost to a voyage. George Cleveland, clerk aboard the *Margaret,* had to mediate through a particularly irritating set of intermediaries in Nagasaki Har-bor in 1801. He described business dealings in Japan "a great affair" and complained that "it was a number of days before the whole was taken away. No person in this country (who has not traded with people who have so little intercourse with the world) can have an idea of the trouble we had in delivering this little invoice which would not have been an hour's work in Salem. We finally, after a great trial of our patience, finished delivering goods, and articles that did not come up to the pat-tern were taken at diminished prices."[46] Salem's captains and supercargoes, experi-encing "imposition to perfection," conveyed their outrage with what they per-ceived as the corrupt practices of the East. After dabbling in the China Trade, some merchants found the labyrinth of regulation so contrary to their ideals of com-mercial virtue that they moved to other waters. Even the unparalleled mercantile genius, Elias Hasket Derby of Salem, found the China Trade more trouble than it was worth. The log of Thomas Ward, captaining the *Minerva* from Salem to Canton in 1809, contributed a petulant view to his colleagues. After sounding Whampoa anchorage, he warned, "You will now or before perhaps have some applications for the birth of ship Comprador, and they are all without exception a set of cheats, & this they will vouch for, if you should doubt their rascality. . . . They will expect a Cumshaw of 260 or 280 dollars for the Liberty of cheating you out of twice that sum, & that too with your consent as it were, as you are knowing to the fact, without having the power to prevent it." Middlemen such as the Hong merchant Consuiqua, for instance, epitomized the vices of the East; Ward described him as "Rich—roguish—insinuating—polite—sends some excellent cargoes—some bad Cargoes—not attentive enough to business and a man with whom you cannot talk with safety, as he will promise everything & perform what he pleases—not to be seen always." Thus, "having immersed the Ship in roguery," the Salem supercargo who emerged in the subtext of such depictions, in contrast to the "stubborn and unfeeling mandarin," became a paragon of both commerce and virtue.[47] We can imagine ourselves slouched in one of the many coffeehouses that favored merchants or at the Salem Athenaeum, overhearing the advice merchant Dudley Pickman would give to Capt. Benjamin Shreve, about to cast off in the *New Hazard* in 1815: "Hooqua does business for [the] Perkins house, [and is] considered very rich, close, to be depended on. . . . I should prefer him to any of those now in the Hong who were there when I was at Canton. Ponqua [is] too poor to deal with. Chunqua Mr Ingersoll [thinks is] 'a big Rogue' [and] I should have nothing to do with him. Conseequa [is] a very uncertain man; I should not have perfect confidence in him, [though] some of the Philadelphians are very fond of him."[48]

In the early republic, the worldly man of commerce not only did business with a variety of people; he might also shape the public consciousness toward a clearer appreciation for other cultures. Describing the East thus, mariners represented themselves as discerning, sophisticated, and cosmopolitan—in brief, as citizens of the world. And, as citizens of the world, their literary appraisals of the "other" brought to the community of American readers a measure of tolerance that could be disarming. With its Chinese motifs in architecture, its kimono-clad ladies riding in lacquered palanquins, its spice-scented coffeehouses, its collection of Samoan war clubs, hookah pipes, and hubble-bubbles housed in athenaeum and marine society, China Trade Salem was an oasis of cosmopolitan experience and attitude in provincial America.

Against the worldly warnings about Eastern corruption one heard in the streets of Salem, there was also a remarkable measure of tolerance and even appreciation for the peoples of the Pacific, particularly in the journals of the first generations of expatriate Salemites. One reads a sense of noble simplicity in the mundane ways of everyday life on the island of Guam, as in Capt. William Haswell's

1801 visit on the island of Guam, we have the following detailed observations: "The houses are small, but very cleanly, and are built of a kind of basket work, with cocoanut leaves and are about twelve feet from the ground. Their furniture consists of two or three hammocks of net work, and the same number of mats, a chest, one frying pan, a large copper pan, and a few earthen jars. Near their houses is a large row of wicker baskets in piles six feet high for their fowls to lay their eggs and set in, the breed of which they are very careful to preserve. The fire place is under a small shed near the house to shelter it from the rain. Their food is chiefly shell fish and plaintains, cocoanuts and a kind of small potatoes which they dry and make flour of, and it makes good bread when new."⁴⁹

Encountering "many canoes of a singular construction filled with natives nearly naked [as they] came off to trade away their fruit," the *Tartar's* supercargo, William Augustus Rogers, found the native people "honest, intelligent and good natured,"⁵⁰ and John Crowninshield "found the people very civil & accomodating & they behaved much better than I had any idea of & in fact as well as any people I ever was amongst. Making proper allowance for the manners & customs."⁵¹ John Crowninshield's reflections on his voyage to Sumatra in 1801 contributed a different view of the East to early American readers. His search for pepper in the *America III* was a commercial success. As portrayed in his log, it was also a demythologizing experience. Instead of the stubborn mandarins and treacherous pirates that Captain Crowninshield expected to find, the Salem mariner represented Eastern peoples as behaving "with the greatest attention & I may say politeness."⁵²

Much of this literature sought to demystify the East. If one were to do business "eastward of Good Hope," one had to quash its myths, understand its realities, and, in particular, render its people humane and civil. The captains and factors who freighted their experiences into the public sphere made the peoples of the East compatible with the commercial civility of the Atlantic community of trading nations. In this vein, the *Salem Gazette* commended the cosmopolitan nature of life aboard the East Indiamen, explaining, "It is no unpleasing sight to see the crew of this ship, Chinese, Malays, Japanese, and Moors, with a few Europeans, all habited according to the different countries to which they belong, and employed together as brethren; it is thus commerce binds, and unites all the nations of the globe with a golden chain."⁵³ Yet, for every Consuiqua, there was a Houqua, whom Capt. Thomas Ward, sailing the *Minerva* out of Salem in 1809, described as "very rich, sends good cargoes & [is] just in all his dealings, in short is a man of honour and veracity. . . . Houqua is rather dear, loves flattery & can be coaxed."⁵⁴ Captain Shreve found Eshing, a Canton silk merchant, very dependable, and Synchong, the porcelain merchant, the "dearest," and also a first-rate business associate.⁵⁵ The fastidious Miss Low found it possible to gain a new respect even for her expatriate British cousins in Macao. Following a visit from Lady Claridge, she admitted, "I have altered my opinion of the English entirely.

We have found none stiff, as we anticipated; on the contrary, affable, polite, and pleasant."[56]

Some maritime writers couched their representations of the exotic "other" as commanding pleas for tolerance. John Crowninshield was one who felt particularly outraged by lurid fables of treachery reported in many travelogues. Clearly writing for the public sphere, he used the voyage of *America III* to Sumatra in 1801 to dash the stereotypes to which early American readers were increasingly being exposed. Captain Crowninshield's log gave Americans a view of Sumatrans who were "remarkable civil to us & behave[d] in every respect with the greatest propriety." Such civility made trade possible. Although Crowninshield was after pepper, he and his crew needed provisions and craved souvenirs, so it was helpful that the Sumatrans "all as we passed treated us with the greatest civility & plenty salams & offering of us any of there little things which they have for sale." In Crowninshield's mind, civility, commerce, and progress went together. The plea for tolerance that completes the Sumatran leg of his log demonstrates further the interconnectedness of this culture of commerce. As *America III*'s log stated,

> [I]n the name of common sence where is the place we could have loaded so large a ship (650 tons) as ours so soon as we did labouring under so many disadvantages. no platform layed nor bulk heads up. a large quantity of ballest all our provisions & water casks in lower hold & all our water to fill. . . . I may venture to say that there is no part of America nor in no port I was ever in before where we could have made such dispatch— this ought to confirm to any reasonable person that these people, these Mallays (worse than Algerians) are quite different people from what we have been taught to beleave them to be—& as to port charges not one dollar except for poltry &c—I can say with propriety it is the best place I ever was in for a Merchant. we must beleave when we are convinced & must be convinced when the thing is demonstrated by facts unquestionable.

For citizens of the world like Captain Crowninshield, for whom reputation was as important as capital in enterprise, the myth of Sumatran piracy was both undeserved and unjust. Furthermore, in the mind of the Yankee trader, such characterizations defied commercial logic. As his 1809 log insisted, "representing them as worse than savages robbing vessels of there property. massacring the crews &c &c. how inconsistent with reason & common sence."[57]

Mythological Salem?

Could Dorothy Hawes have told tales that Harriet Low never knew? As Salem's eastern star was eclipsed by the smoke of inland, western manufactory and locomotive, the grandchildren of overseas mariners wanted to believe in the lost glory of their community. They told each other and themselves how Salem vessels had been so familiar in foreign harbors that the Spice Islands had become known as the Salem East Indies, and throughout the East, the name of their city had became a synonym for the entire country. Later historians claimed to find in the archives of the Peabody Essex Museum "an engaging map, likely drawn by a Chinese artist about 1800, which depicts the United States from the Atlantic to the Mississippi as 'SALEM,' and of a map held by native merchant of Calcutta, noting only two names—Salem stretched across the map and Boston as a dot."[58] Yet, today, these significant historical documents cannot be located. Nor can support be found for other yarns that represent Salem as citizen of the world.

In our histories, in our national consciousness, China Trade Salem came to stand for a set of distinctly American values. Represented as adventurous and cosmopolitan, Salem's voyagers were seagoing paladins, striking back against the pirates of the Pacific and Indian Oceans and the Arabian Sea. In newspaper reports of autumn 1806, Capt. William Story and the crew of the *Marquis de Sumereulas* were national heroes. Surprised and overpowered by Malay proas (canoes) off Sumatra, the crew of the *Marquis* were driven back into the ship's hold to await their execution. Defiantly, readers were told, they "rallied and another effort was about to be made. The injunction was given [by their captain] that if they did not succeed, and the Malays took possession of the ship, a match should be applied to the magazine to blow her up." But "the natives had retreated, which was immediately discovered by the crew who got on deck with the expectation of a deadly contest."[59] This story was repeated again and again in tavern talk and coffeehouse conversations. Around dining room tables, Salem children also regaled grandchildren with the July 1799 account that Hasket Derby sent his father, the renowned Salem merchant Elias Hasket Derby. Young Derby was caught in the confused tumult of the Napoleonic Wars that made American vessels targets of both sides. When, on "July 28th in the afternoon we found ourselves approaching a fleet of upwards of fifty sail," Hasket made a daring decision: "We run directly for their centre . . . to avoid any apprehension of a want of confidence." Memories like this lingered, and long after Napoleon was dead, Salem stood as a land of courageous and liberty-loving people. As late as 1855, the *Salem Evening Journal* was retelling an 1808 story in which the crew of the bark *Active,* of Salem, had been hauled aboard a British letter-of-marque vessel, but the crew overpowered their captors, and all returned to Salem.[60]

Today, Salem celebrates its maritime past. The replica 1797 *Friendship* trails its cable between Derby and Central wharves, the red-bricked Daniel Low building sits proudly alongside the 1803 Asiatic Bank, a short stroll from the granite hall of the 1799 East India Marine Society, and Hawthorne's 1819 customhouse and Derby's 1760 mansion draw busloads of tourists. Local families trace their lines back to the Pickmans and Goodhues and Lows, and one greets the descendants of Ingersolls and Bowditches along cobbled walks of Pickman and Rogers Streets, before homes that housed Crowninshields, Storys, and Wards. How do we reconcile the unrecoverable maps and suspect yarns with a true history of this place? Dorothy Hawes suggested a way. Four hundred journals and ships' logs still rest, almost lovingly preserved, in the Phillips Library of what was once the East India Society. The memories they hold transcend the mythology of Salem. They have become the vessels that ply the waters between Salem and Bombay or Canton, and the reader is their cargo.

Expatriate testimonies, incorporating the memories and longing of those away from home, can carry the reader to fresh perspectives on the study of *place*. As Salemites transferred their lives to passages in India, in China, in Sumatra, the memories they imported transformed Salem into a place of cosmopolitan sensibility and the American public sphere into a domain of global dimensions. The journals of Capt. Dudley Pickman and Miss Harriet Low plotted a course of imbricated orientalism that was traveled soon after by a new generation of American writers. Hawthorne captured the universalist sense of the times while sojourning at Arezzo, Italy, in 1858, tracing his inspiration to the Salem town pump, from whose waters "a rill gushed forth that meandered as far as England, as far as India, besides tasting pleasantly in every town and village in our country."[61] In strikingly similar language, Thoreau, earlier and more expansively, expressed the emergent global sensibility of this age in *Walden:* "Thus it appears that the sweltering inhabitants of . . . Madras and Bombay and Calcutta, drink at my well. In the morning I bathe my intellect in the stupendous and cosmogonal philosophy of the Bhagavat-Geeta. . . . I lay down the book and go to my well for water, and lo! There I meet the servant of the Brahmin . . . and our buckets as it were grate together in the same well. The pure Walden water is mingled with the sacred water of the Ganges."[62] Thoreau, like Hawthorne, understood that Americans were drinking at Salem's well. Later generations of American writers, artists, collectors, and historians would follow them there. American culture drinks at Salem's well still.

Notes

I wish to thank colleagues Nancy Lusignan Schultz, Robert Booth, and Matthew McKenzie and research assistant LaGina Austin for their comments on and contributions to this essay.

1. Dorothy Schurman Hawes, "To the Farthest Gulf. Outline of the Old China Trade," *Essex Institute Historical Collection* 77, no. 2 (April 1941): 101–42 and 77, no. 3 (July 1941): 218–53. Her articles were later brought together and republished as *To the Farthest Gulf: The Story of the American China Trade* (Ipswich, Mass.: Ipswich Press, 1990).

2. This was a time when one had to be nominated for membership to the National Geographic Society.

3. Salem was incorporated as a city in 1836. Her famous seal depicts an Asian man, holding a parasol, against a setting of palm trees and a merchant vessel, encompassed by the motto "To the farthest ports of the rich East."

4. Dirk Jan Struik, *Yankee Science in the Making* (New York: Collier Books, 1962), 106.

5. Robert G. Albion et al., *New England and the Sea* (Middletown, Conn.: Wesleyan University Press, 1972), 60.

6. James Duncan Phillips, *Pepper and Pirates: Adventures in the Sumatra Pepper Trade of Salem* (Boston: Houghton Mifflin, 1949), xi.

7. During the 1786–1787 season, the five American vessels lying to at Canton included the *Experiment,* the *Empress of China,* and the *Hope* of New York, the *Canton* of Philadelphia, and the *Grand Turk* of Salem. The *Turk,* sent to the East by the eminent merchant Elias Hasket Derby, was the first Massachusetts vessel to sail to Asian waters. Hawes, 132.

8. Robert E. Peabody, *The Log of the Grand Turks* (Boston: Houghton Mifflin, 1926), 48.

9. Ralph D. Paine, *The Ships and Sailors of Old Salem* (Boston: Charles E. Lauriat, 1924), 150, 278, 148.

10. Capt. John White, *Franklin,* c. 1819, cited in Charles E. Trow, *The Old Shipmasters of Salem* (New York: G. P. Putnam's Sons, 1905), 221.

11. Cited in Susan S. Bean, *Yankee India: American Commercial and Cultural Encounters with India in the Age of Sail, 1784–1860* (Salem, Mass.: Peabody Essex Museum, 2001), 107, 117.

12. Paine, 144–45.

13. Howard Corning, ed., "John Crowninshield in the *America III,* at Sumatra, 1801," *Essex Institute Historical Collections* 80, no. 16 (1944): 355.

14. Capt. Dudley Pickman, *Derby,* 1803, cited in Bean, 109.

15. William B. Ardiff, "The Ship *Putnam,*" *Essex Institute Historical Collections* 96, no. 25 (1960): 116–17.

16. Harriet Low, Journal, October 7, 1829, Phillips Library, Peabody Essex Museum, Salem, Massachusetts.

17. Paine, 149.

18. Ardiff, 119–20.

19. Capt. Dudley Pickman, *Belisarius,* 1799–1800, cited in Bean, 102. A country vessel was a private merchantman that plied the South Seas, often carrying opium between India and China.

20. Capt. William Rogers, September 10, 1817, cited in Bean, 143.

21. Low, Journal, May 24, 1829; May 31, 1829.

22. Low, Journal, June 7, 1829; October 12, 1829.

23. Rogers, September 10, 1817, cited in Bean, 143–44.

24. Rogers, cited in Bean, 144.

25. Low, Journal, October 10, 1829.

26. Rogers, 1817–1818, cited in Bean, 137.

27. Today, in the Phillips Library of the Peabody Essex Museum in Salem, we can find over four hundred of these records and an assortment of newspapers.

28. Pickman, 1803, cited in Bean, 110–11.

29. *Salem Mercury,* July 31, 1787. Pickman's journal does not elaborate on the "extraordinary" nature of Indian marriage rituals.

30. Pickman, 1803, cited in Bean, 117.

31. Pickman, 1803, cited in Bean, 110–11.

32. *Salem Mercury,* February 19, 1788.

33. *Salem Gazette,* May 16, 1797.

34. Pickman, 1803, cited in Bean, 110.

35. Rogers, 1817–1818, cited in Bean, 145.

36. *Salem Gazette,* August 28, 1792.

37. Dudley Pickman to Capt. Benjamin Shreve, *New Hazard,* Salem, 1815, cited in Carl L. Crossman, *The Decorative Arts of the China Trade: Paintings, Furnishings, and Exotic Curiosities* (Woodbridge, England: Antique Collectors' Club, 1997), 29–30.

38. Pickman, cited in Bean, 111–12.

39. Low, Journal, August 26, 1829; September 30, 1829; September 7–8, 1829.

40. Hubert H. Hoeltje, "Captain Nathaniel Hathorne: Father of the Famous Salem Novelist," *Essex Institute Historical Collections* 89, no. 21 (1953): 352–53. "Yellow-jack" was the maritime term for yellow fever.

41. Bean, 141.

42. Low, Journal, August 26, 1829.

43. Quotation from Paine, 242–43.

44. Nathaniel Bowditch, *Early American-Philippine Trade: The Journal of Nathaniel Bowditch in Manila, 1796,* ed. Thomas R. McHale and Mary C. McHale, Monograph no. 2 (New Haven: Yale University Southeast Asia Series, 1962), 38–39.

45. Joseph B. Felt, *Annals of Salem,* 1827, cited in Paine, 184–85.

46. Cited in Paine, 226.

47. Walter Muir Whitehill, ed., "Remarks on the Canton Trade and the Manner of Transacting Business," *Essex Institute Historical Collections* 73, no. 4 (1937): 305–7.

48. Dudley Pickman to Capt. Benjamin Shreve, *New Hazard,* Salem, 1815, cited in Crossman, 30.

49. William Haswell journal, *Lydia,* 1801, cited in Paine, 247.

50. Rogers, 1817–1818, cited in Bean, 144.

51. Corning, 155.

52. Corning, 150.

53. *Salem Gazette,* August 30, 1785.

54. Whitehill, 307.

55. Crossman, 29.

56. Low, Journal, October 15, 1829.

57. Corning, 144, 150, 155. It would seem that most mariners did not intend to publish their ships' logs, composed as they are of little more than identification of position and comments on weather and climate. A few logs, however, contain enough philosophical and editorial comment that the historian may assume the writer intended these materials to provide a basis for publication or oration.

58. David L. Ferguson, *Cleopatra's Barge: The Crowninshield Story* (Boston: Little Brown, 1976), 9; Charles E. Trow, *The Old Shipmasters of Salem* (New York: G. P. Putnam's Sons, 1905),

45. Ferguson writes that the map was intended as an indispensable guide for Asians who were interested in American affairs.

59. Felt's *Annals,* cited in Paine, 185.

60. Cited in Paine, 159, 186.

61. Quoted in Luther S. Luedtke, *Nathaniel Hawthorne and the Romance of the Orient* (Bloomington: Indiana University Press, 1989), xvi.

62. Quoted in Arthur Christy, *The Orient in American Transcendentalism: A Study of Emerson, Thoreau, and Alcott* (New York: Octagon, 1969), 23–24.

Classroom chair. Photo by Kim Mimnaugh.

Chapter Six

Salem as the Nation's Schoolhouse

REBECCA R. NOEL

> *As the two children grew apace,*
> *it behoved their strange guardian to take some thought*
> *for their education. So far as little Elsie was concerned, however, he seemed*
> *utterly indifferent to her having any instruction, having imbibed no modern ideas re-*
> *specting feminine capacities and privileges, but regarding woman, whether in the bud or*
> *blossom, as the plaything of man's idler moments; the helpmate, but in a humble capac-*
> *ity, of his daily life. He sometimes bade her go to the kitchen and take lessons of crusty*
> *Hannah, in breadmaking, sweeping, dusting, washing, the coarser needlework, and such*
> *other things as she would require to know, when she came to be a woman; but carelessly*
> *allowed her to gather up the crumbs of such instruction as he bestowed on her playmate,*
> *Ned, and thus learn to read, write, and cypher—which, to say the truth, in the*
> *way of scholarship, was about as far as little Elsie cared to go.*

—Nathaniel Hawthorne, *Doctor Grimshawe's Secret*

 HEN education in Salem is considered through the theme of place, it is clear that the town itself was a school. As in other English colonial towns, early settlers learned by necessity to alter European techniques for farming and gardening, fishing and navigation, and building and manufacturing. Yet life in Salem remained uncommonly instructive even compared to nearby settlements. The town's emergent cosmopolitan nature enriched Salem childhoods with an informal education that was global in scope. Learning took place on the lanes and wharves, in cent shops and curiosity-filled parlors. Salem's boys and girls read clouds, stars, tide pools, and ships' flags at a glance; spoke a patois of Eastern terms such as *chow* and *chop, bandana* and *bazaar;* met people of all colors and longitudes in the streets; familiarly handled Chinese silks and Sumatran spices; and munched on the town's famous maritime-themed candies, Black Jacks and Gibraltars. Outside any schoolhouse, Salem offered lively lessons to stimulate the mind.

The successful seaport also developed an unusual class structure. A near aristocracy of wealthy sea captains and merchants wedged in a small town center meant that Salem's capital was not tied up in land. Early artisan, finance, and retail sectors allowed for broader economic strength than in Marblehead or Gloucester. Salem arrived later at large-scale manufacturing than neighboring Lynn, but it always hosted an underclass of transient mariners, odd-jobbers, and servants, white and black.[1] These conditions—great available wealth but a society widely divided in class—could have helped or hindered education in Salem. Over time, they did both. While Salem offered unique opportunities for education outside the classroom, its first two centuries of formal education, up to about 1860, richly express how location interacts with social institutions—in this case, how the town of Salem shaped its schools and the schools shaped the town.

Eager Beginnings

Founded in 1629 by religious purists who insisted on reading and interpreting the Bible their own way, Massachusetts is deeply imbued with educational ambition. The speedy planting of the future nation's first college (Harvard, 1636) shows this sense of urgency. A 1642 law required every town's selectmen to be vigilant against the "'barbarism'" of an unlettered child. On pain of a £5 fine, a 1647 law required towns of fifty households to hire a reading and writing teacher—going beyond the basic literacy handled by the family—while towns like Salem of at least one hundred households had to hire a Latin grammar master to prepare boys for the college at Cambridge.[2]

Salem formed a leading edge of educational enthusiasm even in Massachusetts. Sharing the spirit of the colony's law, Salem anticipated it: in 1637, the Reverend John Fisk began the town's Latin or "Grammar" School. When Colonel Endicott moved for a town meeting in 1641 to discuss a "free" school—meaning that indigent students need not pay the teacher's "rate"—Salem became the first town in Massachusetts, and the second in the future United States, to take official steps toward free schooling.[3] With its unusual year-round calendar, the town also secured rare teacher retention. Except for one year, two successive masters handled the Grammar School from 1640 to 1698. Salem's financial assets, municipal and personal, aided the school as well. Beginning about 1677, Salem dedicated the income from rent of common lands on Baker's Island and the Misery Islands to the use of the school. The Beverly and Marblehead ferry concessions and rents of town land at Ryall Side, the Burying Point, and elsewhere were later added to the school revenues. Moreover, five members of the Brown family gave and bequeathed several hundred pounds from 1678 to 1719. As intended, the town applied the interest from this endowment to help pay the schoolmaster, ensuring free access for poor lads and a cheaper rate for the rest. Salem's intense commitment to schooling, though forward-looking for its times, also had a stern side. Posted on the meetinghouse in December 1673 were five men's names. The men had failed to ensure their families' literacy, so their children were offered in service to anyone who could supply them with education and a calling. Mixing fluidly with faraway people, ports, and products, and busy at home with high-level finance and trade, Salem strongly valued an educated populace.[4]

By 1700, lower-level schooling had begun to seem necessary, both in town and in outlying areas of then-sprawling Salem. Perhaps those five delinquent householders had too much company. Salem Village (later Danvers), Ryall Side (now part of Beverly), the "Middle Precinct" (now in Peabody), and Will Hill (now Middleton), three to eight road miles from Salem's wharves, began receiving town funds for lower-level schooling. After a fitful start, an "English" school—covering reading, writing, and ciphering somewhat above the primary level—opened in the center of town in 1712, downstairs from the room where the witches were tried. In 1729, town moderator Samuel Brown made a groundbreaking three-level donation: £120 to the Grammar School, £60 to the English School, and £60 to endow a new half-year "woman's school," a coeducational primary school with a female teacher.[5]

Salem's school system by 1730 was, structurally speaking, at least a century ahead of its time. The Latin or Grammar School had a long history, and the central English School was permanently established. In having a long school calendar, in providing multilevel schooling, and in hiring women to handle primary education, the town already boasted developments urged by educational reformers in nineteenth-century New England. But those reformers, deeply concerned about underfunded, lower-level "district" schools, would quickly have spotted the hierarchy that kept the rural schools more primary in level. Judging from the future careers of some of their teachers, the rural schools may have achieved some high-end work—for as long as those teachers stayed. Widow Catherine Daland taught reliably in the Village and the Middle Precinct for £5 a year. Capable men facing that salary left for posts as a Latin master earning £70–£90 annually or as an in-town English master earning £10–£30. The central part of town also discovered the economy of paying women to deliver primary schooling and of using town funds to send poor children to female-taught private schools.[6]

Several women served as teachers in the eighteenth century, both public and private. In addition to Daland, widow Abigail Fowler taught for fifty years beginning around 1720, and others were active before 1770. The town's wealth and its high proportion of widows—perhaps a quarter of the adult female population in 1785—churned out a steady supply of literate women seeking employment. Early women teachers probably gained their educations in home settings, but the early 1770s saw a surge in provisions for formal female education. In 1773, the English School assistant advertised that he would teach young ladies to write and cipher at 11 A.M. and 5 P.M., when the boys were away, an arrangement that became widespread later in the eighteenth century. Salem had again jumped into the vanguard, if the hourlong lessons can be considered progress. But girls did not have only those narrow chances for schooling in 1770s Salem. Five individuals opened private schools in those years, for girls, boys, and both.[7]

The Challenge to Public Education: The Rise of Private Schools

Perhaps no one realized at the time that these for-profit teachers were opening a new era as well. Beginning around 1770, and for the next seven decades, small private schools sprouted all over town. Salem never produced a celebrated academy with a grand building, such as those found in Andover and elsewhere. Most Salem private schools were one- or two-teacher proprietary institutions, of a few types. Select schools taught by women, also called "dame schools," usually handled primary- and middle-level students, mostly girls. Overlapping with a day-care function, these schools often met in the teacher's kitchen, where her chores punctuated the school day. A few dame (and some male-taught) schools refined academic and aesthetic abilities in older girls. Coeducational private schools run by men, perhaps with female or male assistants, targeted the middle and upper levels, including some college preparatory work for the oldest boys. Men also opened upper-level private schools for boys only, sometimes one-on-one, with college preparation as the major task. A well-born child would progress through a series of such institutions as the schools were outgrown or as the teachers moved on.

Nathaniel Hawthorne's journey through Salem's private schools was typical. At age three and three-quarters, in 1808, he began at a dame school. He changed to a "master's" school when nearly six and moved on to a higher-level establishment after two years. Here he studied geography, literature, and Latin until he was smashed in the foot by a ball. He was too lame to attend school for over a year, although his teacher paid him academic house calls. From early 1815 to spring 1818, records are murky but suggest at least occasional schooling. Hawthorne next briefly and unhappily tried a small boarding school run by a minister in Maine in 1818. Back in Salem, he enrolled in an advanced-level school, whose teacher convinced his family to outfit him for college. Hawthorne accordingly withdrew after eight months to study with a Salem lawyer. A year and a half readied him for Bowdoin College, where he began in September 1821. The writer who later claimed he had successfully malingered because of "a grievous disinclination to go to school," and who even charged that "much of the time, there were no schools within reach," had attended five or six schools and studied privately with at least one teacher.[8]

This differentiated pattern swelled the ranks of private schools. The Reverend William Bentley took regular notice of the syndrome in his insightful four-volume diary, listing the principal establishments and declaring that there were too many dame schools to count. Likewise, Salem chronicler Joseph B. Felt records four new private schools for young ladies, three coeducational schools, and schools for un-specified gender from 1782 to 1800. Felt finds another 29 new private schools open-ing from 1801 to 1806, 12 of these headed by women and intended for female stu-dents, and 75 more—35 of these by and for women—at least advertised between 1806 and 1820. A few featured breathtaking teacher salaries. Jacob Knapp began a private academy for boys in 1803 at an initial salary of $1,200, raised to $2,000 af-ter three years. Several leading families had arranged the school and hired Knapp, making him one of the few private teachers with a guaranteed salary. This com-pensation humbled public school pay: the Grammar master earned $700, the En-glish masters $650, and the female primary teachers $100 per year. Although the nearby Lynn Academy catered only to elite Federalist families, in academy-mad Salem even populist Jeffersonians (including Bentley) favored private schools along with their Federalist rivals. All told, over 80 different private teachers from about 1770 to 1840 are named in select major sources, surely a fraction of the ac-tual total.[9]

Clearly, schooling was an active and lucrative industry in Salem. The School Committee recognized the challenge and tried to keep up. Except that several recent Latin masters turned out to be Tories, the Revolution hardly disrupted schooling in Salem.[10] In the next years, opportunities for public schooling ex-panded. The English School split into three in 1785: the Centre English School, housed in a new building on Court Street (now Washington), with the Latin School on the second floor; an East English School on the Common; and the West English School on Dean Street (now part of Flint). In 1793, the practice of teach-ing girls for bits of the day, part of the year, became the official policy of all three English Schools. (Decades later, two elderly women who had attended the one-hour schools described their education as "picking up the crumbs left by the boys.") Three public coeducational primary schools were established in 1801, a de-velopment in which Salem outpaced Boston by nearly twenty years.[11]

Also in 1801, the Latin School broadened its curriculum to include writing, arithmetic, English grammar, composition, and geography. This expansion rec-ognized the need for a more practical education, which also inspired special navi-gation schools in the evenings—one subsidized by wealthy merchant Elias Has-ket Derby, free for sixty young seamen. In 1807, the town opened the North Fields English School, across the North River, and a primary-level "African school" (dis-cussed below). In 1816 the English schools' curriculum grew to include English grammar and geography, and in 1819 the Grammar School got a new building on Broad Street while residents of the South Fields, across the South River, got an En-glish School of their own. A second English School opened in the eastern part of town in 1822. By then, Salem's fifteen public schools still did not serve older girls or African Americans well. But the overall system was gaining both capacity and complexity, still strikingly ahead of many Massachusetts towns.[12]

Yet competition from private schools remained stiff. Both Felt and Bentley reflected on the trend. In his list of private-school teachers, Felt quietly inserted his own name: he ran a select school in the 1810s. The chronicler's private-school experience seems manifested in his discussion of elite academies. "This enterprise might seem too exclusive for our Republican institutions," he began. He continued, a little defensively, "Still, while it made greater room in the public schools, and, consequently rendered them more useful, it promoted the cause of education and required no more for its undertakers, than they had a right to obtain with their own property." Bentley's thoughts varied. He had taught in public schools before arriving in Salem, and in 1786 he taught the East English School until a replacement was hired for John Watson, who had left to resume teaching privately. Still he confessed to Watson, "Tho' I prefer a private to a public School & would urge all who can afford the former, to endeavor after it, yet so great a majority cannot afford the expence, that I feel myself obliged to declare that I am zealous to establish the liberal institution of a FREE SCHOOL upon the best foundation." Over the last twenty years of his life, Bentley visited the public schools annually as a clergyman, then quarterly for several years as a member of the School Committee; but he also engaged in private tutoring himself. Around 1798, he began commenting frequently on the increase in private schools, at one point attributing the private-school boom to inadequacies in public-school teachers. But in 1807, he was surprised when four private teachers applied for the new post at the planned North Fields English School. He guessed that the contracted salaries of public schools made them appealing, since most private teachers survived on fluctuating tuition.[13]

As Salem's fortunes waned as a result of the 1807 embargo and 1808–1809 nonimportation acts—trade duties collected fell by almost half from one decade to the next—the town slid into the irreversible decline so poignantly depicted by Hawthorne in his preface to *The Scarlet Letter*. Bentley noticed a corresponding downturn in the private-school sector. Knapp's posh academy was closing, and teachers fled the profession. The demise of private academies caused the public-school population to swell. "Most of the private schools are thin & several [private] school houses shut & sold," Bentley reported in 1811. "The whole air of extravagance is gone & the Common [i.e., public] schools are better filled." By 1818, the economic slump had worsened in Salem, so that in Bentley's memory the period around 1810 seemed a time of comparative luxury. At the start of the depression, some families still had ample resources to continue sending their children to the private schools, as Bentley affirmed: "The richest families had private schools." But within a decade, he noted, "The value of money now begins to be felt by the men of the learned profession . . . & they have excited a wish for greater benefits from municipal establishments." Bentley, however, still saw the private schools as playing an important role in setting a higher standard for

Salem's public schools. He concluded in 1819, "These Schools serve to keep up ambition in our public Schools for these are much better as our private schools multiply."[14]

Despite economic struggles, private schools as a group remained healthy enough to continue their dominance over public schools. The town responded partly by making conditions attractive for public-school teachers. Male teachers got generous raises in the 1820s; the Grammar master's salary hit $1,200 in 1824, and the "usher" or first assistant there saw his pay shoot from $600 to $750 to $900 in five years. The timing of these increases was not random. Public- and private-school teachers in Salem played a dizzying game of musical chairs in these years, swapping jobs and opening their own schools with great rapidity. With all these defections, it is not surprising that the Salem School Committee used pay raises to try to retain its schoolmasters. The Grammar School usher, whose salary had zoomed up, nonetheless left to become the principal of a new boys' high school in 1827—and then went private in 1830 after all. That usher was Henry Kemble Oliver, an important Salem teacher for several decades. Oliver served on the School Committee in the 1840s and made important contributions to public education among many other public activities. Even with his clear commitment to public education, Oliver ran a private school for girls on Federal Street from 1830 to 1848. A dedication to public schools was not yet necessary to prove civic-mindedness in Salem, even for an involved citizen like Oliver.[15]

Salem officials worked valiantly to maintain the town's place as a leader of educational innovation in Massachusetts, keeping itself abreast or ahead of state developments. In 1827, the School Committee obeyed a new state law directing larger towns to open a high school. This law replaced the 1647 statute requiring a Latin grammar school. Now municipalities of over four thousand inhabitants had to hire a schoolmaster to teach history, rhetoric, logic, Latin, and Greek, in addition to the broadened array of lower studies also mandated for smaller towns. In its rapid compliance with the 1827 law, Salem again stood out. Nine other Essex County communities met the threshold for a high school, but only Newburyport, in 1831, joined Salem in doing so at first. Statewide, only three towns had met their requirement to establish a high school for ten months of each year by 1830: Salem, Worcester, and Boston. So much did towns lag that the law was softened repeatedly over the next few years, whereupon some newly complying towns promptly shut their high schools. Though Salem's new high school made it lawful to close the Latin School, both endured, a testimonial to the significant place of education in Salem.[16]

And there was more school making afoot in 1827 Salem. The School Committee created two female high schools at the same time as it founded the high school for boys. This innovation relieved the English schoolmasters of the uncompensated burden of teaching girls part-time, and, like the new boys' high school, it met the competitive challenge posed by the many private schools in town. Certainly there was a demand for advanced education for girls, or none would have trudged to the English schools for one-hour sessions. An anonymous grumbler wrote in the *Salem Register* that public educational offerings for Salem's girls were among the weakest in the state. Not coincidentally, among higher-level private schools, four-fifths of the students, perhaps eight hundred, were girls. The two new girls' "high schools" admitted students age nine and up—the age of admission was twelve for the boys' high school—and the course of study was only two years long. The schoolmasters there were paid $500 per year, half of what Oliver earned at the new boys' high school. Still, it was an impressive start and decades ahead of public secondary education for girls in most other towns.[17]

One more change arrived early in Salem. In 1829, the School Committee banned corporal punishment at the high schools and the Latin School. Students from the years preceding the ban recalled rampant floggings. Master Parker at the Latin School "scorned the ferule, relying on the cowhide ever active in his experienced hands." At the North Fields English School (not subject to the ban), Master Dodge resorted to corporal punishment daily, as students of the 1820s later claimed. For infractions from whispering during prayers to failing at lessons, the corpulent Dodge plied his wood ferule on the palms and his "red dragoon," a nickname for a cowhide, on the legs and back. Seeking variety, he would tie unruly students together by quill strings, force them to hold up his heavy legs as he reclined in his armchair, and lock them in his own basement over lunchtime (where they raided his cake and fruit supply). Often he drew chalk circles on the floor, giving students the option of a flogging or licking up a circle. One student who balked at this choice of lickings reported that Dodge "knocked me to the floor, and seizing me by the flax on my head, jammed my face repeatedly into the [chalk] ring, and then kicked me under one of the benches, where I lay until the school was dismissed and the teacher had taken his departure." A year after the ban was imposed, then Latin master Thomas Eames was fired over it. Educational reformer Elizabeth Palmer Peabody remembered her brothers describing Eames as "a most severe master, flogging for mistakes in recitations." As Felt gently explained, "Mr. Eames closes his connection with the Latin School. He did not think, as the committee did, about the order for the exclusion of corporal punishment."[18]

Private schools imposed corporal punishment too. In 1808, teacher Benjamin Tappan beat a student so badly one day that a doctor had to be called. Although the boy remained in the school, the family was only partly successful in keeping the incident quiet. Even a Quaker schoolmaster, John Southwick, flogged occasionally, and hard. Susannah Babbidge taught and disciplined young children for fifty years, reaching for a long switch when she grew too large to chase her charges. Perhaps by trying to eradicate floggings from the public schools, the School Committee was seeking another competitive advantage. Outside of Salem, corporal punishment persisted in schools for decades longer, past Horace Mann's confrontation with Boston's public schoolmasters over flogging in the 1840s. Salemites from captains to cabin boys knew, too, that flogging on ships was common discipline; indeed, it survived the 1850 congressional ban.[19]

By 1830 Salem's race between public and private schools was in full cry. It took another dozen years for the public schools to gain the edge. As of 1834 the number of public schools had risen to nineteen; but three years later, in 1837, there were still seventy private schools in Salem—more than there had been a decade before. Since the new high schools had opened in 1827, private-school enrollment had held steady at just under 1,700, including 1,000 girls at all levels. Over 1,200 students now attended public schools, with only 480 girls. In other words, the number of boys in public and private schools was nearly equal, but the enrollment of girls in private schools was double that of the public schools. Felt discussed this gender pattern in his chronicle. Public schools for boys improved earlier than those for girls, starting from the 1816 English school curriculum expansion. But Felt also thought wealthy families had judged that "where there is a smaller number of pupils, as under private instructors, there will be less contact with faults in principle and deportment." Without needing to say it, Felt implied that moral purity and social refinement mattered more for girls than for boys among Salem's elite.[20]

This common understanding points again to Salem's shared culture around private schooling. Thoughtful reminiscences reflect the customs, the gestures, the hidden objectives, and the perceptions that persisted across the decades. Eleanor Putnam (a pseudonym) penned an especially revealing memoir of her privileged dame school, which was run by two austere spinsters for midsized children. Admission to this exclusive school was generations in the making: "I have reason to believe that I was not accepted without a thorough examination of family documents, and that the scale was finally turned in my favor by the production of an ancestress who was down in the witch records as having testified against some poor old goody or other." Her successful application ensured permanent social status. She sensed that she could even "elope with a grocer, become a spiritualistic medium, or start a woman's bank" once she had the elite credential.[21]

While the curriculum of a dame school varied by level, it always included lessons in socialization. In Putnam's school—which met, as most dame schools did, in the teachers' fancy home—this agenda took a decidedly gendered form: "At recess we [girls] did not go to romp rudely out-of-doors, but amused ourselves in the house with A Ship from Canton and The Genteel Lady, as became well-bred children." But well-bred boys were different. At recess, the ladies instructed the two enrolled boys to holler outside: "Miss Emily seemed to think that boys must go somewhere occasionally to shout, as a whale must come up to blow," she chuckled. But, in fact, "[t]he boys never did shout. I fancy they were too much depressed by the great gentility of everything." Commanded again to act like boys against the restraints of class, "When there had been a fall of moist snow, the boys would sometimes snowball each other in a perfunctory way, being bidden to the sport by Miss Lucy; and on such occasions we of the gentler sex were allowed to go and look upon the stirring sight from the back-chamber window." One of these boys seemed to understand that class ultimately trumped gender. "It was his standing grievance that he went to a private school. He one day confided to me that his cousin, who went to the Broad Street [public] school, had been thrown down in a foot-ball rush, and had had three teeth knocked in. He added that a fellow could have some fun at a public school, but that Miss Witherspoon's was a baby-class." Putnam and her female classmates drank in the teachings of their school. "[Q]uarrels and sharp words seem to have been practically unknown," she concluded. "[W]e were little gentlewomen in school, whatever we may have been out of it."[22]

Like a secret society that appears to avoid, but constantly seeks attention from those not invited, Salem's private schools relied on and reinforced the town's distinctive class structure. Class injunctions at Salem's private schools were seldom written, but often spoken, and enforced by raised eyebrows most of all. Even the common habit of bringing students up a side outdoor staircase—of a showy, elegant house—conveys the cloistered, exclusive, but only superficially secretive nature of these schools. Salem's chroniclers frequently use the term *famous* to describe the top establishments, implying the fanfare and gossip the schools received in their day (and the localized perspective of these upper-class writers). Fame derived too, over time, from the eminent careers of the schools' teachers and graduates.

The teachers earned both class status and income from running a private school. For some female teachers, their own education, their family's illustrious Salem history, their homes, and their polite manners formed a cultural capital that had outlasted their family's fortune. The best way to cash in on this capital was to sell their upper-class polish to the next generation of social peers. Others had retained their family wealth, but had little to do: life expectancy in sea captain families was under fifty for men, over sixty-five for women.[23] Putnam's teachers fit the profile. Their late brother, a ship captain, had stocked their august house with fine seafaring artifacts like "a whale's tooth curiously carved, an ivory-tinted ostrich egg, and a lump of golden amber in which a tiny hapless fly was mysteriously imprisoned," plus "a never quite dissipated odor of sandal-wood and camphor"—museum-quality materials for a captain-class education.[24]

For generations, attending these elite schools was an instinctive, unquestioned part of growing up wealthy in Salem. In 1865, for example, Hawthorne's sister reflected on his lengthy education. "It was much more expensive than it would be to do the same things now, because the public schools were not good then," she explained flatly. "[O]f course he never went to them."[25]

Horace Mann in Salem: The Beginnings of National School Reform

This "of course" symbolized the challenge facing Horace Mann and other public-school reformers in the late 1830s. Mann became the founding secretary of the Massachusetts Board of Education in 1837, charged with improving the public schools. Acquainted with Salem as a city of learning and science, he scheduled it last on his opening tour of the state. Yet to his dismay, he was coolly received in Salem when he spoke on the hot topic of common school reform.

In his private journal, Mann sniped at Salem's apparent lack of interest in public-school progress. "Met the convention; though that is almost too great a word to apply to so small a number of men," he wrote on November 10, 1837. "[O]ne of the poorest conventions I have had." That was a large statement, as Mann had by this time spoken before dozens of school conventions across the state. The secretary had collided with the wall surrounding Salem's private-school culture—the source of Elizabeth Hawthorne's "of course." Salem-reared Mary Peabody Mann, Mann's later wife, reflected on that initial Salem convention in her 1865 biography. "One gentleman, who made one of the first speeches, questioned the expediency of endeavoring to get the educated classes to patronize public schools," she reported. "He spoke, he said, in the interest of mothers who preferred private schools for their children; and he believed the reasons that they had for this would always prevail: they would have their children grow up in intimacies with those of their own class." The speaker's frankness is telling. The private-school idea had become so deeply—and unapologetically—embedded in Salem's class structure that it seemed timeless, inarguable, and natural.[26]

Salem's apparent early foot-dragging on Mann-era reform made it again anomalous. Most communities that challenged Mann's program were economically underdeveloped; towns with larger merchant and professional classes embraced reform with relative ease. Salem had not grasped the dual democratic agenda of common school reform, what Mary Peabody Mann called "the American side of th[e] question." Improved public schools would give the needy classes the tools to succeed, while also softening class differences by helping all types of children know each other. The proof of progress in public education would be when the richest families sent their own children there, especially girls. But with 56 percent of Salem's schoolchildren attending private schools in 1837, and their families shrinking away from the common touch, a new burst of investment in the public schools would not flow forth upon casual request.[27]

Mann's "remarkable address" in 1837 did capture Salem's attention, as evidenced by the invitation that he repeat it at the Lyceum that evening. Over the next few years, he kept up the pressure, heady praise set against hints of shame, and Salem began to come around. Mann was always irked at resistance among those able to help, and he was probably well informed on developments in Salem because of his friendship with the Peabody family, upgraded in 1843 when he and Mary wed. For both of these reasons, he made an example of Salem. Discussions of Salem's schools appeared in his *Annual Reports,* which circulated statewide, nationally, and internationally. He described Salem's running start on his pet project of school building reform in his *Second Annual Report,* prepared in the fall of 1838. "A year ago"—at the time of his disappointing visit—"the schoolhouses in that city were without ventilation, and many of them with such seats as excited vivid ideas of corporal punishment, and almost prompted one to ask the children for what offence they had been committed," he began a little sharply. Then came Salem's reward: public applause. "At an expense of about two thousand dollars, the seats in all the schoolhouses, except one, have been reconstructed, and provisions for ventilation have been made. I am told, that the effect in the quiet, attention and proficiency of the pupils, was immediately manifested." Moreover, at least nine articles about the town appeared in his widely read biweekly *Common School Journal* from 1839 to 1845, where the *Annual Reports* were also reprinted. The attention was so disproportionate that one story was sheepishly entitled "Salem Schools—Again."[28]

Salem's educational prospects brightened further with the election of Stephen C. Phillips as the city's second mayor in late 1838. Phillips made improvement of the public schools a priority, reproaching the private-school problem from the outset. Waxing numerical in his first inaugural address, Phillips pointed out that nineteen public schools now educated 1,565 children at $5.67 per student, while sixty-four private schools handled 1,469 students at $13.47 each. These numbers also showed that the public schools averaged more than three times the size of the private schools. He continued that the number of students in public schools had gradually been increasing, and those in private schools declining, so that the public schools were now filled to overflowing—though no additional principal teachers or teacher salary increases had met the new need. Then, piquing Salem's competitive pride, he compared the city to others in Massachusetts. When public-school expenditures were considered relative to property values rather than to population, property-rich Salem ranked next to last—and the lowest-spending town, Nantucket, had since raced nearly to the top of the list. In 1837–1838, Salem had spent about $0.12 per $100 of valuation, compared to the statewide average of $0.18 and the Essex County average of $0.22. Certain towns left Salem particularly far behind: New Bedford spent $0.36, Charlestown $0.51, Lowell $0.58, and Lynn $0.72—six times what Salem appropriated.[29]

Phillips also marked a contrast between Salem and Boston. While regular attendees of Salem's public and private schools were about equal in number, in Boston public-school students outnumbered private by more than two to one. In Essex County, the ratio of public to private students was higher still, and in Massachusetts as a whole, there were five public-school students for every student in private school. Phillips implied that Salem harbored an undeserved self-satisfaction over its public education provisions. Instead, he jibed, "[o]ur distinction . . . consists in having long pursued the policy of rearing, multiplying, and sub-dividing the private schools, to an unparalleled extent." In short, "we have been struggling against a divided public sentiment, to advance the public schools to the same condition which they have easily attained in other places, where private schools have enjoyed less favor." He finished by suggesting that the "struggle" would be decided that very year.[30]

Between Mann's pressure from above and Phillips's assertive local agitation, Salem surged ahead in public-school appropriations and interest in just a few years, despite tough economic times. Mann published Mayor Phillips's second inaugural address in the *Common School Journal* in 1840. In his introductory paragraph, Mann again congratulated Salem's efforts. The editor gushed, "During the past year, five schoolhouses have been enlarged, altered, or repaired. The salaries of all the male teachers, except one, have been increased. Encouragement is given, that the female teachers shall soon be more liberally compensated for their services." In addition to the zealous Mayor Phillips and "a most intelligent school committee," Mann flattered Salem's elite: "what is most fortunate of all, the most generous and public-spirited people of the city harmonize with them."[31]

In two ways, the advancement of Salem's public schools also depended on women. Salem had realized early that it could institute a system of primary schools using women as teachers, which seemed appropriate to the tender ages of the students and was pleasingly cheap. Like other towns, Salem systematically underpaid its female teachers in the primary schools: those "mistresses" earned about $150 for teaching some seventy students each, with no assistants, when the salaries of the masters, who did have assistants, had just been reduced from $750 to $700. A few female assistants had worked in the English schools since 1835. Now the state was codifying the practice with an 1839 law that required the use of female assistants at the secondary level in schools of over one hundred pupils. Salem duly hired female assistants, at $150 per year, to teach alongside the masters of the grammar and high schools. With undercompensated female teachers, Salem could expand its teaching staff economically at the next levels.[32]

Education for girls was the other crucial frontier. If the public schools could improve enough to convince parents—especially mothers—that even their daughters would thrive there, the private-school market would finally wane. Girls could attend coeducational public primary schools and, since 1827, the two "Female High Schools." The boys' English schools began to admit girls in 1835, when seventeen girls transferred from the West Female High School to the North Fields English School to equalize enrollment. This opening moment of secondary coeducation in Salem (at least for white students) also tacitly conceded that the Female High Schools were really more on the level of the English Schools. By 1841, there was still no true girls' high school, but five available second-level institutions showed stirrings of real competition with the ubiquitous girls' private schools.[33]

Supporters of public schools also hoped that a splashy public celebration would draw genteel students away from the cloistered private sector. Late in 1841 the School Committee voted to unite the two east English schools and the Centre English School into one. To inaugurate the new "Union" (or "East") School on Essex Street, as well as a new coeducational English School on Aborn Street, Salem carried off a gigantic festival on March 1, 1842. The Union School was opened to visitors in the morning, followed by a march of almost two thousand students to Mechanic Hall at 11 A.M. for a public exhibition. Addresses followed at 2 P.M., and Horace Mann spoke to a large and "delighted" audience at 7 P.M. Afternoon speakers included teachers and ministers from Boston, where schools were closed for Salem's event. Salem students composed five songs, everyone's favorite being "[t]he song of the 'little totties,' as mothers call them, from one of the primary schools."

For two hours, Mayor Phillips congratulated the School Committee's work since his accession: "The six grammar [i.e., English] schools, that lacked everything but pupils, were transformed into as many palaces, well arranged, well furnished, well ventilated, and some of them probably unequalled by any in the world." Along with its own extensive coverage, the *Salem Gazette* included an article about the festival from the *Boston Courier*, which hailed Salem (incorrectly) as "the city, that had the honor of establishing the first free school in the world." Mann devoted two long *Common School Journal* articles to the event. He noted that "though Salem had started later in the race, yet she was no longer to be found by looking for her in the rear"—another intentional goad. Reproducing floor plans, curricula, song lyrics, and speakers' addresses, he crowned the Union building "the most perfect schoolhouse in the country."[34]

But Salem, Phillips, and Mann were not done, even for 1842. Mayor Phillips returned his three years of salary, $2,400, for the beautification of the Boys' English High School and the Latin School. Mann covered the developments in his article "Salem Schools—Again," which began, "When shall we have done with the Salem schools? says the reader. We reply, Not while the Salem schools afford examples of excellence and models for imitation, superior to any to be found in any other part of the country." He painstakingly detailed all the Latin and Greek inscriptions and astronomical diagrams on the walls and ceilings, the latter "preferable to the opportunities which are afforded, in some of our old schoolhouses, for studying astronomy through the chinks in a leaky roof." In sum, Mann believed, "Nothing now seems to be wanting to the complete success of the movement in Salem, in favor of Public Schools."[35]

Whether Mann meant this applause sincerely or was deploying it to keep Salem inspired, the attention paid to public schooling in the years 1838–1842 seemed to be working. An 1843 tally showed a remarkable shift. Now 972 private-school students occupied forty-nine private schools while 2,256 children attended the twenty-eight public schools. In other words, about a quarter of the private schools had closed in just four years, and nearly 500 students had been lost to the private sector at the same time as the total enrolled population had grown by 200. And even counting just regular attendees of the public schools, estimated at 2,000, more than twice as many children attended the public as the private schools. In terms of market share, the public-school sector now claimed about 70 percent of the children in school. Although the cost per pupil was still over twice as much in the private sector, the total public-school outlay for salaries and fuel alone, excluding the new buildings and equipment, exceeded all spending for private schools. Just a few years before, the private total had doubled the public. By 1843, spending and enrollments showed that the tide had finally turned in favor of public schools.[36]

The schools continued to advance in the next several years. In 1845, Salem's girls got their long-overdue public high school. Henry Kemble Oliver suggested a ready funding source: hiring women as principals for the existing female secondary schools at $300 per year would free up enough money for a girls' high school with a male principal earning $800. The scheme allowed career advancement, again underpaid, to two female teachers. (Surrounded by female-run academies, Salem's leading men knew that women could head a school.) Oliver's plan also called for a female-headed primary school to be attached to the new high school, similar to a normal school, to train primary and assistant secondary teachers. In the same year, with too many schools for the old geographic naming pattern, all the schools received honorific names. The English schools officially became "Grammar Schools" around the same time. In 1854, the Fisk (or Latin) and Bowditch (or Boys' English High) Schools—located in the same Broad Street building since the latter was founded in 1827—merged under the name Bowditch. Admission requirements and the first-year curriculum were made identical. College-bound Latin students would gain access to a broader education, and classical languages would be available to the practically minded English High School students. Two years later, the Saltonstall School, Salem's new high school for girls, was merged with Bowditch. Called the Salem Classical and High School, or simply the High School, the institution signified the liberalizing of college curricula and the upgrading of education for girls—although declining enrollments at the Bowditch School and dissatisfaction with Saltonstall also led to the union.[37]

Salem continued to host large numbers of private schools for some time, but in many ways the public schools had finally won acceptance. Elizabeth Hawthorne's suggestion that the public schools—or their reputation—later improved finds corroboration in a roster of English High School boys featuring eminent Salem names: Ropes, Felt, Manning, Peabody, Barstow, Skerry, Devereux, Endicott, Rantoul, and Very. Stephen C. Phillips sent three sons there; merchant Jonathan Tucker had experienced the usual march through private schools in his own boyhood, but his three sons attended Boys' English as well. Public schools had permanently eclipsed the private sector by the time of the Civil War. The share of enrolled children attending public schools grew steadily: 76 percent by 1846, 80 percent by 1851, and 82 percent by 1875, although the dame school tradition survived into the late nineteenth century for younger girls. Even top-drawer Eleanor Putnam could see the change. Describing the 1860s, Putnam claimed that "it would have been unutterably vulgar to allow one's children to go to any but a private school"—but then she added, "until they were old enough to enter the higher grades." This qualified endorsement rewarded years of work, publicity, and investment by school reformers (as well as taxpayers). A private-school culture that seemed inflexible and eternal was blending into a widened Salem culture accessible to all residents walking through the front door.[38]

Salem's Integrated Schools

With the barriers between private and public students collapsing, another obstacle remained before the door to equal educational opportunity could swing open for all of Salem's children. In 1844, the city mandated racial integration in all of its public schools, the first municipality in Massachusetts to do so. But this sudden reform was actually decades in the making.

Slavery in Massachusetts petered out just after the Revolution, and many of Salem's African Americans built humble cottages in a section of Salem unflatteringly called "Roast Meat Hill" or "Knocker's Hole." The black population fluctuated from 173 in 1765 to 202 in 1800, down to 167 in 1810, and up to 282 in 1837. Even the latter growth lagged far behind the increase in the white population: whites outnumbered blacks by 40 to 1 in 1765 and nearly 60 to 1 in 1837. The African American community did develop a socioeconomic range, from mariners or shipboard cooks, earning sporadic and below-subsistence wages, to garden or stable hands, housepainters or chimney sweeps, or domestic servants, to respectable barbers or, especially, chefs and caterers, including a few women. An African Society gathered in 1805, providing music for weddings and funerals, celebrating the dates when European countries had abolished slavery, urging black men to vote, and hobnobbing with the also genteel Boston African Society. Well-dressed or destitute, all black Salemites confronted the indignities of northern

Jim Crow. Restricted in where they could walk, sit in church, and be buried, African Americans often found stagecoaches off-limits and railroad cars segregated. In periodic neighborhood raids, whites drove away scores of allegedly unruly blacks.[39]

As soon as the public primary schools opened, a few black children apparently attended along with whites, and black boys, at least, were found at all of the English schools in the 1790s—some near the top of the class. The Reverend William Bentley remarked especially on Titus Augustus at the Centre English School in 1793, "who read, & shew writings equal to any," and Isaac Augustus at the same school in 1794, who "attracted notice by a very decent hand writing," then an attainment of the first import. But no students of color seem to have climbed the Centre School stairs to the Latin School, with its college preparatory mission. White boys visited African American houses near the school at lunch to watch feats of dexterity, hear stories, and tease various residents, perhaps including the Augustus boys' father. And street gangs pitted "Knocker's Hole barbarians" (a white resident's term) against groups of boys from white neighborhoods, suggesting racial tensions that may have persisted in school.[40]

In 1807, a backlash among poor whites managed to oust African American children from the public schools altogether. A crusading white minister, the Reverend Joshua Spaulding, approached School Committeeman Bentley to help establish a primary school exclusively for black children. The committee approved the school and, after hesitating, hired a "mulatto" woman who could read but not write. Chloe Minns was both capable and dedicated, serving from 1807 to 1823. She learned to write within three years and impressed Bentley favorably each time he visited her school. When he officiated at her 1817 marriage to Schuyler Lawrence, a successful caterer, the minister wrote that she "has acquitted herself with great honour, as to her manners & as to her instructions." (He also lauded the now Mrs. Lawrence and her husband as "the first grade of Africans in all our New England towns.") Spaulding held weekly meetings with black parents, and both he and Bentley continued their interest in the school's progress.[41]

During Mrs. Minns Lawrence's tenure, only a primary school was regularly available to the African American population, although the English schools seem to have accepted black boys at times. After she retired, public education for black children seems to have lapsed for nearly three years. During this period, a few children of color apparently attended the primary school near their neighborhood. Then in 1826, a coeducational "writing" or English school under a black male teacher—by gendered definition, then, a school of a higher level—was opened instead. Seen in one light, this school meant that girls of color got a head start on their Caucasian townswomen, who did not have a full-day secondary public school until the Female High Schools opened in 1827. But the African Writing School was no prize. It was now the only official choice for Salem's black children, enrolling as many as seventy students from ages four to twenty-two. Those who had been attending their nearby primary school were cast out; only fifteen students lived near the new school, while the rest walked from all corners of Salem. This unsatisfactory solution lasted only one year, and the city refused a request from black parents to revive the African American primary school. Again a few children made it into public primary or English schools, a few families found the money for private tutors, and the rest went without. Perhaps Salem's white parents were again more fastidious for their girls. The North Fields English School enrolled York Morris, "a colored lad," at some point between 1826 and 1831. But when an African American girl qualified for admission to the East Female High School in May 1830, she was not allowed to enter. Blacks protested, a legal opinion confirmed her right to attend, and she was admitted after a two-month struggle.[42]

This was the uneasy situation encountered by Sarah Parker Remond in the early 1830s. Daughter of upscale caterer John Remond and sister of the future prominent abolitionist Charles Lenox Remond, she later earned her own fame as an abolitionist lecturer and eventually became a physician. As an adult, Sarah Remond recalled her attempts to secure schooling in Salem. "My strongest desire through life has been to be educated," she began. The eight Remond children learned to read and write at home, but the family had few books. The Remonds unsuccessfully sought for their children the same kind of education that had traditionally appealed to genteel Salemites: "Again and again my mother would endeavor to have us placed in some private school, but being colored we were refused." Finally she and two siblings were allowed into a public primary school, where they met superficial courtesy. After quickly learning the primary-school material and passing the examination, the young Remonds entered the girls' high school for their district. They fared well in lessons and comportment and found the students and instructors again mostly tolerant.[43]

Shortly, however, the Remonds learned that the School Committee was considering establishing a separate school for colored children. They may not have known the extent of the opposition. Some 176 whites had signed a petition protesting the presence of black students at East Female High School, avowing, "we have no disposition to injure the colored citizens, we are willing to be taxed for their improvement, but not at the expense of our own or our children's feelings." Young Sarah certainly did know that the city's proposed solution was a throwback. Students of all ages and levels would be lumped together, in a single inconvenient location—reversing two centuries of development in Salem's public-school system. Worse, she felt, "it was publicly branding us with degradation."

John Remond beseeched the School Committee not to go forward with their plan. When bad news came, the children's teacher at least did not minimize the insult. He announced the Remonds' expulsion to the whole class, intentionally provoking sympathy. But it helped little: Sarah was speechless, then "wept bitter tears," then grew furious. The teacher walked the Remonds home to tell their parents that "he was pained by the course taken by the school committee, but added it was owing to the prejudice against color which existed in the community. He also said we were among his best pupils." Writing in 1861, Remond had not forgotten the wound inflicted on that day. "Years have elapsed since this occurred, but the memory of it is as fresh as ever in my mind, and, like the scarlet letter of Hester, is engraved on my heart. We had been expelled from the school on the sole ground of our complexion." Rather than attend "an inferior exclusive public school," the Remond family left Salem, where they had lived for decades.[44]

The "inferior exclusive" school that opened in 1834 showed traces of sincere effort on Salem's part. The school met in the upstairs chamber of the Centre English School, formerly the Latin School room (vacated fifteen years earlier as decrepit). The teacher was William B. Dodge, founding master of the North Fields English School since 1807. Early in his career, he had received favorable reports, but student reminiscences of his cruel and indolent ways, described above, suggest that perhaps his better teaching days were behind him. Dodge had taken an interest in the black community since 1815 and served as president of the Essex County Anti-Slavery Society at the same time as he was teaching in the African American school. He spent eight years making a go of the new school, handling from sixty to one hundred students at all levels. Dodge suffered no pay cut in his transfer and earned standard raises. Thus, with even primary-level black students now attending a master's school, segregation deprived Salem of the savings usually accrued by assigning primary schooling to low-paid women. While white children cost the city an average of $7 each in teacher salary per year, black children cost as much as $11.67 each. Racial discrimination apparently ran deeper than gendered thrift.[45]

When Dodge retired in 1841, his replacement did earn a lower salary than other schoolmasters, $500 instead of $700. Neither did the twenty-six-year-old Thomas B. Perkins earn the limited respect of Salem's African American parents that Dodge had seemingly held. In the same year, a new schoolhouse for the African American school was voted "on the city land, opening into Mill street, and called Gravel Pit," as Felt's chronicle unappealingly described it, but it was much closer to the neighborhood where most African Americans lived. A new schoolhouse was not enough. Empowered by statewide integration victories pertaining to marriage and train travel, black parents in Salem again called for integration of the schools. Late in 1843, an upstanding black Salemite called on a member of the School Committee in person. "I have two grandchildren whom I wish to put into the [local white] primary school!" he began. When the committeeman denied the entry on the grounds of the children's color, the grandfather replied, "I do not recognize any distinction. I demand, as a citizen, to put my children to school. I have lived in this city many years, demeaned myself well and paid my taxes." The official still blocked the admission, but he also visited the family's home and took up the conversation with the man's wife and daughter. The family's message held firm despite their disappointment. "We do not allow and so help us, we never will allow, for a moment, that our children or any colored children, can with justice be shut out from participating freely in the fair competition in all the advantages of the public school. A distinct school is more debasing than none. We have feelings in common with our fellow men!"[46]

News of the committeeman's refusal traveled quickly among Salem's African Americans, who now definitively rejected the school provided by the city. As two-thirds of the sixty students played strategic hooky, supporters of the school scrambled to pin the plummeting attendance on the new schoolmaster. The School Committee's investigation concluded that the African American population felt "almost a universal disquietude" about the separate school, and a petition submitted by black residents in December of 1843 described it as an "intolerable grievance." In February 1844, former mayor Stephen C. Phillips helped engineer an amenable School Committee, which promptly voted to integrate the schools.[47]

Two factors bolstered the committee's action. The previous year, abolitionists in Nantucket had stacked the School Committee there and enabled the integration of the grammar school, though not the primary schools. The *Salem Register* quoted the Nantucket School Committee's language: "Go child of color and take your place in the school, you are equally as well entitled to it as any other child; take it and improve it to the utmost and God protect the right." Editorializing in similar rhetoric, the *Register* additionally pointed out the savings of abolishing the separate school, believing the new teacher earned as much as Dodge had. (The *Salem Gazette* sniffed that it supported frugality, "but not of that sordid kind.")[48] Second, Salem's black community had crucially helped their own cause by withdrawing their children from the segregated school. The School Committee recognized the impact of that strategy. "*Resolved,* That it is not for the public interest to incur the expense of supporting a separate school for the purpose of educating so small a number of scholars as have attended the school for colored children during the past year," the committee wrote in explaining their decision.[49]

To strengthen the case for integration, Phillips solicited a legal opinion from Boston attorney Richard C. Fletcher. On March 21, 1844, Fletcher submitted a ringing brief that spelled the end of school segregation in Salem and pioneered integration statewide. Fletcher sketched the history of Salem's schools in terms gratifying to its sense of itself as an educational innovator: "Our free school system originated with our Pilgrim Fathers and, until introduced by them, was unknown to the civilized world." Elaborating further on Salem's recent achievements in class integration, Fletcher pointed out that the city's public schools had brought rich and poor together: "The poorest man in the community may look to the free schools as the means of preparing his children for places of public trust and distinction. Many from the humblest ranks of life, in each successive generation, by means of these schools, with the blessing of Heaven are advanced to opulence and power." In fact, this mingling was the very cornerstone of American democracy. Without it, only the rich would have access to schooling, the downtrodden would rebel, and the government would crumble. Fletcher contrasted the city's action in abolishing the separate African American school with a mythological American equality. As he cited the state's constitution, court cases, taxation requirements, and voting regulations, he concluded that "neither the constitution nor laws of this Commonwealth make any distinction between a colored person and a white person."

Fletcher also anticipated the argument, applied successfully in *Plessy v. Ferguson* (1896) and unsuccessfully in *Brown v. Board of Education* (1954), that a separate African American school could be equal in quality to an all-white school. "I think it would be easy to show that this is not the case," he said dryly, contending that segregated facilities were legally irrelevant no matter their amenities. "The colored children are lawfully entitled to the benefits of the free schools, and are not bound to accept an equivalent." Moreover, an exclusive institution was "not a public school, but a school for a particular class," and hence an unlawful recipient of tax money. In sum, Fletcher entirely rejected the notion of separate schooling for children of color.[50]

Whether Salem's African American residents appreciated being compared to "the poorest man in the community," the 1844 decision stood, and Salem became the first municipality in the state to integrate its schools both fully and permanently. The nation would not catch up to Salem's achievements in integrating its schoolhouses for another 110 years, when the Supreme Court ruled in the *Brown* decision that separate schools could never be equal.

Charlotte Forten and the Salem Normal School

Salem's integrated schools brought national attention. Indeed, they drew Charlotte Forten from Philadelphia in 1854, at the age of sixteen. From a family of famous and wealthy abolitionists, but excluded from public schools because she was African American, Charlotte traveled to Salem to complete her education. She boarded with her family's abolitionist contacts, the Remonds, who had returned to Salem despite their earlier difficulties. Charles, his wife Amy, Sarah, and another brother hosted every renowned abolitionist passing through Salem. Engaging avidly in the household's stimulating political conversation, Charlotte also enrolled in the all-girls Higginson Grammar School, formerly the West Female High School.[51]

In May of 1854, Charlotte began a journal that was soon thick with anguish

Charlotte Forten. Pencil drawing by Tracie Fitzgerald, Salem State College Class of 2002. Photo by Kim Mimnaugh.

over slavery and race prejudice amid her views on books, art, and friends. She recorded her horror at the fugitive Anthony Burns's conviction and return to slavery—a Boston application of the 1850 Fugitive Slave Law—alongside her concerns that few of her classmates could understand her despair. Meanwhile she pitched into her lessons, helped out in the classroom, and took field trips with her class: to the Essex Institute, to Marblehead Beach with Hawthorne's sister as a guest. Charlotte quickly grew to love her teacher, Mary Shepard, an inspiring educator and an abolitionist who became a lifelong friend. Always she kept up a ferocious pace of reading and lecture going and talking about the awful subject that gripped her heart and mind. Although her equanimity and her father's support wavered at times, Charlotte persisted, determined to raise humanity through teaching. In February 1855, she concluded her studies at Higginson with a "dreaded examination day" and a series of parties.[52] The following week, she took the Normal School examination and passed it, to her great relief.

When Charlotte enrolled at the Salem Normal School (the future Salem State College), she was entering a new and momentous institution. Massachusetts had established three normal schools in previous years: Lexington in 1839 (later located at West Newton, then Framingham), for women; Barre in 1839 (later in Westfield), for men; and Bridgewater in 1840, coeducational. Academies had included teacher-training departments for some time, but the normal schools in Massachusetts pioneered in self-consciously importing the Prussian and French "norms" of teaching how to teach and in using state funds to educate teachers for local public schools. A large private gift launched the first three schools, with matching state funds. The legislature's 1853 vote to create another normal school for female students in Essex County amounted to a second generation of normal schooling: the first school founded since the original trio more than a dozen years earlier, and the first originated entirely with public funds. The newest normal school was no longer an experiment, but a known function of state government. The Board of Education chose Salem in June 1853, noting its transportation facilities and Salem's history as a center for learning and culture. The city offered the site then occupied by the Registry of Deeds and contributed beyond its share to the state appropriation, while the Eastern Railroad Corporation added a sizable gift.[53]

On September 13, 1854, the building opened for students, with dedication ceremonies the next day. A square, hip-roofed brick edifice at the corner of Summer and Broad Streets, it stood next door to the boys' Bowditch School. The new school was instantly besieged with applicants; the first class enrolled an impressive seventy-two students (including Rebecca Manning, Hawthorne's cousin), of whom about 80 percent lived near enough to commute. Two classes per year would enter. The three-term course lasted a year and a half, with studies of subjects and teaching methods keyed to the public common schools of the Commonwealth, which meant primary and lower-level secondary schools. Tuition was

Salem Normal School following an 1871 renovation. Courtesy of Salem State College Archives.

free, most texts were supplied as well, and a special fund defrayed living expenses for students in need. But the clear expectation was that all graduates would teach in Massachusetts for at least three years to repay the state's investment.[54]

Charlotte was not the first African American student to attend a state normal school in Massachusetts, but she was the first student of color at Salem Normal School.[55] She entered with the school's second class on March 13, 1855. Within days, her future there was in doubt. Her father wrote to demand that she withdraw, apparently troubled by a projected conundrum. Unless Charlotte could get work as a teacher in Massachusetts, the school's free tuition might have to be repaid. Principal Richard Edwards assured her she would be employable in the public schools, and her former teacher, Mary Shepard, promised financial support and wrote to her father separately. Her father soon relented.[56]

Charlotte enjoyed her studies at Salem Normal School, but friendships lagged. Politically mature and most comfortable with adults, Charlotte lamented that "among all my school companions there is not a single one who gives me her full and entire sympathy. My studies are my truest friends." Actual slights tormented her at other points. "I have met girls in the schoolroom[—] they have been thoroughly kind and cordial to me,—perhaps the next day met them in the street—they feared to recognize me." These experiences left her bitter. "I wonder that every colored person is not a misanthrope," she seethed. "Surely we have everything to make us hate mankind." Although Charlotte never found a bosom friend among her Normal School classmates, she became less isolated over time. She wrote a stirring hymn for the February 1856 graduation, and her classmates elected her to write the poem for their own July commencement. She was nervous about the assignment and more nervous about her future. Principal Edwards was urging her to stay for a fourth term in advanced study, but, still worried that she would not be hired as a teacher, she began making alternate plans.[57]

Then, in June of 1856, everything changed. Charlotte got a job. For $200 per year, she would serve as one of two assistant teachers at the coeducational Epes Grammar School. She was "astounded" that "this conservative, aristocratic old city of Salem!!!" would hire her, and she gratefully suspected Edwards's intercession.[58] Not since Chloe Minns Lawrence and her successor, the "colored man" who taught in the African Writing School in 1826–1827, had Salem hired an African American teacher, and never to teach white students.[59] Now its faculty was integrating to match its schools, if a dozen years later. Charlotte would start immediately, missing the last month of her final Normal School term, but she would be allowed to take part in the examinations and graduate. The first several days were hot, humid, and difficult. Her young pupils brought her flowers daily and acted up hourly. On the whole, Charlotte wrote after a week, "I find a teacher's life not nearly as pleasant as a scholar's." By the time of her examinations, Charlotte felt real fondness for her Normal School days. She passed a "very pleasant evening" with her graduating class at Mr. Edwards's home, suffered through the examination, and read her poem at the exercises.[60] Praised by the *Salem Register* as "skillfully written and gracefully delivered," the poem was later published in *The Liberator*.[61]

Charlotte visited the "dear Normal School" frequently that fall. She worked hard at teaching, continued to read and attend lectures, and studied Latin and French throughout the winter. In the spring, the reportedly "very popular" teacher and the students played ball and took walks to relieve their spring fever. As summer approached, she found her weariness beyond even the usual lot of a teacher. On a doctor's advice, she spent the summer recuperating in Philadelphia. Charlotte's health was erratic over the next five years. After that first twelve-month stint, she taught in Salem from September of 1857 to March of 1858; from May of 1859 to the spring of 1860, at Higginson as Shepard's assistant; from early September to late October of 1860, after which she became gravely ill for a time; and as a fill-in during the summer of 1862. Between engagements, she returned to her relatives in Philadelphia.[62]

As Charlotte left her Salem post in March 1858, the *Salem Register* wrote a long commendation. Noting her color—as one of "that hated race" enduring "maltreatment by our own people"—it continued, "She passed through the Higgins[on] Grammar School with decided éclat, and subsequently entered the State Normal School, and graduated with success. In both these schools, she had secured, in no common degree, the respect and interest of her teachers, and of her fellow pupils." Hired as the Epes assistant, Miss Forten "was graciously received by the parents of the district, and soon endeared herself to the pupils (white) under her charge. From the beginning, her connection with the school has been of the

happiest and most useful character, disturbed, we believe, by no unpleasant circumstance." Then the *Register* ungenerously shifted the approbation away from
the pioneering young teacher: "We do not mention it so much to praise Miss
Forten as to give credit to the community and to the school committee that sanc-
tioned this experiment. It is honorable to our city, and to the school committee
which appointed her." Strategic or clumsy perhaps, the tribute was also true.[63]

Charlotte resumed her own education during one of her periods as a Salem
teacher. While assisting Shepard in 1859–1860 and taking German lessons, she attended the new Advanced Course at the Normal School. Designed to prepare her
for teaching at a high school, the courses included "Latin, French, mathematics,
history of the United States, and Mental Philosophy." Although her health failed
after a few months, Charlotte wrote of this interlude, "I was never so happy. I enjoyed life perfectly." She remained in frequent contact with the world of abolitionists and reformers as well. During her years in Salem and Philadelphia, she met
Susan B. Anthony, corresponded and became friends with John Greenleaf Whit-
tier, and enjoyed her brief encounters with Beverly-born writer Lucy Larcom and
Salem-linked reformer Elizabeth Palmer Peabody. What finally drew Charlotte
away from Salem was the opportunity to teach recently freed slaves in the Civil
War South. For two years, her Salem public schooling, her Normal School education, and her Salem teaching experience were transmitted directly to the people
she had championed from afar all her life.[64]

Charlotte's beloved Salem Normal School was well begun. By 1863, it topped
the other Massachusetts normal schools in enrollment, as it would do consistently
for nearly thirty years. The second principal, Alpheus Crosby, appealed to Salem's
wealthy in 1857 and secured thousands of valuable books for the library, as well as
many natural history specimens, including a skeleton. At the quarter-century celebration in 1880, Principal Daniel Hagar noted that over two thousand women had
attended the school and that most graduates engaged in teaching in Massachusetts.
Some alumnae, however, were teaching as far away as Africa, Asia, New Zealand,
and the Sandwich Islands, and one was a county superintendent in Kansas. Although Salem Normal School faced many daunting challenges, this center of learning has remained true to its mission of providing educational opportunities for all
of the Commonwealth's citizens, regardless of race and gender, for 150 years. After
moving to its current campus in 1896, it became a four-year school in 1921, a teachers' college in 1932, and a liberal arts institution in 1960—what we know today as
Salem State College. Celebrating its sesquicentennial in 2004, the college has
maintained its dedication to training teachers, and has added a wide array of un-
dergraduate and graduate programs. Its first female African American graduate is
appropriately commemorated on campus in the library's Forten Hall.[65]

Salem's schools may not have received many African American students at
first. In its thirty-year history (including ten years after official integration), Boys'
English High School apparently enrolled one student of color. Elsewhere, Boston

activists quoted from Fletcher's report in failed legislative attempts to integrate the capital's public schools. When they pursued the effort in court instead, Charles Sumner used Fletcher's opinion in his brief for the famous school integration case of *Roberts v. City of Boston* before the Supreme Judicial Court of Massachusetts in 1849, assisted by Salem-born Robert C. Morris, the nation's second black lawyer. The Supreme Judicial Court—with Fletcher himself, now a justice, necessarily re-cused—decided 4 to 0 against Roberts in their 1850 opinion, which backfired for a century in the judicial branch. Cases like *Plessy v. Ferguson* in 1896 and others as late as 1949 drew on the language and precedent of *Roberts* in upholding separate but equal public facilities for minority groups, until the 1954 United States Supreme Court decision in *Brown v. Board of Education.* However, following school integration in Salem, Nantucket, Lowell, New Bedford, and Worcester, in 1855 Massachusetts became the first state to outlaw racial discrimination in all public-school admissions—a statewide legislative correction to the judicial calamity of *Roberts*. As Salem had gone, so finally went Massachusetts, Boston included.[66] In time, the nation would follow.

Today, Salem is the site of three private schools, and a new charter school is planned for 2004. Salem's ten public schools represent the new as well as the old. Enrollment is approximately 4 percent African American, 3 percent Asian Ameri-can, and 28 percent Hispanic; indeed, as many as twenty different languages are spoken in Salem's homes. Recent immigration continues the city's long multicul-tural heritage and its schools' legacy as laboratories of social democracy in the way that antebellum reformers had envisioned. Two Salem schools have recently been singled out statewide as Exemplary Schools. Along with this mix of cultures and languages, Salem remains connected to its distinguished educational traditions. The educating city carries its lively history into the present, and students attend schools with the names of Witchcraft Heights, Bowditch, Saltonstall, Bentley—and Horace Mann.[67]

Notes

1. Christine Leigh Heyrman, *Commerce and Culture: The Maritime Communities of Colo-nial Massachusetts, 1690–1750* (New York: W. W. Norton and Co., 1984), 68, 70, 207, 224–43, 253, 273, 284; Paul G. Faler, *Mechanics and Manufacturers in the Early Industrial Revolution: Lynn, Massachusetts, 1780–1860* (Albany: State University of New York Press, 1981); Douglas Lamar Jones, *Village and Seaport: Migration and Society in Eighteenth-Century Massachusetts* (Hanover, N.H.: Published for Tufts University by University Press of New England, 1981), 4–9, 52.

2. Joseph B. Felt, *Annals of Salem,* 2nd ed. (Salem: W. and S. B. Ives, 1845), I, 430–32.

3. According to Felt (I, 426–29), one free school appears in the records of Virginia in 1621, and a sketchy document hints at similar plans in Boston in 1636, apparently not followed up. There is no evidence that Salem's school actually achieved free status until about 1644. By con-

trast, Lawrence A. Cremin, *American Education: The Colonial Experience, 1607–1783* (New York: Harper and Row Publishers, 1970), 184, notes that Boston had a free school in 1641, and other towns did soon after, and does not mention Salem among early free school towns. Cremen also (181–82) calls Salem's early grammar school a "petty school," but I find no other evidence to support this designation. Fully free public education did not appear in Massachusetts until 1768.

4. Felt, I, 432–47, 450; Sidney Perley, *The History of Salem, Massachusetts,* vol. II, *1638–1670* (Salem: Sidney Perley, 1926), 91–96; vol. III, *1671–1716* (Salem: Sidney Perley, 1928), 111–12, 159. For one year, c. 1671–1672, Daniel Andrew taught the grammar school; in 1692, he was accused of being a witch. Felt, I, 433; Paul Boyer and Stephen Nissenbaum, *Salem Possessed: The Social Origins of Witchcraft* (Cambridge, Mass., and London: Harvard University Press, 1974), 121. Most towns provided schooling for only three or four months in summer and two or three months in winter. In the late eighteenth century, Salem's calendar was actually reduced and a few vacations were added. For the typical transiency of teachers, see Cremin, 188–89.

5. Felt, I, 440–47; Perley, III, 75–77, 356, 377–79, 392, 402, 410; "Diary of Rev. Joseph Green, of Salem Village," communicated by Samuel P. Fowler, *Essex Institute Historical Collections* 10: 73–104. The English school met downstairs in the town house, where the Grammar School had long met; the building, made of timbers from Salem's first meetinghouse, hosted the witch trials in the courtroom upstairs. "Report of the Committee on the Authenticity of the First Meeting House in Salem," *Essex Institute Historical Collections* 39: 224–25, 241–42, 248. Inspired by Brown's gesture, town treasurer Benjamin Lynde Jr. returned and augmented his salary for the Grammar School too. Brown's 1731 will gave additional funds to these schools. "Extracts from the Salem School Committee Records," *Essex Institute Historical Collections* 91: 29–32, 36–45.

6. For salaries and Widow Daland (or Dealland), see n. 5; Samuel Andrew (or Andrews) leaped from the Village school to the Grammar School, and John Gerrish left the Village school for the English school (Felt, I, 442–44); on town funds being used to sponsor poor children at private female-taught schools, see Felt, I, 449–52, and "Extracts from the Salem School Committee Records," *Essex Institute Historical Collections* 49.

7. Felt, I, 449–52; Perley (III, 97 n) also mentions Abigail Allen, "baptized Dec. 18, 1726; conducted a school; died, unmarried, June —, 1760." Census for 1785 discussed in Edwin Haviland Miller, *Salem Is My Dwelling Place: A Life of Nathaniel Hawthorne* (Iowa City: University of Iowa Press, 1991), 11, where he notes a population of 6,665, with 419 widows and 3,095 children under sixteen. If 52 percent of the over-sixteen population were female, a low guess, then 22.6 percent of women over sixteen were widows—still low, given women between age sixteen and "adult." Medford began part-day schooling for girls in 1766; Salem may have been second. Carl F. Kaestle, *Pillars of the Republic: Common Schools and American Society, 1780–1860* (New York: Hill and Wang, 1983), 28.

8. Margaret B. Moore, *The Salem World of Nathaniel Hawthorne* (Columbia and London: University of Missouri Press, 1998), 76–101, quotation 77; Miller, 47–53; Arlin Turner, *Nathaniel Hawthorne: A Biography* (New York and Oxford: Oxford University Press, 1980), 18–30.

9. Felt, I, 452–77; William Bentley, *The Diary of William Bentley, D.D.*, 4 vols. (Salem, Mass.: Essex Institute, 1905–1914); Faler, 47. In brief, private teachers appear in *Essex Institute Historical Collections* at 4: 2–13; 5: 53–56, 145–52, 193–96, 197–202, 247–54; 6: 93–108; 7: 241–43; 13: 81–89; 21: 1–12, 211–24; 36: 233–44; 42: 82–84; 49: 193–209, 289–304; 50: 289–96; 51: 297–305; 74: 365–72; and see Hawthorne sources in n. 7, 8.

10. Peter Frye (1747–1751), Jonathan Sewall (1751–1756), William Walter (1756–1758), and

Nathan Goodale (1759–1770) provided nearly a quarter-century of Latin scholars with instruction and then took a Loyalist side in the Revolution: Charles Northend, "Old Time Salem Schoolmaster," parts 1–4, 7, *Salem Register,* June 18, 1891; June 22, 1891; June 25, 1891; June 29, 1891; "Postscript," July 9, 1891.

11. Felt, I, 453, 456–58; quotation, Mrs. John W. Perkins, "Early Schools and Schoolmasters," Essex Institute Local History Class, Peabody Essex Museum, Lecture 33 (January 29, 1895), 23; Stanley K. Schultz, *The Culture Factory: Boston Public Schools, 1789–1860* (New York: Oxford University Press, 1973), 30–44.

12. Felt, I, 456, 460–70; Bentley, IV, 526–27, 537–38, 571, 588–89, 600.

13. Felt, I, 459 (quotations), 461; Bentley, I, ix, 31–32 (quotation); II, 140, 269–70, 459; III, 54, 92, 291, 315; IV, 485; Moore, 85.

14. Trade duties declined from over $7 million in 1800–1810 to under $4 million in 1810–1820. Miller, 12. Bentley, III, 456; IV, 69 (quotation), 392, 506 (quotation), 617 (quotation).

15. Felt I, 466–76. The charismatic Henry Kemble Oliver spent twenty-five years as a teacher and became a sought-after lecturer on educational topics. His public service included school committee member and mayor of both Salem and Lawrence, and school superintendent in Lawrence (the latter service so generous that several Lawrence public schools were named after him); member of the State Board of Education; state treasurer during the Civil War; chief of the Massachusetts Labor Bureau and Labor Reform candidate for governor; deputy state constable in charge of child labor; and commissions up to adjutant general of the Massachusetts Infantry (making him "General Oliver" after 1846). He composed many published hymns, often named after Salem locations, including the then well-known "Federal Street." Henry Kemble Oliver Papers, Peabody Essex Museum.

16. Maris A. Vinovskis, *The Origins of Public High Schools: A Reexamination of the Beverly High School Controversy* (Madison: University of Wisconsin Press, 1985), 60–62; Alexander James Inglis, *The Rise of the High School in Massachusetts* (New York: Teachers College, Columbia University, 1911), 38, 72. Salem's Boys' English High School did face a near-closure in 1831, but it survived. Emit Duncan Grizzell, *Origin and Development of the High School in New England before 1865* (New York: The Macmillan Company, 1923), 65–66.

17. In 1812, 295 girls were enrolled in the English schools on this part-time basis; I found no later enrollment figures. Felt, I, 463, 473–75; *Salem Register* for May 21, 1827, cited in Kaestle, 28; Grizzell, 64–69.

18. Felt, I, 475–76; *Salem Gazette,* June 11, 1869, 2; "90 Years Old: The Old North School's Proud Record," *Salem Daily Gazette,* October 5, 1897, 5; Ruth M. Baylor, *Elizabeth Palmer Peabody, Kindergarten Pioneer* (Philadelphia: University of Pennsylvania Press, 1965), 48–49; for Eames's view, see "Extracts from the Salem School Committee Records," 55–61. Regrettably, the huge educational contributions of Elizabeth Palmer Peabody lie beyond the scope of this article, since she spent her most productive years outside Salem. See Baylor; Bruce A. Ronda, *Elizabeth Palmer Peabody: A Reformer on Her Own Terms* (Cambridge, Mass., and London: Harvard University Press, 1999); Louise Hall Tharp, *The Peabody Sisters of Salem* (Boston: Little, Brown, 1950).

19. Bentley, III, 367; "Rantoul Genealogy, &c.," *Essex Institute Historical Collections* 5: 149, 152; Benjamin F. Browne, "Some Notes upon Mr. Rantoul's Reminiscences," *Essex Institute Historical Collections* 5: 198, 201; Benjamin F. Browne, "Youthful Recollections of Salem," *Essex Institute Historical Collections* 51: 53–54; Jonathan Messerli, *Horace Mann: A Biography* (New York: Knopf, 1972), 404–7, 412–21; W. Jeffrey Bolster, *Black Jacks: African American Seamen in the Age*

of Sail (Cambridge: Harvard University Press, 1997), 72–73, 180; Myra C. Glenn, "The Naval Reform Campaign against Flogging: A Case Study in Changing Attitudes toward Corporal Punishment, 1830–1850," *American Quarterly* 35 (1983): 408–25.

20. Felt, I, 478–79, 470 (quotation).

21. Eleanor Putnam [Helen (Vose) Bates], *Old Salem,* ed. Arlo Bates (Boston and New York: Houghton, Mifflin and Company, 1887), 45–46, and see 43–62. Other first-person reminiscences of dame schools, drawn upon in the next paragraphs, include M. C. D. Silsbee, *A Half Century in Salem* (Boston and New York: Houghton, Mifflin and Company, 1887), 47–58; Caroline Howard King, *When I Lived in Salem, 1822–1866* (Brattleboro, Vt.: Stephen Daye Press, 1937), 141–64; Mary Harrod Northend, *Memories of Old Salem, Drawn from the Letters of a Great-Grandmother* (New York: Moffatt, Yard and Company, 1917), 101, 104–13, apparently a partly fictionalized account; "Two Salem Dame Schools," *Essex Institute Historical Collections* 42: 82–84; "Rantoul Genealogy," 149; Browne, "Some Notes," 198–99; and, from nearby Beverly, Lucy Larcom, *A New England Girlhood, Outlined from Memory* (Boston: Northeastern University Press, 1986), 39–48. To place these establishments in the tradition of "needle schools" for elite girls, see Elysa Engelman, "Needlecraft and Wollstonecraft: A Case Study of Women's Rights and Education in Federal-Period Salem, Massachusetts," in *Painted with Thread: The Art of American Embroidery,* ed. Paula Bradstreet Richter (Salem, Mass.: Peabody Essex Museum, 2000), 141–57; and Betty Ring, *Let Virtue Be a Guide to Thee: Needlework in the Education of Rhode Island Women, 1730–1830* (Providence: Rhode Island Historical Society, 1983).

22. Putnam, 50–53.

23. Bernard Farber, *Guardians of Virtue: Salem Families in 1800* (New York and London: Basic Books, Inc., Publishers, 1972), 45–46.

24. Putnam, 58–59.

25. Quoted in Moore, 76.

26. Mary Peabody Mann, *Life of Horace Mann* (Washington, D.C.: National Education Association of the United States, 1937), 91–92.

27. Vinovskis, 27; Michael B. Katz, *The Irony of Early School Reform: Educational Innovation in Mid-Nineteenth Century Massachusetts* (Boston: Beacon Press, 1968), 48, 61; Mann, 92; Kaestle, 59, 116. For a comparable analysis, see Joan M. Maloney, *Salem Normal School, 1854–1905: A Tradition of Excellence* (Acton, Mass.: Tapestry Press, 1990), 3.

28. Mann, 92; *Second Annual Report of the Board of Education. Together with the Second Annual Report of the Secretary of the Board* (Boston: Dutton and Wentworth, State Printers, 1839), 30–31. See "Salem Schools—Again," *Common School Journal* 4 (October 1, 1842): 299–304. In addition to articles cited separately below, see "Salem Schools," *Common School Journal* 6 (December 16, 1844): 377–80; and "Prizes in Schools," *Common School Journal* 7 (February 1, 1845): 33–41. Grizzell (68) agrees that Mann's efforts were "particularly noticeable in Salem."

29. Inaugural Address of Mayor Stephen C. Phillips, in "Public Schools in Salem," *Common School Journal* 1 (May 1, 1839): 133–35.

30. "Public Schools in Salem," 134–35.

31. "Inaugural Address of the Hon. Stephen C. Phillips, Mayor of Salem," *Common School Journal* 2 (July 1, 1840): 204–5.

32. Maloney, 11–12, but I question her claim, 201 n. 24, that female assistants had worked at Boys' English High School as early as 1827, in view of Rufus Putnam's comments in *Catalogue*

of Members of the Late English High School, of Salem, Massachusetts (Salem: George Creamer et al., 1857), 19; Felt, I, 480; Kaestle, 124–25.

33. "90 Years Old," 5; Chas. S. Osgood and H. M. Batchelder, *Historical Sketch of Salem* (Salem: Essex Institute, 1879), 104–5; Grizzell, 69.

34. *Salem Gazette,* March 4, 1842, 2; "East Schoolhouse, in Salem," *Common School Journal* 4 (March 1, 1842): 74–80; "School Celebration at Salem," *Common School Journal* 4 (April 15, 1842): 113–24 (quotations 113; note that Mayor Phillips was the source of the claim that Salem established "the first free school in the world," 113).

35. *Common School Journal* 4 (October 1, 1842): 299–304 (quotations 299).

36. Felt, I, 482–83. These figures leave a few points unspoken. There were nearly 700 youngsters not enrolled in any school, as well as over 250 who attended sporadically. Also, the numbers included only students aged four to sixteen, whereas private schools, especially, were likely to enroll pupils both younger and older than those ages. Salem's private-school enrollment might have suffered partly from the Panic of 1837 in this period and the emergence of boarding schools elsewhere, but my analysis strongly suggests that the growing acceptance of public schooling among the wealthy contributed most to the turnaround.

37. "Salem Schools," *Common School Journal* 7 (September 1, 1845): 267–68, and note Oliver's generosity in facilitating a public school that would compete with his own proprietary girls' academy; Grizzell, 69–70; on the disappointing performance of the girls' high school, see Maloney, 12, 15–16. The new Union or East School became the Phillips School; the Latin School became the Fisk School; the Boys' or English High School became the Bowditch School; the new girls' high school became the Saltonstall School; the West English School became the Hacker School; the North, or North Fields, English School became the Pickering School; the South, or South Fields, English School became the Browne School; the West Female High School became the Higginson School; the East Female High School became the Bentley School; and the new Aborn Street English School became the Epes School. Osgood and Batchelder, 105. On the mergers, see *Catalogue of Members,* 33; Maloney, 12, 15–16, 27. Maloney emphasizes fiscal difficulties in Salem as a bar to improvements in the public schools (12–16, 75–76), while Vinovskis (116) claims that nearby Beverly's troubles with sustaining public schools stemmed from its poverty compared to wealthy Salem.

38. See rosters of students and parents throughout *Catalogue of Members;* "Old Schools and School-Teachers of Salem," communicated by Jona. Tucker, *Essex Institute Historical Collections* 7: 241–43; Kaestle, 59, 116; Carl F. Kaestle and Maris A. Vinovskis, *Education and Social Change in Nineteenth-Century Massachusetts* (Cambridge, England: Cambridge University Press, 1980), 19; 1851 percentage derived from figures in Maloney, 14; James Duncan Phillips, *Salem in the Eighteenth Century* (Boston and New York: Houghton Mifflin Company, 1937), 345–46; Putnam, 45.

39. Arthur O. White, "Salem's Antebellum Black Community: Seedbed of the School Integration Movement," *Essex Institute Historical Collections* 108: 99–103, 99 n. 2, 105; Henry M. Brooks, "Some Localities about Salem," *Essex Institute Historical Collections* 31: 114–17; see also Oliver Thayer, "Early Recollections of the Upper Portion of Essex Street," *Essex Institute Historical Collections* 21: 211. Although these population figures might not be exact, especially regarding mariners, the general picture conveyed is valid. For comparison with Boston, see James Oliver Horton and Lois E. Horton, *Black Bostonians: Family Life and Community Struggle in the Antebellum North* (New York and London: Holmes and Meier, 1999), and George A. Levesque,

Black Boston: African American Life and Culture in Urban America, 1750–1860 (New York and London: Garland Publishing, Inc., 1994).

40. Bentley, II, 31, 96, 146; Browne, "Some Notes," 199–200, mentioning Sampson Augustus; Charles T. Brooks, "Augustus Story, A Memorial Paper Read before the Essex Institute, Monday Evening, May 14, 1883," *Essex Institute Historical Collections* 20: 124; Thayer, 220.

41. Bentley, IV, 435–36 (quotations); III, 382, 456, 500; White, 105–7; Felt, I, 460–61.

42. Felt, I, 476–77; White, 107–8; "90 Years," 5. This York Morris may have been the son of an earlier Salemite by that name, who was active in encouraging black men to vote Federalist (along with John Remond) and was also the father of future attorney Robert C. Morris, discussed below. Brooks, "Some Localities," 115; Horton and Horton, 60.

43. Sarah Parker Remond, "A Colored Lady Lecturer," *The English Woman's Journal* 7 (June 1, 1861): 269–75 (quotations 270). See also Ruth Bogin, "Sarah Parker Remond: Black Abolitionist from Salem," *Essex Institute Historical Collections* 110: 120–50; Dorothy B. Porter, "Sarah Parker Remond, Abolitionist and Physician," *Journal of Negro History* 20 (July 1935): 287–93; and Benjamin Quarles, *Black Abolitionists* (New York: Oxford University Press, 1969), 139–40.

44. White, 108–9; see "Extracts from the Salem School Committee Records," 71; Felt, I, 478; Remond, 270–71. The Remonds moved to Newport, Rhode Island, but they fared no better in seeking public education for their children. Eventually some better-off African American families started a private school in Newport, where Sarah obtained a modicum of additional schooling. Remond, 271.

45. White, 109–10, but note that I have extrapolated from White's arithmetic to derive the cost per student in the African American school; Bentley, III, 380, 397, 499, 537, 546; IV, 111, 190; Felt, I, 481.

46. Felt, I, 481; White, 110, quoting *Salem Register,* March 14, 1844.

47. White, 111, quoting *Salem Register,* March 14, 1844.

48. White, 111–12, quoting *Salem Register,* March 7, 1844, and *Salem Gazette,* March 21, 1844.

49. "Resolutions of the Salem School Committee," *Common School Journal* 7 (October 15, 1844): 326.

50. "Resolutions of the Salem School Committee," *Common School Journal* 7 (October 15, 1844): 326–28.

51. Ray Allen Billington, Introduction to *The Journal of Charlotte Forten* (New York: Collier Books, 1953), 20–23.

52. Billington, 70.

53. Kaestle, 129–30; *100 Years of Progress in the Training of Teachers: State Teachers College at Salem, Massachusetts, 1854–1954* (Salem, Mass.: Salem State Teachers College, 1954), 24; Maloney, 1, 5–9, 18–20. "Salem Normal School" was the commonly used name, while "State Normal School at Salem" was the official name.

54. *100 Years,* 24; *Eighteenth Annual Report of the Board of Education, Together with the Eighteenth Annual Report of the Secretary of the Board* (Boston: William White, Printer to the State, 1855), 22–34; *Catalogue of the Instructors and Students in the State Normal School at Salem. For the Term ending February, 1856* (Salem: Wm. Ives and Geo. W. Pease, Printers, 1856), 12; Maloney, 6, 40–41.

55. Cloe Lee enrolled at the West Newton Normal School in 1847 and met resistance among

both the students and the town. She was supported by the school's then principal, famous abolitionist Samuel J. May (uncle of Louisa May Alcott). When the usual boarding establishments would not accept her, she lived with Horace Mann himself, over the protests of his sister-in-law Sophia Peabody Hawthorne. Gwendolyn Luella Rosemond and Joan M. Maloney, "To Educate the Heart," *Sextant* 3 (1988): 4; Messerli, 446–47, 447–48 nn. 8–9.

56. Billington, 71–72, 80.

57. Billington, 72–75, 80–81, 245–46 n. 56.

58. Billington, 82.

59. Felt, I, 473.

60. Billington, 82–83.

61. *Salem Register,* July 24, 1856, quoted in Billington, 248 n. 6, and see 83.

62. Billington, 85–94, 98, 100, 109–32. My time line, derived from Forten's diary extracts, differs from Billington's.

63. *Salem Register,* quoted in *The Liberator* for March 26, 1858, in turn quoted in Billington, 26–27.

64. *100 Years,* 25; *Register and Circular of the State Normal School at Salem, Mass., for the Spring and Summer Term, 1860* (n.p., July 1860), 3; Billington, 131 (quotation), 27–39, 99, 102, 107, 120, 132, 135–225. Beginning in the fall of 1862, Charlotte taught in Port Royal, South Carolina, in the famous Sea Islands social experiment, and elsewhere in the South for nearly two years, returning to Philadelphia in spring 1864. In later years, she continued to read, learn, write for publication, and likely teach in that city. She married at forty-one, in 1878, the Reverend Francis J. Grimké, son of a slave mother and plantation-owner father whose sisters, Sarah and Angelina Grimké, were celebrated abolitionists. He and Charlotte lived in Washington, D.C., and briefly in Florida. She died in 1914.

65. Maloney, 79, 84–86, and throughout; *100 Years; Proceedings of the Quarter-Centennial Celebration of the State Normal School at Salem, Mass.* (Salem, Mass.: Observer Steam Printing Rooms, 1880); Rosemond and Maloney, 2–8; Ronald L. Lycette, ed., *A Salem Chronicle: The Evolution of a College* (Salem, Mass.: Salem State College, 1982). I thank Salem State College archivist Susan MacKenzie Edwards for her assistance.

66. George William Jackson entered with the twenty-first class on March 6, 1848, but died on July 1, 1850. Principal Rufus Putnam identified him as "colored" at the school's closing festival and obliquely mentioned a "pleasant" anecdote involving him. *Catalogue of Members,* 26, 51. Cross-referencing the school's rosters of students and parents from the *Catalogue* against Salem city directories listing "People of Color" separately from white residents yields no additional black students. *The Salem Directory, and City Register . . .* (Salem: Published by Henry Whipple, 1837; 1842; 1846). On statewide integration, see White, 116–18.

67. From Massachusetts Department of Education: School District Profile for Salem; "Board of Education grants five new charters," February 25, 2003; Information Services and Technology Student Information Management System, Individual School Report Format, October 1, 2001, Table Three—Enrollment by Race; Saltonstall School named Exemplary, "Education Commissioner Selects 14 Exemplary Schools," May 18, 2001; Bentley Elementary School named Exemplary, "15 Massachusetts Schools Honored for Improvement," June 14, 2002, and "Panel Report: Compass School Candidate Review, Bentley Elementary School—Salem Public Schools," 2002; and Massachusetts Department of Housing and Community Development, Salem Profile (2002), 1.

Salem antique shop window. Photo by Kim Mimnaugh.

Chapter Seven

Salem as Hawthorne's Creation

NANCY LUSIGNAN SCHULTZ

[B]y my control over light and darkness,
I cause the dusk, and then the starless night, to brood over the street;
and summon forth again the bellman, with his lantern casting a gleam about
his footsteps, to pace wearily from corner to corner, and shout
drowsily the hour to drowsy or dreaming ears.

—Nathaniel Hawthorne, "Main-street"

ATHANIEL Hawthorne invented Salem, Massachusetts. Wandering his native city's oak-lined avenues and waterfront alleys during his boyhood, recalling the faces of family and friends from his lodgings at Maine's Bowdoin College, immersing himself in dusty historical records at the Salem Athenaeum, peering out of the windows of the Custom House where he suffered through his job as an appointed government official, gazing westward from Europe back across the Atlantic toward his birthplace, Hawthorne built a powerful image of Salem in his imagination. This vision was so vividly conveyed to his readers that this native son has permanently invested Salem with its particular sense of place. His works constructed a literary Salem so powerful that, even today, the literal Salem is shaped by it. In Hawthorne's Salem, actual and fictional characters cross paths woven into a number of historical periods. The smell of fish mixes with the stench of stagnant water under rotting wharves. A few barges and workboats bob lazily at wooden docks. East Indiamen sail into the rising sun, building empires. Ladies ascend marble steps to attend evening lectures, and perfume wafts from the sweep of their fine Eastern silk gowns. Redcoats drink in its taverns. Steeple-hatted Puritans glumly tread its cobblestone streets, while Indians and Satan lurk in surrounding forests.

The writer's gift to his readers—and to other writers who followed him—was this populous picture of Salem—truly, the capital city of what Henry James called the "haunted world of Hawthorne's imagination."[1] Nearly two centuries later, we imagine a place called Salem in all the complexity that Hawthorne bestowed upon it. The writer's son-in-law, George Parsons Lathrop, in his 1876 book, *A Study of*

163

Hawthorne, conceived of nineteenth-century Salem as a diorama of old New England history.[2] Beyond that, Salem can represent a microcosm of the American experience. Its history links it directly to an English heritage of America. Like America, Salem metamorphosed from a wilderness-ringed outpost to a cosmopolitan hub. Nineteenth-century industrialization upended Salem's social order, as it did the nation's. But mainly, Salem embodies the Puritan vision and religious foundations of America, a place where those seeking religious freedom developed an iron intolerance of others, and whose grandchildren succumbed to a deadly mass hysteria. Hawthorne, himself a descendant of a judge in the Salem Witch Trials, dwelled especially on this latter aspect of the town's history. From his fictional depiction of the city, "Salem" has developed into a dominant American icon and literary metaphor.[3] Even more significant than Hawthorne's remarkable sketches of local color, or his clever weaving together of family history and the town's founding days, was his creation of Salem as a concept that then belied, and has since defied, the town's actual history. "Alice Doane's Appeal," "Young Goodman Brown," "Main-street," "The Custom House," *The House of the Seven Gables,* and other Hawthorne works have forged the world's image of Salem as a distinctive site, and as a symbol for America.

Generations of Americans have shifted uneasily in their seats, slogging through some of this required reading in high school and college literature classes. The setting of these frequently anthologized and oft-assigned texts is conflated in the memories of the graduates, so that a Hawthorne novel set in Boston, *The Scarlet Letter,* is popularly recollected as a Salem story. School field trips to Salem complete the identification of witch hysteria with Hawthorne when students tour the Witch Museum and the House of the Seven Gables in a single day. By the end of high school, many students have read *The Scarlet Letter* and Arthur Miller's *The Crucible* in the same English class, and both are remembered as Salem stories. Hawthorne scholars might not recognize how deeply this misconception runs, but as a literature teacher at Salem State College for two decades, I have seen this composite of Hawthorne's Salem take shape in unexpected venues. Tourists seek out Hester Prynne's cottage on the edge of town, freshmen wonder if Dimmesdale climbed a scaffold erected on the Salem Common, and once, I heard a job candidate lecture about a single tombstone marking the lovers' sunken grave in an old Salem cemetery. It is clear that these versions of Hawthorne's tales are not the same as the canonical masterpieces studied by scholars of American literature.[4] Out of this condensed popular memory created by readers' experiences with Hawthorne, a composite "Salem Village" has emerged, a literary construct of the place. This composite—at once the Salem Village from which Young Goodman Brown made his fateful errand into the wilderness and the Salem of myth and memory—functions on many levels in American culture and merits its own cultural history. This chapter explores Hawthorne's creation of Salem as icon and metaphor and the subsequent availability of his invented Salem to other writers.

ટ્ઝ

The coincidence of Hawthorne's birth in Salem on Independence Day in 1804 marks him as a quintessential American writer. Hawthorne had a patriotic birthday, having been born on the Fourth of July, and his works helped fulfill young America's ambitions for a literature of its own.[5] Yet, while writers such as Emily Dickinson, Harriet Beecher Stowe, Herman Melville, Edgar Allan Poe, Walt Whitman, and Hawthorne inscribed poetry and prose that would appear at mid-century, part of the glorious flowering that F. O. Matthiessen termed the "American Renaissance," Salem was falling into deep decline.[6] Its three decades of glory began after the Revolutionary War, rose with the fortunes of the China Trade, and fell with the 1807 Embargo, a year before the death of Hawthorne's seafaring father, in Surinam, of yellow fever. Yet Hawthorne's representation of Salem resurrected the town from obscurity, and in fact created it as a place that looms large in American cultural memory.

Hawthorne's works strengthened the popular association of Salem with both the witch trials and magic. Because of the wide availability of tales such as "Alice Doane's Appeal," "Main-street," "Young Goodman Brown," and *The House of the Seven Gables,* which explore magical powers of Salem residents, popular culture continues to conceive of Salem in the terms Hawthorne set out. Hawthorne helped create the aura of mystery that to this day helps shape Salem's status as a popular icon. In "Main-street," which is Essex Street in Salem, Hawthorne's narrator evokes one of the community's earliest specters, the "Tidy Man," or tithing-man, a town officer in the first settlement charged with the prevention of disorderly conduct, a boogeyman whom the narrator depicts as nabbing Puritan children at play: "What native of Naumkeag, whose recollections go back more than thirty years, does not still shudder at that dark ogre of his infancy, who perhaps had long ceased to have an actual existence, but still lived in his childish belief, in a horrible idea, and in the nurse's threat, as the Tidy Man!"[7] Salem, where the natural is transformed into the supernatural, casts a long shadow throughout American history, and shapes from its darkness still haunt American culture. One significant idea that Hawthorne's Salem represents, then, is that of a *satanic space* that emerged from a *sacred space,* as the memory of Gallows Hill crowded out the Puritan "citty upon a Hill."

Hawthorne's world of supernatural characters, such as the members of Satan's congregation Young Goodman Brown believes he meets in the forest or the wizard family of Maules in *The House of the Seven Gables,* not only have defined Salem but also have made possible the commodification of its history. Hawthorne's works construct a Salem in which the witch trials are prominent in the town's history and in the author's own ancestry. Busloads of tourists pour into the city's streets each summer and especially at Halloween to see, in part, this spooky Salem, home to crystal shops and tarot card readers. Salem lurked as a backdrop and setting for such television programs as *Bewitched* and films such as the classic *Horror Hotel* (1960), *Psyched by the 4-D Witch* (1972), the adaptation of Stephen King's thriller, *Salem's Lot* (1979), *Three Sovereigns for Sarah* (1985), and Walt Disney's *Hocus Pocus* (1993). *Yahoo! Movies* not only classifies *The Scarlet Letter* (1934) as a Salem movie, but goes further to claim, "This *faithful adaptation* of Nathaniel Hawthorne's 1851 novel about a woman who is forced to wear a scarlet letter A on her bosom because she has an illicit affair is *a damning depiction of Puritan life in 17th Century Salem, Massachusetts*" (my italics).[8] Hawthorne's writings have shaped both the image and the marketing of Salem and still define our distinctive sense of it as a cauldron of the occult, where its enshrining event, the Salem witch trials, is constantly reenacted, as "Main-street"'s narrator suggests: "Hurry on the accused witches to the gallows, ere they do more mischief!—ere they fling out their withered arms, and scatter pestilence by handfuls among the crowd—ere, as their parting legacy, they cast a blight over the land so that henceforth it may bear no fruit nor blade of grass, and be fit for nothing but a sepulchre for their unhallowed carcasses!"[9] Today, the streets of "Witch City" are lined with hawkers of this history, and some would see this "blight" as fulfillment of Hawthorne's dire prediction.

More important than the supernatural allure that Hawthorne bequeathed to our perception of Salem, however, is its central role in the formation and articulation of American identity. This identity is represented by early Salem's Puritan intolerance and religious narrowness, and it continues to suggest an ironic counterpoint to the national myth of religious freedom. The opening of *The Scarlet Letter* makes its classic sardonic observation about the founding of utopias like Salem: "The founders of a new colony, whatever Utopia of human virtue and happiness they might originally project, have invariably recognized it among their earliest practical necessities to allot a portion of the virgin soil as a cemetery, and another portion as the site of a prison."[10] Like the town beadle who throws open the prison door to let Hester Prynne pass out of the darkness of her cell, Salem, for Hawthorne, came to represent "the whole dismal severity of the Puritanic code of law."[11] Hawthorne allegorized Salem, turning it into a powerful metaphor that captured a certain undercurrent in the American psyche and its residue of shame, which the writer termed its "persecuting spirit."[12] Hawthorne remains our dark prophet, reminding us of our sinister history, and warning that its dangerous seeds only lie dormant in the rich soil of American culture. His metaphoric *Salem* evokes the legacy of persecution that resonates throughout American culture; in fact, the name itself is synonymous with witch hunts. Salem, therefore, has been a powerful symbol for many generations of Americans.

During the fifties, a full century after the "American Renaissance"—in Senator McCarthy's America—Hawthorne's stories of Salem furnished the metaphor that stood in dark times for the state of the nation. The historical actions of the Puritans, to be sure, offered a clear warning to subsequent generations of the dangers of extremism, persecution, and intolerance. But it was Hawthorne who breathed life into the metaphor of witch-hunting, by presenting the image of Boston's Puritans banishing a young mother and infant from their community and affixing on her bosom a scarlet badge of shame. The witch trials of Salem were Arthur Miller's subject in 1953, but it was Hester Prynne's mark of sex and shame that provided a template of Salem as Cold War metaphor.[13] One hundred years after the decade in which Hawthorne produced *The Scarlet Letter* and *The House of the Seven Gables, The Blithedale Romance* and *The Marble Faun,* Miller built on the available literary legacy of place and used Salem as the location for his stunning critique of post–World War II America. Several of Hawthorne's works suggest that Salem is America; Miller's *The Crucible* makes Salem stand for America, as well.[14]

Hawthorne's Salem

For most Americans today, *Salem* connotes Salem, Massachusetts. There are other towns and cities named Salem, including the biblical city of peace for which the Massachusetts Bay Colony was named:

> His abode has been established in Salem,
> His dwelling place in Zion.
> There he broke the flashing arrows,
> the shield, the sword, and the weapons of war.

In addition to this Salem from Psalm 76, just to the north of Salem, Massachusetts, lies neighboring Salem, New Hampshire, and the name can be found gracing other cities and towns throughout the nation. The capital city in Northwest Oregon, on the Willamette River, with more than triple the population, bears the name *Salem.* And in central Tamil Nadu, in South India, a city called Salem is home to over half a million people.[15] The connotations of Salem, Massachusetts, probably rank above those of the ancient city of Jerusalem in Old Testament texts; the link between *Salem* and the witch trials is probably even more widespread.

Hawthorne set Salem firmly into our imaginations by emphasizing two main aspects of the town's history: the witch hysteria and the rise and fall of Salem's glory days. His fascination with Puritan imagination and temperament informed his treatment of Salem past and present. Salem, in Hawthorne's view, was prophetic of the battle between good and evil in American culture, and this association is part of his legacy. Penning his myth of origin in "The May-pole of Merry Mount," in which the customs of Merry Olde England are cast aside in favor of the perpetual dourness of the Puritans, Hawthorne's narrator knowingly intones: "The future complexion of New England was involved in this important quarrel. Should the grisly saints establish their jurisdiction over the gay sinners, then would their spirits darken all the clime, and make it a land of clouded visages, of hard toil, of sermon and psalm, for ever. But should the banner-staff of Merry Mount be fortunate, sunshine would break upon the hills, and flowers would beautify the forest, and late posterity do homage to the May-Pole!"[16] Hawthorne depicts this defining moment as a choice between two extremes: "Jollity and gloom," he writes, "were contending for an empire." At the end of "The May-pole of Merry Mount," of course, gloom wins the contest in the forest. But far more than the new republic ever could, Hawthorne, at least in the popular conception of him, eschewed jollity and embraced gloom.

An example of Hawthorne's tendency to bleak pessimism may be seen in the deserted, abandoned wharves he portrays in his preface to *The Scarlet Letter*, "The Custom House." In this quasi memoir, the author bemoans the challenge of raising "an image of the old town's brighter aspect, when India was a new region, and only Salem knew the way thither" from remains that he characterizes alternately as a "corpse" and "dry bones."[17] Hawthorne's famous anecdote of finding the scarlet letter in a dusty corner of the Custom House conveys to readers around the globe the idea that a teeming seaport community had experienced a devastating reversal in commerce, revenue, and population. "In my native town of Salem," Hawthorne writes, "at the head of what, half a century ago, in the days of old King Derby, was a bustling wharf,—but which is now burdened with decayed wooden warehouses, and exhibits few or no symptoms of commercial life; except, perhaps, a bark or brig, halfway down its melancholy length, discharging hides."[18]

But the Salem of 1850 was not quite as empty as Hawthorne's works suggest. In 1850, the city's population was about twenty thousand. In 1800, the period that Hawthorne characterizes as teeming with people and activities, Salem's population was ten thousand. When *The Scarlet Letter* appeared in 1850, the number of people living in Salem had swelled to more than twice the size it had been during the heyday of the China Trade. While the port of Salem may have been relatively underused during this period, ships were clearly arriving elsewhere, to the port of Boston, for example, bringing new immigrants, many from Ireland. It is likely that the waves of immigration, increasing through the first decades of the 1800s, account for the fact that during Hawthorne's lifetime Salem's population had actually doubled. It has taken the century and a half since Hawthorne's death for Salem's population to double again, to today's population of forty thousand.[19] Hawthorne's works have contributed to the mythology of Salem's history.

In the same way that Hawthorne has shaped our view of Salem, he has also shaped our view of the Puritans. Several of his stories portray the Salem of the first settlement from the vantage point of its fall from maritime dominance.

Hawthorne's Puritans were narrow and intolerant, struggling under their inherited burdens of religious divisions. In his rendition, Salem's settlers brought centuries-old European fears to a virgin land and planted them in its rich soil. The witch hysteria was only one portion of its dark harvest. In Hawthorne's hands, the events of Salem's founding days laid the groundwork for its enshrining event: the witch hysteria. In this mythic conception, these original sins continued to plague the community, and Salem's rise to global prominence was inevitably followed hard by retribution. The Custom House's dust and decay are the residue of Salem's fall from grace by the 1850s—just three-quarters of a century after the nation's founding. *The House of the Seven Gables* (1851) develops this theme of the dark harvest within the microcosmic world of the novel.

ટੈ

The story of the Salem witch trials was already widely available in nineteenth-century schoolbooks as a cautionary tale about religious excess—a metaphor ripe for exploitation in American literature and culture.[20] The nineteenth century is famously a time for "reform" movements—anti-Catholicism, anti-Mormonism, anti-Masonism, anti-Shakerism—and the period is generally marked by intense paranoia about new religious groups. Thus Hawthorne seized on readily available cultural material, but he turned it into something of his own. First in stories and later in novels, he cast the witch trials as the enshrining event in the foundation of the nation. Hawthorne made a parable of Salem's brief but brilliant rise to world prominence—its run as a real contender for the seat of the nation's capital, its wealth and cosmopolitan citizenry, its loss of national prominence, and finally, its fall into decay and grim nineteenth-century industrialization. In this parable, Salem became Rome—and Hawthorne helped forge the idea that America's far-flung empire had shrunk. Two empires, Salem's and America's, were in decline. In July 1853, he took his quest for mythic origins back to England when his college friend President Franklin Pierce appointed him consul in Liverpool. From 1857 to 1859, he lived in Rome and Florence, soaking up their great antique civilizations. The Italian setting of his novel *The Marble Faun* completed his imaginative iden-tification of America's decline with Rome's (though Hawthorne takes pains in that text to explicitly deny the connection).

Hawthorne writes often about Puritans, and he is also partly responsible for his readers' conception of him as a Puritan, admitting in "The Custom House" that "strong traits of their nature have intertwined themselves with mine."[21] Commentators on Hawthorne from his own day until ours note the way this Puritan vision infuses nearly everything he wrote. After reading *The Scarlet Letter,* his contemporary E. A. Duyckinck remarked that its severe moral "is a sounder bit of Puritan divinity than we have been of late accustomed to hear from the degenerate successors of Cotton Mather." Duyckinck concludes that the "spirit of his old Puritan ancestors, to whom he refers in the preface, lives in Nathaniel Hawthorne."[22] Henry James concurs, writing, in 1879, about *The Scarlet Letter* that "Puritanism, in a word is there, not only objectively, as Hawthorne tried to place it there, but subjectively as well. Not, I mean in his judgment of his characters, in any harshness of prejudice, or in the obtrusion of a moral lesson; but in the very quality of his own vision, in a certain coldness and exclusiveness of treatment."[23] Duyckinck and James share the view that Puritanism pervades Hawthorne's imagination— and I would add the reminder that Hawthorne's Puritanism is itself partly his own invention. The twentieth-century writer Jorge Luis Borges observed that Hawthorne's "Puritan desire to make a fable out of each and every imagining induced him to add morals and sometimes to falsify and to deform them."[24] Because Borges believed Hawthorne was essentially a Puritan, he suspected that Hawthorne regarded writing as "frivolous or . . . even sinful."[25] (Hawthorne admits as much in "The Custom House," calling himself an "idler" and imagining his horrified ancestors asking, "What is he? . . . A writer of storybooks! . . . Why, the degenerate fellow might as well have been a fiddler!")[26] Locating Hawthorne's guilt about writing in ancient tensions between theology and aesthetics, Borges claims that Hawthorne solved his dilemma by composing "moralities and fables" and by making "art a function of the conscience."[27]

Proponents of semiotic theory, the study of signs and symbols in systems of communication, argue that "there is no objective 'reality' that we can know apart from the language that we use to make sense of it."[28] Duyckinck, James, and Borges identify a significant reason why the sign *Salem* is so strongly identified with Hawthorne: this author, who writes so abundantly and memorably about the Puritans, seems never to be able to shake the Puritan worldview from his imagination, an attachment to his ancestors that he himself termed his "sensuous sympathy of dust for dust."[29] We have already discussed some of the reasons that readers mistakenly assume that *The Scarlet Letter* is set in Salem. Hawthorne's iron-willed depiction of the events in the novel is also a factor in the misperception. In much the same way as the popular imagination has transferred the identity of Mary Shelley's mad scientist Victor Frankenstein to the monster he created, Hawthorne's *Scarlet Letter,* in popular culture at least, is a Salem story.

Hawthorne had complex, ambivalent feelings about Salem as a place. In *Our Old Home* (1863), a reflection on his experience in England, he recalls Salem fondly as "my own dear native place."[30] After being fired from his post in the Custom House, he confessed, "This old town of Salem . . . possesses, or did possess, a hold on my affections, the force of which I have never realized during my seasons of actual residence here."[31] But in reflecting on the town in January 1841, he admitted to his future wife Sophia: "I ought to love Salem better than I do; for the people have always had a pretty generous faith in me, ever since they knew me at all."[32] Near the end of his stay at Brook Farm, in November 1841, he wrote to Sophia, lashing out at his native place: "I am intolerably weary of this old town. . . . Dost Thou not think it is really the most hateful place in all the world? My mind becomes heavy and nerveless, the moment I set foot in its precincts. Nothing makes me wonder more than that I found it possible to write all my tales in this same region of sleepy-head and stupidity."[33] At the end of his life, Nathaniel Hawthorne fled from Salem—after his return from England, he lived in Concord, Massachusetts, and, in 1864, died in Plymouth, New Hampshire. The author so closely associated with Salem is not even buried here, but in Concord.

"A Tentative Map of the Known World": Place in Hawthorne's Fiction

[T]he novel and its place have become one . . . [and] the same thing, like the explorer's tentative map of the known world.

—Eudora Welty

Given Hawthorne's deep connections to Salem, it is surprising that his own son, Julian, claimed that his father's "instinct for localities was not strongly developed." Furthermore, Julian averred that "there is comparatively little to be gained by the most conscientious consideration of the localities in which, for lack of better, the characters of Hawthorne's stories are seen and developed."[34] Salem, however, offered Hawthorne ideal material. It shaped him as a writer, and Hawthorne, in turn, shaped its *genius loci*. This sense of place was so powerful that later writers such as Mary E. Wilkins Freeman, Shirley Jackson, Arthur Miller, and the contemporary writer Bharati Mukherjee have profitably turned to Salem as a setting.[35] Eudora Welty's classic essay, "Place in Fiction," written in 1956, a century after Hawthorne reached his full powers as a novelist, offers a way of understanding how Hawthorne was able to infuse so much power into his depictions of Salem and how the town of Salem shaped Hawthorne's work.

Welty agrees with the common perception that place can give a novel its "regional" flavor, but she claims that its significance moves far beyond that. "Place," she writes, is where the writer "has his roots," and she connects location of the novel intimately with a writer's point of view, arguing that fiction is inextricably bound up in the local: "The internal reason for that is surely that feelings are bound up in place. . . . The truth is, fiction depends for its life on Place. Location is the cross-roads of circumstance."[36] But why are feelings so bound up in place? Welty pushes her exploration of the question to assert: "Place has a more lasting identity than we have, and we unswervingly tend to attach ourselves to identity."[37] This connection to identity is a key idea for thinking about the significance of place in fiction, in history, or in life. The place where our most momentous events happen—our birth and death—can continue to be a marker of our existence after we have passed on—in permanent records in city hall, or in the graveyard. In this sense, place can function as a monument to individual identity as well as to the histories of individuals and their communities.

It is this intersection of place and identity that made Hawthorne able to portray Salem so vividly—and that specifically influenced his writing of *The House of the Seven Gables.* Hawthorne recognized the power of the setting, writing in "The Custom House," "This long connection of a family with one spot, as its place of birth and burial, creates a kindred between the human being and the locality, quite independent of any charm in the scenery or moral circumstances that surround him. It is not love, but instinct."38 Hawthorne could not uproot himself from Salem, and this fact both fed and stemmed his creativity. T. S. Eliot articulated this paradox as "the difficult fact that [the] soil which produced him with his essential flavor is the soil which produced, just as inevitably, the environment which stunted him."39 Salem remained for good and ill, in Welty's term, Hawthorne's "heart's field."40

In plumbing the depths of his birthplace and its history, Hawthorne received what Welty calls "original awareness" in Salem. His obsessive explorations of Salem's history—and therefore America's—sharpened his awareness once he became an expatriate. Welty notes, "It is both natural and sensible that the place where we have our roots should become the setting, the first and primary proving-ground, of our fiction."41 Salem was Hawthorne's proving ground, the setting that most enriched his works. Welty observes that a writer's origins help him tap into the universal, and they promote his authenticity. As much as any other writer, Hawthorne seems to have anticipated her advice: "'Consider the source' [and] . . . base validity on point of origin."42

We have seen that historical events can enshrine a place; so can writers. Welty might concur: "Can anyone well explain otherwise what makes a given dot on the map come passionately alive, for good and all, in a novel . . . like one of those Novae that suddenly blaze with inexplicable fire in the heavens?"43 There is no question that Hawthorne permanently ignited Salem's blaze on the map of the American consciousness. Hawthorne's distinguishing mark, argued Henry James, was his feeling for the "latent romance of New England."44 The Salem author indeed created memorable New Englanders, such as Uncle Venner in *The House of the Seven Gables* and the narrator of "The Village Uncle" who romanticized a seaside town and its picturesque inhabitants.45 But Hawthorne's story "The Sister Years" (1838) goes further in suggesting a reason that Salem exerted such power on his imagination. Here, the narrator claims that everything he might need to know about America he could find in Salem: "[I]t would make you laugh to see how the game of politics, of which the Capitol at Washington is the great chess-board, is here played in miniature. Burning Ambition finds its fuel here; here Patriotism speaks boldly in the people's behalf, and virtuous Economy demands retrenchment in the emoluments of a lamplighter; here the Aldermen range their senatorial dignity around the Mayor's chair of state, and the Common Council feel that they have liberty in charge. In short, human weakness and strength, passion and policy, Man's tendencies, his aims and modes of pursuing them, his individual character and his character in the mass, may be studied almost as well here as on the theatre of the nations."[46] His concept of Salem as a kind of America writ small inspired Hawthorne to portray this dot on the map with unusual power.

In "The Sister Years," a dialogue takes place in Salem on New Year's Eve 1838 between the outgoing elder "Sister Year" and her young sister, the "New Year." Sister New Year disparages Salem as "ancient and time-worn," but the elder Year argues that during 1838 in Salem a New City Hall has been built, the railroad has opened, and

> Old Salem now wears a much livelier expression than when I first beheld her. Strangers rumble down from Boston by hundreds at a time. New faces throng in Essex Street. Railroad hacks and omnibuses rattle over the pavements. There is a perceptible increase in oyster shops, and other establishments for the accommodation of a transitory diurnal multitude. But a more important change awaits the venerable town. An immense accumulation of musty prejudices will be carried off by the free circulation of society. A peculiarity of character, of which the inhabitants themselves are hardly sensible, will be rubbed down and worn away by the attrition of foreign substances. Much of the result will be good; there will likewise be a few things not so good. Whether for better or worse, there will be a probable diminution of the moral influence of wealth, and the sway of an aristocratic class, which, from an era beyond my memory, has held firmer dominion here than in any other New England town.[47]

In many ways, the elder Sister Year is offering an argument closely allied with that of progressively thinking characters like Holgrave and Clifford in *The House of the Seven Gables,* a fervent hope that Salem, like the nation, will throw off its prejudices and embrace social reform. "The Sister Years" is set in the period just before Hawthorne took part in the transcendental experiment at Brook Farm. But ultimately, Hawthorne rejected the idealism of this story and retreated into the pessimism of *The Scarlet Letter* at midcentury. The forward-looking Salem envisioned by the narrator of "The Sister Years" and articulated by liberal thinkers such as Holgrave and Clifford in *The House of the Seven Gables* is proposed as a hypothetical model of Salem—but then Hawthorne rejects this construct of the community.

Hawthorne's famous Salem novel, *The House of the Seven Gables,* tells the story of a curse visited on the wealthy Pyncheon family by a member of the impoverished Maule family who is accused of witchcraft. It ends with the figure of a democratic marriage between the humble Maules and the elite Pyncheons—the union of Holgrave and Phoebe—and with Hepzibah Pyncheon having learned to give up some of her aristocratic pretensions. But as generations of Hawthorne scholars have pointed out, the large inheritance that passes to the couple as they begin their married life immediately begins to push them back into a world of Salem gentility.[48] Comfortably married to a rich Salem heiress, the groom brushes off his reform instincts like so many crumbs from the wedding cake. True, the overt theme of Hawthorne's novel is redemption, and technically the marriage of Holgrave and Phoebe blunts the generational curse of the Salem witch trials. But in discussing Salem as a place where an inheritance ensures that families can remain in firm dominion and power—even more so than in other New England towns—the passage cited earlier from "The Sister Years" presciently echoes Holgrave and Phoebe's likely marriage vows: "for better or worse." The liberal's prediction of a "diminution of the moral influence of wealth, and the sway of an aristocratic class" is clearly not the outcome of *The House of the Seven Gables,* though the snobbish Judge Pyncheon lies dead.

Hawthorne's chosen ending holds up a mirror to the lineage of power held by the richest families in Salem, and the novel's conclusion has been, at least until recently, criticized by generations of critics. Anthony Trollope bemoaned its formulaic "hurrying up of the marriage, and all the dollars which they inherit from the wicked Judge." F. O. Matthiessen, at a loss to explain why Hawthorne would let the novel "drift away into unreal complacence," decides that the author must have somehow "overlooked the fact that he was sowing all over again the same seeds of evil."[49] But readers who find the ending unsatisfying have missed the latent power of the novel's Salem setting. *The House of the Seven Gables* is not America writ large, but America writ small, Salem-style. The book is about what Hawthorne saw occurring in his native town, events that he may have seen as falling outside the democratizing developments in antebellum American culture at large. To paraphrase Welty, it is the particularity, the specificity of place, that is the focus of the novelist's attention. While American literature scholars now look to Hawthorne to articulate national themes, Hawthorne chose to remain firmly anchored in the local—in the life of Salem itself. The tenaciousness of the aristocracy in Salem and its "peculiarity of character," not Jacksonian reform movements in America, dictated the novel's conclusion. Holgrave enjoys the wealth that largely eluded Hawthorne throughout his life, and the novel's ending is consistent with the materialism of Salem's history.

But there is a way in which Holgrave's progressive bachelor visions did eventually become a reality, at least in Salem's historic House of the Seven Gables. American Studies scholar Joseph A. Conforti points out the irony that this particular Hawthorne novel has now become enshrined as Salem's literary site. Activist Caroline Emmerton's Colonial Revival "restoration" of Salem's House of the Seven Gables was part of her effort to provide social services to settle and Americanize

View of the House of the Seven Gables from Hawthorne's 1804 birthplace. Photo by Kim Mimnaugh.

immigrants at the turn of the twentieth century. Conforti notes that Emmerton's dual cultural and economic mission at the site "played several historical tricks on Hawthorne, not the least of which was to use the conservative writer's work and literary reputation in the cause of social reform."[50] For both historical and philosophical reasons, the House of the Seven Gables is not Hawthorne's house.

Salem Revisited: Arthur Miller's *The Crucible*

Nowhere in twentieth-century literature is the impact of Hawthorne's Salem felt more strongly than in Arthur Miller's *The Crucible*. As he conceived of the play, Miller recalled that gradually, "[a] living connection between myself and Salem, and between Salem and Washington, was made in my mind—for whatever else they might be, I saw that the [House Un-American Activities Committee] hearings in Washington were profoundly and even avowedly ritualistic."[51] In his introductory remarks to the play, Arthur Miller called the "crying-out" of 1692 "one of the strangest and most awful chapters in human history."[52] The play opens in the Salem bedroom of a widower, the Reverend Samuel Parris, in spring 1692. Recalling, perhaps, the group of gossips that surrounds the prison door as Hester steps forth with her scarlet A blazing in the noonday sun, Miller writes, "This predilection for minding other people's business was time-honored among the people of Salem, and it undoubtedly created many of the suspicions which were to feed the coming madness."[53]

Furthermore, Miller notes: "Sex, sin, and the Devil were early linked, and so they continued to be in Salem, and are today."[54] These themes are associated with Hawthorne's "composite" Salem, with his most famous novel, *The Scarlet Letter*, being largely about sex, sin, and the devil. At the height of the Cold War, and at the critical moment of Rev. John Hale's arrival on stage, Miller stops the action of the play to lecture: "Our opposites are always robed in sexual sin, and it is from this unconscious conviction that demonology gains both its attractive sensuality and its capacity to infuriate and frighten."[55] Miller's analysis in part explains the response of the Puritans of Boston to Hester Prynne. It also explains why demonization has had peculiar power in American history, especially during the mid-nineteenth century, when Hawthorne was writing, and in Miller's time one hundred years later. Hawthorne's treatment of the Puritan colony established numerous parallels for Miller to exploit: New England had its Scarlet A, its courts of Oyer and Terminer, its spectral evidence, its accused goodwives, its Gallows Hill; Miller's America had its blacklists, its House Un-American Activities Committee (HUAC), McCarthy's list, its Hollywood Ten, and its televised hearings. Miller's setting and didactic use of the Puritans of Salem grow directly out of Hawthorne's similar usage. Just as the Puritans used persecution as a way of enforcing a narrow conformity, so McCarthy and his followers sought to persecute and punish in order to free America from the shadow of enemies real and imagined.

Generations of students have been taught in literature classes that Hawthorne's stories helped forge the allegory of the virgin but untamed land and that he transformed the forest into a metaphor for moral darkness. While forests surrounded colonial Salem, Miller's use of it as a symbolic setting owes much to Hawthorne: "The edge of the wilderness was close by. The American continent stretched endlessly west, and it was full of mystery for them. It stood, dark and threatening, over their shoulders night and day, for out of it Indian tribes marauded from time to time. . . . the Salem folk believed that the virgin forest was the Devil's last preserve, his home base and the citadel of his final stand. To the best of their knowledge the American forest was the last place on earth that was not paying homage to God."[56] Miller's "dark and threatening" forest connects the paranoia of his age to Hawthorne's imaginary world in *The Scarlet Letter,* as well as to earlier lawless wilderness scenes in such works as "Roger Malvin's Burial" and "Young Goodman Brown." In a world gone MAD (Mutually Assured Destruction), Miller brooded as Americans retreated behind the palisaded protection of the North American Aerospace Defense Command (NORAD) and hunted for the Reds on Senator McCarthy's blacklist. Miller's canvas was America's nervous age, a "time of confusion [that] had been brought upon them by deep and darkling forces." He captured this confusion in his dark, dank image of the American forest, from which, "as in Salem, wonders are brought forth."[57]

Railing against the political climate of his time, Miller adapted Hawthorne's didactic tone as well. Hawthorne's stern moralizing stance perfectly suited Miller's purposes to illuminate the darkness that surrounded him. *The Crucible* stands as a scathing political critique of 1950s America, and it presages some of the paranoia of our own day, when dissent is often discouraged. Miller writes of the puritanical view of good and evil that pervades American politics: "[I]n America any man who is not reactionary in his views is open to the charge of alliance with the Red hell. . . . A political policy is equated with moral right, and opposition to it with diabolical malevolence."[58] The warning that Arthur Miller puts into the voice of his character, Deputy Governor Danforth, has been eerily echoed in the contemporary language of antiterrorism: "[A] person is either with this court or he must be counted against it, there be no road between. This is a sharp time, now, a precise time—we live no longer in the dusky afternoon when evil mixed itself with good and befuddled the world. Now, by God's light, the shining sun is up, and them that fear not light will praise it."[59] Miller sums up the central flaw of Puritan Salem, Hawthorne's Salem, McCarthy's America, and possibly our own age, as well: "They believed, in short, that they held in their steady hands the candle that would light the world. We have inherited this belief, and it has helped and hurt us."[60] In part, what Nathaniel Hawthorne's and Arthur Miller's "Salems" tell us today is to beware. Fear and paranoia have found the soil of America to be always a rich seed ground.

Writing during the Cold War era of the 1950s, Eudora Welty located the source of our deep attachment to place, which, she argued, is connected with feel-

ings of profound joy or tragedy. The meaningfulness of a place depends on its continuation as an extension of our identity. But the fragility of place, apparent in the
1950s and apparent today as terrorist alerts are coded yellow, orange, or red, is this:
"It's only too easy to conceive that a bomb that could destroy all trace of places as
we know them, in life and through books, could also destroy all feelings as we
know them, so irretrievably and so happily are recognition, memory, history, valor,
love, all the instincts of poetry and praise, worship and endeavor, bound up in
Place."[61] A sense of place creates our sense of self.

Nathaniel Hawthorne as Salem's Creation

Hawthorne's dark tale "Alice Doane's Appeal" illustrates the ways in which he
both built on and embroidered the sense of place that is Salem. Here, the story-
teller creates ambiance for his parable of fratricide and incestuous passion by nar-
rating it from the crest of Gallows Hill, overlooking the populous Salem of the
1830s at sundown. With the aid of the "peaceful glory and tender gloom of the declining sun," says the narrator, "we threw, in imagination, a veil of deep forest over
the land, and pictured a few scattered villages, and this old town itself a village, as
when the prince of hell bore sway here." From the very spot upon which executions of witches were carried out—"the most execrable scene that our history
blushes to record"—Salem 1830 is imaginatively transformed into rustic Salem
Village 1692. This historical contextualizing of his crime story, the narrator hopes,
will suitably impress his listeners, two young women who have accompanied him
to the hill. In an early aside to the reader, the narrator expresses some professional
jealousy over the success of a historian who will be able to "keep his name alive"
with his "antiquarian lore," a newly published account of the Salem witch trials.[62]
When the narrator deems his own story has not had the desired effect on the young
ladies, he decides to ascertain "whether truth were more powerful than fiction" and
spins out his own version of the witch hysteria.

Here, he meets with more success, recording with satisfaction that "their
nerves were trembling, and sweeter victory still, I had . . . found the well-spring of
their tears."[63] The deepening darkness of night falling over Salem and the chill cast
by the narrator's deft storytelling complete the identification between Salem's
bleak history and crimes committed here and elsewhere. Furthermore, the story-
teller adds to his own effectiveness by building on the available legacy of place.
Like the narrative frame of "Alice Doane's Appeal," Salem as a place wraps around
and infuses all of Hawthorne's work. Hawthorne's Salem retains its evocative
power over readers. The sense of place he created has been available to generations
of writers who followed him, especially those who, like Miller, wished to examine
essential truths about America. This Salem remains a powerful force in American
literature and culture.

What Welty noted about place in fiction also proved true of Hawthorne's character—Salem both confined and defined it. Hawthorne, indeed, invented Salem, but Salem, too, invented Hawthorne. Jane Tompkins, in *Sensational Designs,* presents a startling example of the many Hawthornes that have emerged in American literary history, some more connected to Salem than others. The 1932 edition of *Century Readings in American Literature* was published with a biographical sketch of a "shy and solitary" Hawthorne, "writing, dreaming and wandering about the city at night." This portrait illustrates the way Hawthorne is identified with, and indeed, is metamorphosed into, a personification of Salem itself. The Hawthorne of *Century Readings* was a "pale night flower" blooming amidst the "old decay and ruin" of Salem's "glory departed." Tompkins points out the dramatic contrast between the Salem Hawthorne of the 1932 *Century Readings* and the "healthy" Hawthorne of the 1979 *Norton Anthology,* which includes a revisionist biography of the author. In characterizing Hawthorne, revisionists creatively used the word *healthy* to connote tramping around, drinking, smoking, and card playing. This revised Hawthorne is not Salem's solitary prisoner, but a Hawthorne who actually socialized, flirted, and traveled "as far as Detroit."[64] The writer, like the city of his birth, is mythologized by this place, and in American memory.

Hawthorne eventually left Salem and could never bring himself to return. Whatever the struggle was within him, he alluded to it only obliquely. He characterized his ambivalent feelings for Salem as a "strange, indolent, unjoyous attachment," expanding on Salem's power over him in words found near the end of "The Custom House": "[M]y old native town will loom upon me through the haze of memory, a mist brooding over and around it; as if it were no portion of the real earth, but an overgrown village in cloudland, with only imaginary inhabitants to people its wooden houses, and walk its homely lanes, and the unpicturesque prolixity of its main street. Henceforth, it ceases to be a reality in my life. I am a citizen of somewhere else."[65] In a peculiar way, Hawthorne's choice meant that he would cease to be a reality in Salem's life as well, a fate he divined when he expressed the hope at the end of "The Custom House" that Salem's future generations might recall him kindly as "the scribbler of bygone days" and point out the town pump as a site made famous in his works.[66] But when he left, he, too, became one of Salem's "imaginary inhabitants." Because he chose to be "a citizen of somewhere else," we glimpse him now only "through the haze of memory."

You can follow the same oak-lined avenues and waterfront alleys that he wandered. You can walk the streets of Salem looking for Hawthorne's presence, but you will find only traces of him. His vacant chair and writing desk still sit in the Custom House, as if awaiting his return. You can run your fingers over a small bas-relief image of his face and sip from a drinking fountain marking the site of the old town pump at the corner of Washington and Essex. You can sojourn at the Hawthorne Hotel and dine in its upscale restaurant, Nathaniel's. Through the windows of this elegant dining room, you can gaze at his bronzed image, brooding over Hawthorne Boulevard. You can peruse collections of his tales in Salem's

Statue of Nathaniel Hawthorne, Hawthorne Boulevard. Photo by Margaret Press.

bookstores and museum shops. You will not find him. Because he refused to build his house in Salem, Salem built one for him. The House of the Seven Gables is a place linked to Nathaniel Hawthorne, but it is not his house. An authentic remnant of the man, his 1804 birthplace, was moved from its site on Union Street to sit literally in the shadow of the tourist attraction known to locals as H7G. Hawthorne's decision to abandon Salem left an empty chair in the Custom House as his memorial, and Salem's myths would fill it.

Notes

I wish to thank Asenath Blake, Lucinda Damon-Bach, Frank Devlin, Patricia Johnston, Elizabeth Kenney, Dane Morrison, Christine Rawlins, Arthur Riss, Jackson Schultz, J. D. Scrimgeour, Peter Walker, and David Watters for their kind assistance.

1. Preface, *The Complete Short Stories of Nathaniel Hawthorne* (New York: Doubleday, 1959).

2. Hawthorne and his New England legacy are further explored by scholars such as Edward L. Ayers and Peter S. Onuf, eds., *All over the Map: Rethinking American Regions* (Baltimore:

Johns Hopkins University Press, 1996); Dona Brown, *Inventing New England: Regional Tourism in the Nineteeth Century* (Washington, D.C.: Smithsonian Institution Press, 1995); Joseph Conforti, *Imagining New England* (Chapel Hill: University of North Carolina Press, 2001); Michael C. Steiner and Clarence Mondale, eds., *Region and Regionalism in the United States: A Source Book for Humanities and Social Sciences* (New York: Garland, 1988); Perry D. Westbrook, *A Literary History of New England* (Bethlehem: Lehigh University Press, 1988); and Hilda White, *Truth Is My Country: Portraits of Eight New England Authors* (New York: Doubleday, 1971). For specific studies of Hawthorne in Salem, see K. David Goss, Richard B. Trask, Bryant F. Tolles Jr., Joseph Flibbert, and Jim McAllister, *Salem: Cornerstones of a Historic City* (Beverly, Mass.: Commonwealth Editions, 1999); and Margaret Moore, *The Salem World of Nathaniel Hawthorne* (Columbia: Missouri University Press, 1998).

3. Other factors strengthened the use of Salem as a synonym for Puritan intolerance during the nineteenth century, including the 1820 republication of Cotton Mather's *Magnalia Christi Americana* (1702). See also Lawrence I. Buell's *New England Literary Culture: From Revolution through Renaissance* (Cambridge: Cambridge University Press, 1986).

4. Since one can find a great deal of scholarship on Hawthorne and his works elsewhere, this essay will not attempt to survey the critical tradition. For an excellent survey, see Pierre A. Walker's essay, "Why We Still Read Hawthorne 150 Years Later," posted on the *Hawthorne in Salem* website at *http://www.hawthorneinsalem.org/ScholarsForum/MMD2004.html*. In addition to a continuous blossoming of new editions of Hawthorne's novel and stories, some new books about the author include Otto and Katharine Bird, *From Witchery to Sanctity: The Religious Vicissitudes of the Hawthornes* (South Bend, Ind.: St. Augustine's Press, 2003); Richard Kopley, *The Threads of the Scarlet Letter: A Study of Hawthorne's Transformative Art* (Newark, N.J.: University of Delaware Press, 2003); Nathaniel Hawthorne, *Twenty Days with Julian by Papa* (New York: New York Review of Books, 2003); and Harold Bloom and Aislin Goodman, eds., *Nathaniel Hawthorne (Bloom's Biocritiques)* (Broomall, Penn.: Chelsea House, 2003).

5. The emergence of an American national identity, especially through Salem's contact with the East, is discussed in Dane Morrison's essay in this collection, "Salem as Citizen of the World." For a seminal discussion of Hawthorne and the development of national identity, see Lauren Berlant, *The Anatomy of National Fantasy: Hawthorne, Utopia, and Everyday Life* (Chicago: Chicago University Press, 1991).

6. F. O. Matthiessen, *American Renaissance: Art and Expression in the Age of Emerson and Whitman* (London: Oxford University Press, 1941).

7. In *Nathaniel Hawthorne's Tales*, ed. James McIntosh (New York: W. W. Norton, 1987), 221.

8. *http://movies.yahoo.com/shop?d=hv&cf=info&id=1800114797*, retrieved July 27, 2003. The movie poster for *Horror Hotel* capitalizes on Salem's long history with a tagline of "300 years old! Human blood keeps them alive forever!" The film features the "fetching Venetia Stevenson . . . as Nan Barlow, a young college student who is writing a paper on witchcraft. On winter break, Nan travels to New England to do some research and, on one of her professor's recommendations, stays in a small hotel run by the spirit of an undead witch. Soon, Nan finds that the rest of the hotel's boarders are witches as well and that she is about to become their annual Candalmas Eve sacrifice." *Psyched by the 4-D Witch* is billed as "a psychic, acid-fueled freakout about a young woman who becomes inhabited by the nymphomaniac spirit of a Salem witch."

9. *Tales*, 227–28.

10. Nathaniel Hawthorne, *The Scarlet Letter,* ed. Ross C. Murfin (Boston: Bedford/St. Martin's, 1991), 53.

11. *The Scarlet Letter,* 56.

12. "The Custom House," in *The Scarlet Letter,* 27.

13. This connection between *The Scarlet Letter* and *The Crucible* has been noticed by film critics. See Sergio Rizzo's "'Hystorical' Puritanism: Contemporary Cinematic Adaptations of Nathaniel Hawthorne's *The Scarlet Letter* and Arthur Miller's *The Crucible,*" in *Classics in Film and Fiction,* ed. Deborah Cartnell, I. Q. Hunter, Heidi Kaye, and Imelda Whelehan (London: Pluto, 2000), 93–115. See also Mikos Trocsanya, "Two Views of American Puritanism: Hawthorne's *The Scarlet Letter* and Miller's *The Crucible,*" in *The Origins and Originality of American Culture,* ed. Frank Tabor (Budapest: Akademiai Kiado, 1984), 63–71; and Herbert Bergman, "The Interior of a Heart: *The Crucible* and *The Scarlet Letter,*" *University College Quarterly* (East Lansing, Mich.) 15, no. 4 (1970): 27–32.

14. See Arthur Miller, "Why I Wrote 'The Crucible,'" *New Yorker,* October 21, 1996, 158–64.

15. The population of Salem, Oregon, is about 100,000; Salem in Tamil Nadu, India, has a population of approximately 515,000.

16. *Tales,* 93.

17. "The Custom House," 41. For a landmark essay on the connection between "The Custom House" and *The Scarlet Letter,* see Stephen Nissenbaum, "The Firing of Nathaniel Hawthorne," *Essex Institute Historical Collections* 114 (1978): 57–86.

18. "The Custom House," 23.

19. Salem's population in 1850 was 20,264, and its population in 2002 was 39,192. *City of Salem, Massachusetts Manual of City Government—2000.* In 1800, Boston's population was about 25,000. However, by 1850 it had jumped to almost 137,000. *http://physics.bu.edu/~redner/projects/population/cities/boston.html,* retrieved July 21, 2003.

20. See Gretchen Adams, "The Specter of Salem in American Culture" (Ph.D. diss., University of New Hampshire, 2001).

21. "The Custom House," 27.

22. See J. Donald Crowley, ed., *Hawthorne: The Critical Heritage* (New York: Barnes, 1971), 156–57. Quoted in Ross C. Murfin, "Introduction: The Critical Background," in *The Scarlet Letter,* 207.

23. Henry James, *Hawthorne* (1879; reprint, New York: AMS, 1968), 112–14. Quoted in Murfin, "Introduction," 209.

24. Jorge Luis Borges, "Nathaniel Hawthorne," in *Tales,* 407.

25. Borges, 411.

26. "The Custom House," 27.

27. Borges, 411.

28. Donald E. Hall, *Literary and Cultural Theory: From Basic Principles to Advanced Applications* (Boston: Houghton Mifflin, 2001), 137.

29. "The Custom House," 26.

30. Nathaniel Hawthorne, *The Centenary Edition of the Works of Nathaniel Hawthorne,* ed. William Charvat et al., 23 vols. (Columbus: Ohio State University Press, 1962–1997), V, 165. Quoted in Moore, 2.

31. "The Custom House," 26.

32. Hawthorne, *Centenary Edition*, XV, 518. Quoted in Moore, 2.

33. Hawthorne, *Centenary Edition*, XV, 596. Quoted in Moore, 2.

34. Julian Hawthorne, "The Salem of Hawthorne," *Century Magazine* 28, no. 1 (May 1884): 3.

35. Mary E. Wilkins Freeman's play, *Giles Corey, Yeoman,* appeared in 1892. Her 1894 novel *Pembroke* is set in a New England village much like Salem. Shirley Jackson's haunting New England short story "The Lottery" was published in 1948. Bharati Mukherjee's 1993 novel, *The Holder of the World,* situates some of its story in Salem and makes explicit reference to Hawthorne.

36. Eudora Welty, *Three Papers on Fiction* (Northampton, Mass.: Smith College, 1962), 2–3.

37. Welty, 3.

38. "The Custom House," 28.

39. Quoted in Matthiessen, 334.

40. Welty, 3.

41. Welty, 12.

42. Welty, 4.

43. Welty, 7.

44. James, "Nathaniel Hawthorne," in Hawthorne, *Complete Short Stories,* 1.

45. "The Village Uncle" was set in Swampscott, Massachusetts, not Salem.

46. Hawthorne, *Complete Short Stories,* 168.

47. Hawthorne, *Complete Short Stories,* 168–69.

48. For further reading about Hawthorne and the rise of middle-class values in America, see T. Walter Herbert, *Dearest Beloved: The Hawthornes and the Making of the Middle Class Family* (Berkeley: University of California Press, 1993), especially chapter 6, "Democratic Mythmaking in *The House of the Seven Gables.*"

49. Matthiessen, 331–34. Anthony Trollope quoted in Matthiessen, 332.

50. Conforti, 252.

51. Quoted in William Klingaman, "The Crucible," *Encyclopedia of the McCarthy Era* (New York: Facts on File, 1996), 96–97.

52. Arthur Miller, *The Crucible: A Play in Four Acts* (New York: Penguin, 1952), np.

53. Miller, 5.

54. Miller, 35.

55. Miller, 36.

56. Miller, 5.

57. Miller, 6.

58. Miller, 34.

59. Miller, 94.

60. Miller, 5.

61. Welty, 6.

62. Hawthorne, "Alice Doane's Appeal," in *Complete Short Stories,* 557.

63. Hawthorne, "Alice Doane's Appeal," 563–64.

64. Jane Tompkins, *Sensational Designs: The Cultural Work of American Fiction, 1790–1860* (New York: Oxford University Press, 1985), 196–97.

65. "The Custom House," 28, 53.

66. "The Custom House," 53.

Garden gate, Salem, Massachusetts. Photo by Kim Mimnaugh.

Chapter Eight

Salem as Architectural Mecca

JOHN V. GOFF

There was a day, and not very long ago, neither, when I stood at my counting-room window, and watched the signal flags of three of my own ships entering the harbor, from the East Indies, from Liverpool, and from up the Straits.

—Nathaniel Hawthorne, "The Canterbury Pilgrims"

ECCA is the great holy city in the East to which devout Moslems turn for inspiration. Extended to popular culture, the name can also signify any place "regarded as the center of an activity or interest." In "Salem as Architectural Mecca," we will consider how the old New England seaport town of Salem, Massachusetts, looked distantly across the oceans to take some of its longest-lasting and most character-defining architectural cues from the East, principally China, with which it traded extensively after the Revolutionary War. We will further consider the degree to which Salem evolved a unique New England and American architecture based in part upon its interpretation of ancient Chinese design motifs. Finally, we will discuss the ways in which Salem was "discovered" and commercially valued in the 1870s as an important repository of Early American architectural designs and details after the Colonial Revival developed as America's most popular architectural style. By looking distantly east and then becoming an East Coast place to which others looked for inspiration, Salem both evolved an exceptional New England architecture and became a Mecca for architects seeking to raise the level of the Colonial Revival style throughout the United States.[1]

Salem Looks to the East

Salem was a prosperous maritime community almost continuously from its founding in 1626. Yet, after the Revolutionary War was concluded in 1783, economic recession plagued the young United States. John Adams, then ambassador to England, advised all Americans to look to the fabled East Indies to gain new profits. Wise merchants, heeding his call, looked beyond the traditional spheres of trade with Europe, Africa, the West Indies, and South America to establish exotic new trade routes in distant India, the East Indies, and the East.[2]

Much has been written about the exceptional Chinese silks, spices, ivory, porcelains, silver, fans, textiles, and luxury goods that were brought to New England in China Trade ships two hundred years ago, allowing Salem merchants to earn vast profits, build impressive Federal style mansions, and retire in high style. Scholars have proposed that as late as 1850 a fifth of every household's goods in Salem came from China. Small wonder that some of the old seaport's private homes are still crammed with China Trade furnishings. Furthermore, visitors to Salem can still admire hand-painted Chinese wallpaper in the Assembly House on Federal Street, mint condition Canton china brought in 1818 to the Ropes Mansion, and a building full of Asian export art in Salem's Peabody Essex Museum. Crosby Forbes, writing about the museum's new Asian Export Art building in 1988, concluded: "One of the most important contributions of the new wing is that it provides a base camp for further exploration of Asian export art—one of the last major fields of the decorative arts that remains to be explored." In this essay, we shall explore the distinctive architecture of Salem that was derived from Asian export art. We will suggest ways that Salem has been marked by the motifs of the Celestial Kingdom and will demonstrate how the China Trade legacy continues to shape the city's sense of itself as a seaport still connected to "the farthest ports of the rich East."[3]

The China Trade made Salem. One observer who lived amidst Salem's glory days was Marianne Cabot Devereux Silsbee (1812–1889), who boasted in her delightful memoir, *A Half Century in Salem,* "In the early days of this [nineteenth] century, the sun did not shine on a more prosperous town." Her recollections tell us something about the influence of the East Indies trade that dramatically elevated Salem sailors and merchants: "The East India trade had opened the avenue on which indominatable [*sic*] merchants strode with rapid steps to wealth and honor. Derbys, Peabodys, Dodges, Pickmans, Wests, Crowninshields, Forresters, Grays, Silsbees, and probably many others were amassing fortunes more or less splendid. Forests of masts rose at the Derby and Crowninshield wharves; the men worked with a will, and their wives and daughters aided them by a wise economy."[4]

The China Trade made Salem not just prosperous but distinctive, imbuing the seaport with a cosmopolitan and sophisticated spirit. Historian Ping Chia Kuo captures this worldly atmosphere in 1930 in his study, "Canton and Salem." Ping reveals the ways in which the new trade connections with China had the additional consequence of "spreading Chinese culture into the heart of old New England." He quotes a poem by William Wetmore Story that illustrates Salem residents' enthusiasm and receptiveness to integrating Eastern culture into their own:

> Ah me, how many an autumn day
> We watched with palpitating breast,
> Some stately ship, from India or Cathay,
> Laden with spicy odors from the East,
> Come sailing up the bay![5]

As Ping shows, trade with the East had profound consequences for "old New England." The Eastern influence dramatically expanded Salemites' sensibilities, filling their cupboards, influencing their literature, and challenging their fundamental sense of place. Most visibly, images, impressions, and motifs from "all the gorgeous East," in Hawthorne's words, changed the way Salem looked. Salemites borrowed extensively from their experiences in the Indian Ocean, Pacific Ocean, and South China Sea to renovate their houses, their gardens, and their civic arenas. Architecture has a profound impact upon sense of place, because the purpose of the built environment is both to provide shelter and to uplift the human spirit. Long after a building or place is constructed to meet a specific set of design needs for one generation, it may survive to influence subsequent generations and continue to define and express the community's "sense of place." This is usually the case when a town's "best" or most valued edifices are cherished and preserved as local landmarks. A community's values, goals, and aspirations are all safeguarded in the act of preservation, allowing subsequent generations to reflect upon the things that distinguish their landscapes and cityscapes and to consider the meaning of the landmarks and commemorative moments that have bound their times and space. Landmarks become treasured reference points in the built environment, allowing new growth to be measured against ideals, standards, and pieces of civilizations from the past.[6]

Why did home owners, builders, and architects in old Salem incorporate Chinese motifs in their American architecture? Why did subsequent generations of Salem home owners and architects further elaborate these Asian motif designs in subsequent decades? These are challenging questions for the architectural historian, particularly because, until recently, few if any practitioners acknowledged *any* Eastern influences in the brick and clapboard that defines the city. More research is certainly required. It would be exciting to uncover records in which early home owners, designers, and builders put on paper their philosophies and goals for new architectural designs.[7]

In the absence of such written records, I have utilized the methods of both the historic site archaeologist and the architectural historian to attempt to "allow mute objects to speak." From these studies, it appears that visual and architectural repetitions and patterns in Salem's built environment provide ample evidence of Chinese influences on Salem's architecture. One finds in Salem example after example of the adoption and adaptation of place-specific and uniquely "Salem" coin-type windows, window muntins, and wrought iron fence and railing patterns throughout the Federal period and after.[8]

These exotic elements likely became favored design motifs in Salem because, during the Federal period, a majority of the finest houses were built by Salem merchants, sea captains, and sailors who had voyaged to Eastern waters and derived a significant percentage of their wealth from the fabled China Trade. Sailors and their families were proud of the great distances they had sailed. One can find in the Plummer Hall reading room of the Peabody Essex Museum over four hundred ships' logs and journals that frequently describe in respectful terms the philosophies, customs, and traditions that distinguished the Chinese. Relics from Eastern ports were likely kept as reminders of other places, peoples, and adventures. This history is reflected in the Chinese motifs that later generations of architects developed after the Colonial Revival style became popular after 1870.[9]

Colonial Revival architects sought ways to better integrate new construction with the old as a way of celebrating Salem's history and esteemed building traditions. They succeeded in identifying, preserving, and continuing these traditions and in integrating expressions of Salem's pride, global outreach, and economic prosperity. The Chinese symbols, especially those connected to "prosperity," became a source of pride for many Salem residents—not simply the owners and builders of landmarks with Chinese references and architectural influences.[10]

Five Categories of Chinese Architectural Influences

In walking through the residential quarters of Salem, we can observe what other architectural historians have overlooked. At least five distinct classes of so-called traditional New England architecture include representations drawn from ancient Chinese design. What is striking is that all of these are found in Salem. Given Salem's intimate ties to the East, it is likely that Salem's mariners first brought these design motifs to their home port, and from there they spread throughout New England. Along Lafayette Street, Washington Square, and Chestnut Street, famous as "the most beautiful street in America," we can see the following:

1. "China coin" type windows. These are either round or oval and have many variations (e.g., quatrefoil, flower, fish, bat, diamond center, cross center, curved lozenge, etc.). We can trace this imagery back to a distinguished and ancient symbol for "coin" or "prosperity." Salem's merchants and mariners would have seen these over the shop doors of Cantonese (Guangzhou) merchants and introduced them when they returned home.[11]

2. Chinese "stick" type fences and balustrades. These depict sticks arranged in panel designs, millstone dress, double rhombus, and Endless Knot designs.

3. Window and fence designs based upon "overlapping ovals" and lenticular-shaped elements.

4. Colonial Revival style windows and sidelights with small diamond panes alternating with tall vertical rectangles and compressed hexagons. These appear to have derived from the patterns in glazed doors of China cabinets, which in turn derived from Eastern influence and Chinese lattice designs.

5. Colonial Revival octagonal leaded glass windows. Some of these appear to have been designed to imitate fine Chinese porcelain plates.

Transcending these five specific motif categories, we see in Salem's architecture profound historical significance: the motivation and tendency of old New England's China Trade families and their craftsmen to borrow China's highly ornate and complex designs. We find these imitations in Salem's window muntins, fences, stair balusters, and exterior balustrades. All of these elements allude to, and were evolved from, carved lattice patterns in Chinese architecture and from Chinese goods such as fans, ivories, silk patterns, and furniture. While most of America's Federal period architecture is generally known to have evolved from early American study of Scottish and Western prototypes, such as works by Robert and James Adam, I contend that a number of specific design motifs derive as well from Salem's early commerce with the East.

We will begin by looking at the "Chinese coin" motif that has become known as the "Salem" motif.[12]

Salem's Merchant Princes Bring Eastern Designs to Salem

Salem was the birthplace of New England's China Trade. Indeed, there were direct parallels between the Salem families who profited most from the Eastern trade and the homes that prominently feature Chinese designs. Initially, just a few "merchant princes" monopolized New England's trade with China, but very quickly dozens of Salem families competed to earn their fair share of new wealth and prestige. The merchant credited with opening New England's China Trade was Salem's Elias Hasket Derby, reportedly America's first millionaire. Under the command of Capt. Ebenezer West, Derby's *Grand Turk* made the first voyage from New England to India and China between 1785 and 1787. In February 1789, Derby dispatched the *Astrea* to China, the first ship to directly sail from Salem to Canton. These voyages inaugurated a great era of maritime adventure and prosperity, benefiting the "merchant princes" whose names now grace the town's streets: Derby, West, Dodge, Pickman, Forrester, and Boardman.[13]

Salem's interest in all things Chinese became especially heightened by 1799, when the East India Marine Society was founded to better develop Salem's trade links and cultural ties with the "Celestial" or "Flowery" Kingdom and Canton. A new round of Chinese fever seized Salem, resulting in houses being retrofitted with Chinese balustrades. Three examples included the Pickman-Orne House, the Curwen-Ward-Bowditch House, and the Hodges House, then all located on Essex Street, the principal avenue downtown. By 1799, Derby had also accumulated sufficient wealth to build a spectacular Federal style mansion in downtown Salem at Derby Square. While Derby's house no longer stands and cannot be studied in detail, Ping noted that "Elias Hasket Derby used Chinese images to assist in ornamenting his house." Whether these were prints or patterns or other elements, it is now difficult to say.[14]

Eastern Origins of the Coin Motif

Using the visual comparative method of the architectural historian, it is possible to directly trace one of Salem's most "signature" architectural motifs—the China coin symbol—to ancient China. One of the oldest and most enduring symbols in Chinese and Eastern art and culture, the metal coin (*qian*), or cash, is represented variously as: (1) a circle with a square hole at the center; or (2) a circle with a diamond at the center; or (3) a circle with a curved lozenge at the center. These symbols all evolved in China to mean "coin," "cash," "wealth," or "prosperity," because ancient Chinese coins of copper and brass were round, with punched square holes at the center, which allowed them to be stored on strings.[15]

In the East, great attention was put on multiplying riches and wealth. The Chinese came to hold sacred Liu Hai, a benevolent deity who was often pictured as swinging a string of coins and accompanied by a three-legged toad. They also evolved the notion of a money-tree where drooping branches strung with coins would make wealth freely available to the blessed.[16] To invoke and symbolize both the multiplication of wealth and good luck, the ancient Chinese also adopted a coded symbol of two coins, intertwined. This symbol was (and is) variously marked in Chinese export goods and porcelain, woven into rugs and tapestries, or simply knotted into string or fabric.[17] Lydia Chen, the authority on traditional Chinese knotting techniques, observes: "The [Chinese] double coin knot is a knotted representation of an often employed decorative motif, composed of two antique Chinese coins overlapping one another. Merchants [in China] once took the design to mean prosperity, hanging it over the entrance to their shops, hoping to attract wealth. Used elsewhere, the double coin motif connotes not only prosperity, but longevity as well."[18] On Chinese porcelains, the double-coin motif typically employed curved lozenge coins, each turned 45 degrees so the curves were mostly horizontal and vertical, and intertwined, such as are found on ceramic, barrel-shaped garden seats. Because the curve of the lozenge matches the curve of the circle, the coins intertwine, indicating a multiplication of wealth and blessing. During the first thirty years of

Chinese prosperity god Liu Hai with string of coins. Courtesy of John Goff.

Salem's involvement with the China Trade (1787–1817), its residents saw a vast array of Eastern material artifacts adorned with exotic symbols, and they were particularly fascinated with the China coin. They began collecting Chinese coins and other artifacts for education and recreation. As late as 1850, for example, fancy painted paper Chinese fans were being shipped to Salem. These objects introduced the fan shape, painted scenes of Chinese harbors, black and gold decorative panels (resembling what was later called "Japanned" goods), and specific Chinese symbols—including both the three-legged toad and the circle-with-curved-lozenge symbols for Liu Hai and for wealth, prosperity, and blessing. The fans, porcelains, and papers that displayed these motifs were given mostly to the ladies in Salem, who admired and kept the fans and other ornaments as rare treasures.[19]

Chinese fan depicting Salem vessels in Whampoa Anchorage. Courtesy of Peabody Essex Museum.

The Andrew-Safford House, 1818–1819

Dominating the west side of the Salem Common, also known as Washington Square, is the Andrew-Safford House, built in 1818–1819. There we can see some of the earliest and best-preserved examples of China coin motifs. Gerald W. R. Ward speculated in 1976 that the fanlight above the front door was "gracefully divided into ovals and ellipses," but the pattern more closely resembles three curved lozenge-type Chinese coins, touching both each other and the overarching fan.[20]

John Andrew (1774–1829) was a merchant with Archer and Andrew and a commission merchant in Russia who owned stock in Salem's East India Marine Hall Corporation. He imported fragrant sandalwood to Salem in ships sailing from the East.[21] Since the newly built Andrew-Safford House was considered to have been the most costly residence in New England, it has been commonly assumed that Mr. Andrew acquired all his fortune in business. However, Mrs. Andrew, née Catharine Forrester, was Simon Forrester's daughter. In 1817, just prior to building the new mansion, the Andrews inherited a grand fortune from Forrester, reportedly "the richest man in Salem." Much Forrester wealth had been generated through the China Trade. Forrester's first ship, *Perseverence,* for example, returned to Boston in 1802 with Eastern tea, satin, and nankin cloths, netting an almost unheard-of sum of $21,000 in a single voyage. The *Perseverence* was also one of the chief Salem importers of fine Chinese porcelains and ceramics.[22]

When the Andrews began developing their new Salem house, the Reverend William Bentley remarked that Captain Forrester's "money will serve to decorate Washington Square."[23] We can infer, then, that the coin motifs utilized in the windows of the house paid tribute to the old captain's Eastern connections. The China Trade theme likely explains, as well, the Chinese fan-shaped louvred ornaments in the balustrade. These elements correspond to the alignment of major window openings in the main front and sides of the house. In some of the interior windows of the house, curved lozenge coins were utilized as additional fanlight accents (with two other coins and standing alone), while one of the more elaborate windows has designs resembling a flying bat.[24]

In *Friends of the House: Furniture from China's Towns and Villages* (1995), Nancy Berliner and Sarah Handler demonstrate that the Chinese "auspicious characters and carvings" were "a visual vocabulary . . . read as easily as a written language." They further note that the Chinese sometimes mixed coin and bat motifs to signify "blessings in front of your eyes." In the Chinese phrase *fuzai yan quiam, fu* is homophonous with "bat" and "blessings," while *yan* is homophonous with "coin" and "eye." Thus the shapes for "bat" and "coin" could (when understood) secretly stand for—and help one to focus upon—blessings and prosperity in front of one's eyes.[25]

The Humphrey Devereaux House, 1826–1827

Turning our steps in the direction of Chestnut Street, we come to the Humphrey Devereaux House. Eight years after the three-coin fanlight design was installed above the front door of the Andrew-Safford House, a nearly identical three-coin fanlight was built above the front door of 26 Chestnut Street.[26] Devereaux is thought to have been a Salem mariner. In both the Andrew-Safford House and the Devereaux House, we see a direct early-nineteenth-century adaptation of both the circle and curved lozenge shape to mean "coin" and the placement over the entrance to invoke prosperity and blessing. This imitation was likely fueled by Salem's focus upon prosperity and "making it" in the world, as well as by the superstitious nature of those who went to sea in the Great Age of Sail. With death, disease, accident, piracy, enemy attack, changes in weather affecting market conditions, and storm and shipwreck so easily at hand, sailors took special care to invoke blessings, particularly when they returned from sea to retire in a grand new home. Eastern auspicious symbols likely exerted strong appeal in Salem, since they both reminded one of the spectacular past—and memories of "all the gorgeous East"—while safeguarding the home, its occupants, and their future.[27]

Humphrey Devereaux House. Photo by Kim Mimnaugh.

The John Bertram House, c. 1840

Walking back near Washington Square, we come to the John Bertram House at 24 Winter Street. Captain Bertram's house is famed for a most unusual fanlight that features five framed double-circled quatrefoil shapes of various sizes. The quatrefoil shape is traditionally used to symbolize the persimmon in Chinese art, and the fruit is used in the East to represent "business" or "affairs"; the Chinese words for both (*shi*) are homophonous. Persimmon red is an auspicious color in Chinese tradition, and the fruit's four top leaves trace a quatrefoil shape around the stem. Persimmon shapes, "double-circled" and placed above front doors of Chinese homes and shops, invoked, as did coins, a blessing for "prosperity in business" or "success in worldly affairs." The persimmon motif seems to have worked its effect for John Bertram—the captain retired with enormous wealth and is remembered as one of the last of Salem's great sea captains in the Eastern trade. By the 1850s, the fabulously wealthy Bertram constructed an even more elaborate home—the imported brownstone Italianate style mansion that currently serves as the Salem Public Library at 370 Essex Street.[28]

The John P. Peabody House, 1874

During the 1870s, a new American architectural style—the Colonial Revival—developed, spearheaded by Boston architects such as Robert Peabody of Peabody and Stearns in Boston, Arthur Little, and John Benson. Through the North Shore roots of some of these pioneer Colonial Revival architects, and because of access to Salem and the North Shore by the new railroad trains, Salem's historic architecture increasingly became appreciated for representing the best of American and Early American outlook and culture. Colonial Revival architects became excited by Salem's architecture and culture as a new symbol of America's best. New architectural works were created to continue and further develop Salem's great architectural traditions from the Great Age of Sail.

North of Chestnut Street, we come to one of New England's earliest and finest houses designed in the new Colonial Revival style: the John P. Peabody House at 15 Summer Street, built in 1874. The Peabody House is a fine gambrel-roofed neo-Georgian edifice, sort of a miniaturized copy of the pre–Revolutionary War era Cabot-Endicott-Low House at 365 Essex Street. Evidencing Federal period references, one of the J. P. Peabody House's most attractive features is the design of the sidelights near the front door. They present an entire visual essay based upon the China coin motif. A large and elongated oval Chinese coin shape is framed at top and bottom by smaller arrangements of two smaller circles, sandwiched between two medium-sized, round Chinese coins.[29]

Peabody House. Photo by Kim Mimnaugh.

The Pickman-Loring-Emmerton House, 1885

Heading west from Summer Street, we arrive at the Pickman-Loring-Emmerton House at 328 Essex Street. By 1885, Colonial Revival architect Arthur Little (1852–1925) of neighboring Swampscott was practicing in Boston and Salem, commissioned by the George R. Emmerton family to remodel and expand the old Pickman House, or Loring-Emmerton House, as it is currently known. George R. Emmerton, a Salem merchant and president of Merchant's National Bank, married Mary Jane Bertram, a descendant of the wealthy Capt. John Bertram. At the time of remodeling, Emmerton was also "a member of the firm of Ropes, Emmerton & Co.," East India trade "successors of the house of John Bertram." Continuing the great Bertram family's love of Salem history and philanthropy, the Emmertons left a remarkable legacy, including improvements to 328 Essex Street and a daughter, Caroline Osgood Emmerton, who preserved the House of the Seven Gables.[30]

Prior to designing new additions to the Pickman-Loring-Emmerton House, Arthur Little learned the art of Colonial Revival design while working beside Robert Peabody in the office of Peabody and Stearns in Boston. In Salem, Little visited the Andrew-Safford House upon the Salem Common, and from it he derived the inspiration to erect large colossal columns in his addition to 328 Essex. Little apparently also studied with great interest the use of the single-circled China

Pickman-Loring-Emmerton House. Photo by Kim Mimnaugh.

coin motif in the Andrew-Safford House—as well as the double-circled and five-quatrefoil fanlight in the John Bertram House on Winter Street and the more elaborate new China coin composition at 15 Summer Street.[31]

From all of these, Arthur Little designed an exceptional fanlight and series of sidelights for the Pickman-Loring-Emmerton House. The fanlight displays five linked, round China coins—all double-circled and centered with additional circles—while the sidelights are like the 15 Summer Street sidelights but now also double-circled in old Peabody or Bertram House manner, and additionally enhanced with new oval and round centers.

Little here referenced the earlier traditions and did them the proverbial one better by creating new layers of concentricity, complexity, and splendor. Bryant Tolles concluded that "Little's interiors . . . are spectacular exhibitions of Colonial Revival ornamentation and illustrate the ambitious tastes of Gilded Age America." It should be noted that Little's exterior work was equally spectacular. By referencing and building upon old Salem architectural motifs from the Great Age of Sail, Little's structure suggested both history and prosperity.[32]

The Saunders-Barker House, 1893

A wonderful counterpoint to the Pickman-Loring-Emmerton House is the Saunders-Barker House, which we find at 39 Chestnut Street. The Saunders-Barker House has a fanlight with five double-circled quatrefoils, a clear copy of the c. 1840 John Bertram House fanlight on Winter Street. Yet it also has China coin motifs integrated into a fine window at the second-floor level and elaborate sidelights that mix quatrefoils and double-circled ovals. Arthur Little renovated 39 Chestnut Street in 1893 for William G. Barker, owner of a lumber company in Boston. Little likely found great pleasure knowing he was able to build "new" compositions based upon his earlier studies of the Bertram House fanlight prepared for the Emmertons.[33]

Benson and Little's Studio Building, c. 1885

Arthur Little was not the only Colonial Revival architect in Salem to become excited by the expressive possibilities of the Chinese coin motif during the 1880s. John P. Benson (1865–1947) also made some significant contributions. Benson grew up on the Salem Common in the Benson House at 46 Washington Square. It was filled with Chinese porcelains that Benson's sea captain forebears brought home from their voyages to the Orient. John Benson later apprenticed with Arthur Little, in Boston and Salem, between 1884 and 1886, while the Emmerton House was being expanded. Arthur and John's brothers Phillip Little and Frank W. Benson were tightly connected as friends, classmates, and pioneer American impressionists after the two opened a studio together in the "Studio Building" nearby at 2 Chestnut Street, Salem, in 1885. John Benson discovered Salem as a source for new Colonial Revival inspirations as early as April 1884, when, while in Little's employ, he worked on Little's projects in Manchester by the Sea. The young Colonial Revival architect in training wrote to a prominent Salem antiques collector and instructor that "I catch on to everything old fashioned that I see, and I am beginning to see what a fine old place Salem is."[34]

The remarkably picturesque China coin–embellished cast iron railing on the Studio Building in Salem is tentatively attributed to architects John Benson and Arthur Little, from c. 1885. Both Colonial Revival architects were experimenting with China coin adaptations for the nearby Pickman-Loring-Emmerton House in the mid-1880s, while their artist brothers were first getting professionally established at 2 Chestnut Street. Stylistic similarity, date coincidence, and family connections suggest that John Benson and Arthur Little jointly designed the exceptional China coin railing for their brothers Frank W. Benson and Phillip Little in about 1885. The railing was a good advertisement of the artists' interest in reconnecting with Salem's finest heritage at a time when 2 Chestnut Street faced the Salem Railroad Station, and it was seen by five artists who worked at 2 Chestnut Street, as well as by many other businessmen, residents, and commuters. In 1886, both Frank Benson, the artist, and John Benson, the architect, boarded at the Benson House on the Common, when not otherwise employed. In summarizing Frank Benson's impressionist painting techniques, Dean Lahikainen noted, "By

Cast iron railing, Chestnut Street. Photo by John Goff.

using antique furniture, 'colonial' architectural details and Japanese [and Chinese] porcelains and screens [Frank] Benson created images of an elegant modern world that looked to the American past for inspiration." The new China coin metal balcony railing at 2 Chestnut Street apparently allowed the Benson and Little families to extend the old Eastern flavor to the outdoors and to attain similar goals in Colonial Revival architecture as in impressionist art.[35]

The Wheatland-Phillips House, 1896

Continuing along Chestnut Street, the Wheatland-Phillips House comes into view. After completing his architectural training under Arthur Little in the 1880s, John Benson became an accomplished Colonial Revival architect in his own right. The Wheatland-Phillips House, designed for Mrs. Stephen G. Wheatland at 30 Chestnut Street in 1896, represents one of John Benson's most significant commissions in Salem. Bryant Tolles noted, "The facade is executed with such well-proportioned historical accuracy that the house gives the impression of being an original late 18th-century building." A variety of China coin design in the first-floor sidelight windows completes the illusion that this is a "period" building of unique Salem origin.[36]

The Henry Perkins Benson House, 1898

Strolling along elegant, tree-lined Hamilton Street, we come to one of Salem's most spectacular Colonial Revival homes, at 7 Hamilton. Designed in 1898 by John Benson for his brother Henry, then a Salem manufacturer, the Henry Perkins Benson House was constructed with a very complex and wonderful China coin motif in its sidelights by the front door—an appropriate "welcome" for a house that, as late as 1940, contained a parlor in which the Bensons ritually took tea on antique lacquered Chinese tables.[37]

Whereas Mr. and Mrs. John and Catharine Andrew, in 1818, utilized three Chinese coins in horizontal format in a semielliptical fanlight above their front door to achieve desired expression, architect John Benson working in Salem eighty years later utilized two columns of three Chinese coins each in vertical format (six coins total) as sidelights to ornament the new house built for Henry Perkins Benson. Following Arthur Little's example, Benson also made the China coin sidelights more complex and beautiful by introducing further elaborations on all earlier designs. Whereas most of the earliest China coin designs in Salem were scribed around with single circles, and later Joseph Peabody's house used double scribed circles, Benson went the next logical step in 1898 to make sure all of his principal China coins were framed by triple concentric circles. Additional coins were implied by using small coin-size circles to keep the concentric circles together—and

Wheatland-Phillips House. Photo by Kim Mimnaugh.

also by creating midsize half coins at each of the four corners framing each China coin. Architect John Benson's China coin sidelights used at 7 Hamilton Street were among the most wonderful ever created in Salem—and they elevated the design and building tradition to a whole new level.[38]

The Z. Augustus Gallup House, c. 1890

Not far from the Henry Perkins Benson House is the Z. Augustus Gallup House at 357 Essex Street in Salem. The Gallup House is another bold, forward-looking Colonial Revival style house that makes multiple references to Salem's unique historic architecture. It was likely built between 1886 and 1890 for the history-minded Mr. Gallup, who managed the Naumkeag Clothing Company. The Gallup House has some extraordinary details on the front, including wreaths that apparently derive from Salem City Hall and swags that reference Salem architect Samuel McIntire's work from the 1780s. Yet one of the most remarkable features of 357 Essex Street is its huge display of nine exceptional Victorian era leaded glass designs, all joined, in the west wall of the house. The window composition on the Gallup House is arranged in three columns, in A-B-A fashion. The center column displays China coin motifs, as well as what appears to be a ribbon on a pearl, which may be a reference to the "Eight Treasures" in traditional Eastern and Chinese belief. In the Chinese scholarly tradition, the pearl—with ribbon—was the First Treasure, and the coin—with or without ribbon—the Second Treasure. Elsewhere in the side windows, the Gallup House displays scrolls, wreaths, 45-degree-turned Chinese coins, and family crests—evident appeals for deriving new strength from history and from Salem's identity as a prosperous Federal era China Trade seaport.[39]

The Nathan P. Gifford House, 1892–1893

The Nathan P. Gifford House at 377 Essex Street in Salem is a close cousin to the nearby Gallup House. The two houses have similar massing, hip roofs, colossal pilasters, and cornices enriched with both wreath and garland ornaments. Built for Nathan P. Gifford, who owned a Salem "planing mill and moulding mill and lumber [yard]," the Gifford House front, constructed in 1892–1893, was likely designed by the same Colonial Revival architect who designed the Gallup House. It is also most significant for containing rare "transitional" designs of China coin motifs in both exterior and interior sidelights and transom windows.[40]

The Gifford House exterior sidelights and transom windows are significant because they clearly represent the evolution of new "extended" or "stretched" China coin designs created by systematically breaking the pattern apart and elongating it. Some "stretched" and round-ended China coin patterns were evolved, which may have been prototypes to the later development of oval coin designs. In

Transom window depicting China coin motif from the Nathan P. Gifford House.
Photo by Kim Mimnaugh.

creating new transom windows spaced to have lozenge shapes aligning with the left and right door frames of the door below, the Gifford House likely also influenced the design of the later transom window in the Mrs. Emma S. Almy House at 395 Lafayette Street, described below.[41]

The Gifford House's interior transom and sidelight windows are additionally significant because they demonstrate the work of a Colonial Revival architect evolving a whole new "flower" kind of geometry from the China coin shape. By observing that the curved lozenge-within-circle of the Chinese coin motif defines four lenticular or "petal" shapes—intersecting at north, east, south, and west compass points on the major circle—and then reorienting those petals to be radial rather than tangential, the architect or window designer of the Nathan P. Gifford House appears to have evolved a very colorful, new round-centered "flower" design from the traditional China coin shape.[42]

The Thomas A. Devine House, c. 1892

An additional Colonial Revival style house of interest in Salem, dating from about 1892, is the Thomas A. Devine House at 278 Lafayette Street, built for a "wholesale dealer in Family Wines, Gins and Brandies." In the Devine House, some of the most picturesque elements are transom windows placed above first-floor windows that depict pairs of Chinese coins and what might possibly be fish. Was it entirely coincidental that, in Chinese belief, fish were also commonly used to invoke abundance and wealth? Wolfram Eberhard informs us, "The Chinese word for fish (*yu*) is phonetically identical with the word meaning 'abundance, affluence' (*yu*): so the fish [like the coin] symbolizes wealth." C. A. S. Williams further notes: "The fish is symbolically employed [in Chinese culture] as the emblem of wealth or abundance, on account of the similarity in the pronunciation of the words yu . . . fish, and yu . . . superfluity, and also because fish are extremely plentiful in Chinese waters. Owing to its reproductive powers it is [also] a symbol of regeneration, and, as it is happy in its own element or sphere, so it has come to be the emblem of harmony and connubial bliss; a brace of fish is presented amongst other articles as a betrothal gift to the family of the bride elect on account of its auspicious significance." Clearly, the China coin windows at 278 Lafayette Street were custom-designed to be elements of great beauty and wonder. Perhaps they were additionally designed to invoke abundance, prosperity, and blessing, in the age-old Salem and East mercantile traditions.[43]

The House at 1 Laurel Street, c. 1895

In some Victorian era Salem houses, such as at the Colonial Revival and Shingle style house we observe at 1 Laurel Street, architects in about 1890 delighted in both the China coin shape and the curved lozenge shape for new accent window use and were apparently aware of their Eastern origins. The house at 1 Laurel Street displays a fine leaded glass window in its front door that has eight curved and interconnected lozenge shapes that are positioned around what appears to be a pearl on a ribbon or Chinese "Precious Thing." On a side wall, 1 Laurel Street also uses nice China coin windows to accent a series of three windows arranged in A-B-A composition. A hexagonal or "honeycomb" muntin pattern in a rectangular window sash elsewhere appears to make direct reference to the Eastern tradition of using hexagonal shapes for Chinese lattice, window openings, and lacquerware boxes. Window similarities suggest that the same person who designed the Z. Augustus Gallup House designed 1 Laurel Street. Perhaps both were designed by Arthur Little after the Pickman-Loring-Emmerton House was expanded in 1885.[44]

The China Coin Becomes the "Salem" Motif

As architects in the Victorian era increasingly came to discover Salem and to appreciate Early American architecture as a source of inspiration for developing new Colonial Revival style buildings, Salem became increasingly appreciated for its repository of intact and well-preserved early buildings in the Colonial, Georgian, Federal, and Greek Revival styles. The nation's first architecture school—the Massachusetts Institute of Technology in nearby Boston—established a Summer School in Salem by the 1880s. MIT encouraged its student architects to study historic details and to publish measured drawings of historic Salem buildings in the *American Architect and Building News* and other professional publications.[45]

In some of these publications, Salem's ancient China coin architectural motif was documented and labeled the "Salem motif." Thereafter it achieved an even wider pattern of use, particularly in new buildings proposed for Salem. No complete survey of Salem's historic architecture has been undertaken in sufficient detail to allow a complete inventory and study of all the newer interpretations. However, a casual inspection of existing houses, buildings, and building details in and around Salem supports eight observations:

Observation 1

During the Victorian era, a number of grand and new stone and brick Salem Colonial Revival style landmarks were erected that utilized the China coin motif in prominent and special windows, evidently to demonstrate a Salem "sense of place," site response, and architectural compatibility. Key examples downtown include the 1889 Peabody block at 120–128 Washington Street, and the 1898 YMCA block on nearby Essex Street. The YMCA, designed by Beverly architect Walter J. Paine, incorporated China coin motifs in interior stained glass windows. A few of Salem's church buildings from the Victorian era—such as the 1888 Wesley

Methodist Church on North Street and the c. 1900 St. Nicholas Russian Orthodox Church at Webb and Forrester Streets—also appear to have utilized the China
coin or "Salem" motif in some smaller windows to make new architecture
uniquely appropriate to Salem.[46]

Observation 2

Within the banking community, the "coin" or "cash" and "prosperity" symbolism of the China coin motif appears to have been remembered, and/or consciously referenced, by a number of Colonial Revival architects. Thus we see that
the coin shape was used in proliferation to ornament sidelights on Victorian
banker R. Rantoul Endicott's house on Broadway Street in Beverly, as well as to
ornament the Beverly National Bank front of 1955 on Cabot Street in Beverly.[47]

Observation 3

Once the China coin shape was documented in the Boston architectural and
national press as a unique "Salem" motif, it was increasingly used by architects to
ornament new houses and more intimate landmarks designed in the Colonial Revival style in and around Salem. If you continue your walks around Salem, you will
see the following:

• The 1802 Pickering Dodge House at 25 Chestnut was fitted about 1890 with
a rear addition bay window with multiple small Chinese coin windows as decorative accents. These were particularly appropriate, both because the Dodges benefited from Salem's East Indies trade, and because the new bay window looked out
at the Humphrey Devereaux House across the street.

• The 1897 Joseph Parsons House at 25 Washington Square North contains
both double-circled round and oval China coins in its sidelights, fitted with small
quatrefoils (or persimmon symbols) at the center. Capt. Joseph Parsons was both
a retired sea captain and a prominent Victorian era Salem builder who constructed
the Salem Five Cents Savings Bank block, aka the Gardner Block, in 1893.

• The c. 1903–1904 Emma S. Almy House at 395 Lafayette Street was built to
be a spectacular Colonial Revival style Salem mansion replete with Chinese
balustrades above the first floor and China coin windows above the front door.

• The c. 1912 John B. Tivnan House at 361 Lafayette Street had double-circled
round and oval Chinese coins in its sidelights—but the curved lozenge centers
were abstracted to a simple cross shape for ease of fabrication and different effect.

• After Salem suffered its Great Fire in 1914, a number of the new buildings
built in the burned district were constructed to show off the China coin or "Salem"
motif. Thus, on Warren Street, three buildings in close proximity (39 Warren
Street, built for the Mahoney family by architect A. G. Richardson, 38 Warren
Street, and 41 Warren Street) all derive much visual character from China coin
windows, treated as special sidelights and accent windows. On Winthrop Street,

Persimmon window motifs, Washington Square. Two views. Photo by Kim Mimnaugh.

south of Broad Street, 30 Winthrop Street and 34 Winthrop Street also display the China coin motif—both as sidelights in a front door composition and as four-keystone framed oval Chinese coin windows, used as decorative accents on the side walls of projecting winter porches. The Salem Rebuilding Commission considered that the finest building it erected after the 1914 fire was the Saltonstall School on Lafayette Street, designed by architect James E. McLaughlin. The front wrought iron railings to the Saltonstall School also utilize the China coin motif as decorative symbol.

• The c. 1920 M. J. Sullivan House at 186 Lafayette Street was built with sidelights that display both round and oval China coin designs. The oval coin also has an oval center, perhaps derived from Arthur Little's Pickman-Loring-Emmerton House design.

• For the 1926 Salem Tercentenary Memorial erected on the Salem Common, Salem-born architect Phillip Horton Smith utilized the ancient China coin shape to provide a new accent in railings of wrought iron.

• The c. 1928 John W. Gauss House at 1 Lafayette Place has remarkably large sidelights that are framed, top and bottom, with geometric patterns based on the China coin motif. The Chinese coin shape was now linked and expanded to be centered between two half coins, thus ending up as "double wide."

• Architect Phillip Horton Smith's designs for the 1920s railings at the Hawthorne Hotel also show a different stylized interpretation of the square hole centered old Chinese coin.

Some of this geometrical experimentation was likely based upon new access to Colonial Revival thought and publications. However, the Colonial Revival architects also took their ideas directly from studying old Salem landmarks.

Observation 4

Oval variants of the China coin motif were also used to ornament sidelights of houses. An example is the Holman Price House, which stands at 330 Essex Street adjacent to the Pickman-Loring-Emmerton House. By the early 1900s, many Colonial Revival architects grew particularly fond of using the oval Chinese coin shape in isolation and of trying out new variations, such as could be had by intersecting the curved lozenge shape with a simple X. For example:

• The Daniel Low and Co. built house at 8 Bott's Court dating from 1896 has a very simple oval Chinese coin window surrounded with a keystoned casing.

• The c. 1750 John Ropes House at 362 Essex Street in Salem was provided with new Chinese-inspired Colonial Revival alterations in about 1900 that put on both a "Chinese" lattice balustrade and a projecting entry pavilion with handsome oval China coin windows.

Another favored combination was simply to center oval coins between circular coins, such as we see at the Gonet Funeral Home on Hawthorne Boulevard.[48]

Railing with coin motif, Salem Common. Photo by Kim Mimnaugh.

Observation 5

A number of Colonial Revival architects and builders became particularly entranced in Salem and elsewhere with combining curved lozenge muntins above and below oval Chinese coin shapes in sidelights flanking front doors.

• The c. 1915 house at 1 Clifton Street (corner of Lafayette) in South Salem fits this pattern; it displays round Chinese coins, curved lozenges, and an oval Chinese coin in A-B-C-B-A pattern.

• The newer c. 1900 Colonial Revival doorway to the old Salem house at 362 Essex Street was promoted nationally as the "House of Mrs. Emery Johnson" in Mary H. Northend's *Historic Doorways of Old Salem,* published in 1926.

• Sidelight muntins of nearly identical design—but crafted in lead, not wood—are also found in the c. 1920 Edward Pols House, maintained as Bowdoin College's headquarters for the philosophy and Latin American studies departments on the Bath Road in Brunswick, Maine.

Once Salem's "Colonial" designs were published in *American Architect and Building News* and in such works as *The Colonial Architecture of Salem* by Frank Cousins and Phil Riley in 1919, the world was free to derive further utility from Salem's architectural details and design traditions.[49]

Observation 6

From the China coin shape, some Victorian era architects working in Salem apparently became taken with the curved lozenge shape as a decorative device, and they produced houses such as that at 44 Linden Street, which utilized the curved lozenge shape as exterior "gingerbread." At 7 or 9 Ocean Street, the curved lozenge shape was also used to hold together a composite pattern of round and partially curved windowpanes in an ornate thirteen-pane window sash leaded glass design. Sidelights to 303 Lafayette Street, built about 1915, also creatively combined shapes of a curved lozenge (from the Chinese coin) with quatrefoil and tripartite fleur-de-lis shapes. Yet the curved lozenge was also used in isolation as a sidelight display by designers such as Samuel McIntire as early as about 1800, when Chinese motifs were especially popular. The Clifford Crowninshield House on the Salem Common evidences the earlier use of this motif.[50]

Observation 7

The notion of Eastern and Chinese design elements excited Federal period architects and builders working in Salem—as well as others who came to Salem much later. Designs that may have originated in the East as a written symbol on paper, silk, cut design in china, or wood meaning "coin" were adopted by American designers to create new window muntins in wood or lead—or railings in permanent wrought iron. The delicate Chinese fan shapes—which were made of fragile silk or paper in the original Chinese fans imported by ship—were made more permanent and rugged for the New England weather by crafting them as fanlights, fan patterns, and fan ornaments in wood.[51]

Observation 8

It appears that neighboring buildings were frequently built with complementary features. As variations of the China coin motif were evolved by the dozens to create new windows and railing designs in Salem, more and more parts of Salem developed houses that "spoke" the same visual language—or a common dialect about a unique history and sense of place. Arthur Little referenced neighboring designs when he evolved his Pickman-Loring-Emmerton sidelights in 1885, and yet they survived to impact the Parsons House sidelights developed twelve years later, which likely evolved quatrefoil centers because of the proximity to 24 Winter Street. Because neighbors spoke with each other and borrowed from each other when new ideas were exciting, we find clusters of China coin houses in different parts of Salem, such as at 30 and 34 Winthrop Street, and at 38, 39, and 41 Warren Street. The Pickering Dodge House at Pickering and Chestnut Streets was altered to better resemble the Humphrey Devereaux House across the street. The Low family's fascination with the China coin motif apparently resulted in special oval Chinese coin windows being adopted in the interior of the Daniel Low Building, as well as at 8 Bott's Court and at 362 Essex Street, which shared the same neighborhood. Over time, the China coin pattern was employed in Salem in many variations to create many beautiful land-marks, all expressing "Salem" and "special place" through their use of that design.[52]

Forrest Street balustrade. Photo by Kim Mimnaugh.

Eastern Elements Contributing to Salem's Sense of Place

In 1941, Margaret R. Sherer, writing in *The China Trade and Its Influences,* noted: "The American China traders brought home an astonishing variety of embellishments for their plain houses of brick and clapboard." A cursory study of historic buildings in Salem suggests that the China Trade brought far more than a "variety of embellishments" to this one New England city. It brought economic recovery after the Revolutionary War, the infusion of vast wealth and prosperity, shiploads upon shiploads of exotic wonders from the East, and the elevation and creation of a new mercantile elite. In time, the China Trade additionally brought to Salem the creation of new institutions such as the East India Marine Society, the building up of many fine mansions and landmarks in town, the learning of Chinese language and customs, and a thorough cultural mixing of East and West.

As Salem derived economic advancement from its coveted China Trade, and as its leading merchants ornamented exteriors as well as interiors of local landmarks with Eastern "embellishments," the Eastern motifs, including the China coin symbol, increasingly became viewed as significant definers and contributors to Salem's "sense of place." By the 1830s, Salemites had latched on to memories of Salem's glory days in the China Trade, compensating for the decline immortalized by Hawthorne in "The Custom House" preface to *The Scarlet Letter.* China Trade symbols, possessions, and lore acquired a new mystique that helped bolster and strengthen the citizenry in trying times.

After 1870, a new generation of American architects promoted the Colonial Revival style to celebrate America's origins. The Colonial Revival designers achieved a new architecture—and new architectural design techniques—that evolved from, and respected, the past. In Salem, they additionally identified and celebrated the ancient China coin motif as a new "Salem" motif. Once that was done, and once it was popularized through national design publications and architectural practice, Early American China Trade design motifs became Salem's gift to the world. Americans no longer looked to the East for inspiration; they looked to Salem. Salem, enriched and built up by its trade connections with the East, was now America's architectural "Mecca."[53]

Notes

1. William Morris, ed., *The American Heritage Dictionary of the English Language* (Boston: Houghton Mifflin, 1978), 813.

2. U.S. Department of the Interior, National Park Service, *Salem: Maritime Salem in the*

Age of Sail, Handbook 126 (Washington, D.C.: U.S. Government Printing Office, 1987); "Salem and the East Indies," *Cobblestone* (September 1988); the entire issue is devoted to Salem.

3. U.S. Department of the Interior; Dorothy Schurman Hawes, *To the Farthest Gulf: The Story of the American China Trade* (Ipswich, Mass.: The Ipswich Press, 1990); Carl L. Crossman, *The China Trade: Export Paintings, Furniture, Silver and Other Objects* (Princeton: The Pyne Press, 1972); Samuel Chamberlain, *A Stroll through Historic Salem* (New York: Hastings House, 1969), 87, 95; H. A. Crosby Forbes, "Asian Export Art in the Peabody Museum of Salem," *Antiques* (August 1988).

4. M. C. D. Silsbee, *A Half Century in Salem* (Cambridge, Mass.: Riverside Press, 1887), 1.

5. Ping Chia Kuo, "Canton and Salem: The Impact of Chinese Culture upon New England Life during the Post-Revolutionary Era," *New England Quarterly: An Historical Review of New England Life and Letters* 3 (July 1930), 420–42.

6. Kevin Lynch, *What Time Is This Place?* (Cambridge, Mass.: MIT Press, 1972), 22–64.

7. One indicator of the fact that Eastern influences are regularly overlooked is that Chinese, Japanese, Eastern, and Asian styles and elements of architecture are not usually recognized as elements in American architecture, either on state survey forms provided by State Historic Preservation Offices, or in American architectural history building classification texts. See, for example, Marcus Whiffen, *American Architecture since 1780: A Guide to the Styles* (Cambridge, Mass.: MIT Press, 1969, 1988). See also John C. Poppeliers et al., *What Style Is It? A Guide to American Architecture* (Washington, D.C.: The Preservation Press, 1983).

8. Visual comparative techniques were anciently used by Banister Fletcher in his architectural histories, and, appropriately, historic architecture is sometimes called "above-ground archaeology."

9. Increasingly, historians are beginning to appreciate all of Salem, Massachusetts, as a historic maritime community. Maritime activities of past building owners and builders are often reflected in local histories, the deeds record, house histories compiled by Historic Salem, Inc., and the membership records of the Salem Marine Society.

10. One of Salem's best exhibits on the development and impacts of the Colonial Revival in Salem was prepared by the Essex Institute in about 1990, before it merged with the Peabody Museum to form the Peabody Essex Museum in about 1993.

11. Cantonese origins can be inferred from the simple fact that in its earliest years Chinese and American trade was limited to the port of Canton, now Guangzhou, China.

12. The five major categories of influence were realized and defined after making visual comparisons of Salem architectural details with Chinese art motifs from various sources, including C. A. S. Williams, *Outlines of Chinese Symbolism and Art Motives: An alphabetical Compendium of Antique Legends and Beliefs, as Reflected in the Manners and Customs of the Chinese,* 3rd rev. ed. (New York: Dover Publications, 1976); Wolfram Eberhard, *A Dictionary of Chinese Symbols: Hidden Symbols in Chinese Life and Thought* (New York: Routledge and Kegan Paul, 2001); and comparison with motifs found on China Trade antiques preserved at the Peabody Essex Museum.

13. Henry M. Meek, "Historical and Interesting Events [in] Salem, 1626–1897," in *Salem City Directory,* 1897–98, 69.

14. Ping Chia Kuo, 441, 422, 430. The c. 1799 Chinese fever resulted in new Chinese balustrades being fitted to the Pickman-Orne House (aka Bowman's Bakery building) on Essex,

east of North, the Ward-Bowditch (aka Bowditch) House, then located at 312 Essex Street, and the Hodges House, still located on Essex Street at the Orange Street corner. For more on the Bowditch House, see "Bowditch's Salem: A Walking Tour of the Great Age of Sail" (Salem, Mass.: Salem Maritime National Historic Site, 2001).

15. Eberhard, 189–91, 166.

16. Eberhard, 166, 191, 233; Williams, 214. Eberhard states, "One of the most popular Chinese operas is called 'Shaking the Money Tree.' The money-tree, from which coins fall, is a frequent motif in [Chinese] pictures," 191.

17. The two-coin symbol can be found in many porcelain objects preserved in the Asian art collections of the Peabody Essex Museum in Salem, as well as in modern Chinese export barrel-shaped garden seats. It is also reproduced in plastic in Chinese "auspicious" plaques such as that currently displayed in the Sun Garden Chinese Restaurant, located on North Street in Salem.

18. Lydia Chen, *Chinese Knotting* (Rutland, Vt.: Echo Craft Books, 1982), 42.

19. Forbes, photograph of Chinese export art—ornamented fan, n.p.

20. Gerald W. R. Ward, *The Andrew-Safford House: Historic House Booklet No. Six* (Salem, Mass.: Essex Institute, 1976), 9.

21. Ward, 24; also appendix: reproduction of probate listing.

22. Ward; Henry Wyckoff Belknap, "Simon Forrester of Salem and His Descendants," *Essex Institute Historical Collections* (January 1935); William Bentley, *The Diary of William Bentley, D.D.* (Gloucester, Mass.: Peter Smith, 1962), IV, 463; Ping Chia Kuo, 430.

23. Bentley, IV, 510.

24. See Ward.

25. Nancy Berliner and Sarah Handler, *Friends of the House: Furniture from China's Towns and Villages* (Salem, Mass.: Peabody Essex Museum, 1995), 17, 18, 61; Eberhard, 190, presents a slightly different interpretation, hinging upon the Chinese word *qian* for "coin" being homophonous with the Chinese word *qian,* meaning "before."

26. Bryant K. Tolles, *Architecture in Salem* (Salem, Mass.: Essex Institute, 1983), 201; Mary Northend, *Historic Doorways of Old Salem* (Boston and New York: Houghton Mifflin Company, 1926), 74; Kenneth C. Turino and Stephen J. Schier, *Images of America: Salem, Massachusetts* (Dover, N.H.: Arcadia Publishing, 1996), 36. The Devereaux design was nationally popularized as the "Hoffman-Simpson House" doorway in Northend's book.

27. Margaret B. Moore, *The Salem World of Nathaniel Hawthorne* (Columbia: University of Missouri Press, 1998), 149.

28. Historic Salem, Inc. house report on 24 Winter Street; John Bertram materials on exhibit at Salem Public Library. See also Rosamond De Laittre, *John Bertram of Salem, Mass.* (no publisher listed; in Salem Room at Salem Public Library, 1964). De Laittre published transcripts of a diary of Capt. John Bertram. In Bertram's work from 1836, he wrote: "My health was so far restored that I began to extend my business besides my regular trade to Zanzibar and the Red Sea. I had interests in Sumatra, Batavia, Calcutta, and to a small extent to China, a great mistake which came near ruining me." Bad business experiences in China in 1836 might have further motivated Captain Bertram to incorporate "business blessings" in his new house, built about 1840. For the persimmon as quatrefoil—and business—see Eberhard, 232–33.

29. Douglas Shand Tucci, *Built in Boston* (New York: New York Graphic Society, 1976); see

also Karen MacInnis's report on 15 Summer Street prepared for Historic Salem, Inc., 1996. Sadly, the name of the designer who consciously referenced Salem's Federal period China coin windows, Georgian style architecture, and China Trade when designing 15 Summer Street is unknown. It may be that John P. Peabody was a descendant or kin of the famed Salem shipowner Joseph Peabody and/or was related to Boston architect Robert Peabody, who helped conceive the Colonial Revival. For age and stylistic reasons, as well as Peabody family associations, the John P. Peabody House at 15 Summer Street is tentatively attributed to Boston architect Robert Peabody.

30. Tolles, 175; Dean T. Lahikainen, "Redefining Elegance: Benson's Studio Props," in *The Art of Frank W. Benson, American Impressionist* (Salem, Mass.: Peabody Essex Museum, 1999), 79. George R. Emmerton biographical information from Salem city directories and George Granville Putnam, "Salem Vessels and Their Voyages," *Essex Institute Historical Collections* 60 (1924): 43.

31. Donald Coleman, conversation with author, Salem, Mass., June 1992.

32. Tolles, 175–76. Tolles contends the house was built in 1818, and derived its earliest historic name from the occupancy of George B. Loring. Tolles appears to have obtained this information from Frank Cousins and Phil M. Riley, *The Colonial Architecture of Salem* (Boston, Mass.: Little Brown & Co., 1919), 93–94. A more recent title search of the property conducted in 2002, however, proves the house was built c. 1821, and first constructed for William Pickman before being later occupied by the Lorings, Emmertons, and remodeled by Arthur Little.

33. Tolles, 210. Mr. Tolles documents the fact that Arthur Little remodeled the Captain Saunders House now at 39 Chestnut Street in 1893. William G. Bowker occupational information from *Salem City Directory,* 1893.

34. Lahikainen, 79. Lahikainen cites John Benson correspondence to Henry Fitz Gilbert Waters, dated April 15, 1884.

35. Lahikainen, 79.

36. Tolles, 197.

37. Robert Booth, historic house report for 7 Hamilton Street, the Henry Perkins Benson House, for Historic Salem, Inc., 2002. Booth further cites Turino and Schier, 17.

38. Field analysis of 7 Hamilton Street sidelight design.

39. The date for the Z. Augustus Gallup House is suggested as being between 1886 and 1890 from a study of Salem city directories of those years and of city atlases of earlier periods. The directories also evidence Gallup's strong patriotic and historical feelings; the Naumkeag Clothing Company in 1890, for example, took out a full-page ad using an image of Revolutionary War era fifers and drummers to herald the company's democratic pricing structure: one price for all.

40. The dates for the Nathan P. Gifford House alterations are documented as being 1892–1893 from Historic Salem, Inc. house report and archival information. The Salem city directories provide more information on Gifford's business ownership.

41. Field analysis of Gifford House window designs.

42. Field analysis of Gifford House window designs. The Queen Anne style, which was popular in the 1890s at the same time as the Colonial Revival, often favored flower designs in architectural designs; the Chinese were also said to come from the "Flowery" or Celestial Kingdom.

43. Salem city directory listings for Thomas A. Devine; Eberhard, 106; Williams, 185.

44. Field analysis of 1 Laurel Street architectural elements. For more on the Eastern "Eight Precious Things," which were a fusion of Taoist, Buddhist, and Confucian beliefs, see Lee Alane, *Chinese Rugs: A Buyer's Guide* (New York: Thames and Hudson, 1953), 114–15.

45. Records of Massachusetts Institute of Technology; *American Architect and Building News,* editions of 1880s, preserved at the Society for the Preservation of New England Antiquities, Harrison Gray Otis House, Boston.

46. Field analyses of listed buildings. See also Tolles, 95, 104, 121, 37. For the Peabody block, see also Turino and Schier, 62.

47. Field analyses of listed buildings, listings in Beverly city directories, and R. Rantoul Endicott House history preserved by current owner.

48. Field analyses of listed buildings; historic house reports on file at Historic Salem, Inc.

49. Field analyses of listed buildings; Northend; Frank Cousins and Phil M. Riley, *The Colonial Architecture of Salem* (Boston: Little, Brown and Co., 1919; reprint, Salem, Mass.: Higginson Book Company, 1989).

50. Field analyses of listed buildings.

51. Comparison of analyses of China Trade material artifacts; field analyses of listed buildings.

52. Field analyses of listed buildings. Daniel Low, the famed jeweler and mail order merchant of Salem, may have been fascinated with the China coin motif in part because he was distantly related to Abiel Abbott Low, of Salem, born in 1811. A. A. Low established both the A. A. Low and A. A. Low and Bro. firms in New York City, which were "long the leading mercantile houses in the . . . [U.S.] engaged in the China trade." A. A. Low first worked in Canton, China, in 1833 while associated with Russell and Co., then the "largest American firm" in Canton. The A. A. Lows of Salem and New York imported Chinese teas and silks in many ships, including the *Samuel Russell, Houqua, Benefactor,* and *The Great Republic.* See A. A. Low obituary in *Salem Gazette,* January 9, 1893, 4, for additional detail. A. A. Low was the son of Seth Low in Salem; Daniel Low, who started the Daniel Low and Co. retail house in Salem, named his son Seth Low, who continued to manage the Daniel Low and Co. business until the mid-twentieth century. See Daniel Low vertical files at Salem Public Library for more detail.

53. Margaret R. Sherer, "The Sea Borne Trade with the East," in *The China Trade and Its Influences* (New York: Metropolitan Museum of Art, 1941), n.p.; Nathaniel Hawthorne, *The Scarlet Letter* (Boston: Ticknor, Reed and Fields, 1850).

THE POINT

Originally surrounded by water on three sides, The Point derives its name from the now vanished Stage or Long Point. This narrow land mass extended into Salem Harbor behind mill buildings that housed a thriving textile industry. During the area's early history, the shores and shallow coves encircling The Point were dotted with fish drying racks and shipyards. As more land was needed for factories and homes, many of these shallow places were filled in, and new streets laid out.

Salem, unlike Lowell or Lawrence, Massachusetts, was never solely a mill town. However, many of the raw materials vital to the development of inland industrial cities passed through Salem; and in the mid 1840s the Naumkeag Steam Cotton Company opened its first mill along Salem's South River. As was the case throughout New England, the growth of factories soon outstripped the supply of local labor in Salem. Though difficult and often dangerous, mill jobs offered immigrants a steady income and a better life. French-Canadians emigrated to Salem and other mill communities during the late 1840s; by the last decades of the 19th century they had become Salem's largest ethnic group.

For many years French was the principal language of The Point, and several French language newspapers appeared here, including the widely read "Courrier de Salem." In recent years many Spanish-speaking immigrants have settled in the neighborhood.

The Great Salem Fire of June 25, 1914 destroyed virtually the whole Point neighborhood as it swept across the city. But the mills were quickly rebuilt and expanded into the vast structures which are still standing today. They continued to produce cotton goods until the mid 1950s, when the textile industry shifted to the south.

Historic marker, the Point neighborhood. Photo by Kim Mimnaugh.

Chapter Nine

Salem as a Global City, 1850–2004

AVIVA CHOMSKY

In my daily walks along the principal
street of my native town, it has often occurred to me,
that, if its growth from infancy upward, and the vicissitude of
characteristic scenes that have passed along this thoroughfare during the more
than two centuries of its existence, could be presented to the eye in a
shifting panorama, it would be an exceedingly effective
method of illustrating the march of time.

—Nathaniel Hawthorne, "Main-street"

 EW visitors to Salem venture much beyond Derby Square's witch shops, the Peabody Essex Museum's East Asian galleries, or Pickering Wharf's pricey antique dealers. Indeed, why would tourists want to see the vacant shell of what had been the world's largest textile mill, or the run-down tenements of the Point neighborhood that once housed generations of French Canadian, Irish, and Polish mill workers? Today, these same triple-deckers are filled with the aromas of Dominican cooking, and the cadences of Spanish fill the streets. On warm summer evenings, neighbors of all ages gather in the streets to listen to music and gossip. The history of the Point has not been written, yet this is also the history of Salem.

Salem's well-known history of Puritans, witches, and the China Trade is certainly a global one. But the Salem that most tourists and most students of history see is one that is frozen in time. Today's Salem reflects this particular version of its history in its museums and shops. But beyond the tourist trail, the lives of today's Salemites have been shaped much more directly by larger economic forces, today known as globalization. In the late nineteenth century, investors built factories, and the city grew as people came to work in them. By the mid-twentieth century, deindustrialization had begun to drain investment away from Salem, as it had from other northeastern cities, just as a new wave of immigrants began. Locally produced items were replaced by imports, so that almost nothing that today's Salemites eat, wear, or use has local origins.

If uniqueness in the American historical landscape characterized Salem's first centuries, similarity to industrializing American cities characterized Salem of the nineteenth and twentieth centuries. Industrialization in the nineteenth century created classic mill towns and brought waves of mostly Catholic immigrants, first from French Canada, then from the peripheries of Europe (Ireland, Italy, Poland). These immigrants created ethnic neighborhoods and institutions, struggled for their rights through labor unions, and assimilated into a new industrial America. Bustling downtowns housed numerous new department stores, as the working class also became a consuming class.

But what was for workers the American dream was for investors the American nightmare. Everything that improved life for workers—better wages, working conditions, education, and life opportunities—challenged manufacturers' access to a cheap, compliant workforce. By the 1960s, America had entered the era of corporate consolidation and deindustrialization, as fewer and fewer giant corporations took over small operations and blithely sought cheaper, less regulated environments in which to carry out production. Suburban malls turned downtown shopping districts into a distant memory. A new generation of immigrants, this time primarily from Latin America and Asia, filled the tenements abandoned by the older generation, which had moved into newly created suburbs. With factory jobs fleeing to the very countries these immigrants were leaving, the newcomers worked in the lower levels of the service economy, cleaning houses and office buildings, taking care of children and yards—that is, making possible the middle-class, two-income lifestyles of the previous generations of immigrants.

All of these trends in modern America—and in Salem—challenge our conception of the meaning of place. Salem is no longer the home of the Naumkeag Steam Cotton Company, Hygrade Sylvania, or Parker Brothers—these factories have closed, having been swallowed up by corporate giants that operate plants in Mexico and China. Like earlier generations of immigrants, today's Dominicans in Salem speak their native language and have created a network of ethnic businesses in what is now Salem's Dominican neighborhood. But unlike previous immigrants, or perhaps just to a greater degree than previous immigrants, today's Dominicans maintain an ethnic nationalism that challenges old notions of assimilation. Almost none of the products that today's Salemites consume are produced locally. The origins of most of what modern Americans buy, touch, eat, and breathe remain invisible—a global version, perhaps, of Marx's "commodity fetishism."[1] But in Salem—again, as in other communities in America—citizens' groups are asking questions and trying to uncover and redefine some of these global connections. Salem citizens have developed ties with the Colombian workers and communities that provide almost half of the coal that fires the Salem Harbor Power Station.

This essay will explore the notion of place in modern Salem through the concept of globalization. Examining three aspects of modern Salem—deindustrialization, Dominican immigration, and the Colombia coal connection—I will argue that globalization has dissolved previous notions of uniqueness and borders of place. At the same time, however, ordinary people around the world are forging new ties that infuse place with new meaning.

Salem as an Industrial City, 1830–1950

Salem's first factories, like those in the rest of New England, produced textiles, shoes, and leather. The giant Naumkeag Steam Cotton Company drew thousands of French Canadian immigrants to Salem. In the smaller shoe and leather factories, Irish workers knew the Boston Street area as "Blubber Hollow," referring to the whale blubber originally used in the tanning process. (Today, Salemites call the same site Gallows Hill, recalling a different Salem experience—the execution of twenty "witches.")[2] The Hygrade Electrical Company and the Parker Brothers Game Company soon joined the other factories, giving Salem a diversified industrial base in the first half of the twentieth century.

The Naumkeag Steam Cotton Company, popularly known as the Naumkeag Mills or the Pequot Mills, began production in 1839, and by 1948 it claimed to be the largest in the world.[3] Most likely, the first workers were young women from northern New England, whom agents had recruited in the rural areas, and chain migration followed.[4] By the end of the century, though, most workers were immigrants. In the 1830s, 95 percent of the women working at one mill in Lowell were native born of native parents; by 1900, only 11 percent of women textile workers in New England were.[5] In Salem, French Canadians formed the largest group of immigrants, followed by Polish and Irish immigrants.[6]

French Canadians poured into Salem to work. The mill employed over 2,000 people, who lived in company-built tenements in what became known as the Point neighborhood. Salem's population swelled to almost 26,000 by 1875 and to over 36,000 in 1915.[7] In its name, *Naumkeag* (recalling the site's old Indian name), in its brand, *Pequot* (recalling a New England tribe), and in its financial backing (1,500 local stockholders), the mill was intensely local.[8] In bringing in immigrant workers, and in eventually closing its Salem facility and transferring production to South Carolina in 1953, Naumkeag's owners exemplified the southward mobility of capital from New England.

Most of New England's textile mills were built along the area's rivers and were powered by water. Salem's Naumkeag mill was the first in New England to seek a different source of power: steam produced by burning coal. Thus the mill imported both coal and cotton from the U.S. South. The capital behind the mill, though in one sense local, also had its origins in the international trade that had built Salem's propertied class.[9]

The June 1914 fire that destroyed Salem's industrial district also leveled the Naumkeag Mill. A company pamphlet described the scene: "A few hours saw the twenty buildings of the Naumkeag Steam Cotton Company reduced to a few stark brick walls with tangled masses of junk that had once been machinery sunk into the basements."[10] However, the disaster did have a silver lining for factory owners. The rebuilt facilities that opened in early 1916 were the most technologically advanced in New England. Steam had been replaced by electricity (though the name remained), and the owners prided themselves on their "progressive" attitudes that kept "the machinery of the mill at its highest state of perfection."[11] It cannot be said that workers shared in the benefits of this modernization. The improvements allowed their employers to consider one-fourth of them to be superfluous, and they subsequently lost their jobs.[12]

To fight displacement and improve working conditions, carders and spinners at Naumkeag organized their first union in 1918.[13] After a brief strike, the management recognized the union, which hired a representative of the local plumbers' union as its business agent. Within a year, the entire mill (except the loom fixers, who had a separate union) was organized, and in the early 1920s the union affiliated with the United Textile Workers (UTW) of America, AFL.[14]

In its first decade, the Naumkeag workers' union followed a collaborative strategy. At Naumkeag, the UTW's approach was to create a union-management cooperation plan to maintain the plant's viability in the face of depression and southern competition. Even in the difficult years of the 1920s, the Naumkeag union maintained workers' allegiance and acceptance of concessions.[15]

In January 1929, however, the mill's workers threatened to rebel against a joint union-management proposal for a "stretch-out"—a notorious cotton industry tactic of increasing the number of machines each worker could tend.[16] Confrontation was delayed only when the union managed to convince both workers and management to agree to implement a "joint research" plan to study, and carry out, the "stretch-out."[17] The eventual plan was less drastic than that proposed by management two years earlier, but it did increase workloads significantly. For several years in the late 1920s and early 1930s, Naumkeag became a national model for labor-management cooperation.[18] After 1933, however, the Naumkeag experience came to stand for the dangers to unions of losing credibility with the workers by identifying too closely with management.[19] Despite its prominence at the time, the Naumkeag experience has been virtually forgotten since the Depression.[20] The guardians of Salem's history have focused on its more exotic elements, and have allowed the neighboring cities of Lynn, Lowell, and Lawrence to become the protagonists of the North Shore's industrial history.

In 1933, workers at Naumkeag voted overwhelmingly to go out on strike. Their union, the UTW, opposed them vociferously, accusing "radicals" and "communists" of mobilizing the workers.[21] Abandoned by their leadership, except for

Labor activist Anne Burlak, 1931.
Courtesy of Sophia Smith Collections,
Smith College Archives.

Local 33 vice president Wilfred Levesque, who took the side of the workers against the union, workers formed a Strike Committee. They established a relief committee and relief headquarters in the Father Matthew Building on Essex Street, and they set up ongoing picket lines at the mill and the bleachery.[22] Five to six hundred workers regularly attended the frequent mass meetings that the Strike Committee organized.[23] For weeks, hundreds of workers picketed, while various officials, in particular Salem mayor George J. Bates, vainly attempted to resolve the matter. In rebelling against a timid union leadership, Salem's workers came to resemble the radical workers of Lawrence, where "many rank-and-filers believed the UTW was more concerned about collecting dues than winning strikes."[24]

Outside support came in the form of the Communist-led National Textile Workers' Union (NTWU), which sent Anne Burlak—described as a "girl communist . . . of Ukrainian parentage though American born, probably less than thirty years of age"—who helped with organizing, plans, and fund-raising.[25] In fact, Burlak was born in 1911, so she would have been twenty-two at the time, and she was secretary of the NTWU. Typically, the NTWU did not have a strong long-term organizational presence, but it would "rush in its forces" to support spontaneous strikes, as in Lawrence, Massachusetts, in 1931 and Paterson, New Jersey, in 1933.[26] As Dorothy Day wrote of her in the *Catholic Worker*, a few months after the Salem strike, "Anne Burlak is apt to have the workers with her, because she is a fine, strapping young girl, blond-haired, rosy cheeked, looking like a Valkyrie as she marches at the head of her strikers. . . . Wherever there is a strike she rushes to the fore. What she's really out for is a good time, otherwise she'd work with the established union and do some of the much-needed organizing work among the southern textile mills, for instance. But she prefers the obstructionist tactics of the Communist Party."[27] Obstructionist or not, Burlak played a key role in the strike and enjoyed widespread support among the workers until almost the very end of the strike.[28]

Several factors stood out in the 1933 Naumkeag strike. Regardless of official criticism—and the real role—of outside organizers, the unity and radicalism of the workers, and their disdain for their union leadership, are notable. Many of the Polish and French Canadian workers shared no common language—meetings were conducted in English, French, and Polish—but there was little ethnic division. Although there were suggestions that the Polish American workers were more profoundly radical in their demands, the apparent leader of the "insurgent" group was Wilfred Levesque, former vice president of the union.[29] The *Salem Evening News* quoted the New York brokerage firm Orvis and Brothers tellingly: "The strike at Salem seems particularly regrettable as the mill management has long been famous for its friendly and close relationship with its employees. Strikers smashed windows last night with a seeming demonstration that friendship has been rather one-sided. Many of the employees cannot speak English and presumably such words as appreciation or gratitude are not in their native vocabularies."[30]

The role of women—and gender issues—in the strike is also notable. One of the key sticking points was the issue of layoffs. The company was determined to violate seniority rules and lay off married women first. The Salem newspaper, the mill, and the union continually blamed these married women as being the ringleaders of the strike.[31] Salem City marshal John C. Harkins told the *Salem Evening News* that "there seem to be a number of women who are *inciting the violence* on the part of the mill strikers. They seem to have forgotten how to act like ladies. If that continues we shall cease to treat them as ladies."[32] It is not clear why the company was so insistent on dismissing the married women in the face of such strong opposition to its proposal; nevertheless, the mill owners were adamant, and the workers, male and female, married and unmarried, were just as firm in their position. Perhaps the company saw a particular group of married women workers as the troublemakers behind the labor unrest, and it was determined to eliminate them. If so, its plan backfired.

During the last few weeks of the strike, the mill, seeing that the Roosevelt administration's new Cotton Textile Code (coming into effect in July) was going to compel it to fulfill much of what the strikers were demanding, began to make concessions. Several hundred workers joined Anne Burlak in rejecting the mill's offers and calling for the strike to continue.[33] It was not until the United States Conciliation Service was able to obtain the mill owners' agreement to virtually all of the strikers' demands, including recognition of their new, independent union, that the strike ended.[34]

Like other textile union victories in New England, however, this one was compromised by another industry strategy: that of seeking a cheaper and more compliant workforce in a new location. Since the 1920s, northern unions had been faced with the challenge of the appeal of poor working conditions in the South to manufacturers. Northern manufacturers responded to the southern challenge by trying to adjust their wages and working conditions downward or by investing in southern plants themselves. William Hartford notes, "In these circumstances, the practice of unionism in one city was as obsolete as the hand-loom. The struggles of southern workers were now their struggles, in ways they had never been before."[35] However, the UTW's attempt at a nationwide general strike in 1934 was "an unqualified disaster."[36] As C. G. Waldrep notes, "The disillusionment, frustration, and, ultimately, fear spawned in the wake of the General Strike became so pervasive in the textile South that workers were able to pass on the package, like an inheritable disease, to their children and grandchildren."[37] The failure of "Operation Dixie"—a final union attempt to establish a presence in the southern textile industry from 1946 to 1953—was also the final blow to New England's textile industry. Factory owners responded with a shift of investment southward in the 1950s, despite the union's growing acquiescence to increased workloads in the interests of modernization and productivity.[38]

While other New England mills were moving south, Naumkeag, too, hedged its bets, opening a mill in Whitney, South Carolina, in 1951.[39] In 1952, workers at the Salem plant, represented by the TWUA-CIO, agreed to increased work assignments.[40] Still, the company argued that the profit margin in Salem was too low. In mid-1953, Rudolph C. Dick, president of the company, announced that the Salem plant would be closing later that year. The entire operation was moved to the plant in Whitney, and the remaining eight hundred workers at the Salem facility were left jobless. Perversely, the company claimed "that the closing was not a case of moving south, since the company had been operating a mill in Whitney, S.C. for two years."[41] Dick also made it clear that Salem's workers would not be invited to move with the company.[42] Globalization in the 1990s, symbolized by the North American Free Trade Agreement (NAFTA), which encouraged the mobility of capital but not of labor, was yet another step in "the path textiles blazed and others followed, from the earliest days of joint-stock corporations to recent years of runaway industry."[43] By the 1970s, the mills of Spartanburg County, South Carolina (where Whitney is located), had also shut their doors.

In 1958, Salem native Ben Lappin, owner and president of Shetland Properties, purchased the former mill and turned it into an office and industrial park.[44] Many of the first Dominicans to arrive in Salem in the 1960s found employment in the small businesses that opened there.

As was the case with the textile industry, Salem's shoe and leather industries also began as local enterprises. Although they imported hides from as far off as Africa and South America, they relied largely on local sources. Before the Civil War, southern slave plantations constituted a significant portion of their markets. The outbreak of war threatened crisis for the industry, but Union Army orders filled the gap. In the mid-nineteenth century, Salem's tanning and currying shops employed 550 workers; by 1886, that number had grown to 850.[45]

The small shoe and leather factories were the first to begin to migrate out of Salem, and their history is eerily predictive of later deindustrialization. In 1914, the same fire that had devastated Naumkeag destroyed most of the leather district. Of the thirty-five factories destroyed or damaged by the fire, three went out of business, four rebuilt on the same site, nine moved to new sites in Salem, fourteen moved to the adjacent towns of Beverly, Marblehead, Peabody, and Lynn, and five moved to neighboring New Hampshire and Maine.[46] Since a sudden catastrophe precipitated the need to relocate, factory owners tried to find sites close by so that they could resume production as quickly as possible.

However, as geographer Robert Donnell observes, the majority of the factories eventually left Salem, drawn to towns throughout the North by less daunting labor costs and less aggressive unionization, as well as by "mechanical inventions and innovations in the industry; transportation improvements; and rent and tax cost differentials plus other economic inducements." For instance, chambers of commerce, boards of trade, and taxpayers associations tempted Salem industrialists with promises of "free rent for a certain period of time, cheap power and lighting expenses, low taxes or no taxes during the first year, and payment of moving expenses."[47] In particular, the factories that relied on less-skilled labor (because they produced lower-quality shoes) tended to take advantage of the opportunity to enjoy nonunion workers, tax breaks, and other economic incentives offered by towns like Hallowell, Maine.[48] Fifty years later, this trend became known as the "race to the bottom," as poor countries vied to attract industry by offering cheaper workers, no unions, lower taxes, and other incentives.

Two of Salem's other main industrial employers, Osram Sylvania and Parker Brothers Games, also had local roots and began with strong local identification. These Salem plants endured until the 1990s, when buyouts placed them in the hands of corporate executives who favored global strategies and made the Salem factories simply pawns in a global game, rather than companies with roots in a community.

Osram Sylvania's roots in Salem date to the beginning of the twentieth century, when Frank Poor and his brothers established the Hygrade Incandescent Lamp Company with its headquarters and main plant in Salem. In 1931, Hygrade merged with two other companies, Nilco and Sylvania, forming the Hygrade Sylvania Corporation. Sylvania built its Loring Avenue plant in 1936, and when Sylvania merged with the General Telephone Company in 1959 to form GTE Sylvania, the plant became part of GTE. The company experienced enormous growth, producing consumer electronics, and, increasingly in its Salem plants, lighting and precision materials. At its peak in 1983, the Loring Avenue plant employed 694 people. Meanwhile, from their headquarters in neighboring Danvers, Massachusetts, Sylvania's managers expanded the corporation across the globe, opening plants in the southeastern United States, Mexico, and Canada.[49]

During the 1990s, however, GTE Sylvania executives increasingly relocated the company's production to what they perceived as more favorable investment climates abroad. In November 1989, management announced that it would be closing the Loring Avenue plant and laying off 555 workers during the following eighteen months.[50] The death knell for GTE Sylvania in Salem and throughout Massachusetts came with a global merger and the signing of NAFTA, which went into effect in January 1994. When Sylvania sold its North American lighting and precision materials operations to Osram GMBH, a Munich-based company, in 1993, the Boston Street plant too was closed. Osram Sylvania closed its last Massachusetts plants in 1998, using provisions of NAFTA to move to Mexico and Canada and to a nonunion plant in Kentucky.[51] In a clear statement of priorities, company president Charles F. Jerabek announced, "These decisions were painful for everybody involved, but because of them, today, we are more cost competitive, and that has allowed us to grow our market share."[52]

Like the tanneries, the chemical and paint factories, and the lead mill on the Salem-Marblehead border, GTE Sylvania left behind an area of soil and groundwater contaminated with heavy metals and other poisons. In the late 1990s, Salem State College purchased the site to construct a new campus there.

Parker Brothers also illustrates the process of globalization. Founded in 1883 by Salemite George S. Parker and incorporated around the turn of the century by Parker and his two brothers, the firm remained in family hands through most of the twentieth century. General Mills bought the company in 1968 but kept it under the management of Randolph P. Barton, the original George Parker's grandson, until 1985.

In 1985 General Mills let its Parker division go, and it ran as an independent company under the leadership of a former General Mills manager. The new management incorporated in Delaware because of its favorable corporate tax laws, and it shut down six plants, including one in neighboring Beverly, cutting the workforce from 6,800 to 2,900. But the Salem plant continued producing, and the company kept 600 workers in Beverly and Salem.[53]

The Tonka Company purchased the company in 1987 for $555 million, acquiring significant debts. In May 1991, the Hasbro Corporation of Pawtucket, Rhode Island, bought out the still-debt-ridden Tonka for $486 million, turning Hasbro into the largest toy maker in the United States. Hasbro soon announced that it would be closing both Tonka's headquarters in Minnesota and the Salem Parker Brothers plant.[54] The signature game Monopoly, among other games, left Salem in October 1991 for Hasbro's Milton Bradley plant in Springfield, Massachusetts.[55]

Hasbro confirmed the following year that it would be closing the Salem plant permanently by December 1993, leaving 370 employees jobless.[56] In 1996, those former employees who remained in Salem watched as the wrecking ball ended Salem's industrial history. Despite the city's attempts to attract commercial or industrial development to the site, the only interested buyers have turned it into a luxury condominium complex.[57]

Salem in a Global Game

The story of Salem's industrialization, and deindustrialization, is a global story, in which Salem as a place is more of an object than a subject, more of a pawn than a player. Local actors made decisions and carried them out, but they made them in historical contexts that structured the options available and the decisions that they made.

Several ironic codas to the Parker Brothers story reveal the conjuncture of global forces in Salem. First, in the summer of 2002, the New England Regional Council of Carpenters organized a protest against Jefferson Properties, the developer of the site, for contracting out the importation of nonunion, mostly Mexican and Central American workers for the construction of the new buildings.[58] Again, this phenomenon mirrors a trend in the U.S. economy: in areas such as the construction industry, where corporations cannot move the labor-intensive portions of their operations abroad, they have sought to import cheaper and more controllable workers.

Meanwhile, Hasbro accelerated the process of globalization by laying off 700 workers from its El Paso plant and moving the operations to Tijuana.[59] In December 1999, the Tijuana plant, too, closed, sending production to independent contractors in Asia. The closure of this plant and of one in Ashford, England, cost 2,200 more jobs.[60] Hasbro's website proudly proclaims the corporate ethics of its global assembly line. Their policies reveal the extent to which labor union gains of the twentieth century have compromised corporate flexibility. In Hasbro's global factories, the bottom line is this: "No person shall be employed in a factory that produces or manufactures any Hasbro product at an age younger than fifteen. . . . Employers must comply with all applicable wage and hour laws. . . . Normal working hours should not exceed forty-eight (48) hours/week with one day off in every seven-day period."[61] Citizens of all countries who are challenging corporate globalization ask a different question: whether the goal of corporate flexibility outweighs societies' commitments to human needs, the protection of children, or the weekend.

Finally, when the plant closed in the early 1990s, many of the workers were in fact recent immigrants from the Dominican Republic. Starting in the 1960s, Salem, like other declining industrial cities of the Northeast, saw a growing wave of Latin American, especially Dominican, immigration. As in other U.S. cities, the presence of Latin American immigrant workers actually encouraged some industries to delay relocating, at least temporarily.[62] The next section of this paper explores the causes, effects, and nature of the Dominican presence in Salem.

The decline of downtown Salem exemplifies the effects of deindustrialization, corporate mergers and buyouts, and population movements. In the middle of the twentieth century, downtown Salem was a bustling shopping district lined with department stores, including Sears and Roebuck, Kresge, FT Woolworth, WT Grant, Almy's, Webber's, and Empire. With the building of the North Shore Shopping Center in Peabody in 1958 and the Liberty Tree Mall in Danvers in 1970, retailers abandoned the downtown area.[63] The growing tourist industry in Salem has meant that instead of empty storefronts, as in so many other New England towns, Salem's Essex Street is lined with souvenir and gift shops. "There are a dozen places you can buy a crystal ball," one Salemite remarked, "but no place to get a pair of socks for your kid."

To shop in Salem's tourist shops today, and scan the labels on the T-shirts, key chains, and assorted knickknacks there, is to uncover signs of these shifts. The souvenirs sport different local themes—witches, tall ships, lighthouses—but their labels betray their origins in the offshore U.S. factories of Mexico, El Salvador, Honduras, Jamaica, and the Dominican Republic. In the sweatshops of the world's poor countries, very young women work unending hours in miserable conditions to sew the "witch city" shirts or stamp "Salem, Massachusetts" on plates, ashtrays, paperweights, and mugs that will be sold to tourists who have the time and income to meander the historic streets of Salem's downtown—the last mainstay of Salem's economy. What they purchase will be a Disneyfied version of Salem's history, a mythological past designed to entertain and awe, but one that obscures as much as it reveals about the lives of Salem's people over the past centuries.

Dominican Migrants in Salem

If Salem's turn-of-the-century immigration and labor history has been downplayed by its tourist industry, its late-twentieth-century Dominican and Puerto Rican immigration is even less known to outsiders. Yet just down the street from the tourist center begins Salem's bustling Latino neighborhood.

Before World War II, millions of immigrants arrived in the United States as the demand for industrial workers seemed insatiable. Those who arrived after 1945 came to a place that was undergoing a process of deindustrialization. Instead of filling the factories—which were in the process of moving to the very countries they were leaving—these new migrants provided the lower-end services in a postindustrial, service economy, allowing large numbers of natives to maintain upwardly mobile lifestyles: construction, lawn maintenance, housekeeping, and restaurant work. Where does Salem, as a place, fit into this larger picture? During the 1960s, the first Dominican migrants arrived in Salem, settling in the triple-deckers of the Point neighborhood that had been abandoned by earlier generations of immigrant industrial workers. By the 1990s, some three thousand Dominicans constituted the largest minority group in Salem (close to 10 percent of the population, and close to 25 percent of the enrollment in Salem's public schools). Salem as a place holds a particular meaning for this latest immigrant wave; in turn, their presence has turned the city into a new kind of transnational community.[64]

Salem's links with Latin America and the Caribbean date back to the earliest colonial times. Salem merchants were involved in the slave trade between Africa and the West Indies directly, and also indirectly by supplying salt cod for the plantations and for the purchase of slaves in Africa. Tituba, whose religion and stories played a key role in initiating the witch scare of the 1600s, was probably an African slave brought from the West Indies, and she has certainly been recreated as such

Mural, the Point neighborhood. Photo by Kim Mimnaugh.

in the popular imagination (including in contemporary Guadeloupan author Maryse Condé's *I, Tituba, Black Witch of Salem*).[65] The pineapple motif that adorns many historic houses symbolizes hospitality: the shipment from the West Indies had arrived, so guests could expect imported foods to be available.

As did earlier migrants to Salem, today's Dominicans must negotiate conflicting loyalties to their homeland and their new home. They have developed a thriving ethnic community, where food, drink, music, and other cultural symbols of the country they left are readily available. What, then, makes today's transnationalism different from the experience of older generations of immigrants in Salem and around the globe?

First, the coherence of the nation-state is quite different in the case of the Dominican Republic. Migrants from Germany, Italy, French Canada, Ireland, or Poland came to Salem at a time when national identities, and in some cases the nation-state itself, were in the process of formation. Personal and cultural ties with the homeland remained strong, but they were not precisely national ties, given the recent and fragile nature of these areas as nation-states. Dominican migrants, however, come from a country with an extraordinarily strong and well-developed sense of national identity that has grown throughout its troubled 150 years as a nation-state.

Second, and not unrelated, is the long and conflictive history of U.S.-Dominican relations. European immigrants had little previous history of connection with the United States. Their countries'—and their peoples'—struggles for independence, borders, and existence were fought against other great powers. For Dominicans, however, their very identity was forged in a struggle *against* U.S. occupation and domination. The United States has occupied and controlled their country for decades, and it continues to play an overwhelmingly powerful role in their homeland.

Thus, Anglo-American identity was forged in the nineteenth century, in its attempts to dominate Spanish-speaking peoples, and Spanish-speaking people's identities were formed in the struggle to resist Anglo domination. As John Fiske wrote in his celebrated essay, "Manifest Destiny," in 1885, "The work which the English race began when it colonized North America is destined to go on until every land on the earth's surface that is not already the seat of an old civilization shall become English in its language, in its religion, in its political habits and traditions." Assimilating into or adopting this Anglo-American identity thus has an entirely different and more troubling cultural meaning for Dominican migrants than it did for earlier generations of Europeans.[66]

The timing of the migration brings many differences. Proximity and technology have meant that recent Dominican migrants have far greater means to maintain close contact with the homeland than did previous generations of European immigrants. Air travel, reliable telephone service, faxes, the Internet, and money-wiring services mean that daily contact can be maintained with the home country, and frequent travel is a realistic option. Dominican newspapers and food products are readily available.

Dominican migrants in Salem share with other Latin American migrants the creation of what sociologist Peggy Levitt terms the "transnational village," in which entire Latin American communities have become multilocal, with cultural, human, and economic exchanges constantly reinforcing ties of transnationality between specific towns and villages in Latin American countries and their U.S. counterparts. Levitt studied links between the Dominican town of Miraflores and Jamaica Plain in Boston, arguing that "it is not merely that numerous individuals live their lives within a social formation that crosses borders; it is that a significant number from a given place of origin and settlement share this experience collectively with one another, transforming the way they think of themselves as a group."[67] Two Dominican towns, Santiago and Baní, have sent large numbers of migrants to Salem, and these migrants have indeed recreated communities there.[68]

Elderly Dominicans recount similar stories of their early experiences in Salem. José Alix claims to be the second Dominican to settle there, in the early 1960s. By 1965 there were six Dominican families in Salem's Point neighborhood, living in a tenement on Dow Street, along with five Puerto Rican families, and one each from Mexico and Panama. They came from Santiago, the Dominican Republic's second-largest city and a major leather producer, and they came encouraged by the owners of Peabody's small leather factories who were seeking experienced leather workers. Word soon spread in Santiago and among Dominicans in New York: there were jobs in the north of Boston area. The pay was better than in New York, and the cost of living was lower. Friends and family members of the early migrants began to fill the Point apartments, and workers poured into Salem's and Peabody's small shoe and leather factories. Manufacturers from the Shetland Industrial Park "used to come out in the streets here [in the Point] looking for workers." Visas were easy to get, especially before 1965: workers just had to ask for letters from the owners of their factories promising jobs for relatives and friends of those already working there.[69]

The first *bodega,* or small supermarket selling Caribbean products, opened on Palmer Street in the early 1970s. "Before that, we had to go all the way to Dorchester to buy plantains!" Alix recalled. In 1978, a second one opened on Palmer Street. Both were owned by Puerto Rican immigrants but stocked the same food items that the Dominicans craved. Other social institutions followed. In 1978 the owner of the Palmer Street *bodega* opened the Club las Antillas at the corner of Palmer and Salem. It moved the following year to 1 Dodge Street, where it remained until it closed in 1998. The club sponsored Salem's first Hispanic Festival in 1980. Johnny Grullón estimates that when he arrived in 1980, in the midst of the festival, there were about three hundred Dominicans living in the Point.[70]

The 1980s saw an explosion of Dominican migrants in Salem and an expansion beyond Santiago that brought many *banilejos,* or Dominicans from the city of Baní on the country's southern coast. *Banilejos* came first to Salem from Jamaica Plain, where they had already established a large community. Urban problems—violence, poor schools—pushed many *banilejos,* especially families with children, toward Salem. Once the Baní relationship was established, more *banilejos* followed directly from the Dominican Republic.[71]

At the same time, the old sources of employment in the leather and shoe industry had shrunk in the 1980s. Dominicans could still find some jobs in light manufacturing, in the Shetland Industrial Park, in the Centennial Industrial Park in Danvers, or at the Parker Brothers plant in Salem. They also moved into the service industry that continues to employ the majority today—"cleaning, in all its forms," explained Javier Rincón, who owns a small janitorial contracting company himself—in hospitals, nursing homes, restaurants, private homes, and office buildings. Salem's Dominicans are sure that the 1990 and 2000 censuses significantly undercounted the city's Dominican population, and they estimate that it is closer to five thousand than the three thousand that the census found.[72]

Families often rely on immigration strategies that keep a family unit together economically, even if the members are separated physically by migration. One or both parents might migrate to Salem, leaving children at home in the Dominican Republic with relatives and sending money back regularly. Or older children might be sent to stay with relatives and attend high school in Salem. In some cases, migration appears more like commuting, with regular return trips incorporated and expected.

Dominican businesses reflect the webs of transnationalism that are being created in Salem. Some businesses recreate aspects of Dominican culture far away from home. By the late 1990s, there were numerous *bodegas* offering a wealth of Dominican and other Latin American products. Many of these products, ironically, are imported not from the Dominican Republic, but from around the tropical world. Mango juice from Egypt, for example, or canned and packaged products made by the New Jersey–based Goya corporation, sit alongside plantains, root vegetables, and prepared sweets like *dulce de leche* made by Dominican producers in Lawrence, Boston, or New York. Some products exported from the United States *to* the Dominican Republic have actually become so fully adopted into the culture as to be sought out by Dominicans abroad as symbols of home, like packaged breakfast cereals or Nestlé's chocolate milk powder. One local supermarket also sells herbal and other remedies and advertises itself as a "*botánica*"—providing products ranging from cod liver oil and gentian violet to saints and other items used in Dominican *santería* ceremonies.[73] Dominican music greets customers, who can also purchase, in addition to the *Salem Evening News* and the *Boston Herald,* two Dominican newspapers, *El Nacional* and *El Listín Diario* (only a day late); one Puerto Rican paper, the *Vocero de Puerto Rico;* and two Latino papers published in the United States, Boston's *El Mundo* and New York's *El Diario*. Dominican restaurants also provide the food, and the atmosphere, of home. A local Catholic church now offers services in Spanish, and two evangelical churches also serve the Dominican community. In all of these ways, small snatches of the Dominican Republic are being recreated in Salem.[74]

Many Dominican business establishments incorporate what anthropologist Sarah Mahler has termed "multiservices" that cater to the immigrant community. The services are specifically geared to the needs of immigrants and include those that allow immigrants to maintain the connection to the home country and those that provide comfortable and accessible ways to survive in the host country. Money wiring, telephone cards, and travel facilitation are all services that Dominican entrepreneurs provide to the Dominican community to help keep exchanges between the Dominican Republic and Salem frequent and alive. In a way, these services create isolation. Linkages between Dominicans in Salem and the home country are more stable and vibrant in some ways than linkages between Dominicans and non-Dominican Salemites. Not only are business, communication, and money kept within the Dominican community in Salem, but they circulate between the Dominican community and the Dominican Republic through the hands of Dominican entrepreneurs.

"I call every day," explained Johnny Grullón, displaying his "phonecard merengue." "You'd have trouble finding anyone who doesn't talk every day." "You can talk a lot for $5," Alix confirmed. Digital cable offers a special "Supercanal Caribe" that brings eight channels from the Caribbean into Salem homes. Interactive shows actually orchestrate call-ins as easily from Salem as from Santiago.[75]

Other aspects of the "multiservice" industry ease the way for Dominicans in Salem to incorporate into American life. A Dominican can cash checks, get an identification card and car insurance, pay income taxes and monthly bills, or have a telephone installed by relying entirely on Dominican intermediaries who charge for their services.

Some analysts have questioned the degree to which these services benefit the Dominican community, as opposed to exploiting it. One study showed that immigrants pay excessive fees to wire money, when using bank transfers would reduce their costs considerably.[76] Another showed that Latino immigrant business operators took advantage of the term *notario*—which is used for *lawyer* in some Latin American contexts but whose English equivalent, *notary*, does not imply any legal training—to suggest qualifications that did not exist and offer help with immigration issues, thus charging significant sums for services that the provider was not really qualified to offer. Newer immigrants may not have the cultural or linguistic resources to access cheaper and/or more legitimate alternatives outside of the immigrant community.[77]

Nonprofit organizations have also grown to fill some of these roles. When the

Salem Harbor Community Development Corporation was founded in 1979, its constituency was mostly the French Canadian community of the Point, and organizers struggled to build links with the growing Dominican community. By the mid-1980s, Dominicans had become its mainstay.[78] In 1990, Dominican activist Johnny Grullón and a Salem Hospital doctor founded Voces to promote AIDS education in Salem's Dominican community. Voces has expanded over its more than a decade of existence and now serves as a sort of social center, especially for older migrants of the first generation. It offers citizenship classes and GED classes, which have graduated 1,200 and 33, respectively.[79] Also in the 1990s, Neighbor to Neighbor, a national community action group that had begun in the 1980s with a focus on solidarity with revolutionary Nicaragua, shifted its emphasis to working with low-income communities in the United States and opened an office in the Point.

These transnational contacts have gradually established Salem as a place in the Dominican imagination. Historically, New York, or "Nueba Yol" as it is rendered in Dominican Spanish, has represented the United States for Dominicans. "Me voy pa' Nueba Yol!" exults the hero, Balbuena, in the Dominican film *Nueba Yol,* echoing the desires and dreams of a wide spectrum of his countrymen.[80] At first, the Dominicans I interviewed categorically denied the importance of Salem as a place for Dominicans. "New York is the United States," they insisted. However, over the course of the conversation they would begin to modify this statement. "Lately people have heard of Massachusetts," one acknowledged. "They may have heard of Lawrence," another admitted. "People do say they're going to Boston." "They may know other North Shore towns, like Lawrence or Lynn." "It's not common knowledge," was the final consensus. "People only come to Salem if they already know somebody here." But with perhaps five thousand Dominicans currently residing in Salem, from three of the country's major cities, and with virtually all of them maintaining continuous, diverse, and multiple contacts with the homeland, the circle of Dominicans who "know somebody here" is probably quite large indeed.

The city of Salem, too, has changed in response to its Dominican population. Major grocery chains have added "Spanish" sections and products. The school system has taken huge strides in developing bilingual programs and drawing in qualified people to staff them. Two Salem elementary schools boast innovative two-way bilingual programs, though the recent passage of a statewide ballot initiative, banning bilingual education, has thrown the future of these programs into question. The schools' Parent Information Center is staffed by Spanish speakers, and the superintendent sponsors several "Hispanic Parents Nights" throughout the year. The city sponsors Hispanic Heritage events, including a parade through the city center each summer. Dominicans have run successfully for various local positions, including the City Council.

Nonetheless, serious barriers remain to true multiculturalism in Salem. The vast majority of Dominicans continue to reside in the run-down Point neighborhood, where many Anglos fear to tread. The 1990 census showed the unemployment rate in the Point to be double that in the rest of Salem (14.7 percent and 7 percent), while household median income ($18,958) was just over half of Salem's average ($32,645). Only 19 percent of Point residents owned their homes, as compared to 46 percent in the rest of the city. Many Anglos are not hesitant to express viscerally racist sentiments toward the newcomers.[81]

One barrier to assimilation is the fact that the experience of Dominican migrants calls into question the very way that the United States conceives of itself as a nation. Several assignments given to children at Salem's Horace Mann School in the 1990s illustrate this. These assignments were all given as part of a "heritage" project celebrating multiculturalism. But they reveal assumptions about American history and identity that contradict the experiences of many Americans, including many Dominicans. The message that they give these children—children who do not conform to the story the teachers want to tell—is that they don't belong here.

• An assignment asked children to draw a picture of their ancestors coming to America on a boat. A youngster dutifully drew his father—a recent immigrant—arriving on a boat. "But I didn't come over on a boat," his father explained patiently. "I came on an airplane." "The teacher said I had to draw you coming on a boat," the child replied.

• An assignment asked children to research the "country" from which their ancestors came. They were given a worksheet to fill out about the country's language, flag, national currency, national dress, dances, customs, traditions, foods, and so forth. One parent asked the teacher how African American or Native American children were supposed to choose a country, and she replied, "Oh, they can just do Africa"—apparently unaware that Africa does not have a national flag or currency! (In this case, the teacher surely expected Dominican children to choose the Dominican Republic, which would have seemed natural to most of the children and their parents, too. However, like U.S.-Americans, Dominicans are mostly the descendants of immigrants, forced and voluntary, from Europe and Africa.)

• An assignment asked children to look in the Yellow Pages to find a business owned by people from the country their ancestors came from, judging by the names of the owner or business. (This would work for a select group of European immigrants, where language and national borders clearly coincide, but a Spanish surname, for example, gives little clue as to the country of origin of the person. Nor, for that matter, does an English surname.)

Teachers reiterate endlessly that "this is a country of immigrants." However, this is *a* history of the United States, rather than *the* history. It is a history that privileges the story of Europeans who came to America and ignores the story of Native Americans, African Americans, Mexicans, and Puerto Ricans, who were conquered, captured, and forcibly incorporated into the country. The assignments listed above all depart from the idea that *all* students identify with one of the several waves of European immigrants to this country.

The history of Latinos in the United States incorporates both stories. Latinos were first forcibly incorporated (with the conquest and annexation of Mexico and Puerto Rico), but they later continued to arrive as immigrants. However, many studies have shown that their experience *as immigrants* is historically more similar to the history of those forcibly incorporated than to the history of European immigrants.[82] For example, Anglo-Americans frequently argue that Dominicans fail to assimilate into Anglo-American culture (assuming the European experience provides the model for the immigrant experience) because they are too recent, because they don't care about learning English, because they travel home too often, and because they don't care about assimilating. Those who make these arguments forget that many Native Americans and African Americans—two groups who have been in this country longer than most others—have never "assimilated" despite an excellent command of the English language and a fine pedigree of longevity. It is to their experience, as conquered peoples, that the Latino experience is more fruitfully compared. Thus transnational identities also reflect the degree of self-denial that it would require to assume an Anglo-American identity.

Anglo resentment seems particularly pointed in the area of language. In November of 2002, Salem voters joined others in Massachusetts in decisively supporting a ballot initiative to dismantle bilingual education in the state. While Salem's teachers lobbied to defend the innovative two-way bilingual programs, they were unable to turn the tide.

Globalization from Below in Salem

Even as corporate mobility has dissolved older notions of place in favor of globalization, ordinary people are weaving their own webs of globalization and new meanings for place. Immigrant transnationalism is only one example of how people's increased mobility has fostered the development of these new meanings.

Salem has also been the site of other forms of globalization from below. Workers at the Naumkeag challenged the company in the early part of the century by forging bonds of solidarity, and ultimately recognizing that these bonds must necessarily extend to workers in the South, or the industry would simply flee to this unorganized region. In the same way, postindustrial citizens, unions, and activists have reached across borders to challenge the "race to the bottom" that pits workers and citizens in different parts of the world against each other in a scramble to lure industries by offering the lowest wages, the lowest taxes, and the maximum corporate flexibility.

In Salem, this movement has focused on the South American country of Colombia. Just as U.S. textile industries moved first to the lower-wage South, and then to even lower-wage countries in Latin America and Asia, so too the less visible energy industry has sought cheaper sources abroad. Two U.S.-based companies, Exxon and Drummond, dominate the production of coal in Colombia. Their entry into Colombian production in the 1980s and 1990s coincided with the shutting down of mines inside the United States. It also coincided with a surge of violence against workers and villagers in the coal-producing areas of Colombia.

In May 2002, a Colombian Wayuu indigenous activist, Remedios Fajardo, visited Salem. She shocked Salem residents with her accounts of her twenty-year struggle for the rights of her people against the world's largest open-pit coal mine, the Cerrejón Zona Norte mine, developed in the 1980s and operated by the U.S.-based Exxon Mobil Corporation. Most of the coal, she explained, was exported to Europe; however, significant amounts were also shipped directly from the mine to Salem Harbor as fuel for Salem's power station. In her words,

> The coal that is mined in El Cerrejón, located on indigenous Wayuu lands in Colombia, comes to Salem to provide electricity, benefiting this city. We want to tell the people of Salem that this coal has its origins in violence. Our communities have suffered greatly. Their human rights have been violated, their territory has been usurped, their houses destroyed and demolished, and they have had to shed their blood in order for this coal to arrive in Salem and other parts of the world. The acts that have been committed by El Cerrejón could be considered as war crimes, and they should be condemned by the world. PG&E [then owner of the power station] has an indirect responsibility, for it is using a mineral that comes from the sacrifice of communities like Tabaco—destroyed last summer—and other communities that are threatened with destruction, like Tamaquito, Roche, Chancleta and Patilla. We beg the city of Salem to express their solidarity with us, because we have a relationship with them because of this situation. Salem can influence PG&E. We would like PG&E, as a customer of the Cerrejón mine, to demand justice for the people who live in the mining zone, who were born and raised in the zone, and who have lived their lives there.[83]

Fajardo brought videotape taken by Colombian journalists in the summer of 2001 as armed security forces moved into the village of Tabaco, on the edge of the mine, and dragged residents out of their homes to bulldoze them to make room for mine expansion.[84]

Salem residents have been highly divided over issues raised by the Salem Harbor Power Station, one of several older, coal-fired plants in New England that have been accused of causing serious environmental damage. Some point out that the plant is the town's major source of tax revenues and that it provides well-paying union jobs for over a hundred local residents. Others argue that the plant pays less than its fair share of taxes, that coal is an inherently dirty and outdated source of energy, and that the town would be better served by developing alternative sources of clean energy.

Fajardo countered that they face the same debates in Colombia. As far as her people, the Wayuu, are concerned, the Cerrejón mine has brought nothing but disaster. The Wayuu had survived as Colombia's largest indigenous group in large part because the arid Guajira peninsula that they called their home had little in the way of resources to attract outsiders to the area. The discovery of coal and the development of the mine brought a huge influx of people and with them displacement, loss of livelihood, and cultural destruction. Dust and blasting, and the concurrent loss of farms and pastureland, meant that the impact of the mine went far beyond the thirty- by five-mile area that the mine itself occupies. Almost no Wayuu were employed by the mine because most of the jobs in the highly mechanized operation required a level of skill and education that few Wayuu were able to reach, in a region with 65 percent illiteracy. Yet, they had strong relations of solidarity, she told us, with Colombia's mine workers. She urged Salem residents to speak with the Colombian mine workers' union to get their perspective.

When the president of that union, Francisco Ramírez, visited Salem several months later, he made a direct request to the various groups he met with: IBEW Local 326, the union at the power plant, the North Shore Labor Council, Salem's mayor, and the recently formed North Shore Colombia Solidarity Committee. "We are not against foreign investment," he told people in Salem. "But we want that investment to be conditioned on the absolute respect for human and labor rights." The only way that could be ensured, he went on, was for consumers of the products—in this case, all of those in Salem involved in the consumption of Colombian coal—to pressure the U.S. companies operating in Colombia. He called upon his different audiences in Salem to monitor human rights conditions in the coal mine and to let the owners know that they would be held responsible for human rights violations.[85]

He told stunned Salemites of the five union leaders who had been killed in 2001 at the Drummond coal mine in Colombia by paramilitary death squads apparently working for the Drummond Company. He explained that in Colombia a labor organizer is killed every other day, making it the most dangerous country in the world in which to be a union activist. He described the four attempts that had already been made on his own life. He brought a study his union had carried out over the course of six years that provided detailed documentation of the correspondence of human rights violations to the activities of foreign companies in the mining and energy sectors. Foreign companies, he claimed, relied on paramilitaries funded directly through U.S. military aid to Colombia to carry out genocide against unarmed social activists in Colombia. Colombia receives more U.S. military aid than any country in the world except Israel and Egypt, and this aid is being used to pursue the neoliberal agenda of making the country profitable for foreign investment. Salem residents are unwitting participants in this drama because every time they switch on a light, they are using coal that has traveled here from Colombian mines.

A visitor to Colombia's Guajira peninsula, and the coal mine, in August 2002 asked residents whether they knew that people in Salem were concerned about the origins of their coal. "Yes," responded Colombian community activist José Julio Pérez, "we know that they are interested in us. We are waiting for them to come and meet with us."[86]

Conclusion

Salem's history is generally written as if it ends in the eighteenth century. In fact, though, Salem in the nineteenth and twentieth centuries reveals a very different city: one of rapid industrialization and immigration, and intense labor struggles; one of deindustrialization in the late twentieth century as factories moved to the U.S. South, and then abroad; one of renewed immigration, this time from Latin America, in the late twentieth century; and one of increasing global ties as virtually everything consumed in the city currently comes from distant shores.

All of these processes are global in nature, but local people and places are intimately involved with them. A visitor to Salem today is likely to see the city's history as it has been constructed by generations of governmental, commercial, and cultural institutions to be served up as a commodity and a tourist attraction. This history will emphasize Salem as a colonial settlement, as home to the infamous witchcraft trials, and as a leader in the global maritime trade.

Yet, this history erases the lives of the vast majority of Salemites. While one might argue that the global forces discussed in this paper have structured their lives, and the individuals involved have been little more than pawns, this interpretation would also erase the human agency that went into the city's history. This human agency belongs not only to the judges, the inventors, and the investors. Workers migrated, labored, and organized collectively and courageously to make better lives for themselves. Whether in Poland or French Canada, in the Dominican Republic, in Colombia, or in Salem itself, working people have made decisions and taken actions to challenge their poverty and restricted opportunity. They have built lives and institutions and have reached out to their neighbors and across borders in their struggle to make a better world. The city of Salem has been an important site where these struggles have occurred in the past and where they continue to be played out to this day.

Notes

1. Karl Marx defined "commodity fetishism" as invisibility of the origins of the products people consume. The product takes on an independent existence, unconnected to the people who labored to extract or produce it. See Karl Marx, "The Fetishism of Commodities," from *Capital;* excerpted in David McLellan, ed., *Karl Marx: Selected Writings,* 2nd ed. (New York: Oxford University Press, 2000), 472–80.

2. Small tanneries had operated in Salem since the 1600s, but the first factories began to move to Blubber Hollow in the late eighteenth century. By the end of the nineteenth century, over a thousand people worked in the leather factories. See Jim McAllister, "Salem Then and Now," in *Salem: Cornerstones of a Historic City,* K. David Goss, Richard B. Trask, Bryant F. Tolles Jr., Joseph Flibbert, and Jim McAlister (Beverly, Mass.: Commonwealth Editions, 1999), 108.

3. Frances Diane Robotti, *Chronicles of Old Salem: A History in Miniature* (New York: Bonanza Books, 1948), 64. Robotti cites an April 26, 1948, letter from George R. Onody, assistant to the president of Naumkeag.

4. Norman Ware, *The Industrial Worker, 1840–1860* (1924; reprint, Chicago: Ivan R. Dee Publisher, 1990), describes the recruitment process in rural New England and the shift to immigrant labor after 1850 on pp. 151–53.

5. Thomas Dublin, *Transforming Women's Work: New England Lives in the Industrial Revolution* (Ithaca: Cornell University Press, 1994), 81, 230.

6. Most histories emphasize the French Canadian presence in Salem and Naumkeag. See Robotti, 69, 82. However, there were also smaller numbers of Irish and Polish immigrants.

7. For numbers employed, see McAllister, 111; for Salem's population, see Robotti, 77, 99. In 1948, the population was 43,000, one-third of those French Canadian immigrants (Robotti, 82).

8. McAllister, 109.

9. Theodore Steinberg, *Nature, Incorporated: Industrialization and the Waters of New England* (Amherst: University of Massachusetts Press, 1994); Clive Jarvis, *The Story of Pequot* (Salem: The Naumkeag Steam Cotton Company, 1929), 28.

10. Jarvis, 29.

11. Jarvis, 29. See also Richmond C. Nyman, *Union-Management Cooperation in the "Stretch Out": Labor Extension at the Pequot Mills* (New Haven: Yale University Press, 1934). Nyman writes that renovations resulted in "a mill far more modern and efficient and desirable to work in than most of the others in the cotton textile industry" (5).

12. Nyman, 14. Textile workers and their unions in New England have been dogged by the problem of modernization and technology from the beginnings of the industry through its demise. If mill owners failed to invest in technology, they would lose out to more productive plants in the South; if they did invest, it was always at the cost of workers' jobs.

13. There is evidence of organizing activity and strikes at Naumkeag as early as the 1850s, however. See Ware, 119, 161, for mentions of organizing and strikes in 1853 and 1857.

14. Nyman, 6; see also Nyman's Chronology, 205.

15. William F. Hartford, *Where Is Our Responsibility? Unions and Economic Change in the New England Textile Industry, 1870–1960* (Amherst: University of Massachusetts Press, 1996), 57; Nyman, 8–9. As one (generally promanagement) study concluded, "The management was genuinely anxious to improve working conditions, interested in the welfare of its workers, and desirous of establishing cordial relations with the Union. Consequently, since the Union was generally wise enough to confine itself to reasonable ends, when it petitioned for changes which would make conditions more agreeable to the workers, arrangements involving concessions from the management were negotiated with little friction." Nyman, 6.

16. The "stretch-out," also known as the "extended labor" or "multiple loom" system, was designed by engineers working for the Cotton Research Company in 1923, who applied new scientific management techniques to mill work. Under this system, the proportion of unskilled workers could rise from 25 percent to 65 percent of the weavers in a mill, and a single weaver could tend seventy-five, rather than thirty-five, automatic looms. See Nyman, 21–23. The stretch-out did more than increase the workload, as one study of the South Carolina textile industry notes: "The stretch-out was an affront to nearly every aspect of textile life. Before, workers had been able to preserve some level of control over their labor. They saw that slipping from their grasp. . . . More important, the stretch-out devastated what patterns of mutual aid had managed to penetrate the red-brick walls of the mills." G. C. Waldrep III, *Southern Workers and the Search for Community: Spartanburg County, South Carolina* (Urbana: University of Illinois Press, 2000), 34.

17. Nyman, 25–33.

18. Nyman notes that the Taylor Society for the promotion of scientific management, the American Federation of Labor, Yale University, Harvard University, and the United Textile Workers all studied and promoted the Naumkeag experience as a model. National media, including the *New York Times,* also promoted the experiment (Nyman, 78–79). The UTW also promoted Naumkeag as a model for collaborative labor-management relations (Nyman, 145).

19. Hartford notes that the TWUA's aim of convincing northern manufacturers to invest in their plants was tempered by Salem's experience:

> To accomplish these aims, union leaders not only had to induce mill owners to make needed investments. They also had to convince both workers and local union officials that facilitating economic modernization was in their best interests. This was an unfamiliar role for labor organizations, and it carried real risks. A program designed to promote economic efficiency could easily be perceived as class collaboration, and if rank-and-filers came to embrace such views, TWUA leaders would lose all credibility.
>
> These were not idle fears. TWUA officials knew that earlier instances of union-management cooperation had sometimes ended badly. At Salem's Pequot Mills, for example, United Textile Worker initiatives during the early thirties to help management increase productivity had resulted in a rank-and-file rebellion against union leaders (Hartford, 104–5).

20. The Yale University Institute of Human Relations carried out a detailed study in 1934 (Nyman).

21. Nyman, 151. According to the *Salem Evening News,* "The union officers assert that a radical element has stirred up the workers to the point of ignoring the national organization. Local

officials went to the point last night of saying that some of the members of the organization were in the pay of radical elements" ("Union Committee and Mill Officials Will Meet This Afternoon," *Salem Evening News,* May 9, 1933). Here the UTW followed a pattern established earlier in Lawrence, where in 1912 and again in 1918 the union opposed radical, immigrant workers when they struck, led by "a diverse left-wing coalition of ex-Wobblies and Christian radicals" (Hartford, 46–47).

22. Nyman, 155; "Strike Committee Again Meeting with Mayor Bates Today," *Salem Evening News,* May 26, 1933.

23. Nyman, 156.

24. Hartford, 64. Even in Fall River, a bastion of collaborative unionism, the union faced defections in the 1920s and early 1930s as it failed to convince workers that it was defending their interests. Hartford, 57. At the Amoskeag mill in Manchester, New Hampshire, after decades of harmonious labor relations, the UTW supported workers when they launched what was to be a most bitter strike because of a similar complex of layoffs, wage reductions, and speed-ups in 1922. Amoskeag workers also ended up disillusioned with the UTW after the failure of the strike, albeit for different reasons: "They feel that they were misled by the union organizers and sold down the river . . . that they had been used and betrayed." Tamara K. Haraven and Randolph Langenbach, *Amoskeag: Life and Work in an American Factory-City* (New York: Pantheon Books, 1978), 296–97, 302.

25. Nyman, 156. The NTWU was established by the Communist Party's Trade Union Unity League in Providence in 1929. See Mari Jo Buhle, Paul Buhle, and Dan Georgakas, eds., *Encyclopedia of the American Left,* section on "Textile Workers Unions," 818.

26. Harvey Klehr, *The Heyday of American Communism: The Depression Decade* (New York: Basic Books, 1984), 42, 128.

27. Dorothy Day, "All in a Day," *Catholic Worker,* October 1933, 5, 6. (Dorothy Day Library on the Web at *http://www.catholicworker.org/dorothyday/*)

28. Robert A. Bakeman, former mayor of Peabody (home of the Danvers bleachery), "a middle aged, eccentric but well educated socialist, a former clergyman, and a labor leader of some experience," also joined the Strike Committee. Nyman, 157. The Nyman (Yale) study felt that his role was quite important; newspaper accounts of the strike do not place much emphasis on his attendance at a few of the negotiating sessions.

29. Ethnic conflict in the Naumkeag mill has not been well documented. In 1927, Polish workers at Naumkeag tried to elect a Polish business agent, but they were blocked by Irish and French Canadian workers. See Nyman, 8. The *Salem Evening News* suggested on several occasions that the Polish workers were the most radical. At an early union meeting, "a Polish-American worker demanded if the French workers were going to stick and this aroused the ire of one of the latter workers who thought 'she had a nerve to ask that question.'" "Strikers Are Firm in Their Determination Not to Return," *Salem Evening News,* May 13, 1933. Late in the strike, a rumor circulated (but was quickly discounted by the Strike Committee) that Franco-American workers were going to separate from the Polish workers in order to return to their jobs. "There was a feeling that many of the Ward One group had been taken over by Anne Burlak," the paper noted ("Insurgent Group of Strikers Block All Efforts to Get Vote," *Salem Evening News,* June 20, 1933; "Strikers' Committee Votes to Bar Burlak from All Activities," *Salem Evening News,* June 22, 1933).

30. "Executive Board Says Mill Strike Illegal; Urge Return to Jobs," *Salem Evening News,* June 2, 1933.

31. "Violence Today Mars Path of Settlement in Pequot Situation," *Salem Evening News,* May 29, 1933; "Used Tear Gas Bombs on Mill Strikers at Willows This Morning," *Salem Evening News,* June 1, 1933; "Pequot Strike Expensive from Pay Standpoint," *Salem Evening News,* June 12, 1933.

32. "Executive Board Says Mill Strike Illegal; Urge Return to Jobs," *Salem Evening News,* June 2, 1933.

33. "Acceptance of Mill Plan May Be Decided by Secret Ballot Vote," *Salem Evening News,* June 16, 1933; "Insurgent Group of Strikers Blocks All Efforts to Get Vote," *Salem Evening News,* June 20, 1933.

34. Nyman, 166–68.

35. He also writes, referring to the 1920s, "Just as southern mills now competed with local corporations, the substandard wages and working conditions of southern workers posed a potentially mortal threat to the well-being of a Fall River operative." Hartford, 57.

36. Hartford, 62.

37. Waldrep, 86.

38. Barbara S. Griffith, *The Crisis of American Labor: Operation Dixie and the Defeat of the CIO* (Philadelphia: Temple University Press, 1988); Hartford, 123–29. In some cases, mill owners directly confronted the union with the threat: accept increased workloads and reduced pay, or the unionized plants would be shut down to move south, as in the case of the somewhat notorious J. P. Stevens (Hartford, 132). The TWUA also carried out research and legislative initiatives to try to publicize, and detain, the financial sleights-of-hand that underlay much of the merger and plant closure movement of the post–World War II period. See Hartford, 176–78.

39. Whitney was a classic mill town in the heart of Spartanburg County, South Carolina. Waldrep describes the history and culture of Spartanburg's mill towns—almost all company towns grown around northern-owned mills—with great depth and eloquence. The map on p. 16 locates Whitney.

40. "Naumkeag to Shut Its Plant in Salem," *New York Times,* August 21, 1953.

41. The decision to move to South Carolina is detailed in reports in the *Salem Evening News* (August 14, 1953; August 17, 1953; August 19, 1953; August 20, 1953) and the *New York Times* (August 15, 1953; August 21, 1953; November 7, 1953). Quote is from the *New York Times,* August 21, 1953.

42. "No Doubt about Pequot Mills Leaving This City," *Salem Evening News,* August 20, 1953.

43. Laurence F. Gross, *The Course of Industrial Decline: The Boott Cotton Mills of Lowell, Massachusetts, 1835–1955* (Baltimore: Johns Hopkins University Press, 1993), 246.

44. Wendy Killeen, "Teen's Memory Burns Bright at JCC," *Boston Globe,* September 13, 1998.

45. McAllister, 108–9. The 1875 census showed Salem's population at 25,958. See Robotti, 77.

46. Robert P. Donnell, "Locational Response to Catastrophe: The Shoe and Leather Industry of Salem, Massachusetts, After the Conflagration of June 25, 1914," Syracuse University Department of Geography Discussion Paper Series, Number 20, July 1976, 6–8. Robotti (97) says that forty-one factories were destroyed.

47. Donnell, 8, 15–16 n. 23.

48. Donnell does not give specific information about unions or strikes at Salem's leather and shoe factories, but Robotti mentions a tannery strike in 1886 and shoe factory strikes in 1910 and 1917 (Robotti, 94, 100, 102). McAllister (108) describes the 1886 strike in more detail: "The workers protested long hours, low wages, and, most importantly, the unwillingness of the owners to negotiate with a union. The strike lasted five months and was marked by many acts of violence against the non-union workers brought in by the tannery owners. One of the strike leaders, George Warren, was found with a bullet in his head, and the workers who joined the Knights of Labor were excommunicated by the Catholic Archdiocese of Boston."

49. The interlocking websites of *sylvania.com* and *osram.com* tell the story of the companies' early histories. See also Teresa M. Hanafin, "GTE to Close Two Bay State Light Plants, 600 Workers to Lose Jobs," *Boston Globe,* November 7, 1989.

50. Hanafin.

51. "Local Trade Unions Count Gains, Losses," *Boston Globe,* September 6, 1998; Kathy McCabe, "Out of Old Jobs, Former Sylvania Workers Seek New Careers," *Boston Globe,* March 7, 1999. Because the job losses were directly related to NAFTA, workers could receive unemployment and retraining benefits under NAFTA and the Transitional Adjustment Assistance Act.

52. Kathy McCabe, "Sylvania's New CEO Voicing Global Thoughts," *Boston Globe,* October 7, 2001.

53. Joseph Menn, "Too Good to Stay Free; Kenner Parker Tries to Dodge a Takeover Try by New World," *Boston Globe,* August 17, 1987.

54. Paul Hemp, "Hasbro Will Post Loss; Tonka Takeover Cited," *Boston Globe,* July 11, 1991.

55. John C. Burke, "Salem Loses Its 56-Year Monopoly Monopoly," *Boston Globe,* June 2, 1991.

56. "Salem Plant to Close," *Boston Globe,* October 10, 1992.

57. Kathy McCabe, "Salem Seeks New Player. Parker Brothers Factory Site, Where Monopoly Once Ruled, Fails to Lure Right Developer," *Boston Globe,* October 26, 1996.

58. Cindy Rodriguez, "Union Alleges Exploitation, Plans Protest at Salem Site," *Boston Globe,* April 22, 2002.

59. "700 to Lose Jobs as Hasbro Plant Moves to Mexico," November 19, 1997, *http://lub bockonline.com/news/111997/LD0867.html.*

60. See "Hasbro Cutting 2,200 Jobs," *CNN Money,* December 7, 1999. *http://money.cnn .com/1999/12/97/companies/hasbro* and "Hasbro to Cut Jobs in Restructuring," Reuters, December 7, 1999; Michael Mello, "Hasbro Cuts Jobs, Closes Plants," Associated Press, December 7, 1999; David Henry, "Holiday Firings Can Have Longterm Impact," *USA Today,* December 9, 1999.

61. Quoted from Hasbro's website, *www.hasbro.com.*

62. Sarah J. Mahler, *American Dreaming: Immigrant Life on the Margins* (Princeton: Princeton University Press, 1995), 10.

63. McAllister, 113–14; Kathy McCabe, "Uncertain Future for 1940 Red-Brick Factory," *Boston Globe,* March 7, 1999.

64. See Saskia Sassen, *The Mobility of Labor and Capital: A Study in International Investment and Labor Flow* (Cambridge, U.K., and New York: Cambridge University Press, 1988). The 1990 census showed Salem with a population of 38,091 with 3,743 minorities (9.83 percent). Massachusetts Institute of Social Economic Research/State Data Center; reprinted in the *Boston Globe,* April 7, 1991.

65. New York: Ballantine Books, 1994; see also Mark Kurlansky, *Cod: A Biography of the Fish that Changed the World* (New York: Penguin, 1997), 82; Elizabeth Donnan, "The New England Slave Trade after the Revolution," *New England Quarterly* 3, no. 2 (April 1930): 251–78; Timothy J. McMillan, "Black Magic: Witchcraft, Race, and Resistance in Colonial New England," *Journal of Black Studies* 25, no. 1 (September 1994): 99–117.

66. For a discussion of immigrant national identity, see Peggy Levitt, *The Transnational Villagers* (Berkeley: University of California Press, 2001), 24; *Harper's New Monthly Magazine* 70 (March 1885): 418.

67. Levitt, 10.

68. Steven Rosenberg, "Point of Contention: Oft-Ignored Neighborhood Fights for, and Earns, Recognition," *Boston Globe,* June 13, 2002. He cites one migrant, truckdriver José Medrano, who "called the Point one big extended family. . . . he points at the Dominican flag hanging from a window on Perkins Street, and mentions that the building is full of old neighbors from Santiago."

69. José Alix and Justo Grullón, interview by author, December 11, 2002.

70. Alix and Grullón, December 11, 2002.

71. Alix and Grullón, December 11, 2002.

72. Alix and Grullón, December 11, 2002. Javier Rincón, interview by author, December 4, 2002. This discrepancy corresponds to what sociologist Peggy Levitt found in Boston, where knowledgeable informants suggested that the Dominican population was "half again" the 7,938 recorded in official figures in 1992. Peggy Levitt, "'A Todos Les Llamo Primo (I Call Everyone Cousin)': The Social Basis for Latino Small Businesses," in *New Migrants in the Marketplace: Boston's Ethnic Entrepreneurs,* ed. Marilyn Halter (Amherst: University of Massachusetts Press, 1995), 122.

73. Dominican *santería* shares many characteristics with other Yoruba-based religions that have flourished in the former slave societies of the Caribbean, though Dominicans tend to emphasize the indigenous Taíno origins of the tradition as well. In *santería* the identities of Yoruba deities were superimposed onto Catholic saints, so that slaves could worship in their own tradition while ostensibly submitting to their masters' Christianity. Syncretic religious forms in the Caribbean (commonly known as *voudun* in the French-speaking Caribbean, and *obeah* in the English-speaking islands) tend to share several common West African characteristics, including the incorporation of drumming, spirit possession, and healing.

74. Although most Dominicans are nominally Catholic and identify themselves as such, the evangelical minority tends to be more actively involved in church activities. Dominican "ethnic entrepreneurs" follow the pattern described by Marilyn Halter, including "marketing of ethnic products, employment of coethnics, relationship to coethnic customers, cultural capital generated through ethnic-based resources, and strategies of capitalization." See Marilyn Halter, "Boston's Immigrants Revisited: The Economic Culture of Ethnic Enterprise," in *New Migrants in the Marketplace,* ed. Marilyn Halter (Amherst: University of Massachusetts Press, 1995), 7.

75. José Alix and Johnny Grullón, interview by author, December 11, 2002.

76. National Consumer Law Center, "Immigrant Justice in the Consumer Marketplace," National Consumer Law Center, 2001.

77. Mahler, chap. 6.

78. Jim Haskell, Salem Harbor CDC, interview by author, December 11, 2002.

79. Johnny Grullón, interview by author, December 11, 2002.

80. Angel Muñiz, *Nueba Yol,* 1996.

81. In 1994, 10 percent of Salem's population was classified as "minority," while 43 percent of the Point's population was. See Elizabeth New Weld, "New Pride in the Point in Salem, A Neighborhood Seizes Control of Its Destiny," *Boston Globe,* November 13, 1994. Weld also cites numerous disparaging remarks made about the Point and its Dominican population by outsiders.

82. See, for example, Rodolfo Acuña, *Occupied America: A History of Chicanos,* 2nd ed. (New York: Harper and Row, 1981); Clara E. Rodríguez, *Puerto Ricans: Born in the U.S.A.* (Boulder: Westview Press, 1995).

83. Remedios Fajardo, May 2002.

84. "The Destruction of Tabaco," which several Salem residents transcribed and translated, has been edited and released by PressurePoint and was shown on Salem Access TV in the summer and fall of 2002.

85. Francisco Ramírez Cuellar, interviews by author, October 2002.

86. José Julio Pérez, interview by Garry Leech, August 2002.

Newspaper vending machine with Witch City motif. Photo by Kim Mimnaugh.

Chapter Ten

Salem as Crime Scene

MARGARET PRESS

*The fiend in his own shape is less hideous than
when he rages in the breast of man.*

—Nathaniel Hawthorne, "Young Goodman Brown"

S a mystery and crime writer, I write about death. But death is just one page. The pages that precede and follow it are about life: people, motivation, circumstance, connections, and setting. My setting is Salem. The devil once lived here.

In the winter of 1692, the Prince of Darkness paid this settlement a visit. He led the townsfolk into a season of suspicion, fear, and bloodshed by exploiting their motivations and manipulating their sorry circumstances. After seven months and twenty executions of innocents, Salem wrestled him to the ground. By and by the citizens planted his grave with splendid houses and wealth born of the golden ages of sail, then of leather, then of percale sheets and Monopoly board games.

We like to think he is now only a memory, glimpsed safely through the windows of the Salem trolley, or from theater seats peering from behind Daniel Day Lewis's sturdy cape as he plays John Proctor on the silver screen. Or flattened between the pages of the countless books that have used the name of this town as a lure.

Despite its name, from the Hebrew word for peace, the tourists who flock to Salem are convinced the city is about witches and death. They walk the old wharves now and admire the Federal period architecture. They buy mugs and T-shirts and wander the museums. But beneath it all they're looking and listening. Salem battled him once. But is Satan really gone for good?

This question, the faint echoes of that battle, and the attempts to reconcile the past foster a tension that colors our perceptions of everything that touches this town. Nathaniel Hawthorne exploited it as a setting. Arthur Miller expanded it to an allegory. Hollywood reduces it to caricature. Every October, fundamentalist

Christians still sound the alarm against the dangers of witchcraft. The local witches cry out against misunderstanding and persecution. The tourists come to view it all.

Add to this mix the visitors' expectations that have evolved to embrace horror, the occult, the weird, and the unexplained. Salem has tried not to disappoint. Pirates and vampires. Hearse tours and Duck tours. Haunted houses and dungeons. Psychics, gypsies, and palm readers. The first elephants on the continent paraded our cobblestoned streets. Siamese twins included Salem on their tours. The magic of the telephone was first demonstrated to a packed, incredulous crowd at the Salem Lyceum Hall. Harry Houdini brought his show to town.[1]

It is a wonderful brew, and from this cauldron wafts a sort of synchronicity one might call the Salem Factor. We find coincidences and connections in the human experience here because we expect them. We look for the extraordinary in events here, and we see it. The Salem Factor is a state of mind.

Specters and spectacles. We confront our worst fears by embracing, diffusing, and celebrating them. Halloween is the holiday. Salem is the arena. And this is my setting.

Crossroads

In her 1956 essay "Place in Fiction," renowned author Eudora Welty states: "Location is the crossroads of circumstance."[2] To know the heart of a place, start with its people and listen to their stories. Every street, every corner has one. Taken together they make up the essence of this town. The ones that engage me are the skirmishes between good and evil, where man is put to the test, particularly when in these battles between light and dark the Salem Factor hovers in the shadows.

Stand, for example, on the corner of Essex Street and Hawthorne Boulevard downtown. Formerly called Main Street, much of Essex follows an ancient thoroughfare that predates the original settlement.[3] From this spot you can see the wonderful confluence of history, incongruity, and irony this town and this crossroads enjoy. Two historic homes share the northwest corner, situated on the grounds of the Peabody Essex Museum. Across the street to the east stands a hotel. The southeast corner is occupied by my dry cleaners. A pub sits on the southwest corner, flanked by a witch shop and a palm reader's establishment. In the middle of Hawthorne Boulevard presides a commanding statue of Nathaniel Hawthorne himself, seated on a rock with one hand on his hip, facing down toward the wharves. This is his intersection.

From this crossroads our stories begin.

Northwest Corner: The Murder of Captain White

At 126 Essex Street sits a yellow Georgian Colonial style house, dating from about 1730. Four generations of Crowninshields grew up within its walls, including "King" George Crowninshield, who had several prominent sons.[4] He also had a couple of grandsons who in the spring of 1830 would achieve their own brand of notoriety.

The second house on the corner, a magnificent brick building at 128 Essex, was commissioned in 1804 by John Gardner. This house is considered to be one of Salem architect Samuel McIntire's finest Federal style homes. From the Corinthian columns framing the front door to the "reclining figure of Plenty with her cornucopia and attendant cherub" carved on an upstairs mantel, the site is an architectural treasure.[5] It also happens to be one of Salem's most notorious crime scenes.

When John Gardner fell on hard times in 1815, ownership passed to Capt. Joseph White, who had amassed immense wealth as a successful shipmaster and Salem merchant. Captain White happened to be not only rich, but old and childless. That made his Last Will and Testament a matter of considerable interest to his nearest living relatives, two nephews and a niece. The niece, Mary Beckford, lived with Captain White as his housekeeper. Over time, the mercurial captain would change his will, favoring one heir or another, as his relationships with them blew hot or cold.

Mrs. Beckford had a ne'er-do-well for a son-in-law, twenty-six-year-old Joseph Knapp. Captain White came to dislike Knapp so much that he rewrote his

Gardner-Pingree House at 128 Essex Street (above left), site of the murder of Captain White. Photo by Margaret Press.

will again, leaving only a token amount to his niece, Mrs. Beckford. By 1830, Knapp apparently felt that his mother-in-law could do with a little help with her inheritance, and that the eighty-two-year-old Captain White was now plenty old enough. Knapp enlisted the aid of his brother Frank, and together they hired the black sheep of the Crowninshield family—grandsons Richard and George—both in their twenties. Joseph Knapp's plan hinged on the misconception that if a man were to die without a will, by law his estate would be divided equally among his closest kin. So, *step one* was: Get rid of the will.

One day in early April of 1830, Joseph Knapp stopped by to see his mother-in-law at Captain White's home. During the visit, he slipped upstairs, located the Captain's trunk, dug out the latest version of the will, and stuffed it into his pocket. Before leaving the house, Knapp unlocked one of the downstairs windows.

Step two: Get rid of the old man. On the night of April 6, 1830, Frank Knapp took up position on Brown Street behind Captain White's garden. Richard Crowninshield let himself in through the downstairs window and stole into Captain White's bedroom on the second floor. As Plenty and her cherub reclined on their nearby mantel, Crowninshield bludgeoned and stabbed the sleeping captain to death, drenching his nightclothes and bedding with blood.

The next edition of the *Salem Gazette* mirrored the agony and fear that subsequently seized the town:

Atrocious Assassination

The painful duty devolves upon us of announcing, that in our peaceful town, which we had hitherto believed to be secure from the midnight assassin, and those crimes of the deepest die which have occasionally stained the annals of European nations, and of some parts of our own country, a MURDER has been perpetrated so horrible and atrocious, that we should in vain search the records of crime in any country for a case exceeding it in enormity.[6]

Two months went by, with police frustrated in their search for the killer. A group of "public-spirited individuals" formed a Committee of Vigilance to aid in the investigation. Handbills were circulated around town, and rewards were offered for information.

The case finally broke when a pickpocket down in New Bedford told local police that Richard Crowninshield had bragged to him about the murder. Crowninshield and his brother George were immediately picked up. The arrest of two grandsons of the elder George Crowninshield shocked the nation.

Richard and his brother refused to say a word to authorities. Richard had

Cartoon of Captain White's murder. Reprinted from Ellms, *Trials of Capt. Joseph J. Knapp, Jr. and George Crowninshield, Esq.*, 1830.

not been so discreet with his friends, however. A second acquaintance to whom Richard had described the killing tried to exploit this knowledge by sending off a blackmail letter to Richard's coconspirators, the Knapp brothers.

Unfortunately for the whole crew, the blackmail letter was intercepted by the Knapps' father, who promptly turned it over to authorities. Joseph and Frank Knapp were arrested and indicted for murder. Also unfortunately for Joseph, the will that he stole was only an old draft. The official copy of Captain White's latest will, leaving the bulk of his estate to his nephew, happened to be safely in the hands of his lawyer.

Joseph Knapp finally confessed to his hand in the murder plot. In mid-June, Richard Crowninshield, already indicted as the principal in the crime, saw the handwriting on the wall and hanged himself in his cell.

The distinguished Daniel Webster was appointed special prosecutor in what would be a landmark and challenging case. Under the law, accessories to murder could only be convicted if the principal had already been convicted, and if they were present aiding and abetting during the commission of the crime. In this instance, the principal—Richard Crowninshield—was now dead, never to be tried. Second, Frank Knapp had been outside on Brown Street behind the house while Richard took care of business inside.

Webster overcame the first hurdle when he successfully moved to have Frank Knapp designated as the principal perpetrator in place of Crowninshield. The trials of the remaining three men moved forward. Frank was the first before the bar.

Joseph Knapp's confession established the motive and plan. Witnesses placed Frank Knapp in the street on the night of the murder. Webster then argued to the jury that "presence" should be taken to mean near enough to aid and abet. Knapp had been waiting at a previously agreed location, close enough to render assistance to Richard Crowninshield. Webster argued: "The perpetrator would derive courage and confidence from the knowledge that his associate was in the place appointed."[7]

Webster's eloquence paid off. The jury returned a verdict of guilty, and Frank Knapp was sentenced to hang. Additionally, legal precedent had been established, broadening the definition of presence at a crime.

Joseph Knapp's trial followed, made easier by the principles established during Frank's trial. Daniel Webster reminded the jury in his close that there were now three deaths deriving from this "dark and bloody tragedy"—Captain White, Richard Crowninshield by his own hand, and Frank Knapp by a hangman's rope. The crime "stands alone in the calendar of human depravity." In his summation Webster struck to the heart of the case: "The object was money—the crime murder—the price blood."[8]

Joseph Knapp followed his brother to the gallows. George Crowninshield alone went free. Insufficient evidence netted him a verdict of Not Guilty. He lived to the age of eighty-two, the same age at which his brother's victim met his demise.

Nathaniel Hawthorne was living and writing in Salem during this time. From his letters and later works it is clear he shared the town's absorption with the case, particularly since he himself was related to both the Crowninshield and White families. Critics believe that portions of *The House of the Seven Gables* found roots in the White murder. *Mr. Higginbotham's Catastrophe,* published in 1834, also appears to have been inspired by the events. In this story, three villains attempt to murder Mr. Higginbotham, who—like White—was wealthy and childless. Higginbotham's sole heir is a niece. And when the selectmen think the old man is dead, they distribute handbills offering a $500 reward for the apprehension of his killers, just as the Salem selectmen did for Captain White.

Hawthorne's tale ends happily. Capt. Joseph White's did not.[9]

The Ghost of Swampscott Road: The Frances Cochran Murder

From Captain White's house, Essex Street heads west for about a mile, then becomes Highland Avenue, bending southwest past Salem Hospital and leading to the neighboring city of Lynn. Until the late 1800s, Highland was called the Salem and Boston Turnpike. Halfway down Highland, in the rocky outcroppings of south Salem, Swampscott Road forks off to the left.

Salem has had its share of unsolved murders. But this fork leads to one that lives on in the memory of a young witness, as well as in the memories of residents not even born at the time it occurred. As a ghost.

Swampscott Road travels southeast for a secluded mile and a half with no intersections or stops. It becomes Danvers Road where it crosses the Swampscott line, ending at a cemetery. There are no houses on the route for most of its length, only woods, ledge, a quarry, and swamps that feed the Forest River. The road is dark and full of curves. One Salem police detective relates that a popular game of his teen years was to drive down it at night and see who could go the longest with their lights off. Another recalls hanging out there with his friends as they scared one another with tales of the White Lady—the ghost of Swampscott Road. In the dark it was spooky. They'd see a far-off light and tell each other that it was Frances Cochran, returned from the dead. But the Salem synchronicity Factor would bring Frances's ghost back to the Criminal Investigation Division once again, fifty years after her murder.

On July 17, 1941, a young bookkeeper for a Lynn leather company stepped off a bus after telling a friend she was going to buy a dress for a dance that night. Through the bus window, the friend watched nineteen-year-old Frances Cochran climb into a large black square-backed car after apparently recognizing the driver. Frances never returned home.

On July 20 her mother contacted the local radio station WESX and appealed for help in finding her daughter. Five feet tall, a hundred pounds, sweet face, curly hair, last seen wearing a dark blue suit with a lobster pin. Less than an hour later, the station received an anonymous call that directed police to a body in the brushes off Swampscott Road. Frances Cochran had been sexually assaulted, beaten, and strangled. Part of her clothes had been set afire. A piece of wood was jammed down her throat. Her purse, watch, and one white shoe were missing. A lobster pin was found in the underbrush nearby.

Police tried in vain to track down the radio station caller. In sensational language reminiscent of the *Salem Gazette* a hundred years earlier, WESX broadcast a passionate plea directed to the tipster: "In the name of humanity and for the sake of the mother and father and brother of this innocent girl who was cruelly tortured and put to ignominious death, [the DA] urges you to come forward and help clear up this heinous crime."[10]

The caller was apparently unmoved. Ultimately, more than a thousand people were questioned. Hundreds of other tips were received and recorded. Police went back to the scene months later when the foliage had dropped to see if evidence might now be visible in the bushes. All they found were dead leaves.

At one point in the investigation, Salem police rounded up a group of middle-aged men who called themselves the Triggers. Apparently this was a loose association of local gentlemen who hung around the woods off Swampscott Road to spy on couples having sex. Sometimes called the Creepers or Ghosters, they would often meet later to compare observations. Many of them had been going down there for years, lurking around the area as early as the 1920s.

A 1941 police report entitled "Triggers, Ghosters and Creepers Night at the Salem Police Station" documented the interviews and included details of the activities in the woods during the period when Frances was missing.[11] The Triggers knew the area intimately. One man was a draftsman and drew police a detailed map of the paths, terrain, and "good observation posts."

The men insisted they were doing nobody any harm by their Peeping Tom activities. They explained they would "rather do that than hang around Lynn and go into a barroom and drink and cause people trouble."[12] The Triggers also happily provided the investigators with details of their past observations. "Saw one guy with a cow once. Trying to make connections."[13] The police took it all down.

Although they had seen all sorts of things down off Swampscott Road, none of the Triggers had seen Frances Cochran, dead or alive.

Fifty years later, in July of 1991, a woman named Janice Knowlton called Salem police detectives. She related that through recent counseling she had been uncovering repressed traumatic memories from her childhood. She believed she had witnessed her father, George Knowlton, kill numerous women around the North Shore. Her theory was that dad brought her along as a youngster to lull women into feeling safe riding with him. During the forties, he had traversed the country, killing in both New England and Los Angeles. Janice Knowlton was positive her father committed the 1947 LA murder of an aspiring actress named Elizabeth Short—dubbed by the media the "Black Dahlia."[14] When she learned about the Cochran case from a local reporter, Jan began to experience flashbacks of a large square-backed car, of walking in the woods with her dad, and of other details relevant to Frances's murder. She recalled fetching a short piece of branch for him.

Jan Knowlton's father died in 1962. His involvement in the murders was never proven. The case of Frances Cochran has yet to be solved.

The Boston Strangler: The Evelyn Corbin Murder

My first lessons in the demographics of Salem came from reading the police logs and obituaries in the local paper. In Captain White's day, between the columns of shipping news, the *Salem Gazette* contained reports of highway robbery, arson, counterfeit bills, and Indians obstructing the U.S. mail. Nowadays, along with the traffic violators and drug arrests, we find the more charming "possession of short lobsters" lending regional flavor.

Names in the obituary column today are Polish, Irish, and French Canadian. Some of the departed worked at Parker Brothers. Others were employed at GE or Sylvania. Like Frances Cochran, many worked in the leather industry—in the Blubber Hollow tanneries or in nearby shoe manufacturing. Or in the weaving sheds at Pequot Mills, working as loomers and producing cotton sheets for the nation. Before people die, they work. Their jobs are part of the fabric of the city.

Evelyn Corbin was part of this fabric. Born in Salem of French Canadian parents, she was employed as a lamp assembler at Sylvania Electric. Evelyn lived for several years in a brick apartment building on Lafayette Street, in an area rebuilt after the Great Fire of 1914 had stripped it of houses and trees. It was there that she was brutally murdered on a foggy September morning in 1963.

What is remarkable in Corbin's case is the tenacity with which this crime is wrongly attributed, in book and movie, and in widespread popular belief. For years many people have assumed Evelyn Corbin was another victim of the Boston Strangler.

On the morning of September 8, 1963, Corbin, a fifty-eight-year-old blond divorcee, had breakfasted with a friend in the building, then returned to her tidy apartment to dress for Mass. Two hours later, she was found strangled on her bed. Two nylon stockings, which Evelyn had purchased at Almy's the day before, were wrapped around her neck. From the ligatures and body position, and from a later confession by Albert DeSalvo, the public and the DA's office were quick to believe this Salem homicide was his handiwork. It was a widely popular and satisfying assumption, particularly since the string of gruesome murders stopped when DeSalvo was arrested and taken off the street.

However, Salem police detectives were never convinced it was DeSalvo. They had a much more likely suspect in mind, a Lynn man named Robert Campbell. An acquaintance living across the street from Evelyn Corbin had put Campbell up the night before the murder. He told police that Campbell had left around 9:30 in the morning with a pocketful of donuts. Campbell later urged the man to change his story and say it had been 11 A.M. because he was "in enough trouble already."[15] Investigators found a donut on the fire escape near Corbin's window.

During the hours after Corbin's murder, Campbell tried without success to get money and clothes, then picked up a teenage girl and drove to New York. The girl left him as soon as they got there. She told police that Campbell had been "irritable" and acted suspiciously during the trip.

Campbell was later arrested and convicted on charges stemming from a separate assault on a woman in Peabody. Salem detectives continued to pursue leads, but were never able to get enough evidence to secure an arrest in the Corbin murder.

Although DeSalvo was never tried for the "Strangler" murders, he too was incarcerated for another conviction. One day in 1973, he called up a psychiatrist he knew and asked him to come for a visit. DeSalvo wanted to tell him who the "real" Boston Strangler was. Unfortunately, before he had the chance, Albert DeSalvo was murdered in his cell.[16]

Southeast Corner: The Essex Cleaners Robbery

Not all crimes are murders, of course. Many others leave their victims with permanent scars and lifelong memories. We return to our intersection for the next story—about one victim who survived, and one who will never die.

On the southeast corner of Essex and Hawthorne is the green facade of the Essex Cleaners. Established in 1944, it is quite possibly the oldest remaining cleaning establishment in Salem. I'm a customer. One thing I've always liked about owner Michael Szczuka is that whenever I plop an armload of dirty clothes onto his counter, he picks through them and hands me back anything that's actually washable. "Save your money," he says. One thing I didn't know about him until recently is that, in addition to his honesty, he also bears a six-inch scar on his abdomen, right next to a faint bullet hole.

Szczuka's grandparents and great-grandparents were among the multitude of Polish emigrants who settled in the Derby Street area of Salem and provided a major part of the city's growing workforce. Michael's dad was a presser employed at the dry cleaners back when it was called the Essex Cleansers. After a while, his father managed to finance and buy the establishment.

Although the family spent most of Michael's childhood in North Salem, Michael moved back down to the Derby Street area in the late sixties. He lived there with a bunch of rock and rollers, right across from witch Laurie Cabot's first store. Unable to afford their own television, he and his roommates would go over to Laurie's place to watch broadcasts of their favorite rock groups.

Michael Szczuka's own entry into the workforce had been at age sixteen when he was a pot washer at the Hawthorne Hotel. In the seventies, he worked as a lobsterman out of Beverly Harbor. When he wasn't out hauling traps, the lanky, brown-haired man helped out in his father's shop.

Saturday, September 30, 1978, was one of those days. Michael had worked alongside his aunt that morning. During the afternoon a friend of his aunt's had dropped by for a chat. Michael took a break to go have pizza with friends.

While he was out, a dark-haired nervous man in his twenties, later identified as Bruno Rivera, came into the store and waved a paper bag and a gun at the aunt, demanding money. She opened the cash register, but managed to slip most of the contents into a wastebasket below. She then handed the perpetrator thirty-one dollars. Disappointed, Rivera pushed behind the counter and herded the women into a back corner. While he was grilling them about where the rest of the money was kept, a customer entered the shop. She was forced at gunpoint to join the group.

That's when Michael returned to the shop. As soon as he stepped inside, Rivera swung the gun toward him. "Come here!" he demanded. Michael joined the group as they huddled back by the cleaning equipment.

Michael Szczuka had several characteristics at that time. He was young, he was foolish, he was in great shape from lobstering, he was concerned about his elderly aunt, and he was, in his words, "ornery." And at that same moment, Bruno Rivera made two mistakes. He transferred the gun to his left hand so he could use his right to collect wallets. Then he turned to Michael and said, "You better not try anything."

Michael took this as a personal challenge. He was only an arm's reach from Rivera, so he lunged at the man. Rivera's gun went off. The first bullet went right through Michael's abdomen. He didn't realize he had been hit, so he continued to struggle with the assailant. Three more shots went off. One into the floor, one into the wall, and one ricocheted off a dress form and through the window overlooking the statue of a startled Nathaniel Hawthorne.

By this time, the nervous intruder was more scared than the ornery Szczuka family. He got up, grasped his paper bag and weapon, and bolted out the door and down the street toward the wharves.

Someone went for help. Thanks to the Salem Factor, a registered nurse happened to be right next door and came in to help Michael until the ambulance came. At the hospital, Michael underwent exploratory surgery. The surgeon removed his organs, looked around, and stuffed them all back in. The bullet had gone clean through. Recovering from major abdominal surgery ended up being far worse for Michael Szczuka than recovering from the gunshot wound.

It turned out that Bruno Rivera was from Lynn, Massachusetts, but had been incarcerated in the Georgia State Penitentiary for some time. In late September he had escaped from prison and made his way home to Massachusetts. And, wouldn't you know it, when Bruno needed money he went north to this city, bypassing the wealthier communities of Swampscott and Marblehead, and landed at the dry cleaners on Hawthorne's intersection.

Bruno almost got away with the robbery. The case went unsolved until 1980 when a snitch named him as the party responsible for the heist. However, by then Bruno had already been picked up on the fugitive charge and shipped back to Georgia. Another couple of years went by until his extradition back to Massachusetts put him in a lineup for Michael Szczuka, his aunt, and the hapless customer to view. The police scrounged together seven men who resembled Bruno for the viewing. A few patrolmen, the dog officer, a guy from Red's Sandwich Shop next door. But Michael managed to pick him out. Bruno was the nervous one.

In April 1982, Rivera was finally indicted. But there was another delay. Before Rivera could be tried, he managed to escape from the Salem jail and was on the run a good many months before a SWAT team caught up with him at his mother's house and returned him for trial.

Bruno Rivera was found guilty of armed robbery and assault with a deadly weapon. Ultimately, he served his time and was released on parole. In the meantime, Michael Szczuka has reexamined his own life in the wake of his near-death experience, and sought the lessons from this incident. No one is indestructible. Don't burden your life with the wounds of bitterness. Szczuka now owns the cleaners, lives in his great-grandfather's original house off Derby Street, and is active in his church. Pictures of his grandparents, his grandchildren, and a few saints fill the wall by his phone. He hopes that Bruno Rivera had his own spiritual awak-

Salem Police Criminal Investigation Division, old Central Street headquarters, 1990. Courtesy of Salem Police Department.

ening as well, and is out somewhere leading a more useful and wiser life. Perhaps Bruno Rivera has pictures of grandchildren on his wall, too.

With a permanent dent in her breastplate, the dress form still stands in his shop.

The Witch Judge: The Case of the Missing Tombstone

From our intersection, the Peabody Essex Museum complex stretches west for two blocks. It includes not only the Gardner and Crowninshield homes on our corner, but a block down—Marine Hall, the oldest operating museum in the country. In back of Marine Hall are Charter Street and the site of the Old Burying Point. Nathaniel Hawthorne has relatives interred there.

Nathaniel's great-great-grandfather was John Hathorne, the infamous Salem magistrate who examined accused witches in 1692. While others later repented their participation in those dark affairs, John Hathorne never did. Stephen Vincent Benét wrote a mythical account of Daniel Webster's greatest trial, in which Webster defends a New Hampshire farmer against the devil himself and graciously allows his adversary to choose the judge. The devil selects none other than Justice John Hathorne, hauled back from the grave to preside once again.[17] No wonder Nathaniel spent so much of his writing life trying to exorcise Hathorne's ghost from the family tree.

Nearly three hundred years after his burial, Justice Hathorne's grave site became the target of an apparent larceny. On a spring day in 1982 a local tour guide discovered that Hathorne's tombstone was missing from the Charter Street Burying Point. He promptly called the *Salem Evening News* to report the disappearance. This was certainly not the worst insult the Hathorne family had ever endured. Nevertheless, it merited concern. The Old Burying Point is a popular tourist destination, and every guidebook and marketing pamphlet lists Hathorne's grave site as one of the cemetery's most significant features. After all, this is the witch city. John Hathorne was the witch judge.

Once the story hit the stands, the case was cracked by quick police action and a bit of suppressed memory retrieval. The missing tombstone turned up across the street in the Salem Police Department armorer's closet. It had been resting comfortably all the while under lock and key. Apparently, the previous week a good citizen noticed the marker had fallen over and, concerned for its safety, had turned it in to the police. Centuries of deterioration had finally taken their toll on poor Hathorne. An irony not escaping the *Evening News:* the good citizen happened to be the owner of the Salem Witch Museum, Biff Michaud.

The police captain who had taken the tombstone into custody explained in a laconic statement to the press: "Michaud was afraid it was going to be stolen or destroyed, so in it went with the shotguns."[18]

The matter was settled out of court. Judge Hathorne recovered his headstone.

Larceny of a Verdict: The Chucky Doucette Story

When asked what police work is like in Salem, members of the department invariably respond that they wouldn't trade it for anywhere else. Current management is effective and fair. The chief is well respected. And Salem is a great place to be a cop. Not so large that cases get lost or the numbers overwhelming. But large enough that they see a little of everything. Salem is a county seat. It has a hospital, a college, and courthouses. Tourists, witches, power plant, harbor. Judges live on Chestnut Street. Homeless live on Crombie Street. Name a crime—you'll find it here. Some tough. Some strange. Rarely boring.

The 1987 murder of a former gas station employee netted some memorable moments during the police investigation. The Salem Factor, however, would take the case on an astonishing journey through the courts. A wild ride that will long endure in the Salem Police Department's memory.

One Saturday afternoon in February 1987, Salem Hospital nurse Shauna Bufalino began to worry about her husband Ray, who had left their apartment earlier that morning with a man Shauna mistrusted. The man was Chucky Doucette.

Ray had worked for Chucky's father at a Canal Street Texaco station in Salem the previous summer. One day, Ray had fallen on the job and injured himself sufficiently to sue for workmen's compensation. Doucette Sr. had no insurance to cover the claim. Chucky had been pressuring Ray to sign a release relieving the station of liability.

Ray also owed Chucky money. Chucky had made dozens of calls to the Bufalinos' home, demanding to be repaid. Shauna was afraid of Doucette, and urged her husband to pay off the debt.

Sometime around nine that morning, Chucky Doucette had stopped by the Bufalinos' apartment on a quiet street behind Parker Brothers, home of the Monopoly board game. The burly Doucette spoke with Ray for a few minutes. Then, both men drove off in separate cars. That was the last time Shauna saw her husband alive.

Early in the afternoon Shauna borrowed a friend's car and went looking for Ray. She traveled routes she knew he frequented. Her search took her through Blubber Hollow and along secluded Harmony Grove Road where it borders the cemetery in Salem. The road follows the North River and the railroad tracks, which serviced the Blubber Hollow tanneries in their heyday a hundred years earlier. As Shauna approached the Peabody line she came upon her husband's beige Chevrolet Citation by the side of the road. Inside, thirty-year-old Raymond Bufalino III was slumped over in the driver's seat with two .38 caliber bullets in his head.

It didn't take Salem police long to locate witnesses. Three neighbors in the Harmony Grove Road area claimed to have seen a man of Doucette's description between 9:30 and 10:30 Saturday morning, in the vicinity of the Citation. One man thought he heard shots around that time. The detectives called Chucky Doucette in for questioning the following day.

On Sunday morning, Doucette told police that a friend had driven him to Bufalino's apartment Saturday morning and would provide an alibi. The detectives contacted the man, who backed up Doucette's story. Later on, however, the man recanted, explaining Doucette had coerced him into lying.

When Doucette's girlfriend was questioned, she related that Chucky had left the house for work Saturday morning around 8 A.M. The girlfriend had gone back to sleep and awoke again around 10 A.M. to find Chucky back in the apartment, naked and dripping from a shower. However, when police interviewed Chucky's father, they learned that Chucky had called in sick that Saturday morning and never showed up at the Texaco station.

The Salem detectives asked Doucette to come in again Sunday evening and submit to chemical tests for blood traces. On the phone they advised him that no amount of scrubbing would get rid of occult blood—blood that's invisible to the eye. Still, to prepare for his second visit to police, Chucky Doucette (a) shaved his moustache and beard, (b) shaved his hairy arms, and (c) soaked his arms and hands in household bleach for ten minutes. The detectives grinned when they saw Chucky's raw, red arms. This was a classic illustration of "consciousness of guilt," evidence which suggests the suspect is hiding something, which is admissible in court, and which can strengthen the prosecutor's case.

Even with all Chucky's efforts, the state police chemist was able to raise traces of blood. The detectives placed Chucky Doucette under arrest.

Meanwhile, police searched in vain for a murder weapon. Salem detectives talked to a second girlfriend, who admitted that Doucette had owned a Ruger .357 Magnum handgun. Chucky had tried to coerce her, too, threatening that she would "get it from the same gun" if she told anyone about the weapon.[19]

Bullet fragments were recovered from the victim during the autopsy. But without Chucky's gun, there was nothing to compare them to, and no way to tie him to the murder. Eventually, Detective Sergeant Paul Tucker managed to track down the previous owner of the gun, a guy named Tony. Tucker went to talk to him.

"Did you ever fire the gun anywhere?" the detective asked.

Turns out he had. Tony had been at a friend's house in Beverly once, back when he still owned the revolver. There was a party going on, and a bit of drinking. Somehow or other, the gun was discharged. Tony remembered that a bullet had lodged in the kitchen wall.

The Salem Criminal Investigation Division and the state police packed up their tools and went with Tony to the Beverly apartment. Sadly, Tony's friend had recently remodeled the kitchen. New wall, new cabinets. When Tony pointed out where the bullet had gone, the detectives took down the new cabinets and sawed into the wall. One of them reached down between the studs, felt around, and with a smile—pulled up a metal fragment.

Neither the mangled bullet in the wall nor the pieces in the victim's head were complete enough to do a ballistics comparison. However, the Salem CID sent the fragments to the FBI for a neutron activation analysis. The results indicated that the bullets came from the same lot.

It was sounding like a pretty solid case. Salem police investigators were totally unprepared for the surprises in store for them in the old Newburyport Courthouse, where Daniel Webster himself had once argued cases.

Judge John T. Ronan presided over the trial of Chucky Doucette in late September and early October of 1988. From the beginning, Judge Ronan gave the prosecution a tough time. He excluded testimony of two witnesses because they had seen Doucette's photo in the newspaper prior to making their ID. Ronan ruled their identification was therefore "made from impure evidence."[20] He threw out evidence from Doucette's car, and an autopsy report establishing time of death during a period for which Doucette had no alibi. Without the autopsy report the defense was free to argue that death had occurred later, after Chucky had returned to his apartment.

The bitterest pill for investigators was Ronan's numerous insinuations that police had fabricated the evidence and had actually conspired to plant the bullet fragment in the kitchen wall. The judge complained that Commonwealth experts were giving inconsistent testimony. He suggested to the jury that the investigation might have been shoddy, if not suspect.

Nevertheless, after one day of deliberation, the jury returned a verdict of guilty of first-degree murder. Chucky Doucette was looking at a mandatory sentence of life without parole.

Not surprisingly, the defense attorney moved that the verdict be reversed due to insufficient evidence, and argued that the Commonwealth's case was distorted and suspicious. In a dramatic turnaround, Judge Ronan concurred with the defense and before a stunned courtroom canceled the guilty verdict.

In a rare number of cases, judges have been known to set aside verdicts, calling for new trials. But this was the first time a judge in Massachusetts had actually reversed a verdict, effectively replacing it with a finding of Not Guilty. The prosecutor and police were outraged. In words they will never forget, Judge Ronan, in justifying his reversal, declared to the courtroom: "These walls—and this court was built in 1804—have never heard such untruths."[21] Chucky Doucette was immediately released.

But the roller-coaster story of Chucky Doucette was just beginning. The DA's office appealed the judge's finding. And in September of 1990 the Supreme Judicial Court in a 5–0 decision overturned Judge Ronan and reinstated the conviction. The case was returned to Ronan to impose sentencing.

On the morning that the SJC decision was reported in the papers, Chucky Doucette vanished. Although his father claimed he had just gone on "vacation," a nationwide manhunt ensued. Ten days later Doucette finally reappeared and surrendered. Judge Ronan had no choice but to sentence him to life. A month later, however, Ronan granted a defense motion for a new trial.

Doucette's attorney succeeded in getting bail reduced in the meantime. Chucky's father put up the Texaco station as collateral, and Chucky was again free. While out on bail, he was arrested for home invasion and armed robbery, in which he left the homeowner beaten and bound. Doucette had drawn another "Go Directly to Jail" card.

As the second trial date drew near, a new judge was assigned to the case and heard motions to suppress evidence. The luck of the draw went to the Commonwealth this time. Judge Patrick Brady ruled to allow most of the evidence that Judge Ronan had tossed out. With the hand he was now dealt, Doucette finally entered into a plea bargain in December 1991, pleading guilty to second-degree murder. Chucky Doucette is presently serving a life sentence with the possibility of parole after fifteen years.

Ultimately, the Attorney General's office reviewed the trial transcripts and Judge Ronan's allegations regarding the investigation and prosecutorial conduct. The AG found no basis for the complaints, and no evidence of wrongdoing on the part of the Salem or state police.

Human motivation. Chucky Doucette's seemed pretty clear. Judge Ronan's will forever remain a mystery.

Northeast Corner: Failure to Appear

From the grisly crime scene off Blubber Hollow, we return to our crossroads for quite a different scene altogether. Directly across Essex Street from my dry cleaners is the Hawthorne Hotel, named for Nathaniel himself. The hotel dates from 1923 and is quite elegant for its size. In October 1990, a séance was held in the hotel ballroom to a standing-room-only crowd.

It happened to be the night I first made my acquaintance with the Salem Police Criminal Investigation Division, shortly after the Doucette conviction had been reinstated. I had nearly completed my first mystery novel and thought to give it authenticity by talking a bit with real detectives. It turns out that real detectives, besides detecting, also do private detail jobs. And in Salem these include crowd control at séances. An hour after I met him down at the station, Detective Conrad Prosniewski excused himself to change into his uniform, buckle on his gun belt, and depart for the Hawthorne Hotel.

October 31, 1990, marked the sixty-fourth anniversary of the death of the great Harry Houdini. Houdini had once promised his wife that after he departed this earth, he would devote his afterlife to finding a way to contact her. He left her with a secret message he'd use so she would know whether any future communication was genuine. Ever since his death, a group of family members and devoted followers pick a spot somewhere around the country to attempt contact, thus far in vain. They select a place that held particular meaning for the escape artist. Back in 1906, Houdini had done a gig in Salem, which included a stunt performed at the old police station on Front Street. So this year his followers chose Salem for their annual event, and as this town is now a Mecca for psychics, they were banking on success.

The participants convened at the Hawthorne late on the night of October 30 for talks and refreshments. At the stroke of midnight they formed into groups, dimmed the lights, and tried for several minutes to invoke the magician's spirit. "Are you there, Harry Houdini?" they called out. "Please show us a sign!"

From the doorway to the ballroom, Detective Prosniewski kept the peace and glanced around for mechanical devices. If Houdini did make an appearance, the policeman wanted to be sure it wasn't with the assistance of ropes and pulleys. The media were present, no doubt looking for the same thing.

Prosniewski heard someone in the room say they felt cold air. Someone else heard clinking. But in the end, the séance organizers concluded they had failed once again to summon the magician. They conveyed their disappointment to the reporters in attendance. Salem of all places should have been a winner. But ironically, they hadn't been able to round up a local medium to lead the invocation that night and had flown one in from the West Coast. The out-of-town psychic's lack of familiarity with Salem may have been their downfall. Maybe the great man got lost.

The next morning the front-page headline of the *Salem Evening News* read: "Harry Houdini snubs slick Salem séance."[22] The night hadn't been a total disappointment, however. Detective Conrad Prosniewski took home a fine black mug with a bright gold inscription:

Halloween Midnight 1990

Harry Houdini 1874–1926

Séance jobs don't turn up that frequently. The most coveted private details in the police department are actually the weekly bingo games. Members of the department are allowed to bid on them in order of their time on the force. First, they are steady and predictable. There's a bingo game every night of the week somewhere in the city. Second, they are indoors. Third, the bingo crowd is not particularly violence-prone. The greatest hazard tends to be the secondhand smoke.

Police officers, despite the salary figures reported annually in the local paper, are not particularly well paid. To earn the published figures, they have to work a lot of overtime and private details. Others frequently work second jobs to feed their families. They deliver heating oil. They repair cars. They run sub shops. They practice law. Perhaps the most unusual moonlighting work in recent years is Officer Chuck Bergman's. Bergman is a medium. He talks to dead people.

Officer Bergman feels he inherited his psychic powers, since both his mother and grandmother possessed the gift. When Chuck was a youngster, he recalls meeting his first apparitions and running to his mother. Any other parent would have told their kid not to worry; there was no such thing as a ghost. Chuck's mother told him not to worry; he'd understand when he was older.

A stint in the navy brought Bergman to the Boston area in his twenties. He found a job working an ambulance in Salem, joining the police department shortly afterward. He now suspects that living in this city contributed to developing his psychic skills. After all, it's a little easier to talk openly about being a medium in Salem than in other places. Within the psychic community he's known for his uncanny ability to unearth specific details when he works—details he has no reason to know.

Bergman has held hundreds of sittings, most with people who have lost children, who never said goodbye to a parent, who want to check on a sister, or who are tormented by a last conversation, needing desperately to take back angry words and heal some old wound. They want to make things right, finish unfinished business, and answer unanswered questions.

Whether the answers actually come from the departed or from Bergman, his clients go home less wounded than when they came. They've heard what they needed to hear and said what they needed to say.

Although most of the department is pretty tolerant, Officer Bergman has learned to brush off occasional ridicule. One can't help but wonder if the Houdini séance would have had a different outcome if Chuck had been available in 1990. At least he could have given the great man better directions.

The Hawthorne Hotel Holdup and Rooftop Secret

A few years before Houdini snubbed it, the Hawthorne Hotel was held up. Robert St. Pierre, the current chief of police, was a hardworking detective at the time. The night manager at the hotel was able to describe one of the perpetrators, whose short blond hair stuck out through the mesh of his nylon-stocking disguise. With the additional aid of a reliable tip, St. Pierre arrested a suspect—Johnny Miller—and held him over the weekend for his arraignment.

The cells at the old police station were cold, and weekends seemed long on the one meal a day prisoners were given. That Sunday, St. Pierre let Johnny sit in the warm detective's office for a while as the detective wrote up reports and warrants. He gave the suspect some donuts and milk, switched on the TV, and turned back to his paperwork. After watching cartoons for a while, Johnny licked the sugar off his fingers and asked St. Pierre what he was doing.

"I'm writing up a search warrant for your house, Johnny."

At that point, Johnny Miller started talking. The donuts and cartoons tactic turned out to be an effective one. Detective St. Pierre secured a confession and later a conviction in the hotel robbery.

For me, however, the real story on this corner is not the hotel itself, but what's on the roof and what's in its window boxes.

From street level, you need to go off a distance to see the roof of the

Hawthorne. There's a shedlike structure on top, perched among chimneys and vents and barely visible. A few years ago a friend took me up there. You take the hotel elevator to the top floor, trudge up a stairwell, then brandish a special members-only key to pass from the hotel to another time and place. Suddenly, you find yourself standing incongruously in a wood-paneled ship's cabin. This is the clubhouse of the Salem Marine Society, founded by a group of sea captains back in 1766. When the hotel was undergoing construction in 1923, the Marine Society's previous home had to be razed. Rebuilding their meetinghouse on the rooftop was the compromise reached with the owners of the hotel.[23]

My friend Peter is an antiestablishment, aging hippie. The sort of guy who would not have fared well during the McCarthy era, or under the scrutiny of the Committee of Vigilance in Hawthorne's time. The closest Peter's livelihood has been to the ocean was the time he worked as a visitor's guide at the Salem Harbor Power Plant. But he's descended from a sea captain and was entitled to join. His photo resides in the big member book with the old and distinguished visages of Salem's most prominent citizens. Sporting an earring and swirling his black cape, Peter climbs up to the clubhouse each year to vote at the annual meetings by dropping black and white balls into the same wooden ballot box the society has been using for hundreds of years. Nathaniel Hawthorne's grandfather voted this way. So did John Gardner, whose house lies across the street, the scene of Captain White's demise. And so did George Crowninshield, whose family's eighteenth-century home sits beside Gardner's and whose grandson Richard forever stained both houses with blood.

The Harp Lady Case: Breach of Warranty

The blossoms in the flower boxes adorning the Hawthorne Hotel never seem to fade. In the spring and summer the boxes are filled with pansies. In the fall they're stuffed with mums. The hotel's secret is to change out the plants frequently. And when they do, someone calls Nina Vickers to find homes for the discards. Nina is a good example of why I write about Salem.

Nina was a practicing attorney until age thirty-two, when she was diagnosed with terminal breast cancer and given six weeks to live. In the hospital, struggling with pain, sadness, and anger, she snatched dinner tray doilies to write her most earnest legal brief—this one to her Maker—listing herself as Plaintiff, For Recovery. She filed a complaint of a Manufacturing Defect and Breach of Warranty, and in pleading her case to God listed all her best qualities and omitted any failings.

Nina apparently won her case. For twenty-eight years since then she's been grabbing life by the balls. During her recovery, she took up the harp, possibly as a hedge against unemployment in the hereafter if her brief was denied. She became so accomplished that eventually she abandoned law and devoted her life to creating beauty. Nina now plays harp regularly at weddings, funerals, train stations, and grocery stores. She performs whatever her audience wants to hear. Andrew Lloyd Webber, Britney Spears, N'Sync. "My Wild Irish Rose" in nursing homes.

Nina's real forte is her costuming. Why play "Memory" on the harp when you can play "Memory" on the harp dressed as a lobster? Nina creates and sews her own incredible collection of outfits. Most include molded heads or quilted tails, and in the case of her red velvet lobster gown with red-tasseled bodice, she sewed a matching coat with two huge stuffed claws, appropriately different in size. "I had to go down to the New England Aquarium to study the claws," she explains. "One's a ripper claw, one's a crusher claw, you know."

She's gone to Crosby's Market in Salem as a silver-sequined seahorse to play Sunday afternoon concerts for customers lined up at the registers. "The head gets a bit hot," she says. The day I met her at her Salem Willows home, she was working on a giant turtle outfit. Her shelves are lined with silk brocades from China, and toile from her secret local fabric shops. Edwardian gowns and angel robes crowd her sewing room. But Nina's most practical garment is her "funeral-wedding dress," which on first blush looks like an elegant black lace empire-style gown. "Sometimes you have these gigs back to back, with no time to change. So—presto!" She rips off the black skirt, Velcroed to the bodice. Underneath is a lovely aquamarine lamé skirt to replace the somber black. She can do it in her van

Nina Vickers at her harp at Crosby's Market. Photo by John Kennard.

between churches, as she shuffles her program, swapping in "Sunrise, Sunset" for "Amazing Grace."

In the early nineties, Nina and her husband acquired the Hawthorne Cove Marina, next door to the New England power plant and one short block from the House of the Seven Gables. Before she agreed to the purchase, Nina questioned the staff to get some background on the marina. She also hoped to find some small omen to help her with her decision. Someone from the marina sent her up the street. "Go talk to Edith at the House of the Seven Gables. She knows all about the history of this place."

Edith did indeed. Nina learned, among other things, that one of the buildings at the marina was haunted. But when the woman introduced herself as Edith Harman, Nina found her sign: this woman had the same name as her mother. She even bore an uncanny resemblance to her. Unable to resist the Salem synchronicity factor, Nina and her husband purchased the marina.

A few years later, Nina realized that what the marina lacked was a garden. So, she knocked on the door of her colossal neighbor, the power plant, and negotiated with them for a small pile of dirt. Then, she bought perennials.

One day she came upon the Hawthorne Hotel gardeners tossing out old plants and convinced them she could help recycle them. Now, every time the hotel is about to cast out seven hundred tired mums, they call Nina and she springs into action. She hustles down to Crosby's Market to round up boxes, calls friends with trucks and strong backs, and leads her army to the hotel to pack up the displaced plants. Nina gives them away to whomever she can. The rest replenish the marina's beds.

Flowers sentenced to wither and die will instead rebloom in the salty breath of Salem Harbor.

Counterpoint: The Thomas Maimoni Story

In mid–July 1991, Essex Cleaners owner Michael Szczuka opened the *Salem Evening News* and was shocked to discover that one of his regular patrons was suspected of murder. Tom Maimoni lived just down the street in Salem Willows— at the eastern end of Essex, where the road changes name alongside Collins Cove.

The 1991 disappearance of Martha Brailsford and the investigation and trial of Thomas Maimoni for her murder were steeped in the Salem Factor. With this case I set aside mystery fiction writing and wrote my first true crime. Synchronicity, rampant in this story, does not make for an effective literary device in fiction.

The case broke the same week Salem detectives were talking to Jan Knowlton about her father's possible connection to the fifty-year-old Cochran murder. The cold case file was sent back to the archives. The Brailsford case was anything but cold.

On a warm summer afternoon, Martha Brailsford, a creative, compassionate designer also from Salem Willows, went out for a short sail with her neighbor Tom. The man, she believed, had recently been widowed and was still grieving. Martha was last seen boarding his sailboat *Counterpoint* as it pulled up to the Willows pier.

When Martha's husband reported her missing, police were soon knocking on Maimoni's door. Maimoni denied having seen Martha that day. The lead investigator was Detective Sergeant Conrad Prosniewski, who had kept the peace during the Houdini séance the previous year. It didn't take long to find witnesses who contradicted Maimoni's story. So, Maimoni tried another. He had let Martha board his boat, he next claimed, but dropped her off around the bend at the Winter Island pier. When Prosniewski mentioned this to another officer, he learned that a boat owner had been ticketed by the harbormaster for tying up at Winter Island all afternoon, in violation of the time limit. The Salem Factor was now shadowing Maimoni everywhere. When Prosniewski looked up the name on the ticket and contacted him, the violator told him he certainly would have noticed if Martha Brailsford had been on the Winter Island pier that afternoon. He happened to be her dentist.

Maimoni tried a third story. He and Martha had been out sailing all afternoon. Somewhere off of Gloucester harbor they were hit by a rogue wave. Martha fell overboard. Maimoni tried in vain to save her. Failing, he returned home. He had been in shock for days, but was now ready to take police out to the scene of the accident and help locate her body.

Fate had other plans. Police Captain Paul Murphy happened to be a friend of Salem's official witch, Laurie Cabot. He gave her a call. There were a lot of miles of water to cover in the area Maimoni had described. Martha had been missing six days. Murphy wanted help. Laurie told him they would be wasting their time. Martha's body was weighted down at the bottom of the ocean behind an island off Marblehead.

While Captain Murphy was on the phone with Laurie, lobsterman Hooper Goodwin was out hauling in his traps behind Cat Island off the tip of Marblehead. As he pulled up the end of one of his trawl lines, he made a grisly discovery. Caught in his trap was an old anchor, tied to the leg of a skeletonized woman. A diving belt was wrapped around her waist. Her clothes were missing. A one-in-a-million chance: with all of Massachusetts Bay and the Atlantic Ocean at his disposal, Tom Maimoni had dumped Martha's body on top of Goodwin's lobster trap. The sea, Salem's lifeblood since the first settlers clung tenaciously to our shores, was now a crime scene.

When news of the discovery was broadcast, Maimoni went on the run. After a nationwide manhunt, he was discovered two days later sleeping in a Maine cabin a few miles from the Canadian border. Turned out the state trooper who arrested him in the farthest corner of Maine had heard about the case the previous week when he happened to attend a workshop with one of the Salem detectives.

While Maimoni was being returned to Salem, investigators were uncovering the house of cards he had built of his life. Although he had told numerous women, including Martha, that his wife had recently died of cancer, Maimoni had been married four times. All wives were alive and well. Maimoni had recently been fired from Parker Brothers Games for incompetence and arguing with female employees. He had also lied about degrees, jobs, and military service. Detectives searching his condo found inflated resumes, fake business cards, and a framed diving certification patch he had never earned.

A year and a half passed before his trial. Tom Maimoni was convicted of second-degree murder and sentenced to life imprisonment. He is eligible for parole in 2006.

This case was too compelling for a writer to ignore. Besides countless instances of the Salem synchronicity factor, there was the central enigma and paradox of Maimoni's sociopath personality. He was a compulsive liar. He invented stories of inflated achievements and unbearable loss, luring the affections and attentions of bright, sympathetic women. He lied to police during the investigation—silly lies that were easily disproved. He lied to the jury during his trial. Straining to appear heroic and brilliant, he was so pathetically absurd that they discounted most of his defense. It would have been easy to convince the jury that he was human and had made a mistake, covering his tracks out of shame and remorse. But Maimoni couldn't tell the truth when it was in his best interests. He had to be superhuman. For Maimoni, being human was too ordinary, and too painful.

In fact, Maimoni's behaviors—hiding the body, lying, and running—were so ingrained, so much a part of his normal reactions to any sort of trouble, that they really didn't prove much. If Martha Brailsford had somehow died of natural causes, Tom would have still tied an anchor to her and dropped her in the ocean. As the prosecutor told me later: "Normally, a guy lies to police, lies on the stand—you've got consciousness of guilt, right? What about when a guy lies all the time? As a way of life? Then what do you got?"

I once asked Maimoni long after the trial if there were anything he regretted. He answered: "Coming to Salem. My grandmother told my mother not to go to Salem because everyone there is possessed. I should never have moved here."

The Salem Factor was also the Salem Defense.[24]

Behind the Badge: The Crossing Guard

Sometimes a story touches me precisely because—despite my expectations to the contrary—it turns out to be quite ordinary. The human journey is the same everywhere. Even when you live in a place called Witchcraft Heights.

May 19, 1992. A mild Tuesday morning. I had talked my way into a ride-along with the then Sergeant Paul Tucker, Detective Sergeant Conrad Prosniewski, and Chief Robert St. Pierre as they embarked on some sort of important mission. My objective was to see what real-life detectives did all day. I had already seen these gentlemen in action. Salem is a little safer for having them on the force. I clutched my notebook and pen with anticipation.

As it turned out, this morning's assignment was to present a plaque to a retiring crossing guard in Witchcraft Heights. I settled into the back seat with a sigh of disappointment. I wanted to ask the guys: *Is this what all your training was for? To go around presenting plaques?* Tucker and the Chief spent the trip talking about allergies and aluminum siding.

We pulled up in front of a trim house on the corner of Belleview Avenue. Despite the neighborhood's moniker, there's no sign of witchcraft here. The Crowley's house was a split-level ranch in an area developed back in the 1960s, when cul-de-sacs and house lots were carved out of the wooded ledge. Lots of aluminum siding here, vinyl shutters, and fake brick facades. Three-quarters of America looks like this. But where else would it be called Witchcraft Heights?

Another cruiser had already arrived. Sergeant Charles Reed of the Traffic Safety Division, and Ed Smith, the principal of Witchcraft Heights Elementary School, were waiting on the sidewalk. The latter was armed with a pile of children's drawings. Sergeant Prosniewski loaded his camera. The chief unwrapped the plaque. We mounted the steps and rang the bell. Someone explained in a low voice that Mr. Crowley was terminally ill. It would be a short visit because he tired very easily.

Inside, I watched from the kitchen doorway, with Mr. Crowley's nurse. The entourage assembled in the small living room along with Mrs. Crowley, his wife of fifty-two years. Chief St. Pierre made his speech. Sergeant Prosniewski shot the presenting of the plaque, a few group photos, and the unveiling of the artwork. The principal held out a drawing that said "WE WILL MISS YOU MR CROWLEY!" with stick figures and cars in primary colors.

Charles A. Crowley had served Salem as a crossing guard for seventeen years after retiring as maintenance foreman at Raytheon. Born and raised in Salem, he had brought his own family up here, as well. He had been a World War II veteran. More importantly, he had also been a former Salem police officer.

Mr. Crowley was visibly touched. When the speeches were over, he rose from his chair and, shaking off the offers of help, he moved slowly down the hallway into his bedroom. He returned a moment later carrying a badge in his hand. Trying to brush away any sticky sentimentality, he handed it without ceremony to St. Pierre.

"Hey, Bob," he said. "Maybe you should recycle this. Some new guy could use it. I don't really need it anymore." The badge said *Salem Police*. It was the shield from his patrolman's hat. A memento proudly treasured for over forty years. A memento his own grandchildren might have appreciated inheriting. But St. Pierre, representing Charles Crowley's other family, accepted it. I was beginning to understand why four police officers took an hour out of their day to make this trip. Mr. Crowley was preparing for his own crossing.

Back outside, the Chief turned to Prosniewski. "Can you rush those photos,

Conrad? I want him to get them as soon as you can. Pick out a couple of the best, and get them framed fast." Crowley's doctor had estimated he had less than two weeks to live. The crime here was failing health and the theft of time.

The drive back was quiet for a while. Then, they resumed the debate on aluminum siding. Life goes on, and police work more than most means bouncing back. Not lingering too long at gravesides. But somewhat reassured to feel the net of support that would enfold each of them and their next-of-kin when they themselves were knocking on heaven's door.

Mr. Crowley passed away on June 7, 1992, two and a half weeks after our visit. Salem's a little safer for its crossing guards, too.

The Southwest Corner: Armed Robbery with Possession of Diminished Capacity

The southwest corner of Essex and Hawthorne represents a true sign of the times. Today, it is an Irish pub. A couple of years ago, it was a restaurant called the Crypt. The Crypt's menus and decor capitalized on the rampant theme of horror and death that tourists in Salem seem to expect as a natural extension of the witchcraft hysteria. A few years before that, the building was an antiques store.

The times are not good for small businesses in Salem. Once a major shopping destination, it has steadily lost shoppers and shops to the nearby malls and the changing patterns of thoroughfares. A story? More like hundreds of stories.

Andrew Mahoney, who grew up in the Greenway Road neighborhood bordering the Salem Hospital, owns the Irish pub. No one has robbed the pub yet, but Andrew has a crime story that hit much closer to home.

Greenway Road dead-ends in a triangle with Emerald Road, forming a quiet, tight-knit enclave where the kids band together and people notice strangers. When Andrew was a kid, the youngest in the group was Justin Petit, whose family lived on Emerald, two doors away from Andrew's. Justin wasn't the brightest kid on the block and was often picked on. As he grew older, he began getting into trouble.

Justin hooked up with a rougher crowd in his late teens and started breaking into homes and businesses. Lacking wheels and a certain amount of sophistication, Justin's targets were frequently in his own neighborhood.

One snowy afternoon in February 1993, Justin—then nineteen—did a solo job that could be a primer on armed robberies. For a target, he picked the convenient Salem Hospital right next door. For his timing, he picked broad daylight after a freshly fallen snow. For his M.O., Justin Petit walked into the hospital lobby and up to the cashier's window, wearing a beret and sunglasses, and brandishing a Daisy Model 45 pellet gun. He handed the frightened cashier a note that read:

IF You Preess any Buzzer or DO SOMething
Stupid. I will shoot anybody in this OFFice

NO COPS
NO Guards
Be calm!!!
And every thing will Be OK.

At the bottom was a little drawing of a dollar bill with a happy face in the middle. Which was helpful, since the note never actually stated what the perpetrator wanted, other than for the cashier to remain calm. Nevertheless, Justin managed to rob the poor woman of the contents of her safe—about four thousand dollars and a bunch of checks.

For his getaway plan, Justin ran out the front door of the hospital, turned left, and—crouching over and clutching the loot to his chest—made a beeline for his mother's house at the base of the hill. He scrambled through two yards of neighbors who—of course—recognized him. At one point he slipped in the snow and dropped his gun. Justin picked himself up and continued on his furtive journey.

Enter the cops. It did not take particularly demanding detective work to follow Justin's trail of fresh footprints in the snow straight from the hospital, down the hill, across Greenway, and through backyards to his home. Along the way they recovered his pellet gun. And inside the Petits' house they found Justin, his elaborate disguise, four thousand dollars stuffed under a bureau, and three drafts of practice holdup notes:

IF YOU PRESS A
IF YOU PRESS A BUZZER OR DO ANYTHING SL

One was blank. Writer's block.

Justin was arrested and taken to the station, where in his enthusiasm he also confessed to robbing a nearby Little Caesar's Pizza on Highland Avenue two weeks earlier. Justin went away for five years.

But Andrew Mahoney's story about his neighbor has another chapter. Five years later, Andrew had opened a coffee shop across the harbor in Beverly. One day, in walked Justin Petit, with the pasty-white look that prison bestows on a man. Five years older, and some bodywork on him. He had been out about a week.

"Hi—remember me?" Justin asked Andrew.

Andrew was taken aback. "Hi Justin. You stayin' outa trouble?"

"Oh yeah," Justin said cheerfully, and handed Andrew two dollars for a cup of coffee. "Keep the change."

Some hours later, Salem police detectives got a call from the state police. Apparently someone had sideswiped a car in the parking lot of a Super Stop & Shop in nearby Woburn the previous day. A witness had taken down the plate and the car came up leased to Justin Petit. The state police were going by his house to check out the vehicle.

Salem Detective Jim Page took the call. "Justin Petit, huh? Well, by any chance did you have any robberies around there yesterday, too? 'Cause that's what he does."

The trooper was incredulous. As a matter of fact, they had. The Stop & Shop had been held up just moments before the hit-and-run.

Andrew Mahoney read all about it in the *Salem Evening News* the next day. No wonder Justin's tip had been so generous. Those two dollars had been hot.

Justin Petit is not the only special burglar to have graced this city. Over the years Salem police have been blessed with holdup suspects who, for example, walk around with name tags on.[25] One did a few robberies in town wearing his National Guard coat. "How'd you guys find me?" he asked police when they showed up at his door. "Well, possibly the name and unit number on your jacket?" they replied.

Sometimes one can't blame the perpetrators. It is rather the victims that make one wonder. Or customers. Next door to the Irish pub is Fatima's Psychic Studio on Hawthorne Boulevard, owned and operated for the past decade by a local Gypsy family. A fifty-dollar reading turns into two hundred if you need to find yourself a husband or fix your life. The cleansing needed to rid your child of cancer or other curses runs four hundred. Ridding yourself of dark clouds can cost more. If Fatima tells you your chakras are blocked, you're looking at a hundred a piece for unblocking. Cash only, no receipts provided. You have, by the way, seven of those chakras.

Occasionally, upset customers call police when the dark cloud doesn't leave, or the prospective husband doesn't show up, and they start suspecting they're being scammed and manage to overcome embarrassment about their own gullibility. Salem detectives call Fatima's. There's a little dance around what's legal, what's not, and what's just weird. The money is refunded promptly. Even with the refunds, thanks to the Salem Factor, fortune-tellers find this city a lucrative location. Bookstores and restaurants are closing for lack of patrons. But there are enough clouds, curses, and credulity floating around to keep Fatima's in business.

Gallows Hill: The Chad Austin Case

One of the wildest rides in Salem crime scene history has to have been when a bank robber from Barnstead, New Hampshire, blew into town.

After holding up a bank in Portsmouth, New Hampshire, on February 11, 1998, suspect Chad Austin stole a Volkswagen Jetta and led state and local police in New Hampshire and Massachusetts on a high-speed chase for over fifty miles. At clocked speeds up to 118 miles per hour, Austin careened through town after town on the North Shore firing at his growing line of pursuers until once again the Salem Factor struck. The suspect tore south through Beverly, over the bridge, and bounced into—of all places—Salem, headlong toward the Gallows Hill neighborhood. With Salem police now taking up the pursuit, Austin reached the far end of Bridge Street, then headed up narrow Proctor Street. A short block up, Proctor bends to accommodate the rocky ledges at the foot of Gallows Hill. Austin was unable to negotiate the curve and slammed into a utility pole.

Unhurt, the bank robber managed to climb out of the car. Austin continued on foot into the woods behind a housing development and sought cover. Clutching a pink pillowcase filled with nine thousand dollars in cash, he turned to fire at police with a Glock 9-millimeter handgun. Salem police returned fire.

The next thing Austin knew he was crashing through the back door of Paul Hardy, who just so happened to be a corrections officer at the Middleton jail, the jail where both Chucky Doucette and Tom Maimoni had awaited their trials. The thirty-two-year-old Hardy was trained, it just so happened, in subduing armed and dangerous criminals.

By now, the entire nation was watching the live media coverage. Streets were cordoned off, neighbors were evacuated. The Channel 7 News helicopter circled overhead, and crowds of police, reporters, SWAT team members, and FBI hostage negotiators filled the street outside as the world learned that Hardy's four-year-old twin boys were in the house with him.

Phone communication with Austin was quickly set up. By that time, the suspect had made himself comfortable in Hardy's favorite chair and was channel-surfing on Hardy's TV. But as long as his kids were in danger, Hardy didn't dare make a move.

Austin demanded that the police be called off. Salem Police Chief Robert St. Pierre assured him they had stood down. But there was the Channel 7 helicopter overhead, zooming in on Salem's sharpshooters behind cover in the backyard. Austin watched the whole thing and was furious. It set the negotiations back badly.

Channel 7 botched things further by divulging Paul Hardy's occupation on the air to a startled Austin. The element of surprise was now gone. The danger to Hardy's life had now escalated.

After a few tense hours, Hardy and the negotiators were finally able to secure the release of the little boys. No one watching that day will ever forget the scene when the garage door opened and Paul Hardy tried to send his sons out to the waiting arms of police. One boy went running out. The other refused to leave, and sobbing, struggled to return to his father. Just inside the door, Austin could be seen with a gun to Hardy's head. Paul Hardy, his heart breaking, gently pushed his son back out and pulled down the door. As the youngster pounded on the door to get back in, a police officer in a bulletproof vest rushed to grab him up.

Hardy was now free to act. It was not long after when he made his move. The corrections officer lunged at Austin and tackled him to the living room floor. When the police heard gunshots, they stormed the house. Austin was shot in the leg during the struggle, then finally subdued.

When Austin was brought to trial on multiple charges, he surprised everyone by insisting on defending himself. Suave, well dressed, pleasant, articulate, he presented an incongruous picture as he questioned first his former hostage Paul Hardy, then numerous police officers as they took the stand. Captain Paul Tucker, who had fired several rounds at Austin after the latter had opened fire on the police, found the defendant's cross-examination surreal.

"You were trying to kill me," Austin said to him, as he tried to convince jurors that he had taken refuge in Hardy's home in self-defense.

"We were trying to stop you," Tucker countered.

"You were trying to kill me!" Austin repeated.

Austin managed to captivate the jurors and their sympathies enough to cause them to deliberate six entire days before finding him guilty on most counts. On November 4, 1998, the debonair defendant was sentenced to thirty to forty years in prison.

It is often said that the exact location of the executions of accused witches in 1692 will never be known. However, one credible theory places the spot within the small triangle of land in the curve of Proctor Street now occupied by Paul Hardy's cul-de-sac.[26] The space is elevated—a gentler mound than the higher crests of Gallows Hill, with locust trees for hanging and rocky crevasses to receive the bodies of the condemned, denied Christian burial. The wagons bearing the prisoners from Salem Gaol would have traveled Austin's route here, and would have been deterred by the same terrain that was the fleeing robber's downfall. Quite possibly, it was at the exact spot where nineteen innocents met their deaths that Chad Austin's guilty road came to an end, as well.

> *For this was the field where superstition won her darkest triumph;*
> *the high place where our fathers set up their shame,*
> *to the mournful gaze of generations far remote.*
> *The dust of martyrs was beneath our feet.*
> *We stood on Gallows Hill.[27]*

Luminaria

I am riding with Officer John Doyle in the Twenty-Six car, covering the North Salem beat. It is three days before Christmas. So far, it has been a quiet shift. The detectives have taught me that North Salem is referred to as the milk run or the retirement community. The lack of calls means a cop assigned here is "on retirement." Some find good places to pull into and read. "Selective traffic enforcement," they call it. Those who crave action spend their shift cruising all over town, backing up calls from other beats. Officer Doyle is the latter type. We drive every street in Salem that night, but the whole city seems dead. Doyle shows me which neighborhood has the best Christmas decorations on display in their front yards.

We handle a couple of calls, both south of the North River. One is to check on the well-being of a grimy freight engine that, due to the extreme cold, has been left idling for two days on a spur next to Bridge Street.

"So, what's special about Salem?" I ask Doyle.

We're interrupted by a second call—larceny of a pizza on Arbella Street. It's late in the evening. The Patriots have been playing tonight. The pizza shops have been busy with deliveries.

We proceed to the scene of the crime. Doyle gives the ten-dollar dispute his full attention. With skill, patience, and tact he manages to resolve the case to everyone's satisfaction. No one's hurt, no one's arrested. Peace is restored to Arbella Street. Everyone goes back to the game.

We get back in the cruiser. After a while, Officer Doyle remembers my question.

"I'll show you what's special about Salem."

He heads the patrol car up North Street, past the scene of Leslie's Retreat, the 1775 standoff where the first blood of the Revolution was shed. Lt. Col. Alexander Leslie had tried to lead a British regiment up this road in search of cannons suspected to be hidden in the North Fields. He was thwarted at the North River by a raised drawbridge the Salem townsfolk refused to lower. Aside from one superficial bayonet wound sustained by one of the local militiamen, the confrontation ended with Salem—true to its name—peacefully repelling the British seven weeks before Lexington and Concord heard that first shot.[28]

Crossing the bridge is a lot easier in this century. A few blocks up, Doyle turns onto Dearborn Street. It is the night of the Northfield neighborhood's annual luminaria display. Stretched out ahead of us, the street curbs are lined on both sides with white bags and candles, every seven feet. Not a parked car in sight. In the dark the effect is magical. We cruise slowly down Dearborn, past the house where Nathaniel Hawthorne lived when Captain White was murdered. Doyle makes a left onto Lee. These side streets, too, are lined with candles. We drive up and down the neighborhood where patriots once hid cannons from the British. On one block we find a small crowd of carolers. Officer Doyle rolls down his window to hear their song. He shuts off the engine for a moment. "Long time since I heard carolers," he says.

He proceeds further north and swings by Cabot Farms and the Kernwood Marina. Then, he pulls over for a while to check for speeders coming off the Kernwood Bridge.

"This city is real quiet at night. You drive down streets and see a few lights in the windows—blue flickering from people's TVs." The night crew patrol works four days, then two days off. But the four days are split between the 12 to 8 A.M. shift and the 4 to 12 P.M. shift. It's hell on your body. Not only is your sleep schedule in turmoil, your stomach is constantly confused. When Doyle has to wake up at 11 P.M. to get ready for a midnight shift, he shuffles into his kitchen and mutters, "Am I supposed to have cereal now?"

The night's too peaceful even to net a speeder. We head back south toward Essex Street and the station beyond. But Doyle detours by the luminaria again. When we get to the intersection of Moulton and Dearborn he pulls to a stop. Ahead of us in the street are two people with a camera and tripod, focusing down the street in the hope of capturing forever the ephemeral magic of the candles. As a courtesy Officer Doyle extinguishes his headlights. We wait in the middle of the crossroads—lines of lanterns along the curbs in all directions around us. The couple finish their shot and turn to thank the man in the cruiser. In tonight's battle of light against dark, the winner is clear.

And I am thinking of Nina Vickers, her own bright light shining down at the Willows. Defying her sentence of death, celebrating survival in an anatomically correct lobster outfit, playing her harp for weary passengers as they file down the cold platform at the train station. Salem's cumulative myths and memories give it a sense of place unlike any other destination. As Nina plays her 1,001 songs and keeps death at bay, Salem, like an American Scheherazade, spins 1,001 tales.

Is dying any different in Salem? Probably not. But in the mind's eye, surely living is.

Notes

I wish to express my deepest appreciation to the following for generous assistance, invaluable insights, and inspiring stories: Detective Sergeant Conrad Prosniewski, Captain Paul Tucker, Chief Robert St. Pierre, Officers John Doyle, Charles Bergman, Mike Fecteau, and Detective James Page from the Salem Police Department, Chief James Carney of the Marblehead Police Department, Assistant District Attorney Kevin Mitchell of the Essex County District Attorney's Office, Teddi DiCanio, Sharyn Giardi, Nelson Dionne, Nina Vickers, Michael Szczuka, John Kennard, Jeannette Lauritsen, Eric Lauritsen, Andrew Mahoney, Sara Press, Peter Bates, Loretta Rainville, Marsha Blythe-Brown, and Cynthia Victory.

1. Jim McAllister, *Salem: From Naumkeag to Witch City* (Beverly, Mass.: Commonwealth Editions, 2000).

2. Eudora Welty, "Place in Fiction," *On Writing* (New York: Modern Library, 2002).

3. Sidney Perley, *The History of Salem, Massachusetts,* 3 vols. (Salem, Mass.: Sidney Perley, 1924).

4. K. David Goss, Richard B. Trask, Bryant F. Tolles Jr., Joseph Flibbert, and Jim McAllister, *Salem: Cornerstones of a Historic City* (Beverly, Mass.: Commonwealth Editions, 1999).

5. Gerald W. R. Ward, "The Gardner-Pingree House," *Historic House Booklet Number Five* (Salem, Mass.: Essex Institute, 1976).

6. *Salem Gazette,* April 9, 1830.

7. Stephen G. Christianson, "John Francis Knapp and Joseph Jenkins Knapp Trials: 1830," in *Great American Trials,* ed. Edward W. Knappman (Detroit: Visible Ink Press, 1993), 85.

8. *Trials of Capt. Joseph J. Knapp, Jr. and George Crowninshield, Esq. for the Murder of Capt. Joseph White of Salem on the Night of the Sixth of April, 1830* (Boston: Charles Ellms, 1830).

9. For additional information on the Captain White case, see the *Salem Gazette,* April–August 1830, and Daniel Webster, *The Papers of Daniel Webster: Correspondence,* vol. 3, 1830–1834, ed. Charles M. Wiltse and David G. Allen (Hanover: University Press of New England, 1977).

10. Transcript, WESX news broadcast in Cochran case file, undated.

11. Police report, August 15, 1941, Cochran case file.

12. Police report, August 15, 1941, Cochran case file.

13. Police report, August 15, 1941, Cochran case file.

14. Janice Knowlton with Michael Newton, *Daddy Was the Black Dahlia Killer* (New York: Pocketbooks, 1995).

15. Salem Police interview notes, Corbin case file.

16. Susan Kelly, *The Boston Stranglers: The Public Conviction of Albert DeSalvo and the True Story of Eleven Shocking Murders* (New York: Carol Publishing Group, 1995).

17. Stephen Vincent Benét, *The Devil and Daniel Webster* (New York: Holt, Rinehart and Winston, 1965).

18. Rollie Corneau, "'Missing' Hathorne Marker Found Locked in Salem Police Gun Closet," *Salem Evening News,* April 30, 1982.

19. Coverage of Bufalino murder and Doucette trial in the *Salem Evening News* and *Peabody Times,* 1987–1991, and Captain Paul Tucker, personal communication.

20. Coverage of Bufalino murder and Doucette trial in the *Salem Evening News* and *Peabody Times,* 1987–1991, and Captain Paul Tucker, personal communication.

21. Coverage of Bufalino murder and Doucette trial in the *Salem Evening News* and *Peabody Times,* 1987–1991, and Captain Paul Tucker, personal communication.

22. "Not a Ghost of a Chance: Harry Houdini Snubs Slick Salem Séance," *Salem Evening News,* October 31, 1990.

23. For more information on the Salem Marine Society and their clubhouse, see Jim McAllister, "Vessel Cabin Replica Hidden at Top of Hotel," *Salem Evening News,* June 20, 2001, and the *History of the Marine Society at Salem* (Salem, Mass.: The Marine Society at Salem, 1998).

24. For further information on the Maimoni case, see Margaret Press with Joan Noble Pinkham, *Counterpoint: A Murder in Massachusetts Bay* (Omaha: Addicus Books, 1996). Reprinted as *A Scream on the Water: A True Story of Murder in Salem* (New York: St. Martin's Paperbacks, 1997).

25. Ron Agrella and Jeffrey McMenemy, "Bungling Bandits, Maimoni Moments: A Look at 1993's Quirky Crimes," *Peabody Times,* December 31, 1993.

26. William Story and Arthur Venditti, *The Witchcraft Hysteria of Salem Town and Salem Village in 1692* (Peabody, Mass.: Willart Publishing, 1991).

27. Nathaniel Hawthorne, "Alice Doane's Appeal," *The Snow-Image and Uncollected Tales* (Columbus: Ohio State University Press, 1974).

28. Jim McAllister, "Leslie's Retreat: Baffled British," *Salem Evening News,* February 23, 2000.

Window display in downtown Salem shop. Photo by Kim Mimnaugh.

Chapter Eleven

Salem as Witch City

FRANCES HILL

And here, in dark, funereal stone, should rise another monument,
sadly commemorative of the errors of an earlier race, and not to be cast down,
while the human heart has one infirmity that may result in crime.

—Nathaniel Hawthorne, "Alice Doane's Appeal"

ALLOWEEN in Salem is the equivalent of Mardi Gras in New Orleans, Christmas in Bethlehem, Easter in Rome, or the *hajj* pilgrimage to Mecca. But in all these cases except Salem's, ancient pagan or religious traditions link the place with the festival. There is no such link between Halloween and this Massachusetts town. There is even less of a link than there might be with other American towns.

Halloween started out as the Celtic New Year's Eve and in time merged with two Roman festivals and the Christian All Saints' Eve, also known as All-hallows Eve, eventually becoming Halloween. The festival was brought from Europe to the New World in colonial times, but not to Salem or anywhere in New England, where the Puritans would never have permitted such unorthodox celebrations. It emigrated to the more easygoing southern colonies. In the nineteenth century, Irish immigrants, with their combined Celtic and Catholic traditions, helped popularize Halloween and spread it through the nation. There was still no particular association with Salem.[1]

There is a different kind of historical link between the town and the festival. Three hundred years ago, twenty innocent people were executed for witchcraft on Salem's Gallows Hill. And Halloween is associated with witches. This link is of course spurious. The journey from witch trials town to "witch city" was the result of confusion, historical accident, and economic pressure.

The Salem witch hysteria started when two little girls, relatives of the Salem Village pastor Samuel Parris, went into fits and, after a few weeks, were diagnosed by a local doctor as being bewitched. (Salem Village covered roughly the geographical area of present-day Danvers.) The girls accused three local misfits, who were interrogated and thrown into prison, of causing these fits by bewitching them. One, the Indian slave Tituba, made a dramatic forced confession. A political faction centered around Parris began to feed the girls the names of their enemies, members of the rival village faction. The rulers of Massachusetts Bay Colony used the accusers to target a dissident preacher, George Burroughs. Meanwhile, the Salem sheriff seized the accuseds' lands and estates. Eventually, after twenty innocent people had been executed and at least one hundred and fifty had been thrown into prison, to languish for months, the whole sorry business was brought to an end.[2]

That ending was a strange, messy affair. No one accepted real responsibility. No one was prosecuted. No one was punished. It was many years before the names of the wronged innocents were cleared. *Five* of them had to wait till 2001.[3] Only one of the judges who'd helped send the twenty to their deaths, Samuel Sewall, made any apology. That came five years later, together with a government proclamation referring to "whatever mistakes" had been made by the witch trials court. Both were read out on a day of fasting and prayer to atone for all the colony's sins, not just those of 1692.[4] As a result of this lack of clarity about innocence and guilt, the myth that there really had been witchcraft in Salem was never totally dispelled. Today, in the teeth of all the evidence, there are still people who argue that some of those who were hanged might have practiced it.[5] As interest grew in modern notions of witchcraft during the latter half of the twentieth century, some of its followers turned their attention to Salem.

In a small way, local businesses there had been trading on the witch link for some time. In the late nineteenth century a fish company sold some of its wares under the brand name *Witch City*. For the two hundredth anniversary of the trials, Essex Street jeweler Daniel Low produced spoons sporting witch motifs. The leading Salem manufacturer Parker Brothers, the makers of Monopoly, produced a board game called "Ye Witchcraft." But they axed it when Salemites thought it in bad taste. By 1900, a popcorn factory, bicycle manufacturer, boat yard, and oil firm were using the *Witch City* name. A fraternal organization was called the "Witches," as was the Salem High School sports team. The Salem VFW Post sponsored the Witch City Drum Corps.[6]

By the 1950s, in a small way, witch trial tourism had begun. During the decade before World War II, the family who owned the house on the site of the old Salem jail, on St. Peter's Street, built a replica of one of the dungeons where the alleged witches were held, using some of the original timbers. They charged visitors a small fee.[7] At the junction of Essex and North Streets the house of one of the trial judges, though by this time used as a pharmacy, was highly valued as the only extant Salem building with a direct link to the trials. When, in 1944, city plans to widen North Street necessitated either demolishing or moving the building, a group of local residents formed themselves into Historic Salem, Inc., a nonprofit organization whose mission was to purchase this and other properties threatened with development. They relocated it by a few yards, restored the house, and opened it to the public. A significant step in Salem's odyssey, from the town where the witch trials were held to "witch city," was taken when the organization re-named the building "The Witch House" to attract as many tourists as possible.

The town's other major attraction was the House of the Seven Gables, open to visitors even before World War I. It is linked indirectly to the witch trials by means of Nathaniel Hawthorne's novel of the same name. The tale deals only obliquely with the witch hunt. But even such a tenuous link played its part in help-ing build Salem's reputation as a place ambiguously connected with witchcraft.

And meanwhile, the Essex Institute, Salem's highly respected—and, at that time, free—library and museum, encouraged visitors to view a witch trials exhibit that included George Jacobs's cane, Philip English's chair, and some witch dun-geon timbers. The institute merged with the equally august Peabody Museum in 1992. The Salem Essex County courthouse still contained the mass of surviving witch trial documents, including the verbatim transcripts of examinations of pris-oners. They were moved to the Essex Institute in 1980, but it was in the court-house, in 1952, that Arthur Miller read through them, gaining material and inspi-ration for *The Crucible*.[8] This hugely successful drama was itself to generate more interest in Salem and the witch trials.

Salemites regarded this view of their town as mildly amusing. The witch tri-als had been a long time ago and, in any case, had started not in Salem but in neighboring Danvers. During the 1960s, growing tourism impinged very little. But in 1970, two episodes of the television sitcom *Bewitched* were filmed in and around Salem and aired nationally at Halloween. At about that same time, several respectable Salem institutions, such as the local paper, the Chamber of Com-merce, and the Police Department, adopted *Witch City* logos.[9]

And then, in 1971, Laurie Cabot came to town.

Ms. Cabot regards herself as a standard-bearer for Wicca, a New Age religion claiming roots in pre-Christian paganism. She was born in California and, by her own account, discovered in childhood she had telepathic and precognitive pow-ers. Everyone is born with such powers, she claims, but most people lose them.[10]

Whatever the truth about Ms. Cabot's otherworldly powers, her earthly ones are self-evident. Always dramatically dressed in black robes and hung about with pentacles and charms, her eyes heavily rimmed with black eye liner, she strikes everyone with her charisma and canniness. Arriving in Salem with an entourage of two children, a boyfriend, and several devotees, she soon established a follow-ing of attractive black-clothed young girls, highly visible around town. She opened a store, called "A Witch Shop," selling witchcraft apparatus. She appeared at local events, gave television interviews, and gained permission from the bemused Mas-sachusetts governor, Michael Dukakis, to dub herself "the official witch of Salem."

Her skill at recruiting the daughters of well-to-do Salem families as witches caused alarm, but by and large Salem accepted her. If its citizens had laughed at her or roughed her up she might have left town and Salem's history would have been different. Instead, she opened more shops.

Ms. Cabot's rationale for coming to Salem was the executions for witchcraft. Some of the victims had practiced it, she claims, though in the form of Wiccan "white magic" rather than the devil worship for which they were convicted and hanged. She half concedes the absence of any evidence for this and agrees, "Most were probably devout Christians." But she adds, "Nevertheless, I think we must claim them as Witches. Certainly they died for our freedom."[11]

There is no reason on earth or in heaven why Wiccans should claim the innocents hanged in Salem "as witches." There is not a shred of evidence that any of them indulged in any form of occultism, malicious or benign. And to suggest they died for Wiccans' freedom is blatantly absurd. They died for refusing falsely to confess to crimes they hadn't committed. In any case, the Wiccan religion, a modern phenomenon despite its claims of ancient origins, hadn't yet been invented.[12]

Another explanation for Ms. Cabot's choice of Salem as professional resting place is that, given its growing connection with witchcraft, she would have every opportunity for collecting a circle of believers and making a living.

Her coming changed Salem in two ways. She was followed by hundreds of Wiccans from all over America, who now form a substantial minority of the city's population. She was also followed by nearly as many entrepreneurs who had observed the success of her witch shops. Tourism, especially at Halloween, took a major leap forward.

Not everyone was pleased. Long-term residents wondered what was happening as the old church that for years had served as an auto museum was reopened, in 1972, as the Witch Museum. As it happens, though always intended as a moneymaking enterprise, this became, and remains, the best educational venue on the witch trials in town. Its twenty-minute show belies the expectation of schlock aroused by the building's mock Gothic appearance, giving an arresting and largely accurate account of the witch trials. A series of tableaux of life-size figures in detailed settings are ranged round the walls of a large room darkened on entry. The tableaux are lighted one by one as a voice-over tells the story of the witch hunt. Though some of the detail is misleading, the viewer comes away with a good overall picture of the horror and extent of the episode. What's more, the museum's education director works closely with schools, answering e-mail questions, conducting virtual classroom seminars, and providing talks and materials. If Salem's citizens had known what was in store for them over the next thirty years, they might have looked on the Witch Museum with respect.

Meanwhile, Halloween was booming all over America, evolving into a nationwide costume party as much as a "fright night."[13] The Great Depression years had been replaced by the postwar spending spree. Ebullient consumerism characterized national holidays and religious tradition. Social critics, in Salem and elsewhere, deplored the commercialization of Christmas, Easter, the Fourth of July, and, of course, Halloween. But Salem had strong economic motives to seize the opportunities offered.

The town had been the first in Massachusetts Bay to be settled, had become a premier seaport, and had remained so for two centuries. When the shipping trade declined, it developed as a center of industry. But in the 1960s, its economy collapsed. Industry moved elsewhere in search of cheaper wages and rents. The last remaining major business, a blanket manufacturer, was bought by a conglomerate and moved south. The new North Shore Mall on the Danvers-Peabody border put Salem's splendid downtown department stores out of business. Halloween, though hated by so many, was an economic godsend.

An attempt to revive downtown commerce in the mid-1970s flopped completely. The city built a multistory car park and the East India Square mall, failing to realize that lifestyles had changed and people preferred shopping in huge suburban malls rather than in dinky town center ones. Half of the new East India Square buildings stayed empty. The new Essex Street walkway, meant to encourage strolling shoppers to buy a wide variety of goods, became a long outdoor stage for Wiccans and hucksters. The shops sold little but Witch City T-shirts, Witch City ice cream, and witchcraft souvenirs.

This town center restructuring gave the city a missed opportunity to commemorate its witch trials history and to encourage the growing number of tourists to focus on *that*. It occurred at the time of the bicentennial, which gave a boost generally to American history tourism. But the City Council tried to dissociate Salem from witchcraft by ignoring 1692 and marking other aspects of its past. The East India Mall could have been named after one of the victims of the witch hunt. A memorial to those victims could have been erected instead of a fountain near the site of the town pump in Essex Street mentioned in a story by Nathaniel Hawthorne.[14] Unfortunately, the city's hope that visitors would turn their attentions from witchcraft to maritime history and Hawthorne was, to put it gently, optimistic.

It was with rather more realism that in 1982 a group of businesses led by the Salem Witch Museum, with the cooperation of the Salem Chamber of Commerce, set up the first Halloween "Haunted Happenings." These included a ball, a pumpkin-carving contest, a haunted house, a haunted ship, and a "witches' brew competition." The irrepressible Laurie Cabot judged the children's costumes for the "horribles' parade" along Essex Street. She was also involved in a "psychic festival" that included tarot card readings and a lecture series on ESP, reincarnation, the occult, and the significance of Halloween.[15]

Many did not approve. One indication of this can be seen in a letter sent out

Salem Witch Museum. Courtesy of Salem Witch Museum. Photo by Tina Jordan.

to townspeople by the Chamber of Commerce the following year saying that "any person or persons arriving at our festival clad in ugly, green-faced, troll-like, blood-dyed or otherwise grotesque costumes will *not* be admitted on the premises and *no* refunds will be given."[16] Residents had complained about traffic jams, difficulties with parking, and overcrowded pavements, but what they objected to most was the tastelessness of it all.

The letter was a cry in the dark. To try to stop people looking grotesque at Halloween is like trying to ban fairy lights at Christmas. The tensions that had mounted through the 1970s between businesses in need of the tourist trade and residents who objected to the invasion of their town by weirdly dressed visitors grew ever more bitter. "Haunted Happenings" escalated from a three-day weekend to a four-day weekend, then to two weeks, then to three. Regulations passed in the 1920s requiring anyone dealing with history tourism to pass a Salem history test fell by the wayside. There was no political will to enforce them, despite many councilors' sympathy for their constituents' complaints. No city office was, or wished to be, responsible. The bottom line was that Salem had no economic base except tourism. Halloween stayed as a free-for-all, as did "witchcraft" business year-round.

Meanwhile, the Essex Institute, once the proud guardian of the witch trials heritage, was distancing itself from the Salem that had evolved from that heritage. Its donors, many of them members of old, well-to-do Salem families, watched with distaste every time the town filled with green-faced, troll-like creatures in search of downmarket thrill. The Essex Institute started charging entry to its library housing the witch trials documents. And it retired most of the witch trials relics. Inquiries about 1692 were received with a distinct lack of zest. The exception was one of the institute's historical house tours of the 1684 John Ward House that included, and still includes, a talk on the witch trials. The institute began stressing that it was the repository of the whole of Salem's history, not merely that of the witch hunt.

When the institute merged with the Peabody Museum, it acquired huge amounts of new funding from a wealthy local businessman. It spent this on expanding and restructuring its buildings with a view to becoming a world-class museum of "art, architecture, and culture." The work, completed in 2003, includes six new art galleries, public gardens, a glass atrium, an auditorium, and an entire reconstructed, early-twentieth-century Chinese merchant's house. The main temporary exhibit in early 2003 was of Korean photography. The museum aims to provide a "new paradigm for Salem," says its press officer, Greg Liakos, who maintains that "1692 is still a deep psychic wound in the community." The museum "feels strongly that the community needs to be telling a different story about itself, inclusive of all the stories."

Nevertheless, the Peabody Essex takes part in Halloween festivities. In 1986, what was then the institute founded a series of story readings called "Eerie Events." Costumed actors tell spooky stories in the atmospheric settings of the historic houses owned by the museum. Eerie Events are in the ancient Halloween storytelling tradition and vastly more tasteful than almost anything else happening in Salem during the festival. But there is no connection between these stories and the witch trials, except in one case, in which the alleged witchcraft of 1692 forms the backdrop. They do nothing to lessen the distance the museum has placed between itself and that part of its heritage.

In the same spirit of distancing itself from the witch trials, the National Parks' Visitors' Center emphasizes its presettlement, architectural, and maritime history, confining books on the witch trials to only a few shelves. Historic Salem, Inc., which had restored and opened the Witch House, also retreated in distaste from Salem's witch trials tourism. By the 1980s, the growing embarrassment among worthy organizations was leaving a vacuum. Visitors to Salem with a genuine but uninformed interest in the witch trials, as opposed to a fascination with witchcraft, had nowhere helpful to go apart from the Witch Museum. Nowhere else welcomed, entertained, and informed them, or pointed them to the places and sites of true historical interest.

Most of these places and sites are in Danvers, which was where the witch hunt began. Few people know that, so Danvers has been spared any association with witchcraft. Ironically, the place has become the industrial and shopping center Salem has ceased to be, and is in no need of a tourist trade. The non-profit-making Danvers Historical Society and Danvers Alarm List Company have managed the historical remains in their care very well. The Rebecca Nurse House, where the most famous of the victims of the witch hunt lived at the time of her arrest, has been splendidly preserved and is open to the public. Its extensive grounds contain the Nurse family cemetery and a replica of the Salem Village meetinghouse.[17] Thanks to the hard work and dedication of local historian Richard Trask, the site of the parsonage where the witch hysteria began has been excavated and is well supplied with explanatory markers and signs.[18] Many other houses associated with the witch trials still exist, though most are privately owned.[19]

But visitors to Salem with an interest in the witch trials have to discover all this for themselves. And that was the case when, in 1992, the tercentenary arrived.

For this, the City Council and local businesses at last built memorials to the victims of the witch hunt. And splendid memorials they were, too. One is in Salem, next to its historic first cemetery, and one in Danvers, opposite the site of the meetinghouse where the first interrogations of witch suspects were held. The playwright Arthur Miller unveiled the design of the Salem memorial in November 1991, and the Nobel laureate Elie Wiesel dedicated the memorial in 1992. A Salem Award was inaugurated and presented to Gregory Allen Williams, a hero of the 1992 Los Angeles riots. Conferences, symposia, and workshops were held on subjects such as the contemporary relevance of the witch trials to civil rights and racial tolerance. Scholars and theologians gave lectures on contemporary instances of witch-hunting. Witchcraft Heights Elementary School performed a play by a Salem State College playwright about the dangers of stereotyping and gossip.[20]

The stated purpose of all this was to honor the innocents who had died and to remind the world of the danger of such atrocities happening again. The unstated purpose was to boost Salem's tourism. The global economy had gone into overdrive and tourism was up everywhere. There seemed no reason why Salem should not benefit as much as Boston, Williamsburg, Virginia, and other historical towns. The difficulty was that tourism in Salem had taken a very different form from that of those other towns, largely exploiting, instead of exploring, its history.

The tercentenary, by concentrating on the historical facts, might have been thought to counter that trend. To some extent, for a while, it did. The committee encouraged the Peabody Essex Museum to mount a display, called Days of Judgment, of documents from the witch trials, with notes and explanations. The new Salem memorial, which gave the names and dates of the victims of the witch hunt and quotations from the moving words they uttered at their examinations and in letters, drew thousands. But a new office of tourism and cultural affairs, founded in 1993 in the wake of the tercentenary, before long found itself as involved in promoting and encouraging Halloween events as much as Salem's witch trials sites. Soon, the previous state of affairs was fully in force again.

The vacuum left by the distancing of the Peabody Essex Museum from the witch trials was still waiting to be filled. Several new "witch trials museums" sprung into being but made no attempt to emulate the Salem Witch Museum's accuracy. Instead, they mounted displays that ignored or travestied the truth. These "history museums" were joined by other attractions, based on targets of morbid fascination other than the witch trials themselves. Salem Witch Village, next to Salem's oldest cemetery and the witch trials memorial, claims to be a museum of witchcraft, "staffed by practicing witches." Dracula's Castle on Lafayette Street offers "a trail of eerie chambers filled with vampires and other creatures of the night." The New England Pirate Museum enables you to "board a full length pirate ship and explore an 80 foot cave" and "see artifacts from sunken ships and private treasures." Boris Karloff's Witch Mansion offers a 3D Terror Show, an "Elvira" lookalike, and a cauldron constructed for the 1985 animated Disney film *The Black Cauldron*. Salem's Museum of Myths and Monsters displays figures representing vampires, werewolves, witches, and ghosts.[21] But none of these tourist traps are offensive in the way the "history museums" are offensive, since they do not trade directly on historical individuals' misery and death. The newer ones are confined to the Pickering Wharf area, which during the 1990s became the chief center for the Halloween, witchcraft, and ghoulish sides of the tourist trade. Laurie Cabot opened her third shop there, "The Cat, Crow and The Crown."

In the late 1990s, what was surely the nadir of tastelessness was reached. A business called "Mass Hysteria Haunted Hearse Tours" provided a vehicle billed in the publicity material as a "luxurious hearse" to take eight visitors, paying substantial sums, to "a netherworld of witches, madmen and the returning dead."[22]

"Come face-to-face with a haunted barge," urges a Salem guidebook, conjuring a bizarre image of a tourist and a ship's figurehead staring at each other, "where a murdered sea captain repeats his last earthly words again and again. Is that his hollow voice you hear in the wind?" The tour, needless to say, does not balk at exploiting the 1692 executions, claiming to "explore 'the pit' where those convicted of witchcraft were buried."[23] Since no one actually knows where the bodies were laid, this claim is false. But even more offensive, to many, is the fact that the tour guide points out the scenes of two recent murders.

The "Mass Hysteria Haunted Hearse Tours" upset enough people for the City Council to try to find some legal reason for closing them down. But it seems there was no law or by-law the tours were breaking. Many people believe that, had tourism not been essential to Salem's economy, permits and licenses would have been less readily granted to vendors and entrepreneurs from the 1970s on. Tourist managers and city councilors blame one another for the current state of affairs, each claiming the other could have prevented things from reaching such depths. Once Laurie Cabot and her Wiccans publicized Salem as witch capital of the world, what followed was more or less inevitable.

Halloween in 2001 and 2002 saw a drop in visitor numbers, following the events of September 11. Yet in 2002, on October 31, the streets seemed to this writer packed to capacity. I had arrived apprehensively, given the impression by locals that I was about to embark on a tour of hell. What I found was a pleasant surprise. There were green faces and trolls in abundance, together with doctors and nurses in blood-spattered uniforms, girls with vampire teeth, numerous black-garbed creatures with scythes, and one very tall man in armor and black wings. But there were also people in grass skirts, Hawaiian garlands, and red wigs, in spangled dresses and red feather boas and flowing white, flower-bedecked robes. Many children wore sausage balloon headgear. The ghoulish and ghostly was only one element in this citywide costume party. Bands delivered mainstream popular music. People danced. It was hard to tell Wiccans from black-clad Halloween visitors, and in many cases they were probably one and the same. There was no sense of threat. No one was drunk. On the contrary, there was a strong sense of innocent, even childlike, fun. A couple of men carried placards saying, "Jesus hates sin," and the Foursquare Gospel Church manned a stall giving out cocoa. But there was no sign of the fundamentalist fervor that afflicted Salem in the 1980s, when Christian and Wiccan parades vied with each other with suspicion and hostility. On the whole, there seemed nothing wrong with this festival. In fact, there seemed quite a lot right with it. People were having a good time without doing harm.

Laurie Cabot was still flourishing. Her hair was getting gray, but the queue for her book signing snaked all the way round Pickering Wharf to the water. Later the Salem Wiccan community celebrated the Celtic New Year with a candlelit procession from Gallows Hill to Essex Street. Returning Wiccans merged with the candlelit tour groups being led round the town center.

One of these, led by local historian Jim McAllister, took as its subject the his-

Tourist bus stop marked by witch motif. Photo by Kim Mimnaugh.

tory of the witch trials. A group of about forty people of all ages, some in Halloween costume, some wearing ordinary clothes, listened attentively to the tales of the young girls' afflictions, the accusations of the innocents, their last brave words on the scaffold, and how the witch hunt was at last brought to an end. Collars were turned up and scarves were wrapped more tightly as the evening wore on. Children huddled next to their parents. But the only real difficulty was the large number of other groups vying for street space and stopping places. However, Mr. McAllister is experienced at circumnavigating competitors.

This is true metaphorically, too. He gave his first tour in 1983, but in the late 1990s, when a large number of candlelit walking tours on "spooky" themes started up, he added a "Terror Trail" to his other tours. It competes directly with the "Haunted Footsteps Ghost Tour," "Vampire and Ghost Hunt Tour," and others. Mr. McAllister narrates stories of hauntings and murders through the centuries as well as such horrors of 1692 as John Proctor's and Martha Carrier's sons being tied neck and heels to force their confessions, and Giles Cory's being crushed to death by stones.

Now, encouragingly, the other candlelit tour operators are moving into Mr. McAllister's original territory. Leah Schmidt, who started a walking tour business in Salem in 1996 with the "Haunted Footsteps Ghost Tour," also runs a "Salem History Tour" and a "Witch Trials Memorial and Cemetery Tour."

Schmidt's "Haunted Footsteps Ghost Tour" at Halloween 2002 was a fascinating mixture of the historical and fanciful. Witch trials history jostled with tales of the supernatural as the tour moved from the Athenaeum, where Nathaniel Hawthorne supposedly saw the ghost of a recently deceased member, to the Joshua Ward House, the "fourth most haunted house in America," where Sheriff George Corwin of 1692 is said to be buried, to the possible site of Giles Cory's death. The abandoned buildings of the recently relocated local jail now occupy this site. The tour added fascinating modern history and sociology to the mix of ingredients, integrating past and present prison conditions. It also included the Howard Street cemetery and its ghosts, though without actually walking along Howard Street. The tour-hating residents there are apparently more alarming than anything that might return from the dead.

Mr. McAllister's and Ms. Schmidt's tours are at the top end of the market. One glimpse of a tour at the lower end was enough to dissuade me from joining it. In the Witch Trials memorial, surrounded by the stone benches commemorating the twenty people who died, a tall, cloaked young man, his face painted white, paced up and down, telling his audience with ghoulish relish, and in detail, of a grisly murder that had supposedly taken place in a house that had once stood on that spot.

In its guided tours, as in other ways, Halloween 2002 was the free-for-all it has always been, despite that 1983 plea for good taste. That has now slightly changed. As a result of the Howard Street tensions, certain tour operators, some Howard Street residents, and representatives from the Salem Chamber of Commerce and City Council held meetings to decide on new regulations to replace the ones long since ignored. There were foreseeable conflicts. Certain residents wanted walking tours banned altogether in residential areas. Businesses maintained that this would breach their constitutional rights. They had avoided serious trouble so far by not walking down Howard Street, where one especially irate lady had threatened to hose down the whole group. But businesses had no wish to continue this self-policing policy. They wanted it made clear that everyone has a right to walk the public streets. They also wanted proposed restrictions on the time a tour may start and end to be reasonable, so that tours could continue till 9 or 10 P.M.

The regulations that were finally passed came into force on January 1, 2003. They are purposely minimal, since the council wanted to keep them enforceable. They stipulate that both the owners of walking tour businesses and the employees acting as their tour guides must be licensed by the city. The guide must wear a badge with the words "licensed public guide" and the number of his or her license. He or she "shall conduct himself [/herself] in an orderly manner at all times when engaged in the business of a guide."[24] But the council has also made clear that it still expects self-policing.

The ordinance says nothing about what the guides may say in their talks. The council maintains that such a regulation would contravene the right to freedom of speech. It seems possible that other rules may be put in place again one day if the conflicts over tastelessness continue to escalate.

However, the best hope for the future is a new policy on the part of the historical institutions that have distanced themselves from the witch trials. The blot on Salem is not its Halloween reveling or witch shops, but the exploitation of Salem's tragic history. If the worthy institutions accept their responsibility to educate and entertain visitors about the trials as well as about the rest of Salem's heritage, there will be less demand for commercial attractions on the subject. Serious historical tourism can and should exist side by side with Wiccan parades and Halloween festivities.

The costumed revelers wandering around Salem at Halloween 2002 had an innocence that can all too easily turn into dangerous cruelty. In Salem in 1692 the search for diversion ended with a dark delight in human suffering. In 2002, as people listened attentively as the white-faced young tour guide gloatingly described death and dismemberment, one could see the same tendency, thankfully leading only to passive enjoyment. It is hard if not impossible to legislate for good taste. But it should not be hard or impossible to inform and entertain about the past with humanity. The best historical tourism shows men and women long ago as just as capable of happiness and pain as the people hearing or watching their stories.

Notes

1. David. J. Skal, *Death Makes a Holiday: A Cultural History of Halloween* (New York: Bloomsbury, 2002).

2. Frances Hill, *A Delusion of Satan: The Full Story of the Salem Witch Trials* (New York: DaCapo Press, 2002).

3. Frances Hill, *Hunting for Witches: A Visitor's Guide to the Salem Witch Trials* (Beverly, Mass.: Commonwealth Editions, 2002), 74.

4. Hill, *Delusion,* 207.

5. Chadwick Hansen, *Witchcraft at Salem* (New York: G. Braziller, 1969), 64–86.

6. Jim McAllister, *Salem: From Naumkeag to Witch City* (Beverly, Mass.: Commonwealth Editions, 2000).

7. McAllister, 125–26.

8. Arthur Miller, *Timebends: A Life* (New York: Grove Press, 1987), 335–36.

9. McAllister.

10. Laurie Cabot with Tom Cowan, *The Power of the Witch* (New York: Delacorte, 1989), 4–5.

11. Cabot, 73.

12. Hill, *Hunting.*

13. Skal, 56–57.

14. Nathaniel Hawthorne, "A Rill from the Town Pump." *Centenary Edition,* vol. 9, 144.

15. John Hardy Wright, *Sorcery in Salem* (Charleston, S.C.: Arcadia Tempus, 1999), 89.

16. Wright, 85.

17. Hill, *Hunting,* 106–10.

18. Hill, *Hunting,* 111.

19. Hill, *Hunting,* 111, 115–16, 120–22.

20. Paul E. Chevedden, "Ushering in the Millennium, Or How an American City Reversed the Past and Single-Handedly Inaugurated the End-time," *Prospects: An Annual of American Cultural Studies* 22 (1997): 35–67.

21. *Salem, Massachusetts: Official Guidebook and Map* (Salem, Mass.: Salem Office of Tourism and Cultural Affairs, 2002), 21, 30–32.

22. *Salem Guidebook,* 33.

23. *Salem Guidebook,* 33.

24. City of Salem, 2002. Ordinance to amend an Ordinance pertaining to Article II Public Guides, Tallahassee, Florida, Municipal Code, 2002.

Logo of the House of the Seven Gables. Photo by Kim Mimnaugh.

Chapter Twelve

Salem's House of the Seven Gables as Historic Site

LORINDA B. R. GOODWIN

But as for the old structure of our story, its white-
oak frame, and its boards, shingles, and crumbling plaster, and
even the huge, clustered chimney in the midst, seemed to constitute only the
least and meanest part of its reality. So much of mankind's varied experience had passed
there—so much had been suffered, and something too, enjoyed—that . . .
it was itself like a great human heart, with a life of its own,
and full of rich and somber reminiscences.

—Nathaniel Hawthorne, *The House of the Seven Gables*

 IRATES. Traitors and revolution. Romance, with Hawthorne's capital "R." Narrow escapes from the slaveholder's chains or the witch-hunter's noose. The most beautiful woman in the village. These are themes we would expect in nineteenth-century novels and histories or in contemporary representations of American history in film and fiction. We certainly would not expect to encounter such drama at any archaeological site outside of *Raiders of the Lost Ark*. But this is exactly what I found at the archaeological project I led at the House of the Seven Gables, both as part of the historical research and as commonly held knowledge about the site. These notions may have roots, sometimes tenuous, in fact, but all of them are part of the truth that the site has generated over the past 350 years. Today, those truths, as well as those facts, are part of the appeal of the Gables, a tourist destination that attracts tens of thousands of visitors to Salem every year.

Every property has many histories, but, unless deeply scrutinized and broadly considered, they seldom extend in importance beyond the owner's family to also become the stories of a city, a colony, or a nation in the way that the House of the Seven Gables does, a house that was built by a merchant and financed through the bustle of trade with the Caribbean, China, India, and Sumatra. Over the centuries, layers of truth, myth, fact, and fiction have built up around this place, making it one of the most storied homes in the country, quite apart from its associations with Nathaniel Hawthorne. Its elastic histories stretch into the web of the American past and have become its principal stock-in-trade.

In this project, I expected that the team's archaeological and historical research would uncover many discrete facts about the house. I also hoped we would be able to explode the larger mythology conferred by Hawthorne on this famous site as well as the smaller ones that have sprung up from within the community. I discovered instead that the stories that have attached themselves to the house form a patina, a part of the thing itself. I learned that it is important to see how these elements of folklore can serve the inhabitants of a house and a town, and can continue to do so for centuries. These other "truths" are also a legitimate subject of our research and must be considered as such. This chapter addresses the multiple histories of the Gables and explores how its folklore and history contribute to the appeal of the house and to our understanding of how history evolves.

Unlike many nationally important and protected historic sites, the Gables, also known as the Turner House, was not originally a public place (aside from the role it played as the workplace of a family deeply involved with the surrounding community). It is different in this respect from Boston Common, Independence Hall, or the Golden Gate Bridge. And unlike Mount Vernon, Monticello, or the Martin Luther King Jr. birthplace, the Turner House was not the home of a nationally well known individual or family. What makes it significant in American culture is its association with Hawthorne, even though he never lived there. So why has this house—and Salem—become so closely associated with Hawthorne in national memory? Partly its significance comes from its use as the setting for Hawthorne's brooding nineteenth-century novel, *The House of the Seven Gables*. But the site has become more broadly connected to a whole constellation of ideas that reveal how the past was remembered in nineteenth-century Salem.

The rest of the importance of the Turner House comes, ultimately, from one source—its location on Salem Harbor. The scenic aspects of the house, particularly the gardens in back, are what attract tourists today. But what drew the Turner family to build their house there was the harbor's role as a means of communication and trade. The Turner family's prominence in overseas trade connected them to the town, the nation, and the world. Indeed, because of the Turner House's proximity to the Atlantic, it is tied into many of the critical shaping events in American history.

Many generations have located themselves in this place, and here, for the archaeologist to uncover, are successive strata of history and identity. In any archaeological site, once these occupation layers have been deposited, they may subsequently be removed or intermingled, altered or lost, and these changes are a part of the story too.

The Archaeological Project

I undertook this project in order to complete work toward my doctoral degree in American Civilization at the University of Pennsylvania. Because the house was so saturated in community history and national importance, I felt that the project was particularly suited to addressing issues in the disciplines of American history and culture, material culture, and social history. I was also interested in how the past at this site was interpreted and presented to the public. Since then, my research on the Turner family has taken me into a wider study of colonial merchants and their cultural expressions, both material and intangible.[1]

The site of the Turner House is directly situated on Salem Harbor, which is still a place of bustling trade today. Although the business may take the shape of light industry, business parks, and tourism rather than oceangoing trade, the harbor is still busy with fishing boats and pleasure craft. The House of the Seven Gables is a tall, dark brown clapboarded house that gives the impression of slumping age; adjacent to it is the flower garden, which leads down to a lawn and the seawall on the harbor. An important tourist draw (second in importance only to the house's history and its architectural significance), the garden is planted in Colonial Revival style raised beds, an interpretation that was established when the site was first opened to the public. Around the garden stand several other historic houses moved from elsewhere in Salem (including Hawthorne's birthplace), and these complete the inventory of the property's assets.

The project at the Turner House took place from May to September of 1991.[2] I worked with professional archaeologist Christy Dolan and a team of local volunteers, who exchanged their time and effort for training in excavating and recording practices. The extensive survey involved strategically locating meter squares across the site to identify the archaeological remains and determine whether they were intact. This also allowed us to keep the historical site safe while allowing visitors both to enjoy the garden and to view our work. The units were located throughout the area of the historical site: several were placed in the garden area (where the work yards of the house originally would have been), some were on the lawn (above the seawall that was rebuilt in the 1970s), and some were abutting the house foundation (to observe architectural information and to pick up on any scatters of material close to the house). One was placed at the back of the house in the attempt to locate a well that was marked on a late-eighteenth-century map, since wells often contain well-preserved materials that were discarded once the well was out of use.

We worked primarily with small tools—mason's trowels, dustpans, and tablespoons—and screened the soil we removed through quarter-inch mesh to recover smaller finds. Recovered artifacts were kept in plastic bags that were marked with the exact horizontal and vertical location of the unit and level (which had been established by mapping the site before work began). The more stable artifacts were washed in water with toothbrushes, then marked with indelible marker and sealed with clear nail polish. Those that were more delicate were carefully brushed or put into containers marked with the location designation.

We followed the natural soil layers (called stratigraphy) until we reached glacially deposited sand—a stratum that underlies the earliest human occupation. Following archaeological procedure, we recorded all of our finds and their contextual associations with photographs, illustrations, and written notes. In the end, we recovered almost seventeen thousand artifacts and faunal remains—including ceramic sherds, bottle glass, window leads, butchered animal bones, personal objects (including buttons, silver-gilt pins, and a fragment of a shoe buckle), nails and other architectural debris, and prehistoric stone tool and pottery fragments, enough to tell us about what life looked like through more than four hundred years of European and Indian life at the site.

The History of the Site—As an Archaeologist Views It

The history of human occupation and use of the Turner site can be described in the way in which an archaeologist discovers archaeological remains, starting with the surface and most recent materials, then continuing downward and deeper into the past to the earliest occupation layers. One literally goes back through time with each occupation. We begin with a particularly important event that took place here: its purchase and restoration by Salem philanthropist Caroline Emmerton in 1908.

Caroline Emmerton and the House of the Seven Gables Settlement Association (1908–Present)

Caroline Emmerton owned the Turner property from 1908. Having visited the place as a child, Emmerton remembered being charmed by "the gaunt old house," describing it as "wonderful and ancient." She planned to use it to fund her local settlement work and, in so doing, to fund the transformation of immigrants into American citizens.[3] In 1908, its age and presumed decay did not detract from its value but created an air of romance, no doubt fostered by Hawthorne's 1851 novel. From 1908 to 1910, Emmerton employed Joseph Chandler, a well-known historical architect, to restore the house to its seventeenth-century appearance (although it was determined that the house originally had eight, not seven, gables). To complete her vision, several more early Salem houses were subsequently brought onto the property. These buildings include the Hooper Hathaway House (a seventeenth-century structure bought and moved in 1911), the Retire Becket House (built c. 1655, bought in 1916, and moved to the grounds in 1924), and Hawthorne's birthplace (constructed c. 1730–1745, moved in 1958).[4]

Part of Caroline Emmerton's restoration efforts are associated with George Francis Dow's historical preservation movement in Salem—especially his reconstruction of the first settlement, now called Salem 1630. Both Emmerton and Dow were interested in the Colonial Revival movement of the early twentieth century, and by preserving the buildings they thought most important, actually built another layer of Salem's history themselves. The historic site as it presently stands is both smaller than the original holdings and a constructed site, save for the Turner House itself, and this in itself is significant, reminding us of how earlier scholars sought to study and interpret the past.

One of the intriguing finds that dates from this period, in addition to some of the trenches and building debris from the architectural restoration, was closely connected with the first use of the site as a tourist destination: peanut shells. In many of the pits, we found peanut shells with early-twentieth-century artifacts, suggesting that peanuts were sold as refreshment to visitors at the site. More importantly, however, was the principal artifact of the site—the restored Turner House and the houses that were moved on to the property—which is indicative of how Caroline Emmerton perceived the site and her settlement work. This imprinted her view of history and contemporary immigration onto the landscape: "The historical and literary associations of the old houses must surely help in making American citizens of our boys and girls."[5]

Susannah Ingersoll (1784–1858)

Caroline Emmerton bought the house from the Upton family, who owned the site from 1883 to 1908; several absentee owners held the property from 1879 to 1883, and Horace Connelly owned the property from 1858 to 1879. The owner with the longest tenancy before that was Susannah Ingersoll, who was born in the house in 1784 and lived there until her death in 1858. It was she who invited her kinsman Nathaniel Hawthorne to the house and, as local legend has it, regaled him with stories of the house's history, inspiring, among other works, *The House of the Seven Gables* (1851) and *The Whole History of Grandfather's Chair* (1840). Legend has it that once, when Hawthorne complained of writer's block, Susannah pointed to an antique chair in the house and suggested he write about that. Although Hawthorne occasionally denied that his novel was based on any place in particular, the similarities between his fictitious house with seven gables and the Turner-Ingersoll House are striking.[6]

Neighborhood rumors suggested that Susannah was a recluse (as a result of an unhappy love affair), and certainly the notion of a lonely woman living in an old house for decades is more than fertile grounds for the imagination, but added to that is the story of Horace Connelly, the adopted son of Susannah. A rumor (circulated by Horace himself, who took the name Ingersoll after Susannah's death) suggested that he was her biological child, but this was rejected by Caroline Emmerton, who said that he lived in the Gables for twenty-one years "as a quack doctor and squandering his substance on dissipation and dissolute friends."[7]

A "secret staircase" is associated with Susannah's life in the house. House tradition has it that Caroline Emmerton was shown a book, marked "Cuffy his book," that was concealed in the secret staircase.[8] This convinced her that Susannah Ingersoll was concealing runaway slaves there. While that is possible, the "secret" staircase was more likely built for the use of servants at the time of the house's construction. Once again, part of the folklore associated with the house was translated into the wider events of United States history.

Secret staircase in the House of the Seven Gables. Photo by Kim Mimnaugh.

Samuel Ingersoll (1782–1804)

Capt. Samuel Ingersoll occupied the house from 1782 to 1804, and, upon his death in 1804, he left it to his wife, Susannah. She, in turn, left it to her daughter, the above-mentioned Susannah, in 1811.[9] As an ambitious man, the captain left his mark on the site after he bought the house from John Turner, Esquire, in 1782. Although his voyages took him away from Salem for long periods of time, while he was at home he made considerable alterations to the house. He tore down the back kitchen ell and constructed both a French drain and a massive seawall, essentially enclosing the house in a nineteenth-century shell. Ingersoll was probably one of the first inhabitants to use the house more as a private residence than a place of business.

One of the reasons that Captain Ingersoll presumably bought the house was its cachet as the former home of one of the most important families in Salem: the Turners. Ingersoll had the money, and was now buying himself a place rooted in Salem's history and maritime tradition. He viewed it as a measure of his success that he now lived in the home of one of the foremost families in town.

The Honorable John Turner, Esquire (1742–1782)

The third generation of John Turners to live at the Turner House, the Honorable John Turner, Esquire, inherited the Turner House in 1742, but probably considered it too old-fashioned for use as anything but a summer retreat and he built a more fashionable house in the center of Salem. John Turner III inherited the foundation and fortune in trade that had been established by his grandfather and maintained by his father, but he was not successful at (or willing to continue) the family business. As the third generation in a prominent Salem family, it appears this John Turner was determined to live the life of a gentleman; he does not seem to have taken any interest in business. He became an Anglican and a Tory, things calculated to mark him as an English gentleman, and moved from the family home. These were actions that trampled on his family's traditions, and worse, offended the Congregationalist and patriotic sensibilities of his neighbors. Eventually, quite possibly through inattention to business, he lost everything, and was forced to ask his friends to help search for employment. In 1759, he used their fond memories of his father to secure the post of naval officer in Salem, one already held by another man.[10] Turner remained in this post until 1772, when it was too dangerous for a Tory to act as a tax collector in rebellious Salem. It was probably his father's reputation and his sons' involvement in the Continental forces that kept him from being driven out of town altogether.

By 1782, the Honorable John had to sell everything to pay his debts; he sold the family house on Turner Street to Captain Ingersoll. At the time of his death in 1786, Turner was living in rented lodgings. While his father's inventory had been worth more than £10,000, John Turner left only £59, most of this accounted for in fine, but very old, clothes.[11] Despite John Turner's initial desire to move away from the bustling port community and his scandalous—some would say traitorous—behavior, the house retained the positive "patina" conferred on it by his father. More than that, the fact that the site had been occupied by the English since the early seventeenth century and by three generations of a locally important family gave it an added cachet, particularly as Salem itself was undergoing a renaissance after the Revolution and was beginning its "golden age" as one of the premier ports in America involved in the Asian and Pacific trades.

Quite possibly the most important change the Honorable John brought to the Turner House was its sale to Samuel Ingersoll. It is sad to think of him trying to distance himself from his family's house, rejecting it as old-fashioned, then being forced by poverty to move back to it, only to have that taken away at the end. It was really his father, Col. John Turner, who left a much more lasting impression on the house and on Salem, with both his deeds and the stories that grew as a result of them.

Col. John Turner (1671–1742)

Col. John Turner cut such a figure that local historians, contemporary with him and later, tend to describe the house itself in terms of him and his tenure.[12] In this sense, Colonel Turner, with his several properties in and around Salem and his social importance, became the *genius loci* for the house, and there are a number of locally known stories about his exploits that render him larger than life.

This John Turner was born in 1671 and reached his majority in 1693. Although his stepfather lost most of the fortune left to the family, after his death, this John Turner seems to have repaired the family fortune through trade with the southern colonies and the Caribbean. He married Mary Kitchen in 1701 and his sisters also married into the most prominent of Salem's merchant families. John became active in local government and the military, ending his military career after achieving the rank of colonel.

By the 1720s, Colonel Turner had acquired all the land between what is now Turner, Hardy, and Derby Streets and renovated and redecorated his house and property to reflect his new status as a member of His Majesty's Council in Boston (held from 1720 to 1740). When Colonel Turner died in 1742, his thirteen-page probate inventory catalogued the house room by room, valuing real and portable property worth more than £10,000. This 1743 document reveals the house's lavish furnishings and luxuries the family used in their renowned entertainments, listing objects ranging from "a silver standing cup washed with gold" valued at over £37 to a "cotton Hammock" in the kitchen chamber.[13]

Like his father before him, Colonel Turner had a connection with pirates, but unlike Captain Turner, Colonel Turner's exploits are actually documented. He and Stephen Sewall, the diarists' brother, led a band of men to take a privateer who had transgressed his letters of marque. Because the threat of attack by native people, European powers, or pirates was very real in the early part of the eighteenth century, I suspect that this had a profound effect on the way he was perceived in the community.

In another instance of his exploits that contributed to his larger-than-life persona, a concealed staircase leading from the first floor to the second is sometimes attributed to his tenure, described as a measure taken to conceal his sisters from the hysteria of the witchcraft trials in 1692. There may be an actual connection between him and the witchcraft trials—a John Turner is described as having been bewitched by Ann Pudeator.[14] Both of these tales (along with others, including an unsubstantiated and untraceable rumor that Colonel Turner kept forty Indian scalps in the attic of his house as trophies) add to the glamour of a successful colonist.

The material connections of his tenure to the house nicely reflect the connections he maintained with other merchants and the elite in town through parties and other entertainments.[15] The seal of a green glass wine bottle, marked "1715," is probably one of the earliest dated examples to be recovered archaeologically. An elegantly made scale weight, labeled "2 Scruple," represents not only the meticulous accounting of his profession but also the Turners' access to delicate scientific equipment and other costly items. These, along with the furniture listed in his probate inventory and the records of his grand entertainments in friends' diaries, show Turner's pride in the place, his own endeavors adding to the solid foundations his father established.

Capt. John Turner (1668–1680)

In 1668, when John Turner purchased the land on which he built the Turner House, Salem was making the transition from a small European hamlet on the New England frontier to a town of some consequence in the Massachusetts Bay Colony. Settlements were clustered along the North and South Rivers and along the harbor, and wharves were beginning to project out into the harbor like the teeth of a comb.

John Turner, described in his will as a "marrenear," was probably born in Boston in 1644 to a shoemaker named Robert Turner and his wife Elizabeth Freestone, both of whom most likely left southeastern England during the Great Migration. John, his younger brother Habakkuk, and his sister Elizabeth moved to Salem when their mother remarried after their father's death, sometime around 1651. Their mother married George Gardner, a merchant whose Salem family had amassed enormous wealth in the Atlantic trade.

Although there were rumors throughout the Salem community that young Captain Turner's rapid accumulation of wealth might be attributed to piracy,[16] it is more likely that his success can be attributed to his family's trade and connections in Salem and in Barbados, where a cousin Turner owned a plantation, probably growing sugarcane. These family connections were vital to every family in Salem because of the trust that could engender trade: having eyes on the ground at a distant port, reliable news from kinfolk whose interests were bound to your own, and family on ships to keep an eye on the investment was the equivalent of CNN and the *Wall Street Journal* in a time before satellite communication and instant messaging. Because of the nature of his trade and the economic conditions of the time, Captain Turner became one of the wealthiest men in the Commonwealth.

Captain Turner and his wife Elizabeth Roberts had five children. The family also had a series of indentured servants living with them. He added a large kitchen ell onto his home, and, later on, an impressive two-and-a-half-story parlor addition that was styled in the new fashion of classically inspired proportion and symmetry, which faced directly out onto the harbor. The Turner family was established in trade, and their Salem house, as well as being built literally to oversee their vessels and business, demonstrated this to everyone with eyes.

The house was no longer just a private residence; because of the Turners' business, it had become a semipublic place, with offices and space enough for meetings about the business in and of the town. Once that happened, I suspect the truths about the house began to subtly change as well.

The landscape around the house was devoted to the management of the Turner family's trade, with storage sheds, ships' supplies, and a countinghouse area near to the Turners' wharf (no longer extant). Although it was certainly used as a garden in the late nineteenth century, it was a long way from the scenery used as a draw to visitors in the twenty-first century.

Captain Turner did not enjoy his new home for long. He died in 1680 at the age of thirty-six, leaving his wife Elizabeth to take charge of their children and the family business, including obtaining the rights to sell hard liquor in town. Later, in 1684, she yielded control of the business to her second husband, Capt. Charles Redford, and he seems to have run the family into debt by the time of his death in 1691.[17]

By this time, the harbor was quite densely settled, and the house occupied as fine a place on it as any. Although John Stilgoe says that the colonial structures in this area were built in the time-tested way of England, I suggest that the Turner family was also using the *retardataire* architecture to create a sense of permanence of English culture and the presence, even the dominance, of their family in Salem.[18] Stilgoe also suggests that the physical shape and organization of the community reflects its social hierarchy; the Turners were in the thick of things in Salem and Massachusetts for several generations.[19] For one of the richest men in the colonies, the house and its location were marks of his success.

Ann More (1637–1668)

Before the construction of the Turner House, both Europeans and Native Americans lived on and used the site. John Smith described the northern coast of what is now Essex County in 1616, writing that it was "a good Countrie, within

The House of the Seven Gables, with historic marker of Hawthorne's birthplace. Photo by Kim Mimnaugh.

their craggie cliffs. . . . Naimkeg [Naumkeag] though it be a more rockie ground . . . is not much inferior."[20] Naumkeag was settled by the English in 1626 by a group from the New England Company led by Roger Conant, and it was renamed Salem (a corruption of the Hebrew *Shalom,* or "peace") about 1630. The first historical records associated with the Turner site reveal that the Salem Town Council granted Ann More, a widowed midwife, three-quarters of an acre of land here for her support in 1637. A small English-style house was built, and here Ann More lived for about thirty years, when she sold part of that property to John Turner around 1668. Archaeology has not revealed any specific material trace of Ann More probably because the Turner House was built over the site of her own, possibly even incorporating part of the structure of her house into the new one.

Although Ann had some family nearby, and her daughter, Mary Grafton, had gone to the council on her behalf, the house and that parcel of land represented Ann More's survival, particularly after she was no longer able to act as a midwife.[21] Presumably born in England, she spent most of her life on that plot of land, far from what she had grown up with, and one wonders whether she viewed her life after England and her husband as independence or isolation.

Native Americans

Even before any of the British settlers arrived in this area around 1626, the site was used by Native Americans. Although the local Indians were practicing maize horticulture in clearings along the coast, the site of the Turner House was used as a temporary campsite, probably because of its access to a rich variety of marine and estuarine resources. Clam and oyster shells, ceramic fragments, projectile points (such as arrowheads) and the flakes (or debitage) from their manufacture, and charcoal are all that remain of their occupation of this site. Not much more can be said about their presence on what would become the Turner House site.[22]

Naumkeag was a center of political and social activities, being at a boundary between the Massachusett and Pawtucket peoples. Although the religious and social systems of the native inhabitants have not survived in the archaeological record (if they had material manifestations, in the first place), the name of the place suggests part of what the area represented to them. Salem was called *Naumkeag* (variously translated as "fishing place" or "eel fishing place") in Algonkian.

Conclusion

The fact that the Turner House, better known as the inspiration for Nathaniel Hawthorne's *The House of the Seven Gables,* is one of Salem's premier tourist destinations should come as little surprise. Its location on the scenic waterfront, its architectural importance as a standing (albeit restored) seventeenth-century building (Abbott Lowell Cummings described the house as one of Essex County's "most ambitious houses"), and the considerable influence of its occupants on Salem in the seventeenth and eighteenth centuries would be more than enough reason to justify its attraction to thousands of tourists a year, but add to that the house's associations with Hawthorne and his literature, as well as the less well known connections of the house with the Salem witchcraft hysteria and the American Revolution, and you have a phenomenon.[23] This historicity and its connection with Hawthorne (who himself had connections with witchcraft trials through his ancestor, Judge Hathorne) were what preserved the Turner House, and they also support the house today, making it into a powerful symbol for Salem and, often by extension, the United States.

It is the way the house is used as a symbol that makes it so appealing on so many levels. As a representative of Salem's start in Atlantic commerce and its brief fluorescence in the China and Pacific trades, as the home of one of the most influential families in Salem, and as a national landmark, the house's history makes it easy for it to be utilized in discussing almost any part of American history. Whereas once it was the tangible assets of the place that drew Indian and English settlers to Naumkeag and the site itself, it is now a matter of what the house has been, and what it now represents of local, state, and national history, that makes it sought after. The location is still important, both for its scenery—the views of Marblehead and the garden are evocative of its colonial maritime past—and the position of the house on the harbor, but no longer because of its presence over-looking one of the busiest and best-known ports in the early modern world. The virtue of the Turner House has been shifted from its material benefits to its symbolic and historic assets, and those are its stock-in-trade today. While some of the stories that the house continues to generate represent historical facts, those that don't are important hints about the way that history is shaped.

Anne Yentsch discusses the way that history is remolded to suit later generations, who take a series of events and alter them to make a more appealing past, creating a positive identity for a house, a neighborhood, or a town by constricting or inflating time lines, emphasizing positive values, and overstating the wealth, titles, or achievement of the inhabitants.[24] In an early article, I used her work to identify this phenomenon at the Turner House, and I take this opportunity to consider more deeply how the tales woven about the Turner House have become a part of it and are valuable clues to the way people use history on any level.[25]

John Turner, possessed of too much wealth too quickly, perhaps was a subject of speculations and rumors of piracy, and these persisted in the historical record. His son, Colonel Turner, a man prominent in town affairs, was noted for his part in vanquishing the pirates who threatened the coast and an Indian threat from the north, and was supposedly married to "the most beautiful belle of the village." It was his achievements that cemented the Turner name in Salem, showing up as a byword for bravery, wealth, hospitality, and civic duty.

John Turner III, usually written about in terms of his father, managed to keep his house intact and his skin untarred during the Revolution, no mean feat for someone who welcomed the royal governor and collected customs for the Crown. By the time the house was purchased by the Ingersolls, who were associated not only with Hawthorne but also possibly with the Underground Railroad, the house had been reified as an antique, a venerable part of Salem's past, and a social marker, and it was being used to speak to the new wealth of Salem as an important port in the global trade with Asia and the Pacific.[26] Although the place (both the Turner House and Salem itself) had fallen on harder times during the later part of the nineteenth century, it retained its cachet as a place of interest through its history.

By the time that Caroline Emmerton bought the place, filled with her childhood recollections, it was ready to be transformed into an American icon and an agency of assimilation according to what was considered the best sociology of the day. Her notions of public service and what it meant to be successfully taught to be an American also expanded into teaching native-born Americans, generations later, about their history.

Peter Ginna has written, "If places can shape history, it is no less true that they are shaped by it, often indelibly."[27] Places can also be understood as cauldrons of historical creation. The Turner House, as Hawthorne's inspiration for *The House of the Seven Gables,* has been for about a century (and will always remain) a tourist destination. As part of a waterfront neighborhood in a storied city, it is a place where local events and personal histories combine with larger ideas to generate important symbolic notions. These notions continue to be employed and to metamorphose in an enduring alchemy that serves the community and, by extension, through tourism, a national audience.

For a while as I worked on my research at the Gables, I was struck by the notion that archaeology was a means of setting facts straight, and that is certainly one goal. I was able to contribute to a redesign of one of the rooms, discuss the wider implications of the merchant elite in Salem in the early modern period, and provide tangible evidence about the lives of the Turners and Ingersolls in the shape of thousands of artifacts, as well as by my own interpretation of the site, which rapidly became part of the history that the Gables uses to describe itself.

What took me much longer to realize was that archaeology was not going to change the community-created "truths" about the house, and those "truths" were just as important as quantifiable facts to the people who lived in and near the house, and perhaps more important, because they fed into the identities that they chose. The folklore and local history of the house and its denizens—however glorified or exaggerated or distorted—have accreted into a wider history, and even if they are not facts, they are important to the culture of the place. Archaeology simultaneously examines these things, puts them into their proper contexts, and reveals other data, which may or may not be interpreted and added to the patina of history, myth, and memory. We do not just look at the past, see how the story of a house changes over time, and "correct it," but we also observe how people actively select and use history to suit themselves. Reputation and history are liquid and can be altered by environment while still being constrained by certain historical facts that do not change. These "truths" change over time according to the needs of a people, in spite of the facts.

Notes

1. Lorinda B. R. Goodwin, *An Archaeology of Manners: The Polite World of the Merchant Elite of Colonial Massachusetts* (New York: Kluwer Academic/Plenum Press, 1999).

2. For the full details of the archaeological project, see Lorinda B. R. Goodwin, "'A Stately Roof to Shelter Them': An Historical Archaeological Investigation of the Turner Family of Eighteenth-Century Salem, Massachusetts" (Ph.D. diss., University of Pennsylvania, 1993); or Lorinda B. R. Goodwin, *Archaeological Site Examination of the Turner House, Salem, Massachusetts* (report prepared for the Massachusetts Historical Commission, 1992). A concise description of the project and the artifacts can be found in Lorinda B. R. Goodwin, "'A Succession of Kaleidoscopic Pictures': Historical Archaeology at the Turner House, Salem, Massachusetts," *Northeast Historical Archaeology* 23 (1994): 8–28.

3. Caroline O. Emmerton, *The Chronicles of Three Old Houses* (1935; reprint, Salem, Mass.: House of the Seven Gables Settlement Association, 1985), 29.

4. Bryant F. Tolles, *Architecture in Salem, An Illustrated Guide* (Salem, Mass.: Essex Institute, 1983), 65–67.

5. Emmerton, 39.

6. Gilbert L. Streeter, "Historic Streets and Colonial Houses," *Essex Institute Historical Collections* 36, no. 3 (1900): 211.

7. Emmerton, 25.

8. Emmerton, 29.

9. William Bentley, *The Diary of William Bentley, D.D., Pastor of the East Church, Salem, Massachusetts,* 4 vols. (Salem, Mass.: Essex Institute, 1907–1914), 216.

10. G. Andrews Moriarty, "The Turner Family of Salem," *Essex Institute Historical Collections* 48, no. 3 (1912): 267.

11. *Essex County* [Massachusetts] *Probate Records* (Volume 361): 354.

12. For example, see Bentley.

13. *Essex County* [Massachusetts] *Probate Records* (docket 28, 367).

14. Katherine W. Richardson, *The Salem Witchcraft Trials* (Salem, Mass.: Essex Institute, 1983), 16.

15. See Goodwin, *Archaeology of Manners,* chap. 4, for an in-depth discussion of the relationship between artifacts and social status among colonial merchants.

16. Samuel Eliot Morison, *The Maritime History of Massachusetts, 1783–1860* (Boston: Houghton Mifflin, 1921), 16; G. Andrews Moriarty, "The Turners of New England and Barbados," *Journal of the Barbados Museum and Historical Society* (1931): 7–14.

17. Moriarty, "Turners of New England and Barbados," 11.

18. John R. Stilgoe, *Common Landscape of America, 1580–1845* (New Haven: Yale University Press, 1982), 45.

19. Stilgoe, 50.

20. James Duncan Phillips, *Salem in the Seventeenth Century* (Boston: Houghton Mifflin, 1933), 15.

21. Henry Wyckoff Belknap, "The Grafton Family of Salem," *Essex Institute Historical Collections* 64, no. 1 (1928): 49–50.

22. Goodwin, "Kaleidoscopic Pictures," 11.

23. Abbott Lowell Cummings, *The Framed Houses of Massachusetts Bay: 1625–1725* (Cambridge, Mass.: Harvard University Press, 1979), 73.

24. Anne E. Yentsch, "Legends, Houses, Families, and Myths: Relationships Between Material Culture and American Ideology," in *Documentary Archaeology in the New World,* ed. Mary C. Beaudry (Cambridge: Cambridge University Press, 1988).

25. Goodwin, "Kaleidoscopic Pictures," 25.

26. See chapter 5 of this volume.

27. Peter Ginna, "Taking Place," in *American Places: Encounters with History,* ed. William E. Leuchtenburg (Oxford: Oxford University Press, 2000), xviii.

Salem Harbor Power Station. Photo by Kim Mimnaugh.

Coda

Montage of Brick and Water

J. D. SCRIMGEOUR

Beating the Bounds (the City Limits)

Hawthorne hated it—the assumptions
of power, the majesty of money,
crushing as brick. Horses, and streets
that narrow near the water, spray
of sea across a face, an ungloved hand,
stones beating each other into smoothness
in the surf, beating the bounds, rounding
brick to pebble, to sand. 1692 . . .

1962. The generals disappearing from their
families for ten days, debating Cuba.
This country that started here, nearly
extinguished. Now, should the masks
get handed out, they'll be gone before
Salem gets any.

Hopeful? What's the difference between
5 years, and 80? The death of a child,
an old woman? Between millions
and thousands? Between boulders,
and pebbles? Sand through the fingers
trickling on a warm, sunscreened leg.
Sand emptied from sneakers
onto the brick porch. Drinking
filtered water, piano blinking
runs of notes. Spill of waves.

❧

Brick

More are cracked than whole
none quite the same color
though they can be painted
usually white or black

they make painful, brief music
chipping, cutting the hand—

they gather in wheelbarrows . . .

and, mortared into the Essex Condos,
they rise out of the downtown,
casting their shadows
over the pedestrian mall.

❧

The Shoreline

On the shoreline swollen gulls stand guard,
while others sit back a few feet,
bellies on the sand—a coffee break.

Several twist and tuck their heads
into the feathers along their side,
as if nursing themselves,
or reaching for their wallets.

Their legs are their proudest parts,
spindly, they concentrate
strength and orange.

Those pairs of mallards frisking in the surf
are too content, and too simple
for these gulls, who will

squabble and cry over french fries,
who will fly off, alone, if the wind
moves them, catches them right.

❧

Cigar Store Indian, Salem, Massachusetts, April 1999

Split from shoulder to gut,
he grins. Only half a man,
he's got no backside, guarding
the five-and-dime's trinkets
behind him, behind glass: a ceramic
Groucho, who looks mulatto,
and a Mark Twain. His grin—
so stupid—at first arouses pity,
but look closer: it's unbelievable.
        Across Washington Street
inside a monolith of brick, someone
named Aracely sells witch-hangings
in an anonymous office. Residents
get loans to delead their houses
before their children become
idiots.
        If he could see,
he'd see down the alley
the building where Bell first
displayed the phone. If he could
remember, he'd remember the murmur
of the river in the distance,
now dry and paved; the warm stink
of horse dung on the cobblestones.
He'd remember those pimple nights
when, kidnapped for thrills,
he lurched in the back of pick-ups.
He was always found—in the woods
a few yards off Route 1A,
or face down on Gallows Hill.
Unlike the Pope, he won't make
the millennium. Gash deepening
and widening, he'll be gone

before this poem is finished,
replaced and used for fuel.

ॐ

Way Back

It used to be.
It used to be.

They've dedicated the little league field
beside Pioneer Village—where men
and women dressed in 17th century clothes
furtively chase two rats that—they say—
someone set free there.

The name: Stephen O'Grady,
beloved coach, killed
by a drunk driver,
outside the bounds.

ॐ

That Guy You See Around Sometimes

Baggy pants, black hair shagged,
unshaven, 22, he holds

his three-year-old's hand into
High Street Park—the one

with no grass behind
what used to be

the St. Mary's Italian
Catholic Church. The boy

lets go for the steps
to the slide as he tells

an older father—the only
other adult there—how

he works at the Hawthorne
Hotel, he'd like to go to college

someday, how the mother
walked out eight months ago—

"wants nothing to do with him,"
chin pointing toward the boy,

voice without bitterness,
just heavy with astonishment

at the world's thoughtlessness—
"Joshua," he calls, "Joshua,"

and moves to catch his son.

Apologies

It is not my story, the story
of my ancestors, Mary T. Estey,
hung for witchcraft, Thomas
Hutchinson, one of the jurors
who found her guilty, it
is not my story, not yet.

No, I write of basements flooded
and duct-taped cars, private schools
in surrounding towns shimmering
with playing fields, their
nutrient-enriched grass like a shag rug,
and public school children that ride
buses to dark, borrowed gyms,
recess on a small asphalt playground
with some painted bases

alongside the college students, passing
class to class, cigarettes and—

Hawthorne hated it all, hated it—
wrote romances in which the good,
the simple good, triumphed. The rule
of order flawed from the start.

ès

Salem in Myth and Memory

The power plant manager
arguing against the new regulations

at the meeting with the state reps.
in the College's 800-seat

auditorium overflowing with
community, saying, "This

is an injustice as bad
as the witchhunts!"
      Some

in the crowd hissing, those
in white helmets applauding.

ès

Overheard

Who said
The food
At Red's
Was good?

ફ્ર

Roll Call

St. Mary's Italian Catholic Church,
closed in 2003, after 85 years—brick.

Salem State College Library—brick.

The boxy mansions of Chestnut Street
("the most beautiful street in America")—brick.

The facade of the old armory before
they demolished it—brick.

The sidewalks that ruin strollers—brick.

Our house, built after the great fire of 1914—
we've been told that between the drywall inside
and the asbestos shingles outside,
a layer of brick.

ફ્ર

Buck-A-Bag

I used to play basketball Saturday mornings,
spend the afternoon reading on a shaded porch.
Now people coo at my back, talk monosyllables
to Guthrie, my nine-month-old in this Unitarian
Universalist church that ministers to gays,
lesbians, and public defenders and which is now
selling old clothes on folding tables and claiming
to sell donuts though I don't see any, and even
if I did, that's not what we're here for, not with 100
chocolate and butterscotch chip cookies at home
for the Fischer-Urkowitzes this evening, as if
they will eat even 10 of them—who are we kidding?—
We make the cookies to eat them ourselves, we make
sure that we'll have enough and so no donuts, no
basketball—no, this is get other people's

trash almost free! Typewriters needing ribbons.
Updike paperbacks. 1000 piece puzzles of Amsterdam
at night with mini-lights that you insert—batteries
not included. A 20, no 10, no 5 dollar bike.

My older son, Aidan, has opened one of the games,
"Where in the World," and is rapidly memorizing
all the countries in Asia, circa 1986. Eileen,
my wife, is being handed not just clothes, but
their histories, from a woman who is emptying
her garbage bag of donations. She just gave
Eileen a pair of shorts that would barely fit
over my wrists. Oh, where is the man
in the gray sweatshirt who wants to give
everything away? I'd pay a quarter for that puzzle,
but not 50 cents, no way.

ᴣ☙

Donna and Deborah

two sisters, one
who never talks, one
who never stops, how

there used to be a market
where CVS is and we'd get
buttah, sure, and meat—

the phone call during the storm:
you tell him he can't shovel snow
in front of your house
look outside, go look outside

they both call Eileen Ellen
Donna says, oh Deborah,
tell them about the owl

oh yeah, we saw an owl
right there on our porch,
real tiny, right up—

her hand, blotchy and curled
stiff from the years
at Sylvania, rises and moves
as if tossing seed—there.

ૐ

Failed Poetry Exercise

If at first you don't succeed
you're doing it wrong. Like teaching:

I give them gum, and a first line.
They offer both back, the gum

already chewed, of course, sweetness
and firmness dispersed in their

arid mouths. And I do care if they
write poems, the way I care

that the cop who died in the crash
had young twins. Kim, straight

from the funeral and its traffic,
didn't want to talk about Hawthorne

seizing the public by the button,
but she did since I'd written it

in my datebook: *March 31. Kim,*
4:00: Hawthorne, button.

Before leaving we both almost wept.

ॐ

Jury Duty

No room
in the County Courthouse,
so they're shuttled across
Federal Street.

The hour rolls by
in the church basement—
the video over
that explains the duties.

Signs abound:
We are all God's children

                                        Proclaim Liberty

            Hope

                    Peace

                            Love

                    Joy

Taped to a pole: *Please put all trash in barrels.*

So many talking . . .
            one man explains solitaire to a woman.

ॐ

Pigeon #3

On the roof of the Senior Center
sit a line of pigeons,
turning their heads
from street to graveyard.

They coo and caw,
sharing info: spilled fries
on Endicott,
cat's out on Winthrop.

That one with the swath
of white on its side, third
from the left, longs to poke
among the cigarette butts

surrounding the trash can,
if only to get away
from the gabbing. Instead,
it ruffles its feathers and

pecks at a noisy neighbor,
then flicks its head
into the gutter and grinds
pebbles in its beak.

ð

Salem to Lynn: A Note

Lynn, you've lost your shoes.
Maybe someone stole them
down Long Beach. Watch

your step, girl, there's glass
and hypodermic needles
in the sand.

ð

July 4

I didn't know about the Horribles Parade
at Salem Willows, and I didn't know
whether the buses were running when the lone
man asked.

Of course, the flags were hacking the sky,
but after a while they stopped and hung,
spent . . .

The scent of lighter fluid in the air . . .

In the slice of park, under a huddle of trees,
a few sit on benches, pigeons walking

at their feet.

The Labontes have a large, sturdy sign
in their front yard. Their name, cursive,
above a painting of Joseph, Mary, and baby Jesus.

And the parking lot sign with "Private" whited out:
Property.

ﷺ

Salem Willows

What is the meaning of life? Which popcorn—
peppermint, caramel, or buttered—
is the best? Miniature golf squeezed
between the tired arcades, teens
driving and skiing and killing
wildly, dying over and over.

For a dime, the aged monkeys
dance in their glass cage, their necks
worn through, fur half gone,
clothes untucked. For a nickel
the drinking test: worming a metal circle
around a curved electrified bar. Are you
Punch Drunk? Pickled?

ﷺ

The Sights

After illicit ejaculation
in a Chestnut Street bedroom,
the bodies pause, then rise
and prepare for the other side
of the shades where the trolley

shimmies and announces facts,
like bricks, canned jokes the mortar.
                                    At dusk,
groups of tourists clutching candles
trudge through the empty downtown
realizing they could be somewhere
else. The guide, draped in cliché black,
can't muster a reason . . .

The bricks, though, clutch the past,
hoping to contain it in sidewalks and walls.
Fragments wash up on Dead Horse Beach
and Forest River, not quite smooth,
and plainly different—more fragile,
less beautiful, than rock.

ঌ

Atlantic Blues

Heard the weather last night
Hurting the shore
Heard the surf last night
Just *hurting* the shore
Don't know why I left
Won't do it no more

Saw the water this morning
A sheet of blue
Saw the water this morning
A long sheet of blue
It's a go-home day
That's what I'm gonna do.

Felt the water today
Rise up past my knees
Felt the cold Atlantic
And an arctic breeze
It's a hard luck world
Take me back, please!

ઢ .

North Street Shell

Have you prayed to Allah today?
read the small sign
over the penny dish

that disappeared from the gas station
after nine-eleven. And when

that October, a customer
asks the Arabic counterman,
"Things going o.k. for you?

Any problems?" He shrugs,
says, "It's o.k.," says
"What're you gonna do?"

ઢ

Walking Winthrop Street

The ice-pocked sidewalk leads me
to walk in the street, and the world
takes on an astonishing balance:

houses the same distance from me,
sidewalks like rails,
and the telephone poles and light poles

rise sheer into the night, the pools
of light in clear patterns. Only
the trees don't line up, spilling their shadows

wherever they fall, hovering
over the wires and bulbs.

❧

The Family

Lynn smokes a pack a day. She married Peabody when she got pregnant. Now they hardly talk. Her children have stolen from her, sold her VCR for drug money. She sits on the stoop each morning, smoking, her bleached hair drying in the sun.

Peabody works in the aged coffee shop. A stained apron. Balding. His brother works with him, and they each plot who will take over the business once the grandmother, who speaks no English, dies.

Salem is the grandmother, tottering, senile. She calls for her sister, long dead, when she wakes in the night. Her hands gnarl the cross round her neck. Teenagers furtively bring her babies to strangle in the shadows of dawn. No one knows what happens then. No one has ever told.

Beverly is ashamed of his brother, but also of himself. Growing up, he was teased for having a girl's name. He's hated working in the shop, him with a college degree. He won't speak Greek, claims he has forgotten, but he listens closely to grandmother's mutterings at the Thanksgiving table.

❧

High Street Park

Whiff of gas near
the bike rack, glass

and chewed gum
in the woodchips,

the usual graffiti
on the plastic slide.

On a black rubber
seat, a note:

This is Megan's swing.

ર્જ

The Masthead

You could have a hundred
gables, your house on the sea
would still be smaller than leaves
of grass. Walt's hallucinating
the dawn and then there's the water,
smacking slow then fast, like
good sex, bodies lost in the music.
Gulls swoop parabolas
to the rails' tangents. Mist
clouds Misery Island. Somewhere
out there he waits. Not Moby Dick,
not Ahab, not even Ishmael, but
the mad composer, harpooning
and being harpooned, salt tang
on his fevered tongue. Pirates
still circle Java, gun runners,
smugglers. Whales, too,
though fewer. Poe's whirlpool
to the North. Iceberg. Death
has an etymology,
but no footnotes. Odysseus
was wrong: you don't bind yourself
and listen, you sing
and wait for an echo.

Contributors

EMERSON W. BAKER II is chair of the History Department of Salem State College. He earned his Ph.D. in history from the College of William and Mary and his B.A. in history from Bates College. He served as managing editor of *American Beginnings: Exploration, Culture and Cartography in the Land of Norumbega* (University of Nebraska Press, 1995) and is coauthor (with John Reid) of *The New England Knight: Sir William Phips, 1651–1695* (University of Toronto Press, 1998). He also directs archaeological excavations on early colonial sites in northern New England.

ROBERT BOOTH is an independent scholar in local history and a business executive. He has done advanced studies in the Preservation Studies Department at Boston University and holds a B.A. in English from Harvard College. He coordinates research for Historic Salem, Inc., and is the author of numerous studies of Essex County, Massachusetts, and of *Boston's Freedom Trail* (Globe Pequot Press, 1982).

AVIVA CHOMSKY is a professor of history and coordinator of Latin American studies at Salem State College. She earned her Ph.D. in history and her B.A. in Spanish and Portuguese from the University of California, Berkeley. Her books include *West Indian Workers and the United Fruit Company in Costa Rica, 1870–1940* (Louisiana State University Press, 1996), *Identity and Struggle at the Margins of the Nation-State* (coedited with Aldo Lauria-Santiago, Duke University Press, 1998), and *The Cuba Reader: History, Culture, Politics* (coedited with Barry Carr and Pamela Maria Smorkaloff, Duke University Press, 2004). Her current book project, inspired by her contribution to this collection, explores the history of labor and immigration in Salem.

JOHN V. GOFF is an architect, a preservationist, and an architectural historian. He earned his M.Arch. from the University of Oregon and his B.A. degrees in history and American civilization from Brown University. He has served as executive director and architectural historian for Historic Salem, Inc., one of the oldest community preservation organizations in the country. He was instrumental in the restoration of the Nathaniel Bowditch House in Salem and is a founder of

Salem Preservation, Inc. He has written extensively on the topic of historic preservation.

LORINDA B. R. GOODWIN is currently a research fellow at the Department of Archaeology, Boston University. She earned her Ph.D. in American civilization from the University of Pennsylvania and her B.A. in archaeological studies from Boston University. She has been a Winterthur research fellow. Her book, *An Archaeology of Manners: The Polite World of the Merchant Elite of Colonial Massachusetts* (Kluwer Academic/Plenum Publishers, 1999), is a study of the manners, material culture, and rise of the merchant class in New England from 1660 to 1760 and includes her archaeological research at the House of the Seven Gables.

FRANCES HILL is the author of *A Delusion of Satan: The Full Story of the Salem Witch Trials, The Salem Witch Trials Reader,* and *Hunting for Witches: A Visitor's Guide to the Salem Witch Trials.* She has also published two novels, *Out of Bounds* and *A Fatal Delusion.* She holds a B.A. in English literature and philosophy from Keele University. She lives in London, but spends every summer in Connecticut.

MATTHEW G. MCKENZIE teaches maritime history at the Sea Education Association and is part of the University of New Hampshire History of Marine Animal Populations (HMAP) project. He earned his Ph.D. in history from the University of New Hampshire and his B.A. in history from Boston University. His current research examines the development and political roles of navigational science and cartography in late-eighteenth- and early-nineteenth-century New England.

KIM MIMNAUGH is a member of the Art Department staff at Salem State College. She received an M.F.A. in photography from the Massachusetts College of Art and a B.A. in photography from Sam Houston State University. She has been a recipient of a fellowship from the New England Foundation for the Arts and the Massachusetts Cultural Council. She is currently working on a series of color photographs of interior spaces.

DANE ANTHONY MORRISON is a professor of history at Salem State College. He earned his Ph.D. in history from Tufts University and his B.A. in history from Boston College. He has been a recipient of an American Philosophical Society fellowship and is a George Washington Distinguished Professor of the Society of the Cincinnati. His books include *A Praying People: Massachusett Acculturation and the Failure of the Puritan Mission, 1600–1690* (Peter Lang, 1995) and *American Indian Studies: An Interdisciplinary Approach to Contemporary Issues* (Peter Lang, 1997). His current book project, *True Yankees: Maritime Discovery and National Identity, 1783–1807,* examines the experiences of Americans abroad during the period of the early republic.

REBECCA R. NOEL is a lecturer in history and literature at Harvard University. She earned her Ph.D. in American and New England studies from Boston University and her B.A. in history from Yale University. She is at work on a book about health reform in schools from the early republic through Reconstruction.

MARGARET PRESS is the author of *Counterpoint: A Murder in Massachusetts Bay* (Addicus Books, 1996), a factual account of a 1991 Salem homicide (re-released in paperback as *A Scream on the Water: A True Story of Murder in Salem* [St. Martin's Press, 1997]). She has also published a Salem-based mystery series (*Requiem for a Postman,* 1992, and *Elegy for a Thief,* 1993, Carroll & Graf). Raised in California, she holds a doctorate in linguistics from the University of California, Los Angeles, with an emphasis on Uto-Aztecan languages. She currently works for a software company in Cambridge and has lived in Salem since 1987.

NANCY LUSIGNAN SCHULTZ is a professor and coordinator of graduate programs in English and American Studies at Salem State College. She earned her Ph.D. in English and American literature from Boston College and her B.A. in English and French from the College of the Holy Cross. She has been the recipient of fellowships from Harvard University and the National Endowment for the Humanities. She is the editor of *Fear Itself: Enemies Real and Imagined in American Culture* (Purdue University Press, 1999) and *Veil of Fear: Nineteenth Century Convent Tales* (Purdue University Press, 1999). She is also the author of *Fire and Roses: The Burning of the Charlestown Convent, 1834,* published in paperback by Northeastern University Press in 2002. Her current book project, *A Capital Miracle,* is a social history of the controversy surrounding miraculous cures in the antebellum American Catholic Church.

J. D. SCRIMGEOUR is a professor of English and coordinator of creative writing at Salem State College. He earned his M.F.A. and Ph.D. in English from Indiana University and his B.A. from Columbia University. He has published numerous works of poetry and is the author of the memoir *Spin Moves.* His essay on teaching at Salem State College, the inspiration for his contribution to this collection, was featured in the *Chronicle of Higher Education.*

CHRISTOPHER WHITE is a lecturer and head tutor in the Committee on the Study of Religion at Harvard University. He received his Ph.D. in religion from Harvard University and his B.A. from the University of California, Davis. His current research examines the history of American liberal Protestant faith and religious practice.

Index